# LUTHER AND THE REFORMATION

# LUTHER AND THE REFORMATION

BY

## JAMES MACKINNON, Ph.D., D.D.
Regius Professor of Ecclesiastical History, University of Edinburgh

VOL. III.

## PROGRESS OF THE MOVEMENT (1521-29)

*NEW YORK*

RUSSELL & RUSSELL · INC

1962

FIRST PUBLISHED IN 1929
PUBLISHED, 1962, BY RUSSELL & RUSSELL, INC.
L. C. CATALOG CARD NO: 62—10691

PRINTED IN THE UNITED STATES OF AMERICA

# PREFACE

THIS volume traces the history of Luther as a Reformer from the Diet of Worms to the Conference of Marburg. These years constitute the second act of the Reformation drama. In the opening scene we see the recluse of the Wartburg directing the movement by his correspondence and continuing and widening the attack on his opponents in a series of controversial writings, dealing with ecclesiastical institutions and usages—Auricular Confession, the Mass, religious Vows, and Monasticism. With his activity as propagandist he combines that of the scholar and the teacher, the chief fruits of which are his translation of the New Testament from the original Greek and his series of sermons in the vernacular for the instruction of the people in the Gospel.

In his absence at the Wartburg his colleagues at Wittenberg attempt to initiate a thoroughgoing reform of religious usages. This reform arouses the opposition of the Elector of Saxony and eventuates in a deadlock and the demand for Luther's return. His reappearance as active leader and his moderating influence mark a victory for the policy of gradual change in virtue of expediency, to which his colleagues, with the exception of Carlstadt, defer. He himself, however, erelong deems the time ripe for more incisive measures and takes in hand the reform of worship, usages, and organisation at Wittenberg and elsewhere.

Meantime the evangelical movement has been taking an ever firmer and wider grip of Germany through the co-operation of a large band of recruits from the secular and regular clergy with the Reformer, who renews from Wittenberg his polemic against the Roman Curia and its literary champions in Germany and elsewhere. The growing strength of the movement is reflected in the refusal of the first Diet of Nürnberg to suppress it and its demand for the convocation of a free General Council in Germany to consider the question of reform. Though the second Diet held in the same city is less recalcitrant, it only undertakes to execute the Edict of Worms " as far as possible," and repeats the demand for a General Council.

Throughout these three years of conflict and expansion, Luther, though an outlaw, has become the dominating force in the empire, and the Reformation, both as a destructive and constructive movement, is bidding fair to eventuate in a revolution of the old order in Church and State. Truly a marvellous tribute to the religious genius, the courage, the daring of the monk who, in his appeal to Scripture and conscience at Worms, had seemed to play the part of a second Hus and invite the doom of the martyr of Constance.

By the year 1524 the movement has quickened the aspiration for political and social as well as religious reform, and though Luther has striven to keep it within the strictly religious sphere, as he conceived it, and has denounced revolutionary violence, the drama widens with the abortive risings of the lesser nobility under Hutten and Sickingen to achieve a political revolution, and of the masses to effect a social as well as a religious Reformation.

As the result, in part, of this complication, the evangelical movement, whilst continuing to gain recruits among the princes and the people in northern Germany, loses something of its initial grandeur as an emancipation from the old religious and social order and ceases to be a national movement. The empire is divided into two antagonistic religious parties which league themselves for or against it. The influence of this antagonism appears in the two Diets of

Spires.   In the first Diet the balance of advantage leans in favour of the adherents of Luther, who begin to organise separate territorial churches.   In the second it falls heavily against them, whilst the evangelical cause is further weakened by the breach between Luther and Erasmus and the outbreak of dissension in the evangelical ranks over the sacramental question.   At this point the curtain falls on the second act of the Reformation drama.   In the fourth and concluding volume the sequel, which constitutes the final act and closes with Luther's death in 1546, will be unfolded.

The author expresses his thanks to the Carnegie Universities' Trust for a guarantee against loss up to a certain amount for the publication of this volume.

# TABLE OF CONTENTS

## CHAPTER I

# Contents

# Contents

# Contents

## CHAPTER VIII

## CONSOLIDATION OF THE EVANGELICAL MOVE-

# Contents

## CHAPTER IX

# Contents

# LUTHER
# AND THE REFORMATION

CHAPTER I

## LUTHER AT THE WARTBURG (1)

### I. Behind the Veil

LATE in the evening of the 4th of May, after a wearisome ride through the Thuringian Forest, Luther arrived in the darkness at the old burg overlooking Eisenach.[1] He was lodged in an isolated apartment which commanded a view of the forest-clad hills from which he had emerged, and his identity was known only to the Warden, Hans von Berlepsch, and the trusty troopers who had been concerned in his capture. To others he was known as Knight George, and in order to fill the part assigned him he was arrayed in a costume befitting his supposed rank, with a gold chain encircling his neck. He grew a beard on his shaven face and a crop of hair on his tonsured crown, was waited on by a couple of pages,[2] and was instructed in knightly deportment by a trusty trooper (*Reitknecht*). "You would with difficulty recognise me," he wrote to Spalatin ten days after his arrival; "in fact, I scarcely know my former self."[3] The Warden was so anxious to preserve the secret of his identity

[1] Enders, iii. 150. Ego die, qua a te avulsus fui, longo itinere novus eques fessus, hora ferme undecima, ad mansionem noctis perveni in tenebris; *cf.* "Tischreden," v. 82 (Weimar ed.).

[2] "Tischreden," iii. 37, ed. Förstemann.

[3] Enders, iii. 155; *cf.* iii. 164, letter to Melanchthon, 26th May, equitem videres ac ipse vix agnosceres.

and his whereabouts that he would not at first permit him to write to his friends at Wittenberg, and he was fain, in obedience to his remonstrances, to tear up the letters he had penned to Melanchthon, Amsdorf, Agricola, Schurf, and others, " for fear of revealing where I am." [4] A week elapsed before the embargo was removed, and he was allowed to assure his colleagues by letters, conveyed to them apparently through Spalatin, that he had been taken to a place of safety—where he did not inform them.[5] These early letters are indefinitely addressed " from the region of the birds," or " the region of the air," or " the hilltop," or " the island of Patmos."

The secret was so well kept that the most conflicting rumours as to his fate flew from mouth to mouth. That he had been seized and carried off somewhere in the Thuringian Forest was known at Worms within a week after the event. But where he had disappeared to, whether he had been captured by friend or enemy, whether he was dead or alive was a mystery, and the mystery naturally gave rise at Worms and elsewhere to the most divergent surmisings. Some suspected that he had been seized at the instigation of Aleander or the Archbishop of Maintz.[6] Aleander saw in this inference a Lutheran device to stir up the people with the cry that the Romanists had violated the imperial safe conduct, and instinctively divined that the Elector " had his hand in the game " in spite of his disclaimer at a sitting of the princes.[7] Others thought of Sickingen or Hector Beheim, a robber knight of Franconia, with whom the Elector was at feud.[8] Luther himself mentions in his letter to Spalatin a prevailing report, which

[4] Enders, iii. 146, 150.

[5] *Ibid.*, iii. 148 f.; *cf.* 154. Luther himself sought to put his enemies off the scent by writing a letter to Spalatin which he should contrive to bring to the notice of Duke George, and which contradicted the rumour that his place of concealment was the Wartburg. *Ibid.*, iii. 201-202.

[6] Kalkoff, " Depeschen," 235-237.

[7] *Ibid.*, 235; *cf.* 211. As late as the 6th of July, Aleander was still in ignorance as to his whereabouts, though he continued to suspect "that Saxon wolf" of concealing him. Brieger, "Aleander und Luther," 245.

[8] " Depeschen," 237, 240-41.

had reached the Wartburg a few days after his arrival, that he had been captured by a party of friendly Franconian nobles.[9] Another tale purported that he had entered Leipzig, the day after his supposed capture, amid the plaudits of the people.[10] An anti-climax to this tale was provided in the story, equally circumstantial and, happily, equally false, that he had been found dead in a silver mine with a dagger through his body.[11] This story raised a storm of anger at Worms where the mob swore vengeance on Aleander and Caracciolo, who were warned by their friends that their lives would not be safe even in the Emperor's arms. " The will of the Lord be done," piously ejaculated Aleander ; " it is His cause that we defend." [12] It evoked a passionate response from many a pious heart all over Germany. Albrecht Dürer, who heard the tragic news in the Netherlands, bewailed in his Diary the untimely fate of " the God-inspired man." " O God, if Luther is dead who will henceforth expound the holy Gospel so clearly to us ? " [13] The same note of passionate anxiety appears in the letter which the jurist and humanist, Gerbellius of Strassburg, addressed to Luther at Wittenberg, telling him of these sinister reports, and of the intense longing of himself and all good and learned men to hear if he was alive and at liberty to write to his friends.[14] This widespread anxiety was erelong dissipated by the assurance indirectly conveyed to his friends far and near that his disappearance was a prearranged device to foil the persecuting policy of his enemies. Already, on the 23rd May, Bucer, writing from Worms, sent a hint of the real facts of the case to Zwingli. " You may take it from me that Luther has indeed been taken captive, but unless I am very much deceived, not at all by his enemies. The thing has been admirably concealed and very prudently carried out." [15]

In view of the popular passion excited by these flying

[9] Enders, iii. 153.
[10] " Depeschen," 238.
[11] *Ibid.*, 238.
[12] *Ibid.*, 238.
[13] Leibschuh, " Albrecht Dürer's Tagebuch," 82-84 (1884) ; Thausing, " Dürer's Briefe, Tagebücher und Reime," 122.
[14] Enders, iii. 159-160, 18th May.
[15] Zwingli, " Opera," vii. 174, ed. Schuler und Schulthess.

rumours, many of Aleander's co-religionists were more than doubtful of the wisdom of the policy of persecution. " Who knows," wrote Luther to Melanchthon, shortly after his arrival in his hiding-place, " what God will effect in His high purpose through this plan of concealment ? The priests and monks who waxed furious against me as a free man have now such fear of me as a captive that they are fain to regret and relax their former foolish zeal. They tremble at the growing menace of the popular hatred, which they know not how to escape. . . . A certain Romanist has written to the Archbishop of Maintz, ' You have got Luther out of the way as you wanted. But the people are so incensed against us that we shall scarcely ransom our lives unless with lighted candles we search for him and invite him to return.' This may have been written in jest. But what if the jest turn out to be serious ? " [16]

Luther was not too happy in his enforced retirement. He feared, he wrote to Melanchthon, lest his disappearance should be regarded as a desertion of the battle.[17] He had only yielded perforce to the advice and will of others and had no greater wish than to expose his throat to the fury of the adversary. He had heard from Spalatin of the preparation of the savage Edict against him and his books. But it will not prove the terrible thing they imagine, except in the hands of blind and boastful men like that Rehoboam of Dresden (Duke George) and his compeer, the Elector Joachim of Brandenburg. " God lives for ever and ever," of whose anger the abominable kingdom of the Roman Antichrist is the horrible spectre. Meanwhile, let Philip realise his vocation as a minister of the Word and man the walls and towers of Jerusalem.[18] The difficulty of adapting himself to the situation, coupled with an invincible confidence in God, also finds expression in the letters to Amsdorf and John Agricola. " Here I sit a strange captive, willing and yet unwilling—willing because God so wills it, unwilling because I should prefer to stand forth in behalf of the Word, but have not yet been found worthy. Wittenberg is hateful

[16] Enders, iii. 147.
[17] Ibid., iii. 148. Verebar ego ne aciem deserere viderer.
[18] Ibid., iii. 148-149.

to its neighbours (Duke George and the Elector Joachim). But the Lord will see to it that His time will come when He will laugh them to scorn. Only let us have faith in Him. Write how it stands with the sermons—what part each takes in order that my hope or fear concerning the Word may increase."[19] " I sit here inactive and out of sorts the whole day long," we read in a letter to Spalatin on the 14th May. He was, however, not so idle as he professed, for he proceeds to tell him that he is reading the Bible in Hebrew and Greek and that he is contemplating writing a work in the vernacular on auricular confession, continuing his commentary on the Psalms and the *Postille*, or popular expositions of the stated lessons from the Gospels and Epistles, and completing the exposition of the *Magnificat* when he shall have received the books about which he had written to Wittenberg.[20] A month later he tells him that he is at once the most inactive (*otiosissimus, i.e.*, free from official duty) and the busiest (*negotiosissimus*) of men. " I am studying Hebrew and Greek and write without inter-mission." He had written expositions of several of the Psalms; had finished the *Magnificat*, which he had begun before the journey to Worms, and the promised work on auricular confession; had elaborated his *Postille* on the Nativity, and was hard at work on his Confutation of Latomus.[21]

The exposition of the 68th Psalm, the first fruit of this literary production at the Wartburg, was penned for the purpose of encouraging his friends at Wittenberg and else-where. The disconsolate Melanchthon had written in doleful strain bewailing his absence and describing the Wittenberg circle as sheep without a shepherd.[22] In reply, Luther sent a spirited message on the 26th May, reminding him how they had often conversed together of faith and hope in the things not seen, bidding him take upon him the mantle of Elijah, sing the song of the Lord in the night, in which he too will join, and not provoke Him to anger by lamentation and faint-heartedness. " For the honour of the Word, and

---

[19] Enders, iii. 151-152.
[20] *Ibid.*, iii. 154; *cf.* 150.
[21] *Ibid.*, iii. 162, 171.
[22] *Ibid.*, iii. 164.

for the confirmation of myself and others, I would rather burn on live coals than, half living and not able to die, rot away here alone. . . . Even if I perish, the Gospel will not perish, in which you now excel me and, like Elisha, succeed Elijah, imbued with a double spirit, which may the Lord impart to you." [23] Passages from the 68th Psalm formed part of the service of the Mass in the chapel of the Wartburg on Ascension Day and Whitsunday (9th and 19th May), and the words, " Let God arise and let his enemies be scattered. Thou hast ascended on high and hast led captivity captive," suggested the exposition as an appropriate message to his friends. The opening verse had formed the exordium of the papal Bull of condemnation, and Luther in turn adapted it to the situation. With a rather facile exegesis, though with increasing evidence of Hebrew scholarship, he sees in these words a prophecy of Christ and the resurrection and the triumph of the Gospel, in spite of its enemies and the difficulties and dangers of the way to heaven. " When Christ died, God did as if He were asleep and saw not the raging Jews who, as the disciples fled and scattered, thought that they had won the day. But God arose and woke Christ from the dead and rallied the disciples, thereby turning the tables on the Jews and putting an end to the glorying of His enemies." [24]

He followed it up with an exposition of Psalm 37 for the benefit of " the poor little flock at Wittenberg." Like St Paul, who from his prison at Rome wrote epistles to comfort and strengthen his converts, he was anxious to guard them from " these wolves, the papists," who malign them as heretics and would fain tear them in pieces. He is absolutely certain that what he has taught them is the true and pure Gospel, for which he has borne testimony at Augsburg, Leipzig, and Worms, and from which his enemies flee as the bats and owls around the Wartburg do the light. They fear discussion and think that they have settled the matter by declaring him and his adherents Wiclifites,

---

[23] Enders, iii. 163. In this reply he enclosed the exposition of the 68th Psalm. Mitto Psalmum istis feriis cantatum (162), with instructions to have it printed or circulated in manuscript.

[24] " Werke," viii. 4-5.

Hussites, heretics. Let them rage and fulminate as they will. He has the Scripture on his side which his opponents handle as skilfully as an ass which would play the harp.[25] With blockheads and sophists like Emser, who wrest the Scriptures to maintain their ecclesiastical nostrums, it is useless to argue. The Scripture, say they, is obscure and not fit for the people to read. On the contrary, no clearer book than the Bible has ever been written, and their distinction between implicit and explicit faith—the faith of the people and the faith of the expert—is a mere subterfuge to keep the people in ignorance and submission to their tyranny. True, there are obscure passages. But these are to be read in the clear light of the Scripture as a whole, which enables every one who will to believe firmly in its teaching. Even the Fathers—Jerome, Augustine, Hilary, for instance—whom they parade as infallible authorities when it suits them, did not lay claim to such authority and recognised the Scripture as the supreme and sole rule of faith. Let the little Wittenberg flock cleave, therefore, to the Word and defy the sophists of Rome, Louvain, Paris, and Leipzig. Grounding on it they will no more esteem and fear the fulminations of the Pope and his satellites than the rock does the raging billows of the sea.[26]

It is thus that Luther himself, firmly grounded in the Scripture as his real Wartburg, breasts the rising storm of persecution and strives to inspire his adherents with his own invincible spirit. The Bible, and the Bible alone, is his battle-cry, and the conviction that he stands for God and His Word is the real secret of the marvellous spiritual resource and power that radiate, in the form of those clandestine communications, all over Germany from the old burg on the height above Eisenach. His claim to a monopoly of correct interpretation sounds rather naïve, inasmuch as his own exegesis is at times artlessly subjective, though here again his growing familiarity with the Hebrew text is very noticeable. He is prone to read into Holy Writ what is in his own mind rather than what was in the mind of the Hebrew seer and singer. He does not make due allowance for

---

[25] " Werke," viii. 210-212.    [26] Ibid., viii. 234-239.

honest conviction in others, though the instances he gives of
the ridiculous exegesis of an Emser and others in support of
their ecclesiastical contentions certainly merit the scorn
and contempt which he heaps upon them.   But then Luther,
with his back to the wall, is fighting for his life and his cause,
and without this supreme belief in himself as well as in the
Word he would have lost both.   " Pray for me," he begs
in conclusion, " that I may become truly pious, for, that I
must be separated from you, I would on no account do the
papists a service and Christ a disservice by allowing myself
to be in the least depressed by them.   I am by God's grace
still as mettlesome and defiant as I have ever been.   In
body I suffer a little infirmity.   But this is of no
consequence." [27]

His infirmity was, however, more serious than he cared
to let be generally known.   He had suffered at Worms
from an attack of indigestion.   The strain had told on his
emaciated body and the malady increased with the change
to the Wartburg.   The lack of exercise and the rich diet
which his host insisted on providing resulted in persistent
constipation, with bleeding from the bowels and sleeplessness
—the worst he had hitherto experienced.[28]   It was accompanied by fits of dejection to which he was temperamentally
subject.[29]   Whilst he was penning these courageous messages
to his absent friends and flock, he was himself in danger of
being engulfed in the deep waters of physical and spiritual
misery, and was battling with the old temptation to doubt
and despair (*Anfechtung*).   The malady reached a crisis in
the beginning of July when, for more than a week, his bodily
and mental suffering became unendurable and he thought
of going to Erfurt for medical advice.   " For the last eight
days," he wrote to Melanchthon on the 13th July, " I have
written nothing.   I neither pray nor study, partly on
account of the trials of the flesh, partly because I am tormented with another malady.   If my condition does not
improve, I shall throw off this disguise and go to Erfurt to

[27] " Werke," viii. 240.

[28] Enders, iii. 171.

[29] *Ibid.*, iii. 163.   Animi molestia nondum cessit et prior spiritus ac
fidei infirmitas perseverat.

consult the doctors, and you will see me there. For I can bear this wretchedness no longer. Nay, I would suffer ten serious wounds more easily than this one seemingly slight lesion. Perchance the Lord thus torments me that He may force me out of this hermitage into the public arena."[30] He got relief from the prescription which Spalatin sent him,[31] though he only gradually recovered and suffered from recurring attacks during the next three months.[32] It was only in the beginning of October that he was able to assure Spalatin that the disorder had yielded to the prescribed treatment.[33]

His recovery was facilitated by the rambles and rides in the neighbourhood with which, at the Warden's instigation, he interrupted his solitary life. He sallied forth to gather wild strawberries on the Schlossberg and joined in the chase. In a letter to Spalatin on the 15th August, he tells of one of these parties and how, amid the snares and the dogs worrying the harmless hares and partridges, he was reminded of the bishops and theologians who, under their master the devil, hunt the innocent souls of men which he was striving to save. He had no pleasure in this sanguinary business and tried to rescue a wretched hare by wrapping it in the fold of his mantle. Even then the dogs would not be denied their prey and worried it through the mantle. " So rage the Pope and Satan in order to destroy the souls I have saved, caring nothing for my efforts to rescue them." [34] In his rides in the neighbourhood he was accompanied by his trusty attendant who, as Mathesius tells, was ever on the alert to prevent him spoiling his part as Knight George by relapsing into his old habits as monk and professor. He could not, for instance, refrain at first from laying aside his sword and picking up a book in the inns which they visited, and had to be reminded that the reading of books did not consort with the profession of knighthood. On one occasion in the inn at Reinhardtsbrunn he was actually recognised, and the ready-witted attendant only saved the situation

---

[30] Enders, iii. 189.
[31] *Ibid.*, iii. 199.
[32] *Ibid.*, iii. 204, 214, 216.
[33] *Ibid.*, iii. 236.
[34] *Ibid.*, iii. 219-220.

by adducing a pressing engagement and hurriedly riding off with him.[35]

During these months of physical and mental suffering the devil was an ever present reality. Despite his emancipation from the mediæval religious standpoint, he retained to the full the mediæval belief in magic and satanic apparitions. Behind the Pope, the Emperor, Duke George, Aleander, Eck, and other enemies lurks the devil, whose agents they are and who is ever lying in wait for Luther himself. In the eerie solitude of his apartment in the haunted old burg, as in his cell at Wittenberg, he occasionally makes his presence known in the nocturnal visitations of which he later discoursed in his " Table Talk." He hears him rattling the hazel nuts in the sack which his house attendants had brought him and which he kept in a closed box. When he put out the light and went to bed the nuts would rattle against the beams and his bed would shake. It did not occur to him that the rats might be playing hide-and-seek in the roof. It could only be the devil trying to disturb his sleep. He did not take the visitation very seriously and erelong fell asleep again. Suddenly he was awakened by a terrible racket as if a whole cartload of casks were rumbling down the stair outside his door. This was really very serious. He started up and opened the door. Nothing was to be seen or heard in the stairway. " Is it you, so be it you," he ejaculated according to the formula usual on such occasions, commending himself to Christ and recalling the words of the Psalmist, " Thou hast placed all things under his feet." [36] Again it did not occur to him that he had been dozing over just as the rats had reached the climax of their antics above the rafters or the wind had roared up the stairway. On another occasion Satan takes the form of a black dog which he dreamed or imagined he had found lying in his bed and had thrown out of the window in Christ's name, with the aforementioned formula

---

[35] "T.R.," v. 103; Walch, xv. 2330-2331. In the "Tischreden" the incident occurs in a monastery at Erfurt.

[36] "Tischreden," iii. 37 (ed. Förstemann), and Weimar ed., v. 87.

on his lips.[37]   The story of his having thrown the ink-bottle
on the occasion of one of these satanic apparitions does not
seem to be authentic.   But on his own testimony such
apparitions were by no means infrequent.   " Believe me,"
he wrote to Gerbellius on the 1st November, " that Satan
throws himself in my way again and again in this easeful
solitude.   It is much easier to fight against the incarnate
devil, that is against men, than against the spiritual hosts of
wickedness in heavenly places.   Too often I fall.   But the
right hand of the Most High sustains me." [38]   " There are
many wicked and cunning demons about me here who, as
they say, pass the time for me and cause me trouble,"
we read in a letter to Spalatin of the same date.[39]   His great
talisman, he tells us, when these experiences came to him,
was the Word, and when the Word threatened to fail him he
had recourse to ridicule.   The devil could not stand this
kind of counter-attack, and the coarser the ridicule the
better.[40]

## II. Renewal of the Battle for Reform

Despite the enforced cessation of his public activity,
he followed with an alert interest the trend of events and
strove to foster and direct the movement at Wittenberg
and elsewhere.   In his eagerness to resume the part of active
reformer, he thought of leaving his solitude and establishing
himself at Erfurt, in spite of the papal ban and the imperial
Edict, and was only restrained from carrying out his purpose
by the remonstrance of Spalatin and an outbreak of the pest.[41]
What he was prevented from doing in person he sought to do
by means of a voluminous correspondence with Spalatin,
Melanchthon, Amsdorf, and others at Wittenberg and
elsewhere.   He notes with delight every indication of
progress from whatever quarter it came.   As the prospect
of his return recedes he urges Spalatin and Amsdorf to prevail

---

[37] " T.R.," v. 87-88 ;  Myconius, " Geschichte," 37 ;  Köstlin-Kawerau, " Luther," i. 439-440.

[38] Enders, iii. 240.                    [40] " Tischreden," iii. 37-38.

[39] *Ibid.*, iii. 243.                    [41] Enders, iii. 203.

on Melanchthon to take his place as a preacher of the Gospel. He suggests that he should address the people in the vernacular on feast days and thus restore the custom of the ancient Church and, at the same time, wean them from the drinking habits and amusements usual on these occasions. He sees no force in the objection that he was not in priest's orders. In expounding the Greek New Testament to his students he is *de facto* performing the office of a priest. In any case he is amply entitled to follow the example of Christ Himself who preached in the synagogues, in boats, on the seashore, on the mountain. If the people call him to this work it is of no consequence that he has not been ordained by the bishop. The people need the Word of God above all things, and their need makes it incumbent that he should undertake this vocation. What is there to hinder him from expounding the Word to the citizens in the common tongue as well as to the students in Latin ? [42] He exhorts Melanchthon himself, who felt that his vocation lay more in the professor's chair and the study than in the pulpit, boldly to preach the grace of God and the fact of sin as the great realities. God, he tells him, does not save fictitious, but real sinners. In striving to impress on him this fact he unfortunately makes use of language which, if read apart from the context, is rather equivocal and has often been quoted by the enemy in discredit of his doctrine of justification. " Be a sinner and sin vigorously. But at the same time confide and rejoice still more boldly in Christ, who is the conqueror of sin and death and the world. As long as we live we must needs sin. For this life is not the habitation of righteousness, but, as Peter says, we look for new heavens and a new earth wherein dwelleth righteousness. It suffices that, through the riches of His glory, we acknowledge the Lamb of God who taketh away the sin of the world. From Him sin will never wrench us away even if we commit fornication or murder a thousand times in one day. Think you that so small a price and redemption have been given for our sins by such and so great a Lamb ? " [43]  The case is no doubt hypothetical, and in his insistence on the power of God's

---

[42] Enders, iii. 230-231 ; *cf.* 233.        [43] *Ibid.*, iii. 208-209.

grace to prevail against the fact of man's sin he forgets
for the moment his distinctive doctrine that justification
necessarily involves the moral regeneration of the believer.
This is one of those extreme utterances to which he was at
times prone, and one can only regret that in putting the case
in this way he did not take time to weigh his words, even in
a private letter to one who was not likely to misunderstand
them. In his propensity to utter things on the spur of the
moment Luther, it must be admitted, was at times his
own worst enemy.

He took a keen interest in the reorganisation of the
University, which the Elector and Spalatin carried out
during a midsummer visit to Wittenberg. The theological
faculty was strengthened by the accession of Aurogallus to
the chair of Hebrew, and of Justin Jonas to that of Canon
Law, which he shortly after exchanged for one of Theology,
and which Luther wished to banish from the curriculum.[44]
He thanked God that He has raised up others to fill his place.
His colleagues had now no need of him, and his only concern
is lest Melanchthon should overtax his strength, in spite of
his repeated warnings, and suffer penury for lack of a
sufficient stipend.[45]

He warmly welcomed the work of Oecolampadius on
" Auricular Confession," the appearance of which in the
previous April had stirred the wrath of Aleander,[46] and
expressed his desire to have it translated into German.[47]
The perusal did not, however, render superfluous his own
work on the same subject, which he dispatched to Spalatin
on the 10th June with the request to have it forthwith
printed.[48] This work is the first of the attacks on the
institutions of the Church launched from the Wartburg, in
continuation of the polemic which the journey to Worms
had interrupted. It is not directed against the practice

[44] Melanchthon, "Opera," i. 390 f. On the Reform of the University,
see Friedensburg, " Geschichte der Universität Wittenberg " (1917).
[45] Enders, iii. 190, 199, 203-204.
[46] " Depeschen," 209-210.          [47] Enders, iii. 162, 180.
[48] Enders, iii. 171. Von der Beicht, ob der Papst macht habe zu
gepieten. " Werke," viii. 140 f. The printing proceeded so slowly that
it did not appear till the end of September.

of confession as far as it is enjoined by Scripture, but against the abuse of it as practised and enforced in the mediæval Church. The actual practice, he contends, is based on a perversion of Scripture and is merely an ecclesiastical device to enslave the penitent to the tyranny of Pope and priest, which he denounces in his most violent mood. Hence the attempt, in the first part, to prove from numerous passages in the Old and New Testaments that it is not permissible to go beyond the clear testimony of Scripture in a matter of this kind and introduce and enforce a usage that rests only on human authority. To do so is to depart from and distort the truth, as did the false prophets against whom the true prophets, Christ, and the Apostles warned. It is of no avail to cite the ordinances of General Councils in support of such usages. The ordinances of Councils like that of Nicæa, which, he assumes, limited themselves to the elucidation of the truth from the Scriptures, are indeed valid, inasmuch as they are in accord with God's Word. But in as far as Councils have legislated a multitude of observances merely out of their own heads, their laws have no authority as against that of the Word. " Therefore Councils here or Councils there, if what they ordain is only human doctrine, it is of no validity. . . . I believe in Christ and Paul His Apostle more than in all Councils, even if they were more in number than the sands of the sea and the stars in the heavens. They are to be condemned if they do not base their decisions on the Word of God." [49]

He proceeds, in the second part, to examine the few scriptural passages adduced in support of the existing practice. He makes sport of the far-fetched and forced exegesis which finds in Matt. viii. 4, " Go show thyself to the priest," and Proverbs xxvii. 23, " Be thou diligent to know the state of thy flocks and look well to thy herds," an argument for auricular confession to a priest. Such silly glosses are more worthy of ridicule than refutation. No wonder that the Romanists strive to keep the people from reading the Bible and thus prevent them from finding out for themselves the lies and crass deception with which they seek to bolster

[49] " Werke," viii. 150.

up their unfounded pretensions. James v. 16 enjoins confession not to a priestly confessor, but to one another. John xx 22-23 only confers the power of absolution on the disciples and leaves confession, which it does not in fact mention, to the discretion of the individual Christian. But, says the priest, in order to absolve from sin it is necessary that the penitent should make known his sins. This, retorts Luther, is to demand the impossible, since no one is able to reckon up his sins. Does not the Psalmist say, " Who can understand his errors," and " Mine iniquities are more than the hairs of my head "? Such a demand tends only to misery of conscience, inasmuch as the priestly absolution must needs leave the penitent in doubt and perturbation. Moreover, the system makes him the victim of a priestly tyranny, which serves to enslave the soul as well as fill the priest's pocket and enhance his power. Therefore they are not to be damned who make confession to God alone or to a fellow-Christian as long as they do so with true repentance and faith.[50]

The third part is a plea for freedom from the mechanical and enforced observance of the ecclesiastical canon of the Fourth Lateran Council, which requires all Christians to confess once a year at least. This observance does not make for real reformation of life, but only fosters formalism and hypocrisy. The people should be drawn to confession and communion by the preaching of the Gospel of faith and repentance, and not driven by ecclesiastical enactment. The soul cannot be saved by mere laws and ordinances, but only by influencing the heart and the will. Confession should, therefore, be voluntary. God's grace seeks and requires the longing heart, not mere ecclesiastical obedience, and only in reliance on His grace, not on prescribed works, can peace of conscience be found. Moreover, the power of loosing and binding was given by Christ to the whole Christian community, not to Pope or priesthood, and it pertains to the community to exercise this power, as in the time of the Apostles and long after. He would fain revive the ancient practice and would rather reform than

[50] " Werke," viii. 152 f.

abolish confession, to which he attaches a high religious value for two reasons. It fosters self-humiliation before God and our neighbour, leads to the Cross by which alone we can find a gracious God, and it enables us to participate with full assurance in the promise, "What things soever ye shall loose on earth shall be loosed in heaven." Here we have a true echo of Luther's own experience in his search for a gracious God which began in self-condemnation and ended in the full assurance of the forgiveness of sins in simple trust in God's mercy and love in Christ. "O, if we knew how gracious it makes God that a man should thus abase and humble himself in His honour, we would dig up confession from the earth and fetch it a thousand times over. For the whole Scripture testifies how gracious and loving God is to those who thus abase and condemn themselves." [51] "How grand and sure a thing it is to take God at His own word and feel that we have so strong a support and confidence in His truth that we may freely and boldly urge God Himself with His own word." [52]

He was immensely gratified by Melanchthon's confutation of the fulmination against his teaching which the Theological Faculty of the University of Paris had at last issued on the 15th April.[53] "I have seen the Decree of the Parisian sophists with Philip's Apology," he wrote to Spalatin on the 15th July, "and I rejoice with all my heart." [54] He forthwith determined to translate both into the vernacular, with a characteristic preface and conclusion,[55] and dispatched the translation to Wittenberg.[56] The doctors of the Sorbonne had discovered no less than 104 heresies in his writings and they expressed their opinion of their author in the current

[51] "Werke," viii. 176.

[52] *Ibid.*, viii. 178. Luther elaborated his exegesis of Matt. viii. 4 in the "Evangelium von den Zehn Aussätzigen" at the request of Duke John, the brother of the Elector, which was issued from the press in the beginning of Nov. 1521. "Werke," viii. 340 f.

[53] Melanchthon, "Opera," i. 398 f. ("Corp. Ref."). Adversus Furiosum Parisiensium Theologastrorum Decretum pro Luthero Apologia, June 1521.

[54] Enders, iii. 200.

[55] *Ibid.*, iii. 190.

[56] It was finished in the beginning of Aug. *Ibid.*, iii. 215.

vituperative style. Luther, it is evident from this document, was not singular in claiming a monopoly of the truth against opponents and imputing to them the worst of motives. In this respect he is no better and no worse than the Sorbonne divines who described him as one of those vipers who devour their own mother, the Church. He is a presumptuous blasphemer who claims to know better than all the Fathers, theologians, and Councils of the Church, as if God had reserved to him alone a knowledge of the things necessary to salvation. Such audacity and impiety can only be overcome by prison, ban, and fire, rather than by reason, and this conviction appears to explain why, in condemning him, they do not condescend to argue with him. They simply declare him an arch-heretic and blasphemer like Arius, Manicheus, Wiclif, Hus, and many more agents of the devil. Like all heretics he wrests the Scriptures to please himself, and in so doing has simply renewed the heresies of these diabolic perturbers of the Church. In particular, his book on the " Babylonic Captivity " is as bad as the Koran and can only have been written by an accursed enemy of the Church. They accordingly condemn in virulent terms the long list of articles bearing on faith and morals, drawn from this and his other writings, though significantly enough they pass over his views on the papal power in silence.[57] Their own reputation in this matter was gravely suspect in papal eyes, and the omission of this cardinal heresy from the list rather qualified the approval with which Aleander reported the deliverance to Rome.[58]

Though the Sorbonne doctors were experts in the current art of theological vituperation, they were greatly inferior to Luther in ironic retort and rough humour. " Now we see what our Parisian Masters are capable of when they get thoroughly angry. If I say that the Dean of the Paris Faculty of Theology and his fellow-sophists are unmitigated asses, I shall only give them occasion to draw up another article and say, ' This article is false, foolish, sacrilegious, unchristian, presumptuous, erroneous, heretical, and

[57] " Werke," viii. 268 f.

[58] Brieger, " Aleander und Luther," 237, uno solo hanno fatto male, che de primatu pontificis non hanno fatto mentione alcuna.

personal.' But what else could these furious gentlemen of
the Sorbonne do ? Who could have imagined that there
were such children, such old wives, such fools in the
schools ? " [59] Unlike the Apostles, these blind and mad
schoolmen do not trouble to give reasons for their findings.
In particular, the Scriptures do not seem to exist for them
and they simply wrest his views to suit their arbitrary
conclusions. What passage of Scripture could not be
proved to be heretical on this principle ? But this method
of merely denouncing the views of an opponent and answering
arguments by calling out heretic will not do in these days of
growing enlightenment. · " It won't do any longer, my dear
asses, merely to pass judgments without reasons given, as
you have hitherto done so long and now do. You have so
long led the common man by the nose and plundered him
in body, goods, and soul with your doctrines, that he no
longer can, will, or ought to suffer it. He is becoming
wide awake and is determined to get to the bottom of the
knavery which you have practised on him and still practise
in the name of Holy Church. The time has come of which
it is said, ' Render an account of your stewardship.' " [60]
Since they have set the example he will also declare his
opinion of them without reasons given and will deal with
them far less gently than Melanchthon in his " Apology."
Instead of handling them like Philip with the light plane,
he will dress them down with the peasant's axe. This he
proceeds to do with the lusty vigour and in the homely
language of the peasant. In short, he tells them that they
are the most inveterate blockheads and asses that he has
ever met and he does not neglect to turn to account their
evasion of the crucial question of the papal supremacy.
They have left the papists without a head and have robbed
his opponents of Leipzig, Rome, Cologne, and Louvain
of their idol, " Now then, ye papists of Rome, Cologne,
Louvain, and elsewhere, ye have the judgment of Paris.
Sing and dance and enjoy yourselves over it as ye will,
ye have lost your head." [61] He and his adherents, on the

[59] " Werke," viii. 290-291.    [61] *Ibid.*, viii. 293.
[60] *Ibid.*, viii. 293.

other hand, will none the less be of good cheer and will, like Paul, thank God and take courage.  " My heart is glad and gives thanks to God.  O how whole-heartedly I wish the Pope joy of such defenders, since he is not worthy of better. How has he corrupted and spoiled us poor Christians with his laws !  But now God has begun to pay him back and provides him with such champions, of whom he must be ashamed in his heart.  O how must his heart fail him and the evil spirit tremble that the light has at last dawned which he would fain extinguish, and which the more he seeks to extinguish the brighter it becomes and the more it declares his shame.  Let us, therefore, with joy and full confidence pray, *Manda, Deus, virtuti tuæ.  Confirma hoc, Deus, quod operatus es in nobis.*  The last judgment is, I hope, before our doors." [62]

Having thus drastically settled with the Sorbonne divines, the trend of events led him to revert to more practical matters.  The question of the celibacy of the clergy, both secular and regular, had by this time become an urgent one. One of his old students, Barth. Bernhardi, Provost of the University living of Kemberg in electoral Saxony, had ventured to marry, and a couple of other priests in the dioceses of Magdeburg and Meissen had taken the liberty to do likewise.  These two delinquents were promptly arrested and imprisoned by their ecclesiastical superiors, the Archbishop of Maintz and Magdeburg and the Bishop of Meissen.  The archbishop in addition demanded the extradition of Bernhardi at the hands of the Elector of Saxony.  Instead of complying, the Elector referred the case for report to the Wittenberg jurists, and in July Melanchthon submitted to his legal colleagues a defence in behalf of the accused.  In this document [63] he claimed that the marriage was legitimate on the ground that it was in accordance with scriptural precept and the practice of the ancient Church, which had been perpetuated in the Greek Church down to the present time.  Moreover, in the Western Church celibacy was a late innovation which had been imposed on the Germans without their consent and was an

---

[62] "Werke," viii. 293-294.        [63] " Opera," i. 421 f.

unwarranted oppression of conscience and an infringement
of individual liberty, in deference to mere human tradition.
Even the Canon Law only made its observance binding " in
as far as human frailty would permit." [64] The accused
was besides not conscious that he had explicitly sworn to
observe celibacy, and had found by experience that it was
impossible to do so owing to the infirmity of the flesh.
It was a matter of conscience, and with Scripture and the
practice of the early Church to guide him, he had determined
to free his conscience from the yoke of human tradition
and enter into the estate of wedlock, in accordance with the
divine sanction and ordinance.

Carlstadt improved on Melanchthon's contention in this
document by demanding, in an academic disputation on
the 21st June and in his work " Super Coelibatu," in
amplification of his thesis on the subject, the abolition of
celibacy for monks and nuns as well as for priests. He
even went the length, by a forced interpretation of Scripture
texts like 1 Tim. iii. 2, " The bishop must be the husband
of one wife," of maintaining that only married men should
be ordained as priests and demanding that those who live
in concubinage should be compelled by the bishop to marry.
From 1 Tim. v. 9, " Let none be enrolled as a widow under
threescore years old," he not only condemned the admission
of young persons of both sexes to the monastic life, but
accorded monks and nuns below this age freedom to marry
and live in wedlock in the religious houses. They indeed
commit sin in breaking the vow of chastity. But they sin
still more heinously in transgressing in secret this vow by
their sexual excesses.[65]  " Good God," wrote Luther to
Spalatin on the 6th August on receiving the sheets of
Carlstadt's work, " our Wittenbergers will give wives even
to the monks !  But they will not thrust a wife on me." [66]
He had himself advocated the marriage of priests in the
" Address to the German Nobility " and was prepared
to approve of that of his old student Bernhardi, though he
could not help marvelling at his boldness.[67]  Priestly celibacy

[64] " Opera," i. 435.                    [66] Enders, iii. 215.
[65] Barge, " Karlstadt," i. 265 f.      [67] Ibid., iii. 163, 165, 206.

is, he writes to Melanchthon (1st August), a mere human ordinance and is, therefore, not binding on Christian men. It is contrary to the clear testimony of 1 Tim. iv. 3, in which Paul condemns the false teachers of his time who forbid marriage and whom he denounces as agents of the devil. He would, therefore, on the ground of this explicit testimony, allow priests to exercise liberty in this matter.[68] But he questioned Carlstadt's view, which Melanchthon shared, that monks might also exercise this liberty and was not satisfied with the fanciful and arbitrary exegesis of passages like 1 Tim. iii. 2 and v. 9, with which Carlstadt attempted to justify the marriage of monks as well as priests. He fears that it will expose them and their cause to the calumny and ridicule of the enemy.[69] Moreover, he doubts whether monks and nuns who have voluntarily chosen the celibate state and offered themselves to God have the right equally with priests to break an obligation deliberately taken, except in the case of those who have taken this vow before the age of puberty and without a due sense of what it implies.[70] In thus differentiating between priests and monks in this matter, he does not seem to realise that the former as subdeacons had come under the obligation henceforth to maintain chastity and explicitly renounced their freedom to marry.[71] From the point of view of ecclesiastical law, the distinction was, therefore, really one without a difference, and from the scriptural point of view the argument based on 1 Tim. iv. 3, in favour of the marriage of priests, might also be used in favour of that of monks. At this stage, however, Luther was not prepared to draw this conclusion. He was, indeed, convinced that, if Christ were to return, He would break these chains and abolish all burdensome restrictions tending to hinder the salvation of souls.[72] But he has not yet discovered the explicit testimony of Scripture for which he is

[68] Enders, iii. 206-207.

[69] *Ibid.*, iii. 210-211 ; *cf.* 218.

[70] *Ibid.*, iii. 206-207.

[71] See the condition of ordination as subdeacon given by Kawerau, " Werke," viii. 314.

[72] Enders, iii. 212.

searching and which would enable him to give a definite
decision on the point, though he would fain succour the
miserable victims of the monastic system, who are tormented
with temptations of the flesh.[73] He fears, too, the scandal
to which the wholesale renunciation of vows will give rise
without such a manifest warrant of Scripture.[74] In
particular, he is very dubious as to the effects on both
morality and social order of the argument used by
Melanchthon,[75] that the vow of celibacy is not binding,
simply because it is not possible for human frailty to keep
it.   Might not this argument, he asked, be used as an excuse
for dissolving marriage and breaking all God's commandments at will ?   The question was so important and caused
him such anxiety that he suggested that he and Melanchthon
should secretly meet in some place to discuss it.[76]   It
looks, he jocularly adds, as if Melanchthon in troubling
him with the subject were determined to have his revenge
for his having inflicted a wife on him by forcing him also
to enter the married state.  " But," he adds, " I will take
good care that you shall not succeed." [77]

### III. THE ATTACK ON MONASTICISM

Meanwhile he sent him a long series of theses on the
subject, inscribed to " the bishops and deacons of the
Church at Wittenberg," with the promise to add an elucidation of them later.[78] He envisages it from the standpoint
of his cardinal doctrine of justification by faith.   He starts
by quoting Paul, " Whatsoever is not of faith is sin "
(Romans xiv. 23).   This, he holds, is to be understood

[73] Enders, iii. 207.  Scripturam quæsimus et testimonium divinæ
voluntatis.

[74] *Ibid.*, iii. 206-207.  Scandala etiam vitanda sunt, ubi non est
manifesta scriptura pro nobis, quantumvis licita sunt.

[75] In some supplementary sheets of his " Loci Communes " which,
along with a letter on the subject, he sent him in the beginning of
Sept.   Enders, iii. 222.

[76] *Ibid.*, iii. 222-223.                    [77] *Ibid.*, iii. 227.

[78] *Ibid.*, iii. 226, 9th Sept.  " Themata de Votis," " Werke," viii.
323 f.

of the faith that alone justifies in virtue solely of God's grace and not of man's works. /Those who have vowed themselves to the religious life in order by monastic works to merit salvation have totally misapprehended this fundamental principle of the spiritual life.  By relying on such works instead of on faith in God's mercy, they have grossly erred from the divine way of salvation and are guilty of infidelity and impiety towards God./ There is scarcely one in a thousand in these days who has not taken the monastic vows with the object of earning thereby salvation, and it is probable that they would not have done so if they had known that they could not attain saving righteousness by this means.  Such vows are, therefore, not binding and should be discarded without regard to ecclesiastical authority or the opprobrium of common opinion.[79]  He does not, indeed, condemn the monastic life if adopted freely and in the right religious spirit.  The New Testament is the reign of liberty and faith [80] and leaves the believer free to exercise his liberty in this matter.  Those who, like St Bernard, have taken the monastic vows in a truly religious spirit may do so as long as they do not confide in monastic works for salvation. But this manner of life is liable to lead to the perversion of the Gospel and the perdition of souls,[81] and as practised at the present time it is almost universally pernicious.  It is based not only on ignorance of true faith, but on an unwarranted distinction between the precepts and the counsels of the Gospel, which falsely exalts the monastic life as the state of perfection in depreciation of the ordinary Christian life.  Moreover, it assumes a distinction between the ordinary Christian and the ecclesiastical orders which, as far as Christian life and duty are concerned, does not exist, and is nothing but an ecclesiastical mask.[82] / The great test of Christian living is, next to faith, the love of one's neighbour and active well doing, and to bury oneself in a monastery and shun the ordinary duties of life, on the pretext of obedience to the monastic rule, is to obey Satan

---

[79] " Themata," 43-53.

[80] Novum enim Testamentum regnum est libertatis et fidei, 73.

[81] " Themata," 71-102.

[82] *Ibid.*, 103-115.

rather than God and neglect the Christian law of service for others. ⌊The chains of monastic vows and rules, which stand in the way of common service, ought to be broken, as Samson broke the withes of the Philistines.⌉

In a second series specifically dealing with the question, ⌈whether it is permissible to vow a perpetual vow, which he sent a few days later,[83] he emphatically maintains the negative on the ground of the essential liberty of the Gospel.[84]⌋ All vows, he insists, must be such as are not incompatible with this liberty, which is by divine right and gift, and no vow such as virginity ought to be taken except on the understanding that one is free in accordance with the Gospel to relinquish it.[85] It is of the essence of the Gospel that the principle of liberty be maintained, " Nothing may be done against liberty, but only in behalf of liberty." [86] Moreover, ⌊such vows are merely of human ordinance and institution, and whatever is not prescribed in Scripture is to be avoided.⌉ In view of the danger of the monastic life from the evangelical standpoint, it is far safer for those who have entered it to renounce it.[87]

These theses made a profound impression on his colleagues at Wittenberg.   When the first series arrived, Melanchthon was sitting at dinner with Peter Suaven, Luther's companion on the journey to Worms, and John Bugenhagen.  " These theses," said Bugenhagen, after reading them several times with wrapt attention, " will effect a revolution of the existing order."  " They mean," added Melanchthon, " the beginning of the liberation of the monks." [88]   They sent both series to the press, from which they issued on the 8th October.   The impression which, in book form, they produced far beyond Wittenberg, was deepened by the work on " Monastic Vows," [89] in which he elaborated them and which he finished on the 21st November.   In the course of writing it he was, as he tells Gerbel, bringing forth " a son who should smite the papists, sophists, monks, and Herodists with a rod of iron."  " So many evils does this most wretched

[83] Enders, iii. 232.
[84] " Werke," viii. 330 f.
[85] " Themata," 1-18.
[86] *Ibid.*, 34.
[87] *Ibid.*, 125-128.
[88] " Werke," viii. 317.
[89] " De Votis Monasticis," " Werke," viii. 573 f.

celibacy daily produce in the case of young men and women that nothing more hateful sounds in my ears than the name of nun, monk, priest, and I account the most careworn married life a paradise in comparison." [90]  In the dedication to his father he joyfully announces that his conscience has been liberated from the teaching and superstition of men in this matter.  " Christ has absolved me from the monastic vow and has given me such liberty that, while He has made me the servant of all, I am nevertheless subject to Him alone. . . . What if the Pope shall kill me and condemn me to the lowest hell ?  I desire nothing better than to be damned and never to be absolved by him." [91]

This does not mean that he had determined to disregard his vow.  It only means that he had ceased to regard it as an essential or even a desirable element of piety.  Nor does it mean that he was desirous to escape from the burden of celibacy in order to be free to indulge the sexual appetite. The book was certainly not written from any such motive. He had resolved to remain in his present state, he wrote to Link after its completion.[92]  Nor is his purpose merely to engage in an aggressive polemic against his enemies, but to guide those who were tormented with scruples of conscience and the sense of sin, under the bondage of their vows, and needed enlightenment and counsel.[93]  He had, in fact, as he informed Spalatin on the 22nd November, heard that a number of the monks at Wittenberg had renounced their vows and abandoned the monastery [94]—a tribute to the influence of his theses as well as to the preaching of the Augustinian monk, Zwilling.  He was afraid lest they had done so without sufficient knowledge or reflection, and his anxiety had led him to pen this work in order to regulate and moderate the movement.[95]  He regarded it as the most

[90] Enders, iii. 241, 1st Nov.

[91] " Werke," viii. 576.

[92] Enders, iii. 258, nam et ego in habitu et ritu isto manebo nisi mundus alius fiat.

[93] " Werke," viii. 577 ; cf. 666 and 668.

[94] Enders, iii. 250, and see the letter of the Prior Helt to the Elector, " Opera Melanchthoni," i. 484, 12th Nov. ;  Nik. Müller, " Die Wittenberger Bewegung," 68 (1911).

[95] Ibid., iii. 250.

powerful and irrefutable of all his writings.[96]  It is certainly remarkable for the skill and force, the lucidity and fertility of thought with which he brings his evangelical teaching to bear on the subject, though it should not be forgotten that it had been to a certain extent anticipated by that of Carlstadt.[97]

To this end he gives a clear and concise exposition of his doctrine of justifying faith versus works in the monastic sense,[98] and this doctrine is the touchstone of his attitude on the question. Monasticism, he repeats, is based on a complete misapprehension of the Gospel by which God in His grace grants the remission of sin through faith alone, and not through works of any kind. The notion that salvation can be most surely attained by taking the monastic vows and living in accordance with the rule of the Order is, he maintains, current in all the monasteries, though it is contrary to the views of the better representatives of the monastic life such as St Bernard and St Francis.[99]  " Ask all the votaries of the monastic life why they have taken these vows and you will find them possessed by this impious notion.  They conceive that the grace of baptism (by which the remission of sin is given through faith) is ineffectual and that they must take refuge from shipwreck in the life of penance and strive by this means not only to attain the good and frustrate the effects of sin, but even by a more abundant penance become better than other Christians. That this is their striving is proved by their own testimony. If, say they, I should not find salvation in this way of life, why should I subject myself to it ? " [100]  So inveterate is this current belief that the monks even go the length of regarding their entrance on the monastic life as a second baptism, and believe that the merits arising from it are so great that they assure an immediate entrance into heaven after death and are available for the salvation of others.[1]

From the evangelical point of view, on the other hand,

---

[96] " Werke," viii. 569.

[97] Barge, i. 300.

[98] " Werke," viii. 593-594.

[99] *Ibid.*, viii. 590.

[100] *Ibid.*, viii. 595.

[1] *Ibid.*, viii. 598-600.

this is a reversion to Jewish legalism from which Paul delivered Christianity.[2] In this sense the votaries of the monastic system are apostates from the Gospel. To become a monk is to deny Christ and become a Jew.[3] He applies to them the words of I Tim. iv. 1-2, " In later times men shall fall away from the faith, giving heed to seducing spirits and doctrines of devils." [4] He even goes the length of equating monasticism not only with Judaism, but with Manichæism.[5] It avails not that they seek to justify their legalism by distinguishing between the evangelical counsels and precepts. This distinction is mere quibbling for the purpose of justifying their stupid superstition. It has no basis in the Gospel. The Sermon on the Mount, for instance, is not a series of counsels for the exercise of this so-called higher life, but a series of instructions for all Christians. The common Christian life is the only true Christian life.[6] Moreover, this so-called higher Christian life is a sham and a pretence. No class is more influenced by the common passions of human nature than the monks and nuns who neither are nor can be without concupiscence.[7] Paul, indeed, praises celibacy on the ground that it enables those who practise it to devote themselves to God's service by freeing them from the cares and tribulations of the married state, and in this sense he will not quarrel with it. But Paul leaves it to the free choice of the individual, and only in as far as it is in accord with evangelical liberty is it permissible.[8] This liberty specifically consists in the emancipation of conscience from the tyranny of works in the legalist sense, from the monastic penitential system, not from works which faith brings forth and which Christ operates in the believer.[9] All vows assumed in this legalist spirit, which thus perverts the Gospel of God's grace and infringes the principle of evangelical liberty, are utterly reprehensible and ought straightway to be renounced. He has now no hesitation in demanding this renunciation in the case of monks as well as priests, and the fact that

[2] " Werke," viii. 600-601.
[3] Ibid., viii. 600.
[4] Ibid., viii. 595.
[5] Ibid., viii. 597-598.
[6] Ibid., viii. 580-583.
[7] Ibid., viii. 585.
[8] Ibid., viii. 585.
[9] Ibid., viii. 606-607.

the latter have voluntarily come under the obligation of celibacy no longer avails as an argument in favour of its observance. " I would dare to absolve all monks from their vows and confidently pronounce that these vows are reprehensible and null in God's sight. Formerly, indeed, I was prepared to absolve only priests from the vow of celibacy. But on a closer study of the words of Paul in I Tim. iv. 1-2, I have come to see that they apply generally to all celibates, monks as well as priests." [10]

He has discarded, too, the fear that the renunciation of such vows will prove a danger to social order and morality, inasmuch as evangelical liberty in this matter is concerned solely with the relation between God and the individual, not with the relation between the individual and his neighbour.[11] On the other hand, the monastic system, under the false pretext of what is called " freedom in spiritual things," *i.e.*, the right of children to embrace the monastic life without the consent of parents—of which he himself had wrongly made use when he became a monk—virtually assumes the right to abrogate all social and civil ties and obligations.[12]

His argumentation is largely of a theological character. The decisive test in judging the monastic system is the testimony of Scripture, especially his doctrine of justification by faith. Hence the intensely dogmatic note of the treatise, the marked tendency which, however, he shares with his age, to see nothing but error and perversity on the other side. One feels here, as in many of his other works, that, cogent as many of his arguments are, he would have made out a stronger case if he had been content to eschew the imputation to his opponents of unworthy motives and wholesale wickedness on purely theological grounds. Here, as elsewhere, he is too prone to be the man of one idea. At the same time he by no means neglects to envisage the subject from the practical point of view, and his arguments from this point of view are very forcible. One of the strongest of them is the contention that the monastic

[10] "Werke," viii. 597 ; *cf.* 598.        [12] *Ibid.*, viii. 627.
[11] *Ibid.*, viii. 615.

profession does not square with the monastic practice in regard to the vow of poverty, for instance. The monks stress the obligation of their vows and magnify their virtues above those of the ordinary life of men. But they do not really observe them and their profession is largely hypocritical. Evangelical poverty consists in not being covetous and ministering of our substance freely for the benefit of others. But this vow is, in practice, largely an illusion and a mockery, since no class is more tenacious of its property and its rights and more grasping than the monks.[13] The vow of poverty is thus really a sham. Monastic poverty might more truly be termed abundance.[14] The monasteries are endowed with large possessions and offer an easy means of subsistence. In those monasteries where poverty truly reigns the applications for admission are few enough.[15] Real poverty does not mean the possession of things in common, as the monks pretend, but the lack of subsistence. They fleece the people in order to live in ease and plenty and so hinder the people from succouring the truly poor in their midst.[16] Like locusts this multitude of lazy and useless persons devour the substance of others, whilst rendering service and benefit to none.

Equally objectionable from the practical point of view is the vow of obedience which enjoins obedience only to the superior of the Order, and even so only in the things enjoined by the rule, whereas the Gospel commands obedience to all in the common service of the community.[17] This separation from the Christian community, which leads to the neglect of the practical duties of life under the plea that obedience is better than sacrifice (1 Sam. xv. 22), is not merely a perversion of the words of the prophet, but a travesty of the higher form of religious life which they profess to exemplify. This life consists in active well-doing for the service of others, not in donning a cowl, shaving the head, sleeping in a common dormitory, eating in a common refectory, giving oneself to the formal routine of religious exercises, whilst neglecting the active service commanded

[13] " Werke," viii. 587.
[14] *Ibid.*, viii. 643.
[15] *Ibid.*, viii. 642.
[16] *Ibid.*, viii. 642-645.
[17] *Ibid.*, viii. 586.

by God. It is of no avail to adduce the plea of this so-called higher devotion to the things of the spirit. The best worship of God is the keeping of His commandments,[18] whereas the rendering of a partial obedience under the monastic rule results only in the maintenance of a multitude of lazy and useless people, who, like locusts, devour the substance of others, whilst rendering service to none and making the commandments of God of no effect.[19] The obedience of wives to husbands, children to parents, servants to masters, subjects to rulers is far more in accordance with the Gospel, which teaches us to serve all freely without regulation or limitation. Monastic obedience is, in the words of 2 Tim. iii. 5, merely " a form of godliness, whilst denying the power thereof." [20]

For Luther the vow of chastity is now equally invalid, not merely because it is contrary to evangelical liberty, but because his experience of the monastic life, though not necessarily his own personal experience, has proved that it is impossible to preserve it. He has from his own observation found the most glaring contradiction between profession and practice. He evidently speaks with knowledge when he says that many who, in immature years, have taken this vow have discovered that they are really incapable, by their temperament and the natural disposition to do the evil rather than the good, of keeping it, and he contends that in view of this indisputable fact it should only be taken conditionally.[21] On grounds of common sense as well as Scripture, celibacy, he now maintains, is a matter which ought to be left to the judgment of the individual, and not formally prescribed and maintained apart from temperament and experience. The law of God and nature alike is to increase and multiply, and it is a mistake to attempt mechanically to reverse this law by a rigid rule.[22] In deciding to abandon this vow, immaturely imposed, one is not breaking a divine command, for God has not imposed celibacy as a condition of the spiritual and moral life.[23] His observation has convinced him that the life of solitude

[18] " Werke," viii. 625-626.
[19] Ibid., viii. 623-629.
[20] Ibid., viii. 645 f.
[21] Ibid., viii. 630-632.
[22] Ibid., viii. 630-631.
[23] Ibid., viii. 632.

and mechanical religious observance is not generally favourable to a chaste habit of mind. It tends, in fact, to intensify the passions which assert themselves with all the greater force as the result of artificial repression. It generally produces a morbid state of sexual desire, with evil physical and moral effects which render this so-called monastic chastity an impossibility. Monks and nuns, he says, are usually the victims of the flames of lust and self-pollution.[24] He and many others with him had found by experience that the early stage of the monastic life was peaceful and happy. But this early experience during the year of probation is no guarantee of future immunity from the temptations of the flesh and of the maintenance of the truly chaste mind.[25] For such, marriage is the only remedy. It is a natural and honourable state, and it is a lying invention that one cannot serve God in the married state, as they pretend. Celibacy, on the other hand, leads to a miserable torment of conscience far more than the cares of married life.[26] It is verily a false notion that the true Christian life is only to be found in a monastery. For him monasticism has become in theory and practice largely a pseudo-Christian institution. It is not surprising that Sylvanus in a vision discovered that hell was full of monks![27] He would turn the monasteries into schools for the instruction of youth in faith and religious discipline until they reach mature age.[28] [Whilst leaving the individual free to decide for himself and not condemning the monastic life, if the principle of evangelical faith and liberty is maintained,[29] he concludes that, confiding in the Gospel, these vows may safely be renounced and a return made to the liberty of the Christian faith.] "Let us do the right through good report and ill. The Lord judges the peoples of the earth with equity. Let every man be a liar; let God alone be true."[30]

With these words he sends out this manifesto in which he sets forth with such argumentative force the evangelical, in opposition to the mediæval conception of the Christian

[24] "Werke," viii. 649.
[25] Ibid., viii. 660-661.
[26] Ibid., viii. 665.
[27] Ibid., viii. 657.
[28] Ibid., viii. 641.
[29] Ibid., viii. 616.
[30] Ibid., viii. 54, 666-668.

life. It is a challenge all along the line to the dominant
but effete monastic system and a trumpet call in behalf of
emancipation from this system in accordance with the
teaching of Christ and Paul, and to a certain extent the
dictates of reason and natural law. Luther's Christianity
and his humanity alike have become too large for the limits
of the cloister with its concentration on self, its legalist
conception of God and religion, and its narrow outlook on
life and the world. In spite of its pronouncedly theological
standpoint, the work is a truly human document. It
consecrates the whole of human life as a service of God,
inspired by faith and love of one's neighbour, in opposition
to monastic supernaturalism and formalism. In view of the
far-reaching effects of this principle in the sphere of the
practical life, the attack on monasticism is as much a land-
mark of the evangelical movement as was the attack on
the scholastic theology, the papal absolutism, and the
sacramental system of the Church in the sphere of doctrine.
In the development of Luther's thought the " De Votis
Monasticis " deserves to take rank with the " Commentary
on Romans " and the " Babylonic Captivity."

It is hardly surprising that the cautious Elector hesitated
to launch this new bombshell against the old system by
sending it to the printer at Wittenberg, in accordance with
Luther's directions to Spalatin.[31] Spalatin kept back the
manuscript, instead of forwarding it to Wittenberg, and it
was only in deference to Luther's energetic insistence, coupled
with the threat to write an even more violent philippic,[32]
that he gave way, and the work at length appeared in
February 1522.[33] He was clearly becoming impatient of
these gagging tactics, which only intensified his sense of
the impotence which his exile at the Wartburg imposed on
him. If he could not act, he was determined that neither
the Elector nor Spalatin should assume the right to dictate
what he should write or print. He had, he wrote to Spalatin
on the 9th September, too often practised self-restraint
towards his opponents at their instigation. The Erasmic

[31] Enders, iii. 250; cf. 252.        [33] " Werke," viii. 565-566.
[32] Ibid., iii. 252-253.

style of controversy effected nothing and only confirmed the Romanists in their incorrigibility. The prophet Jeremiah was a better guide in this matter than Erasmus. If he had followed his own inclination at Worms, instead of the advice of Spalatin and other friends, he would have spoken very differently. " I very much fear and am troubled in my conscience that, yielding to your advice and that of other friends, I repressed my spirit at Worms and did not show myself an Elijah in the presence of these idols. They would hear a very different tone if I should once more stand in their presence." [34]

Meanwhile the ideas on the subject to which he had given expression in his theses, and of which the work was the elaboration, had already borne fruit in the monasteries. " If," he had written, " the monks knew that only by faith is salvation attainable, would they not forthwith conclude, what necessity is there for taking these vows and becoming a monk ? " [35] The sequel speedily brought the answer. At a Chapter of the Augustinian Order convened at Wittenberg by Link in the beginning of January 1522 and attended by those favourable to Luther's side of the question the decision was a foregone conclusion. He had taken care to prompt both Link and Lang beforehand as to the policy to be adopted.[36] He did not approve of the precipitate and tumultuous secession from the Wittenberg monastery, and would rather that renunciation should take place with mutual agreement and concord. But he would recall none against his will and would accord full liberty to depart or remain. " Certain I am that you will not do or suffer anything to be done against the Gospel even if all monasteries are to go under. I do not think you can prevent the departure of those who wish to go, and the best plan to adopt at the forthcoming Chapter is, following the example of Cyrus in the case of the Jews, to issue a public declaration granting liberty to go or stay, expelling no one and retaining no one by force." [37] The Chapter, professing

---

[34] Enders, iii. 229-230.
[35] " Werke," viii. 596 ; cf. 603.
[36] Enders, iii. 256-258, 18th and 20th Dec.
[37] Ibid., iii. 258.

to be guided solely by Scripture and not by human traditions, and proclaiming the evangelical principle that whatever
is not of faith is sin, accordingly conceded to all members
of the Order liberty to continue in or renounce the monastic
life. A vow contrary to the Gospel is no vow but an
impiety, though no one should make use of this liberty from
carnal motives but solely on conscientious grounds. Those
who decide to continue in the monastic life may retain the
monastic habit and rule. In the matter of the retention
or the abrogation of ceremonies, respect should be had
to the weaker brethren and charity observed in the spirit
of Paul who became all things to all men, though the
Kingdom of God does not consist in eating and drinking,
but in righteousness, peace, and joy in the Holy Ghost.
Begging and masses for the dead in return for money are,
however, interdicted in deference to the Apostolic command
to abstain from all appearance of evil. Those who are
qualified shall teach the Word of God publicly and privately ;
the others shall engage in manual labour.[38] The decision
was thus in keeping with Luther's mind on the matter in
preference to that of extremists like Zwilling who had
demanded the radical abolition of the monastic system.
Practically, however, it effected this result as far as the
Augustinian Order at Wittenberg was concerned. When
Luther returned in the spring of 1522, Prior Helt was the
sole occupant of the monastery. The provision of 100 gulden
to each of the retiring monks had facilitated the process of
evacuation.[39]

## IV. Communion in both Kinds and the Abuse of the Mass

Carlstadt again took the lead in agitating the question
of communion in both kinds. In an academic disputation
on the 19th July he not only claimed the right of such
communion for every Christian, but maintained that it is

[38] " Opera Melanchthoni," i. 456-458, wrongly dated Oct. 1521.
N. Müller, " Die Wittenberger Bewegung," 147 f.
[39] Hausrath, " Luther's Leben," i. 514.

sinful to partake of the bread alone and not of the wine.
" We are not Hussites, but true Christians who take the
cup as well as the bread." Only in so doing does the Christian
fulfil the ordinance of Christ, and it would be more salutary
not to take communion at all than to take it in one kind.[40]
In another disputation held three days later he attacked
the ceremonial of the Mass and demanded its trenchant
reform.[41] The actual agent of this reform was, however,
not Carlstadt, but Gabriel Zwilling, a native of German
Bohemia and a member of the Augustinian Order, whose
Bohemian origin doubtless contributed to make him an
ardent votary of his teaching. Though inferior to him in
theological erudition he was gifted with a fiery popular
eloquence, and his sermons on the subject packed to over-
flowing the monastery chapel, and, it would seem, also
the parish church. His audience included professors and
students as well as townsfolk, and Melanchthon was a
regular hearer. So deeply was he impressed by these
sermons that he took part along with his students in a
celebration of the communion in both kinds in the parish
church on St Michael's Day (29th September).[42] Zwilling's
hearers spoke of him as " a second Luther " (alter Martinus)
whom God had sent to take the place of the exile at the
Wartburg. The excitement reached a climax on the 6th
October when the impassioned preacher delivered a long
harangue from the monastery pulpit, in which he denounced
the adoration of the Host as idolatry and contended that
the Mass was not an offering anew of the body of Christ in
satisfaction for sin, but a commemoration of His death
which He had instituted for the confirmation of our faith,
and which ought to be celebrated in accordance with His
institution.[43] Whereupon the majority of the monks refused

[40] Barge, " Karlstadt," i. 290-291.      [41] Ibid., i. 292.
[42] See the student Helmann's letter to a friend in Breslau, 8th Oct.,
" Theologische Studien und Kritiken " (1885), 132-135. See also
Nik. Müller, " Wittenberger Bewegung," 15 f. The statement has
been questioned by Kolde, " Luther," ii. 567, but is accepted by Barge, i.
312, and Kawerau, " Luther's Werke," viii. 400, and " Luther's Rückkehr von der Wartburg," 66.
[43] " Studien und Kritiken," 134-135; " Corpus Reformatorum,"
i. 460; cf. 466; Nik. Müller, 28.

to say Mass in the traditional form, and their sympathisers among the students and the citizens determined to receive the communion only in both kinds.[44]   The monks persisted in their refusal in spite of the remonstrances of representatives of the University and the Chapter of the Castle Church,[45] and the intervention of the Elector who, on hearing of the incident on the 8th October, sent his chancellor, Brück, to deal with the situation.  The chancellor appointed a Commission of professors and members of the Chapter to investigate, but he evidently did not take the incident very seriously.   In the conclusion of his report to the Elector on the 11th October he expressed the opinion that the monks would not long remain refractory, since they would erelong feel the consequences of their refusal to say Masses for the dead in their kitchen and cellar and would think better of it.[46]  His cynical prophecy proved, however, to be premature.  On the following Sunday, the 13th October, the indomitable Zwilling again inveighed before an over-flowing audience on the abuse of the Mass in a harangue lasting two hours, and supplemented it after the midday meal with another lasting an hour, " so that all who were present were amazed." [47]  He was ardently supported by a number of Augustinian monks from the Netherlands, and the innovators became so insistent in their demand for communion in both kinds that Prior Helt, in order to evade this innovation, was fain to prohibit the celebration of Mass in the meantime.[48]

The excitement was intensified by another disputation in the University, in which Carlstadt, while insisting on the concession of the cup, now took the side of moderation,[49]

[44] " Studien und Kritiken," 135 ;  " Corp. Ref.," 460.

[45] " Corp. Ref.," i. 460.                    [46] Ibid., i. 460-461.

[47] Letter of Burerius to Beatus Rhenanus, 18th Oct., " Zeitschrift für Kirchen Geschichte," v. 326;  Nik. Müller, 33.

[48] " Corp. Ref.," i. 475.   Helt to the Elector, 30th Oct.;  Nik. Müller, 56.

[49] " Z.K.G.," v. 326.  Burerius thinks that Carlstadt did so in order the better to bring out all that could be said on the question.  Others think that he was playing the part of the weathercock.  Barge defends him against these suppositions and attempts to reconcile his somewhat reserved attitude on this occasion with that of the theses of 19th July.

and Melanchthon and Jonas upheld the radical view. " We must at last make a beginning," argued Melanchthon, " otherwise nothing will be done. He who has once put his hand to the plough must not look back." [50]  The report which the Commission sent to the Elector on the 20th October amply justified the demand for a reform of the Mass. As currently celebrated, " it is one of the greatest sins on earth." As originally instituted, it was a commemoration and sign of Christ's death for the forgiveness of sin, " not a good work whereby an offering is made to God for oneself and others." This is an unwarrantable and utterly perverse assumption of the blind papists. The multiplied celebration of Masses is a mechanical performance which bad priests undertake for the sake of money, and which burdens the conscience of good men. In particular, Masses for the dead ought to be abolished, though private Masses in which the priest celebrates alone may be allowed to continue in deference to weak brethren. Otherwise the original institution ought to be restored and communion in both kinds established in accordance with the express direction of Christ. In conclusion the Commission, assuming the right of the Elector as head of the State to remedy ecclesiastical abuses, exhorts him to take a hand in this reform in accordance with the Gospel and pay no heed to the outcry of " Hussite " or " heretic." [51]

The Elector, it appeared, was by no means prepared to act on this exhortation. In the face of the Edict of Worms it was necessary to refrain as far as possible from further religious agitation and avoid innovations that could only aggravate the danger for himself and his subjects accruing from his determination not to execute the Edict. To countenance the demand for the reform of the Mass and other abuses would be to court the active enmity of his immediate neighbours, Duke George of Saxony and the Electors of Brandenburg and Maintz, and risk the outbreak of a religious war. The situation was undoubtedly a difficult one, and a wary attitude, besides being in accordance with

---

[50] Nik. Müller, 47-48 ;  Barge, i. 323.
[51] " Corp. Ref.," i. 466-470 ;  Nik. Müller, 35 f.

his predilection for a cautious diplomacy, seemed the only alternative from the political point of view. Hence the instruction to his councillor, Dr Beyer, who replaced Brück as negotiator, to submit the question to all the members of the University and Chapter for judgment (25th October). The matter, he was instructed to remind them, concerned the common weal of Christendom and could not be precipitately decided by a few Wittenberg theologians for the whole Church. If the reform in question was really grounded on the Gospel it would undoubtedly make headway and could be accomplished with the common Christian consent. Moreover, there was the practical consideration that the abolition of the Mass would deprive the churches and monasteries of the endowments originally granted for this purpose and involve the Reformers in the charge of spoliation. In addition, such a measure would inevitably provoke discussion and tumult which were at all hazards to be avoided.[52]

The renewal of the discussion only led to a division of opinion between the University and the Chapter. Whilst the conservative majority of the latter declared against the proposed reform, the former, in its final report on the 12th December, renewed in more insistent terms its demand for abolition.[53]

Meanwhile Luther had been taking a keen interest in the discussions at Wittenberg. He had himself, he wrote to Melanchthon on first hearing of the agitation at the beginning of August, been considering the question of restoring communion in both kinds and had determined to take up this reform before all others on his return.[54] He had already dealt with the subject in the "Babylonic Captivity," in which he indicated the right of the Christian to the cup as well as the bread, though he was prepared to submit to the traditional practice on the rather questionable assumption that Christ had not made the use of either obligatory. This was

---

[52] "Corp. Ref.," i. 471-474; Nik. Müller, 50 f.

[53] *Ibid.*, i. 493 f.; Nik. Müller, 84 f. Some of the professors of the Faculties of Arts, Law, and Medicine declined to vote on the ground of their incompetence and left the decision to the Faculty of Theology.

[54] Enders, iii. 208.

the position which he still maintained in the letter to Melanchthon, and he controverted the view of Carlstadt that it was sinful to communicate only in one kind, whilst approving a return to the original institution. On one point he has decidedly made up his mind. He will never again celebrate private Mass.[55] He expressed to Spalatin his disapproval of the daily Mass said by the priest at the Wartburg, and wished that these private celebrations should be diminished if they cannot be at once abolished, since the Mass is by institution a communion and a commemoration which ought to be accompanied by the preaching of the Word and celebrated publicly in the presence of the congregation.[56] The communications both written and verbal, which came to him from Wittenberg,[57] led him in the beginning of November to put his reflections on the subject on paper for the purpose of instructing and confirming his fellow-monks at Wittenberg. Hence the work " On the Abrogation of Private Mass," [58] which he dedicated to them and dispatched to Spalatin on the 11th November.[59]

He greatly rejoices in the movement they have begun, which must expose them to opposition and calumny. He knows by experience how difficult it is to challenge convention and oppose single-handed the doctrines and institutions of centuries. " How often my trembling heart beat within me at the thought of this formidable argument of theirs, ' Are you alone wise ? ' ' Has all the world erred and lived in ignorance so many centuries ? ' ' What if you are wrong and you drag along with you so many to eternal damnation ? ' But Christ at length confirmed me with His own sure and faithful words, so that my heart no longer trembles or palpitates, but defies these papistical arguments no less than the rocky shore bids defiance to the rage and tumult of the waves." [60] A conscience grounded on the Word of

---

[55] Enders, iii. 207-208.

[56] *Ibid.*, iii. 237, 7th Oct.      [57] See " Werke," viii. 411.

[58] " De Abroganda Missa Privata," " Werke," viii. 411 f. German trans. by Luther himself, " Vom Misbrauch der Messe," *ibid.*, viii. 482 f.

[59] Enders, iii. 247.      [60] " Werke," viii. 412.

God as on the rock affords us the infallible certainty of which we are in quest.[61]

He starts by attacking the priestly power and denying on scriptural grounds the papal claim to make laws contrary to Scripture, in virtue of a succession from Peter whom Christ appointed as His immediate successor, and to whom He confided His priestly power. This assumption is a lying invention of the devil. The New Testament knows of only one high priest who offered Himself for us to God.[62] It knows of no priestly order under an earthly high priest, but only of a spiritual priesthood of all Christians in the sense that they can directly approach God, pray to Him, and instruct others.[63] He adduces the relative passages in support of this contention and challenges Pope and priesthood to produce a single iota of evidence to the contrary.[64] The Parisian and Louvain theologians, Emser and others, who have attempted it have produced only the figments of their own arrogance and blasphemies.[65] With the fall of this pretended priesthood the priestly Mass necessarily becomes nothing but impiety and idolatry. It has no scriptural warrant and is based on the traditions of men against which Christ and the Apostles inveigh.[66] It is vain to defend it by saying that it has been ordained by the Church and that what the Church has ordained has been inspired by the Holy Spirit. What certainty have we that priests and doctors have not erred in this institution? Only what the Word of God manifestly proclaims is to be received as certain, and the mere ordinance of the Church, or of those ordaining in its name, is not necessarily authoritative apart from the Word.[67] The New Testament knows of sacrifice, but only in the spiritual sense of offering ourselves body and soul to God in the mortifying of the flesh as our reasonable service (Romans viii. 13 ; xii. 1 ; 1 Peter ii. 3). This spiritual

---

[61] " Werke," viii. 412.

[62] *Ibid.*, viii. 415. Unum et vero solum est nobis sacerdocium Christi, quo ipse obtulit sese pro nobis et nos omnes secum.

[63] *Ibid.*, viii. 415. Hoc sacerdocium spirituale est et omnibus Christianis Commune.

[64] *Ibid.*, viii. 415-416.

[65] *Ibid.*, viii. 416-417.

[66] *Ibid.*, viii. 418.

[67] *Ibid.*, viii. 419-420.

sacrifice is not the office of shaved and anointed priests, but of all Christians who walk the way of the Cross in self-mortification.[68] Here again he challenges his opponents to produce a single passage from the New Testament in which the Mass is represented as an offering, a sacrifice to God. It is only the memorial of Christ's sacrifice which it celebrates.[69] Moreover, in the New Testament, the ministry of the Word, the prophetic function is common to all who have received a message from God and is not the exclusive right and privilege of any class of functionaries. Has not Christ said, " They shall all be taught of God " ? (*Theodidacti*, John vi. 45).[70] Paul, indeed, commands women to be silent in the Church and thus seems to deny that the ministry of the Word is common to all. Paul's prohibition, he answers, applies only to speaking " in the Church," not elsewhere, and is meant to preserve order and decency in the public assembly. Otherwise his command would be contrary to the testimony of the Spirit who spoke through the daughters of Philip and in the canticle of the Blessed Virgin herself.[71]

He then proceeds to examine the Apostolic writings in order to show the antithesis between the New Testament ministry and the Roman Catholic priesthood with its graded hierarchy, its pomp-loving and pampered dignitaries. He pictures this antithesis in vivid and sinister colours and makes ample use of his gift of objurgation. This hierarchical development is the work of Satan pure and simple, who has craftily succeeded in thus transforming the Church into a travesty of the Apostolic institution, and has deceived even those good men who, he admits, have miserably been seduced into accepting this travesty as Christian and Apostolic. On the clear testimony of Scripture this development with its distinction between cleric and laic, its assumption of the indelible character of the clergy, its difference of status and rank, its lust of pomp and power and luxury,

---

[68] " Werke," viii. 420-421.

[69] *Ibid.*, viii. 421. Christus semel se ipsum obtulit non denuo ab ullis offerri, sed memoriam sui sacrificii voluit fieri.

[70] *Ibid.*, viii. 422-424.

[71] *Ibid.*, viii. 424-425.

its greed and hypocrisy, its prohibition of the marriage of the clergy, etc., is totally contrary to and subversive of the simple evangelical ministry of the Apostolic age, when bishop and presbyter designated the same functionaries and these functionaries differed in nothing from other Christians except in their specific office of ministering the Word and sacraments, just as a magistrate differs in no respect from other citizens except in his office of ruling the city.[72] " Thus by the agency of the devil have they violated the Church and the Word of God and by the guile of the serpent have seduced the minds of Christians from the simplicity and purity of Christ." [73]

He next examines the passages relative to the institution of the Lord's Supper in disproof of the traditional conception of it, which his opponents strive to substantiate by appealing to the Fathers, the Church and its General Councils, the papal decretals and the scholastic divines. His line of argument is largely that of the " Babylonic Captivity," whilst steering clear of the scholastic philosophy and theology and restricting himself to the evangelical evidence. From the historic point of view, his plea for a return to the primitive practice is a very forcible one. He condemns the superfluous and meticulous observances regulating the celebration, such as the exact repetition of the prescribed formulas, fasting beforehand, the handling of the elements only with the anointed fingers of the priest, etc. He can find no trace of these in the original institution. Christ and the disciples did not, for instance, celebrate the Eucharist fasting, but after partaking of the evening meal. He will not insist on the abrogation of these customs if the individual conscience is left free in this matter, and the Church refrains from placing the omission of them in the category of mortal sins.[74] In instituting the rite, Christ observed the utmost simplicity and we are bound to follow His example in obedience to the command, " This do in remembrance of me." To transform it into a sacrifice is to radically change and vitiate His institution.[75] The Sacrament is the New Covenant by

---

[72] " Werke," viii. 426-430.

[73] Ibid., viii. 430.

[74] Ibid., viii. 431-434.

[75] Ibid., viii. 434-436.

which Christ assured the forgiveness of sin through the shedding of His blood, and the believer in commemorating His death does not offer a sacrifice, but simply accepts in faith His promise and pledge of forgiveness.[76]  Both grammar and common sense can read no other meaning into the words of institution.  He himself, however, hardly observes the rules of grammar and common sense in assuming that in instituting this memorial He actually changed the bread and wine into His body and blood.[77]  In this respect there is still in his thought a remnant of the magical influence, the superadded notions which he condemns so drastically in the current view and practice.[78]

To regard the Sacrament as a sacrifice, instead of a pledge of God's love in Christ, is to beget doubt and fear instead of confidence and joy.  For who can be sure that this so-called sacrifice is acceptable to God ?  From his personal knowledge he avers that this anxiety and un-certainty is the prevailing feeling among the priesthood.[79] In this, as in other respects, the current religion is for Luther a religion of fear and torment of conscience in contrast to the joy and confidence which the gospel of God's grace and love—of which the Eucharist is the promise and pledge—begets in the believer.  " O sweet and potent promise in which His body and blood are given as the pledge of our salvation and the remission of sin.  Behold these are the blessings which are shown forth to you in the Eucharist.  Think you that these can be exhibited by an angry and implacable God, and not rather by a most indulgent, loving, and solicitous Father ?  What greater thing can He possibly promise than the forgiveness of sins ? And what is the remission of sin but grace, salvation, heirship, life, peace, eternal glory in God Himself ?  But for you, O mad and impious papist, how different is the God you would propitiate by this sacrifice of yours in the Mass ! Desist, I beg you, from your worthless propitiations.  There is only one unique propitiation by which God is appeased,

[76] " Werke," viii. 436-437.
[77] Ibid., viii. 435, mutat panem in corpus suum ;  cf. 438.
[78] Ibid., viii. 437-439.
[79] Ibid., viii. 441-442.

so that no hope is left you in any other sacrifice or device except in this one only . . . and faith alone in His body given and blood shed avails." [80]  In vain they seek refuge in the reflection that it is incredible that Luther alone can be right and that all others have erred.  Let them remember the prophet Micaiah and what happened to King Ahab who refused to listen to him.[81]

To the Canon of the Mass he opposes the plain words of the Gospel, and he condemns its sacrificial formulary as the adversary of the Gospel.  The appeal to Gregory the Great, Bernard, Bonaventura and others who approved and used it is not valid against the clear testimony of Scripture. Nothing under heaven is more dangerous than this appeal to the example of the saints, if unsupported by Scripture. The saints, on their own confession, were all sinners and liable to error.  Witness the " Retractions " of Augustine. Even the great Fathers were no infallible oracles to be blindly followed without the exercise of one's own judgment. The wretched superstition which uncritically accepts the legends of the saints and mere human doctrines, to the neglect of God's Word, and of the principle of the Apostle to prove all things has filled Christendom with error and lies.  No less superstitious is the belief in purgatory and the eternal droning of Masses for the dead which ought to be utterly abolished and the primitive institution restored.[82]

He adds a terrific indictment of the Papacy as a travesty of both the law and the Gospel, the patron of every vice and transgression forbidden in the Decalogue.[83]  One feels that on moral grounds at least this travesty deserves and has invited this unmitigated castigation.  The solitary seer, hidden in the Wartburg by a cautious Elector and chafing under the restraint of his pugnative spirit, lets himself go on paper at least without the slightest consideration for anything like judicial moderation.  Theological bias as well as moral indignation is doubtless reflected in this passionate indictment.  For Luther the worst sins of the Pope and the

[80] " Werke," viii. 442.          [82] *Ibid*., viii. 449-457.
[81] *Ibid*., viii. 443.            [83] *Ibid*., viii. 460 f.

bishops lie in the realm of faith rather than of morals.[84] In this respect he still labours under the age-old belief, reflected so tragically in ancient and mediæval ecclesiastical history, that a theological opponent must needs be a monster of iniquity. This imputation his opponents were only too prone to apply to him, and on the same assumption he pays them back with compound interest. He hurls his accusations against them in the passionate conviction that the beliefs, which he holds to be deadly error, must necessarily produce the most baneful moral effects. This is for the Church historian an all too familiar feature of theological controversy in periods of intense feeling and thinking in matters of faith. In fairness even to Antichrist who sits in Peter's chair at the beginning of the sixteenth century, we must make due allowance for the theological bias as well as for the volcanic temperament of the Wartburg seer, which underlies this terrible indictment. Even so, there was material enough in the state of things ecclesiastical under the degenerate papal régime to substantiate this foregone verdict, and with this material to work on, Luther's command of invective and his passionate conviction went straight for the heart of the Antichrist. In spite of its proneness to exaggeration and declaration, one cannot but feel the marvellous fecundity of thought, the sheer moral and spiritual force which were welling forth from this dynamic spirit in the solitude of the Wartburg the waves of a religious revolution. By this mysterious hand were being traced the writing on the walls of the modern Babylon, as he termed Rome. " God hath numbered thy kingdom and finished it. Thou art weighed in the balance and found wanting " (Dan. v. 26-27).

In conclusion, he exhorts his brethren at Wittenberg to go forward in spite of the outcry of the papists, " Look yonder, at Wittenberg, the worship of God has ceased ; the Mass is no longer celebrated ; they have all become heretics and madmen." He hints that they may well also

---

[84] " Werke," viii. 464. Sed hoc detestor, hoc pugno quod, cum sint vice pastorum lupos agunt et verbo rationeque ipsa docendi mandata Dei solvunt, non solum minima sed ipsa maxima et prorsus universa, et sic docent ac perdunt homines. Hic non in mores, sed in fidem peccatur.

turn their attention to that monument of superstition, that Bethaven or house of idols in the Church of All Saints, with its huge store of relics on which the Elector had spent so much of his people's substance. How much better to have spent it on the poor of Saxony ! With this hit at the foolish zeal into which the papists have misguided him, he adroitly mingles appreciation of the Elector's equitable rule and the service he has rendered to the cause of the Gospel. They have reason to thank God that he is no tyrant or fool, but a lover of the truth, under whom they can the better finish the work they have begun. He reminds them of the old prophecy which he heard as a boy, that the Emperor Frederick would erelong deliver the Holy Sepulchre at Jerusalem. The prophecy is at last being fulfilled in " our Frederick," whom the Electors assembled at Frankfurt chose as Emperor. For the sepulchre to be delivered is the Holy Scripture which the papists have buried and which, under this Frederick, has been brought forth into the light. What if he should glory that he himself has been the angel or the Mary Magdalen that has been at the opening of the Holy Sepulchre and has made Wittenberg another Jerusalem ! But enough of this word play. In very deed it has been given to them to look upon the pure grace of the Gospel, and it is theirs zealously to spread the light that others may see it too. Only let them avoid discord and have respect to the weakness of others in the spirit of the Apostolic injunction that it is good not to do anything whereby thy brother stumbleth, whilst following the dictates of conscience without respect to the person or masks of men.[85]

[85] " Werke," viii. 475-476. Barge (" Karlstadt," i. 334 f.) sees in this philippic an incitement to the forcible repression of the Mass. Karl Müller, on the other hand, emphasises the passages counselling moderation in disproof of Barge's conclusion (" Luther und Karlstadt," 23, 1907). At all events the spirit of the work was bellicose enough.

# CHAPTER II

# LUTHER AT THE WARTBURG (2)

## I. The Halle "Idol"

WHILST advising his brethren to act considerately, Luther was evidently at this stage in full sympathy with the active reform party at Wittenberg. He was, in fact, by no means satisfied with the Elector's attitude towards this party and his dissatisfaction was intensified by what he deemed his subservience, on grounds of expediency, to the Archbishop of Maintz. The pointed reference to the Elector's " Bethaven " at Wittenberg was doubtless suggested by the fact that the archbishop had proclaimed an indulgence in connection with an exhibition of the relics in the collegiate church at Halle. To judge from the catalogue, the collection included thousands of articles dating back to the days of Moses and coming down to those of St Thomas of Canterbury, and invested with an indulgence efficacy which was good for a truly fabulous number of years in the world to come. This pious fraud drew crowds to take advantage of the spiritual benefits to be derived from a visit to the exhibition, coupled with fervent prayer and a contribution to the Church. From these contributions the archbishop hoped to pay off his debts and found a new University as a rival to that of Wittenberg.[1] Verily, Luther had some excuse for indulging in these diatribes against " idolatry " which crowd his controversial works and sound so excessive to the more delicate modern ear. Here was the archbishop at his old trade of selling the forgiveness of sins by practising on the superstition of the people ! And here were the people

[1] See Wolters, " Der Abgott zu Halle " (1876), and Hausrath, " Luther," i. 480 f.

as ready as ever to be gulled and fleeced by this wolf in sheep's clothing! No wonder that Luther waxed furious and vowed to smash "that idol at Halle," in spite of the diplomatic caveats of the Elector conveyed to him through Spalatin. "I will not be held back," he wrote on the 7th October, "but will publicly and privately go for that idol of the archbishop with his brothel at Halle."[2]   He set to work and dashed off a philippic "Against the Idol at Halle."[3]

Meanwhile the archbishop had attempted through his secretary, Capito, to induce the Elector to intervene, and Capito had written to Luther himself begging him to desist from his purpose.[4]  Capito also paid a visit to Wittenberg in the endeavour to influence Luther through Melanchthon.[5]  As the result of this diplomatic pressure came a letter from Spalatin on the 11th November, forbidding him, in the Elector's name and in the interest of the public peace, to write against the archbishop.  Luther replied with a point-blank refusal. "I will rather break with you and the prince and all men. If I have resisted the Pope, why should I give way to the Pope's creature?  A fine thing indeed to talk about not disturbing the public peace whilst you suffer the eternal peace of God to be disturbed by these impious and sacrilegious proceedings.  Not so, Spalatin, not so, prince.  But for the sake of Christ's flock, this most grievous wolf must be resisted with all our might as an example to others."  He accordingly sent him the manuscript to be forwarded to Melanchthon for revision and publication, and bluntly told him to beware of keeping it back or trying to persuade Melanchthon from complying with his wishes.  His purpose is fixed and he will listen to no argument to the contrary. Did Christ and the Apostles seek to please men or flinch before the opprobrium of the Gospel?  What if the students have pelted a mendicant monk from Lichtenberg in the streets of Wittenberg, about which Spalatin had evidently written him as an example of the danger of public commotion?  Who can hope to bridle such occasional outbursts?

---

[2] Enders, iii. 237 ; cf. 240.          [4] Enders, iii. 238.
[3] " Wider den Abgott zu Halle."       [5] " Corp. Ref.," i. 462 f.

The Gospel is not to be repressed because of such youthful escapades.[6]

Spalatin, nevertheless, retained the manuscript and Luther determined to challenge the archbishop directly on the subject in a letter on the 1st December, which Melanchthon forwarded to Capito on the 11th.[7] Its tone was very different from that of the two letters which, he reminds him, he had humbly addressed to him on two previous occasions. It is an ultimatum which bluntly treats him as a culprit and threatens to expose his licentious private life, as well as his conduct as a churchman, as the penalty of non-compliance with his demand. Mayhap he has assumed that, now that Luther has disappeared from the arena and is under the imperial ban, he need have no fear of being called to account by him. He is welcome to his assumption. " But I beg your grace to know that I will do what Christian love demands, in spite of the gates of hell, let alone popes, cardinals, and bishops." Now that the abuse of indulgences has been proved to be nothing but fraud and villany, let him cease to rob and deceive the poor people and show himself a bishop instead of a wolf. From the small fire which a poor mendicant monk kindled there has grown a conflagration in which God has passed judgment on the Pope, whose power grows daily smaller, though at first all the world believed that the monk had undertaken a forlorn enterprise. The same God lives still and will know how to cast down a Cardinal of Maintz, even if four emperors were at his back. Let him beware of despising and provoking Him whose might knows no measure. This monk will strive so mightily with God that He who has brought low the Pope will begin a play with the cardinal that he wots not of. He, therefore, gives him due warning. If he does not forthwith suppress the idol at Halle, he will expose him before the whole empire and show it the difference between a bishop and a wolf. He adds the demand that the bishops shall allow the clergy to marry and not tyrannically make use of their power to penalise those who have entered or shall enter into honourable wedlock. At least let them cast

---

[6] Enders, iii. 246-247.     [7] " Corp. Ref.," i. 492.

the beam out of their own eyes and drive away their own harlots before beginning to separate pious married women from their husbands. In regard, in particular, to the archbishop's own sins against chastity, he will no longer observe silence, though he has no inclination or desire to expose his shame and dishonour in this respect. But unless in fourteen days' time he has a satisfactory answer, his book against the idol will go forth to the world.[8]

Within the prescribed interval (reckoning from the 11th December) the archbishop's reply, dated 21st December, was dispatched, along with a soothing epistle from Capito. The archbishop now addresses him as " Dear Doctor " and assures him that he has accepted his letter in good part and avers that he had already removed the cause of it. He adopts the tone of a penitent and promises to act henceforth as becomes a pious churchman and Christian prince, as far as God shall lend him His grace and strength to do so as a poor sinner who can do nothing of himself. " I know well that without God's grace there is no good in me, and I am as profitless and stinking a piece of filth as anyone else, if not more so." He is more than willing to suffer brotherly and Christian reproach and to comply with Luther's demands and make amendment for the future, in reliance on the help of a merciful God.[9]

His abject capitulation is a striking evidence of the moral influence which the outlaw in the Wartburg had come to wield during the interval since he penned his humble petition against the abuse of indulgences to the same high dignitary four years before. This influence was due partly to his own powerful personality, partly to the fact that behind this personality was the force of an awakened public opinion which it materially contributed to foster, and which the archbishop had only too good reason to fear. Moreover, behind Luther lurked the spirit of social restiveness which was finding expression in popular declamation against the overgrown and ill-used wealth, the extortion and tyranny of ecclesiastics who were feudal magnates as well as degenerate churchmen, and for whom the day of reckoning

---

[8] " Werke," 53, 95-99 (Erlangen ed.).        [9] Enders, iii. 266.

was about to dawn in social as well as religious revolution. Assuredly it was high time to profess penitence and promise amendment if the revolutionary spirit, on social as well as religious grounds, might perchance thereby be conjured.

Luther had grave doubts about the sincerity of this abject confession, and he was very unfavourably impressed by the attempt of Capito in an accompanying epistle to remove them. Capito, it seems, had been striving, after the manner of Erasmus, to attain the same result as his bellicose friend in the Wartburg. He had reason to believe that he had made considerable progress in winning the archbishop for his evangelical teaching, and besought him not to endanger the good work by a precipitate and uncompromising attitude.[10] The reference to Erasmus was hardly fitted to predispose him to self-restraint. He had recently, in a letter to Spalatin, condemned what he deemed the time-serving attitude of both Erasmus and Capito,[11] and he now tells him that he can by no means approve the method of promoting the cause of the Gospel by conniving at and excusing the reprehensible conduct of princes, merely in order not to provoke a conflict. This can only result in flattery and denial of the truth. The spirit of truth cannot but reprove and offend, as did Christ whose example we are to follow. This is, indeed, to be done in the spirit of love and in order to save souls. But it pertains to the ministry of the Word, in the first place, to root out and destroy and scatter. Does not Jeremiah pronounce a curse on those who do the work of the Lord deceitfully (xlviii. 10)? If the cardinal really means what he writes, he would hail his letter with the greatest joy and would be ready to prostrate himself at his feet. If, however, as he suspects, he is playing the hypocrite, he will not be deceived by these tricks of Satan. The fact that he has released the married priest of Kemberg, whom he had imprisoned, is no proof to the contrary. For he has only released him after compelling him to separate from his wife, contrary to the Apostolic teaching, whilst shutting his eyes to the abominable clerical immorality prevailing in his dioceses of Maintz, Magdeburg,

[10] Enders, iii. 259-263.    [11] *Ibid.*, iii. 229-230, 9th Sept.

and Halberstadt. His conduct in depriving Knaxdorff, the reforming preacher at Magdeburg, is equally inconsistent with these professions, and has intensified his doubts as to his sincerity. " We will uphold true religion," he tells him in conclusion, " with all our might, whether it offends heaven or hell. There you have Luther, as you have always had him, your most yielding slave if you are a friend of piety, your most inveterate opponent if, along with your cardinal, you persist in making a mockery of sacred things." [12] He will not answer the cardinal's letter as long as he is unable to decide whether he should denounce him as a hypocrite or praise his sincerity. Capito bore him no grudge for this plain speaking, and during a visit to Wittenberg in March 1522 a reconciliation took place between them.[13]

" Vague and uncertain reports " [14] of events at Wittenberg caused him such anxiety that he determined to pay a visit in order to learn at first hand how matters actually stood. It was a dangerous venture, since the route lay in part through the territory of his arch-enemy Duke George, alias " the Rehoboam of Dresden " as he called him. Accompanied by his trusty attendant,[15] he descended on the 3rd December at an inn at Leipzig, and is said to have been recognised, despite his disguise, by a woman in the public room before setting forward on his journey.[16] Next day he rode incognito into Wittenberg and furtively alighted at the house of Amsdorf in which Melanchthon was also quartered. On the previous day the students, reinforced by a number of their fellows from Erfurt and by a party of the citizens, had burst into the parish church " with knives under their cloaks," wrested the Mass books from the hands of the priests who were about to say Mass, and driven them from the altar. Other priests, who in the early morning were celebrating Mass in honour of the Virgin, had been pelted with stones. On the following

[12] Enders, iii. 279-284, 17th Jan. 1522.
[13] See letter of Burerius to Beatus Rhenanus, " Z.K.G.," v. 333.
[14] Enders, iii. 250.
[15] The contemporary account given in " Z.K.G.," xxii. 124, says he rode with three horses.
[16] Seidemann, " Leipziger Disputation," 99-103.

day, that of Luther's arrival, they renewed the demonstration against the Mass by invading the Franciscan monastery and using threatening and abusive language. As a precaution against these threats the Town Council was fain to send a guard to protect the monastery,[17] in front of which the mob again demonstrated on the 6th.[18] In spite of this electric atmosphere, Luther spent several happy days among his friends and expressed himself in a letter to Spalatin as completely satisfied with all that he had seen and heard.[19] He evidently did not regard these student escapades so tragically as did the Town Council in its reports to the Elector. The only vexing experience he records was the discovery that Spalatin had not sent the manuscripts of his philippics against monasticism, the Mass, and the idol at Halle to Melanchthon for publication, as he had directed. Several months before he had taken it very ill that the Elector had intervened to prevent the public disputation on a series of theses on auricular confession, which he had sent to Wittenberg, and had at the time expressed his irritation to Spalatin in no measured terms.[20] He now penned an angry letter from Wittenberg to the delinquent who, in consequence, while retaining " The Idol," was fain to send the other two to be printed. " I am determined to have what I have written printed, if not at Wittenberg, certainly elsewhere, and if the manuscripts have been lost or retained by you, my mind will be so embittered that I will write much more violently." [21]

He relaxed so far as to agree to defer the publication of " The Idol " in the meantime. But he strongly protested against the policy of subordinating the cause of the Gospel to political expediency. " For the Lord lives in whom you, as is the way with courtiers, have no faith unless He shall moderate His works to suit your convenience. . . . I beseech you, if it is the truth that celibacy and monkery are condemned by the divine Word, as is not doubtful,

[17] " Corp. Ref.," i. 488 f. ; Nik. Müller, 73 f.
[18] Boehmer, " Luther im Lichte der Neueren Forschung," 120.
[19] Enders, iii. 253. Omnia vehementer placent quæ video et audio.
[20] *Ibid.*, iii. 193, 13th July; *cf.* 199, 15th July.
[21] *Ibid.*, iii. 252-253.

why is it not permissible to attempt and carry out the contrary ? Are we only to dispute without end concerning the truth and always refrain from carrying it into effect ? If we are to accomplish nothing more than we have hitherto done, we should cease teaching the truth altogether." [22] Evidently he was determined, as the result of his visit, to force the politicians at Lochau to abandon their elusive, temporising policy and face the question of instituting a practical reformation.

## II. The Warning Against Revolt

At the same time his observation of the revolutionary spirit on the way to Wittenberg had impressed him with the imminent danger of a widespread upheaval on social as well as religious grounds, and before setting out on the return journey he had resolved to address to the people a manifesto against precipitate revolutionary measures.[23] Throughout these months of solitary vigil in the Wartburg rumour and his own reflections have borne in on his mind the spectre of " some fearful tragedy which Satan has in store for Germany." [24] Seer-like he perceives the gathering clouds that portend the thunderstorm of a rising against the dominant system in the Church, and, it may be, the State, and he ever and anon warns his enemies to beware of provoking the judgment of God. A series of riots at Erfurt in the spring and summer of 1521, in which the clergy were roughly handled, was symptomatic of the religious passion which his evangelical teaching and his excommunication and outlawry had quickened over a large part of the empire. More furtive, but still more ominous, was the widespread aspiration for emancipation from the oppressive feudal system in the masses, which this teaching tended to intensify, if it by no means originated. For the

[22] Enders, iii. 254-255.
[23] *Ibid.*, iii. 253. Dominus confortet spiritum eorum qui bene volunt, quamquam *per viam* vexatus rumore vario de nostrorum quorundam importunitate, præstituerim publicam exhortationem edere quamprimum reversus fuero ad eremum meam.
[24] *Ibid.*, iii. 230.

social revolutionary spirit was an inheritance of long standing which it did not create and which mistook in him its prophet. The masses had, nevertheless, some reason to see in him their emancipator from social oppression as well as ecclesiastical abuse and error, and his disappearance had only intensified the determination to have it out with his enemies and theirs. He could denounce the rampant evils in both Church and State with equal verve on occasion, and did not always measure the consequences of his invective. He by no means approved of the use of violence in behalf of either religious or social reform and expressed his disapproval of the Erfurt riots.[25] But he took occasion to point out the madness of the Romanists in ignoring their significance in the face of the signs of the time. " It is obvious, as Erasmus writes, that the people neither can nor will bear longer the yoke of the Pope and the papists. . . . Hitherto they have sought to increase their power by force and oppression. But whether they can maintain this oppression we shall erelong discover by experience." [26] Certain he is that if the Pope persists in repressing the Gospel, Germany will not be without a violent upheaval, and the sooner he attempts it, the sooner will he and his creatures perish and Luther return from the Wartburg. Karsthans, *i.e.*, Jack Mattock, the peasant, is awake, and Germany has many Jack Mattocks, he adds ominously in reference to the popular diatribe under this title against the parsons, which had appeared in the previous year.[27] The same foreboding appears in the dedication of his work on " Auricular Confession " to Franz von Sickingen. Let the papists take warning betimes from the fate of the Canaanites, who spurned Joshua's offer of peace and were annihilated in consequence. The people will not indefinitely bear their tyranny and he disclaims all responsibility for the consequences. All his efforts to reach a peaceful understanding have been in vain. Force is their only alternative, and the time is at hand when they will call for peace in vain. Another will teach them, not like Luther with epistles and words, but with deeds.[28]

[25] Enders, iii. 153, 158, 202.
[26] *Ibid.*, iii. 153.
[27] *Ibid.*, iii. 164.
[28] " Werke," viii. 138-139.

It was the unmistakable portents of the coming upheaval, which he noted on the way between the Wartburg
and Wittenberg, that led him on his return to pen his
" Faithful Exhortation to all Christians to guard themselves
from Tumult and Revolt." He is not sorry to hear of the
alarm of the papists who have so shamelessly oppressed
the people in times bygone and have given Jack Mattock
ample cause to let them feel the weight of his flail and club.
But let them fear more the wrath of God, whose judgments
they have provoked, and who will destroy them by the power
of His Word. In this matter God works by His Word and
Spirit, not by the sword. The falsity and lies of the Antichristian Papacy have been disclosed, and men have only
to understand the truth and the reign of Antichrist will
surely fall. The duty of initiating and carrying through
a reformation belongs to the secular Government and the
Estates,[29] not to the comman man. What is done by such
constituted authority in forbidding what is contrary to the
Gospel and enforcing obedience is not revolt or revolution.
Whilst it has the right to compel the acceptance of necessary
reform, it should eschew violence against the person and
not make use of the sword in the service of religion. Popular
revolt, on the other hand, is inadmissible. It cannot achieve
the betterment it seeks. " For revolt has no reason in it and
usually does more mischief to the innocent than to the
guilty. Therefore no revolt is right, however just the
cause. It results in more damage than betterment. Hence
the institution of government and the power of the sword
to punish the wicked and protect the good. Herr Omnes,
the revolutionary multitude, on the other hand, fails to
discriminate and allows itself to be hurried into the extreme
of injustice. Be guided, therefore, by the powers that be.
So long as they do not act and command hold heart, hand,
and mouth in check and attempt nothing on your own
account. If you can influence them to action, you may do
so. But if they will not, neither may you, and if you
nevertheless do so, you are guilty of wrongdoing and are
much worse than the other party. I hold and always will

---

[29] Die weltlich Ubirkeit und Adel, die Fürsten und Herren.

hold with the party that suffers from revolt, however unjust the cause it represents, and against the party that excites revolt, however just the cause, since revolt can never occur without innocent bloodshed and damage." [30]

Moreover, revolt is a device of the devil in order to discredit the cause of the Gospel. Hence the outcry of the papists over the Erfurt riots, which they falsely ascribe to his teaching. " Those who rightly study and understand my teaching do not resort to revolt. They have not learned it from me. That some do so under the pretext of our name, how can we help this ? How much have the papists done in Christ's name which He not only forbade, but which dishonours Him ? " [31] Shall they, then, undertake nothing for the Gospel if the Government declines to act ? By no means. Let them follow his example and spread the light of truth as the mouthpiece of Christ. " Have I not done more harm to the Pope, bishops, parsons, and monks with the word alone and without the sword than all the emperors, kings, and princes with all their power have ever been able to do ? May not I and every one who speaks the Word of Christ freely claim to be His mouthpiece ? Certain I am that my word is not mine, but His. . . . It is not our work which is now moving the world, for it is not possible that man alone can begin and achieve such a movement. It has come to pass without any plan or counsel and it will go on without these, and the gates of hell shall not hinder it." [32] " Spread and help to spread the Gospel ; teach, speak, write, and preach that human ordinance is nothing ; prevent, counsel that none may become priest, monk, or nun, and that whoever is in this state may forsake it ; give no more money for bulls, candles, bells, pictures, churches, but proclaim that a Christian life consists in faith and love. Go on doing this for a couple of years and you will see what will become of Pope, bishops, cardinals, parsons, monks, nuns, bells, steeples, masses, vigils, cowls, shaven crowns, rules and statutes, and the whole swarm and vermin of the papal régime. They will vanish like smoke." [33]

[30] "Werke," viii. 680.  
[31] Ibid., viii. 681.  
[32] Ibid., viii. 683.  
[33] Ibid., viii. 683-684.

At the same time he warns against mere superficial bluster and pretension on the strength of having read a couple of pages or listened to a single sermon. Such pretentious talkers plume themselves on being " Lutherans," just as the opposite party boast themselves to be papists. " I beg that people will leave my name out of the business and call themselves Christians, not Lutherans. What is Luther ? This teaching is not mine. I have not been crucified for anyone. St Paul would not suffer it that the Christians should be called Pauline or Petrine, but only Christians. How could I, a poor, ill-odoured maggot sack, entertain the idea that Christ's children should call themselves by my unsavoury name ? Not so, dear friend, but let us cast away party names and call ourselves after Christ, whose teaching we possess." [34]

Finally, whilst showing a firm front to the incorrigible enemies of the faith, let them bear with the scruples of the weak about the Mass, etc., for their sake and that of the Gospel.

It may seem strange that Luther, himself the greatest rebel against constituted ecclesiastical authority, the most aggressive protagonist of new ideas, should thus appear in the rôle of the thorough-going pacifist. One is inclined to ask whether the " Exhortation " was not a belated tribute to the Elector's policy of wait and see, a surrender to Spalatin and the politicians, whose mouthpiece Spalatin was in his letters to the Wartburg. Had the aggressive religious leader been himself suddenly transformed into the calculating politician ? The conclusion does not necessarily follow, and there is no real reason for doubting, on this ground, the sincerity of this manifesto on behalf of moderation. For years he had been striving to rouse and educate public opinion against the unreformed Papacy. He had done so at times in very inflammatory language which gleams like lightning here and there in the works in which he challenged and defied the power of the Roman Antichrist. He had regarded himself as the instrument impelled by God to prepare the way by his teaching for an evangelical Reforma-

[34] "Werke," viii. 685.

tion. But whilst proclaiming the truth and striving to win adherents for it, his root conviction had been that God Himself through the power of His Word would establish it. In the " Address to the Nobility " he had so far improved on this indefinite programme as to appeal for the active intervention of the State, in view of the failure of the Church to reform itself and the futility of expecting such a reform on the part of the ecclesiastical authorities. He had based this appeal on the divine institution of the State and the principle of the priesthood of believers, which entitled the State to secure the commonweal in the religious as well as the civil sphere.

This theory also underlies the " Exhortation " and it rules out the irresponsible action of the people in either sphere. While the people may and ought to agitate for reform, it can only be accomplished by its lawful organs—the public authority as directed by the prince and the various classes and bodies on which legislation and administration devolve. He himself claims and has exercised the right of agitation within legal limits and recognises this right in every member of the community. His writings and his correspondence with Spalatin and others furnish ample evidence of the exercise of this right. But beyond this the individual may not go, and it is because of the danger of irresponsible violence on the part of his adherents and the revolutionary spirit seething in the people that the initiation of actual reforms by constituted authority is so emphatically stressed in the " Exhortation." It was certainly not written merely in the interest of the governing classes or for the purpose of backing up the halting policy of the Elector and his councillors. It was not the offspring of either servility or insincerity.

Whether it was altogether logical or feasible is a different question. One feels as if the writer of those burning appeals in behalf of individual liberty and right in the " Babylonic Captivity," for instance, has lost somewhat of the daring and the passion of an earlier time, and is besides rather deficient in logic. To disown and defy the tyranny of Antichrist and stress the right of the individual mind and conscience to independence and freedom, and then inculcate the duty of suffering and deny the right actively to use this liberty to overthrow this tyranny seems rather tame as well as illogical. Similarly one feels as if the subordination of the individual to the State is too absolute and hardly consistent with the emphasis on individual right, which is a fundamental of his teaching. In this respect Luther's view is rather limited. He concerns himself with liberty in the religious sense and does not extend it beyond the things of the spirit. Whilst agreeing with his general principle that revolution has usually no reason in it, this does not necessarily involve the conclusion that the individual is to do nothing but preach, pray, and suffer, refrain from all initiative in deference to constituted authority, and be content to yield it unquestioning obedience. He does not seem to realise that the tyranny of the State might be or become as intolerable as the tyranny of Antichrist, and if he has a remedy against the latter in the exercise of the power of the State, he seems to have none against the former. The great religious reformer has evidently not the genius of the political or social reformer and is apparently prepared to accept the *status quo* in the State, whilst revolting and waging war against that prevailing in the Church.

Moreover, whilst relying on the power of an enlightened public opinion to bring about, through the State, a transformation of the Church, it is rather naïve to assume that the Christian community has not the right to reform itself by organised and combined effort. Suppose the State refuses to perform its function and remains inactive or takes the side of the old order, what will happen to the reform movement ? Is it sufficient to rely, in the face of a powerful organisation like the Papacy and the mediæval Church, on the indefinite power of the Word, great as its effect may be on the conscience and heart of the believer, if the believer may not put his hand to the task of asserting and vindicating his convictions ? One wonders whether, even in the religious sphere, the prophet of Wittenberg has also the gift of organising the movement he has initiated and does not defer too much to State intervention in this matter.

III. THE NEW EVANGELISM AND THE TRANSLATION OF
THE NEW TESTAMENT

It would be a mistake to see in the " Exhortation " any
slackening in his bellicose zeal against the Papacy. Any
doubt on this head is dispelled by the defiant philippic which
he hurled at the papal chair in the shape of an Address to
the Pope prefixed to his translation, with comments, of the
Bull, *Cœna Domini*, in which the Pope annually cursed all
heretics and other evil-doers at Easter. In that of the
preceding Easter (1521), Luther and his adherents were
included in the list of those thus publicly damned. In
response, the heretic sends at the beginning of 1522 to His
Holiness his New Year's Greeting in the sardonic effusion
which he entitled " The Evening Guzzle of the Most Holy
Lord the Pope." [35] The effusion cannot be said to be in
the best of taste. For Luther Rome has become the object
of unmitigated contempt and this contempt he seeks to
impart to the people in terms that would catch the popular
ear. The Latin of the Bull, which it has cost him such
trouble to put into intelligible German, is worthy of a
kitchen boy and can only have been written when the
Pope had supped too well. He trusts the Pope will give
him a cardinal's hat or a bishopric for the pains he has
taken in dressing up this drunken Latin in respectable
German. The translator ought also to get drunk in order
to do justice to the original. The bad language of the
Bull affords additional evidence of the drunken condition
of its author. For what else should one expect of a drunk
man but that he should curse and swear against all the
world without rhyme or reason. He proceeds to adduce
more proofs of the Pope's maudlin unreason in the detailed
comments on the various articles of the Bull, in which he
points out, with stinging sarcasm, the glaring contradictions
between its arrogant claims and lordly tone and the humility,
the lowly and loving spirit of Christ and the Apostles.
Discarding in conclusion the buffoonery of the preface and

[35] " Werke," viii. 691 f.

the comments, he reads the Pope and the papists a plain-spoken lecture on the Gospel which teaches not to curse but to love one's enemies, and on the parody of Christianity which Roman greed and arrogance seek to uphold by force and terror. He quotes from the Vulgate the words of Paul, *Radix omnium malorum avaritia*, " The love of money is the root of all evils," and sardonically remarks that the first letters of these four words spell " Roma." He adds an exposition of the 10th Psalm which, at the risk of being himself accused of a forced exegesis, he takes as a forecast of the wickedness and tyranny of the Roman Antichrist.

He was not content to rely on the popular pamphlet or the controversial treatise for the furtherance of the evangelical cause. V The Word itself being for him the great agent in overthrowing the Papacy and its institutions, it is essential to instruct the people in the Word if the Gospel is to assert its power in the regeneration of the Church and the world. To this end he had, some time after his arrival at the Wartburg, undertaken the task of writing in the vernacular a series of sermons (*Postille*) on the passages from the Gospels and Epistles which were read on Sundays and Feast days throughout the year.[36] On the 19th November he dedicated the collection, which covered the passages from the Gospels and the Epistles from Christmas to Epiphany, to Count Albert of Mansfeld, and prefixed to it " A Short Instruction on what we should seek and expect in the Gospels." [37] He followed it up with a translation of the Latin Advent sermons (*Advent-postille*) which he had written and sent to the press for the benefit of preachers before the journey to Worms, and which he now revised and enlarged in the vernacular for the benefit of the people.[38]

Gospel preaching in the evangelical sense begins with Luther. He deplores the lack of such preaching and

[36] Enders, iii. 171, 190, 204, 214, 218, 220, 235, 240; *cf.* " Werke," viii. 343, where in the dedication of the Evangelium von den Zehn Aussätzigen (17th Sept.) he refers to the accumulating *Postille*.

[37] " Werke," x., Pt. I.[1] These sermons fill the whole of this volume of his works.

[38] Enders, iii. 250, 256, 258. This series, which he completed towards the end of Feb. 1522, is given in " Werke," x., Pt. II.[2]

denounces the fables and scholastic subtleties with which
the parsons and monks delude and mislead the people.
"One blind man leads the other and both fall into the
ditch." [39] He claims that he has rediscovered the Gospel,
and his object in these sermons is to disentangle it from the
load of human doctrines with which the priesthood and the
schoolmen have overlaid it. Hence the polemic against
the current conception of the Gospel which finds expression
in these sermons, though the controversial element is only
incidental. Nor is the claim without foundation. He
undoubtedly strikes a new note, inasmuch as he bases his
message solely on the Word of God, as he interprets it, in
opposition to the mediæval Church. No one but Luther,
or one taught in Luther's school, could have so preached.
Moreover, apart from the distinctive matter of these sermons,
the manner of them is characteristically Lutheran. They
reflect the personality of the preacher all through. The
preacher has no audience before him, for he is buried in the
solitude of the Wartburg. All the same, he writes just as
if he were addressing an ordinary congregation in the Saxon
vernacular. There is no rhetoric, no attempt at mere oratory,
for he is uttering thoughts, convictions on which, he is
absolutely convinced, his own salvation and that of his
hearers depend. But this strength of conviction imparts
to his discourse a spontaneous eloquence, an incisive, arrest-
ing power of appeal, a directness and clarity of expression
which only a preacher aflame with the prophetic fire and
gifted by nature with an utterance adequate to his message
can attain. Such a preacher does not study effect. He only
expresses himself in the conviction that he speaks God's
message, as did the prophets and Apostles of old. To be
thus convinced was undoubtedly the secret of the power of
these sermons.[40]

At the same time, they have other features which
contribute to explain this power. The humanist has displaced the schoolman. Luther has made solid progress in
the knowledge of the original languages since the time when

[39] "Werke," x., Pt. I.[1], 37 ; cf. 50, 54, 140, 181, etc.
[40] On Luther's power as a preacher, see Garvie, "The Christian
Preacher."

he began to expound the Bible to his students at Wittenberg. He has studied the passages he expounds in the original Greek, and he shows a remarkable skill in expressing the meaning of the original in the vernacular. He has an extraordinary gift, which not many scholars possess, of making himself understood by the common man. He is a master of simplification, of popular exposition, in the best sense of the term. He uses the popular proverb and aptly illustrates his theme from the life of the people. Himself a son of the people, he strikes a democratic note which reflects a warm sympathy with and an understanding of the common man. He never loses an opportunity of showing how worthy is the common life lived in a Christian spirit and of reminding his hearers that the world and its wealth only too surely tend to deflect the soul from God and eternity.[41] His distinctive theology is reflected in these sermons. But it is entirely divorced from the subtlety and the jargon of the schools. It is no mere system of belief. It is brought into living touch with religion. It is experimental. It reflects his personal experience of the problem of salvation in the face of God's righteousness and man's sin. It is doctrinal in the sense that it seeks to inculcate the teaching of the Word in the solution of this problem. In this sense it is dogmatic enough, for, like Paul, the preacher is concerned first and foremost with the answer to this problem and knows of no other possible solution than that proclaimed by the great Apostle of the grace of God in Jesus Christ. It is emphatically Christo-centric, as Luther, following the Apostle, has apprehended Christ. " To preach the Gospel is nothing else than to bring Christ to men and men to Christ." [42] He knows nothing of the distinction between the Gospel of Christ and the Gospel about Christ, of any development of the teaching of Jesus by Paul or other Apostle. The whole Bible, in fact, from beginning to end is a testimony to Christ. In spite of his undoubted scholarship he is still apt at times to read more into his texts than they really contain, though his exegesis is in the main relevant. What the New Testament writers do is simply to

[41] "Werke," x., Pt. I.[1], 70, 86, 89.     [42] Ibid., x., Pt. I.[1], 14.

give full expression to what Moses and the prophets foresaw and taught about Christ. " The whole of the Old Testament has nothing in it but Christ." [43]

He nevertheless recognises a certain progression in the unfolding of the Christ revelation which, he thinks, reaches its fullness in Paul. From this point of view he rates Paul above the four evangelists. " I will venture to say that the Gospel is clearer and more fully expressed in Paul's Epistles than in the four Evangelists. The Evangelists have described Christ's life and word. . . . St Paul writes nothing of Christ's life, but he expresses clearly why He came and how we should make use of Him." [44] It is therefore, above all, the Gospel according to Paul that he expounds with such power and conviction in these sermons, in opposition to the moralism which makes the Gospel a law and Christ a second Moses, and to the ecclesiasticism in religion which consists in the performance of prescribed " works," such as fasting, repeating prayers, keeping vigil, almsgiving, founding churches, saying Masses for souls in purgatory, etc., and which he equates with the Phariseeism of the New Testament.[45] " St Paul teaches in this Epistle (Titus ii. 11-15) what Titus and every preacher shall preach to the people, viz., Christ and nothing else, in order that they may know what He is, why He came, and what He has accomplished." [46] Specifically to preach Christ is to proclaim the fact of man's sin and the glad tidings of God's saving gift to sinful man, received in faith unto salvation. The first essential of the reception of this gift is the sense of sin, the distrust of self, and all its works. Be a sinner in order to become a Christian is the great paradox. The Gospel is a message for sinners, not for the self-righteous or those who seek salvation by these Pharisaic works.

This is the kernel of Luther's own preaching to the people, of the new evangelism which, with a rare facility and mastery of simple exposition, he expounds to the common man in the common tongue, and which, as thus expounded, was fitted to appeal to the popular mind. It

[43] "Werke," x., Pt. I.[1], 10 ; cf. 80, 81, 181.

[44] Ibid., x., Pt. I.[1], 47.

[45] Ibid., x., Pt. I.[1], 17, 51.        [46] Ibid., x., Pt. I.[1], 19.

enables us to understand how the Lutheran Reformation, in its primary religious form at least, was emphatically an evangelistic movement, and why it made such a powerful impression on the people. | This evangelism is simply a New Testament, or, more correctly, a Pauline theology as moulded in Luther's own thought and experience in the quest for a gracious God, and adapted to the common understanding. It is born of his own experience of sin, of the futility of "works," moral or ecclesiastical, for salvation, of the sole sufficiency of Christ's work appropriated by faith, the sole efficacy of God's grace in effecting the regeneration of the soul and begetting the new life of faith, from which works spring and which becomes the dynamic of a practical Christian ethic. This ethic is the fruit of the personal reception of Christ as Saviour, and manifests itself in devotion to Him as Master. Luther's opponents had and have much to say in criticism of the theological presuppositions of this Evangelism as tending to Antinomianism, etc. But Luther himself assuredly does not teach a cheap or formal faith, though many of his adherents might too easily in practical life overrate his principle of faith at the expense of his Christian ethic. It is not, he insists, a fruitless faith that Christ brings to the receiving heart. The whole of the Christian life, he reiterates, is but a purification from sin. "For though faith redeems us forthwith from all the guilt of the law and makes us free, there remains the evil disposition in body and soul, which it is the work of faith to purify wholly." [47]

In addition to instructing the people in the Gospel through these sermons, he determined to put into their hands the Gospel itself in the common tongue. He had evidently discussed the project of a translation from the original language with his colleagues during his furtive visit to Wittenberg in the early part of December. They urged that he himself should undertake the task.[48] In his "Table Talk" he says that Melanchthon in particular had urged him to undertake

---

[47] "Werke," x., Pt. I.[1], 52.

[48] Enders, iii. 256. Novum Testamentum vernacula donaturus quam rem postulant nostri.

the work,[49] and his own sense of the superlative importance of providing an accurate version for popular use disposed him all the more readily to comply with the request. / " I long that every town should have its own interpreter," he wrote to Lang on the 18th December, after his return, " and that the tongue, hand, eyes, ears, and hearts of all should be occupied with this book alone." [50] / Lang himself, to whom he had owed his knowledge of the elements of the Greek language, had already in the previous year published a translation of Matthew from the Greek text of Erasmus. While Luther encouraged him to continue what he had begun,[51] his own plan embraced the whole Bible, not portions of it. Such a translation in the common tongue was, indeed, already in existence and had appeared in various editions during the fifteenth century and early years of the sixteenth.[52] But this translation had been made from the Vulgate and was thus but a translation of what was itself a faulty rendering of the original, and Luther had the advantage of being able to use for the New Testament the text of Erasmus (second edition, 1519). He also used a text sent him by Gerbel which was, however, practically that of Erasmus.[53] On this text he set to work within a few days after his return.[54] He laboured with such intense assiduity that he had worked through the whole of the New Testament by the end of February 1522.[55]

Truly a herculean performance and a striking testimony to his productive capacity which enabled him at the same time to translate and enlarge his Latin *Postille*. He felt at times, as he wrote to Amsdorf, that he had undertaken a burden beyond his powers.[56] | It was not merely a question of turning one literary form into another, but of rendering it in an idiom which the people could readily understand and which should, nevertheless, convey, in an apposite style,

---

[49] " Tischreden," iv. 709.
[50] Enders, iii. 256.          [51] *Ibid.*, iii. 256.
[52] Moeller, " History of the Christian Church," ii. 543.
[53] Enders, iii. 241.          [54] *Ibid.*, iii. 258.
[55] *Ibid.*, iii. 325.
[56] *Ibid.*, iii. 271. Interim Biblia transferam, quamquam onus susceperim supra vires.

the sense of the original. |The variety and divergence of dialects in German made the selection of a uniform medium peculiarly difficult. As a basis he chose the official language of the Saxon Chancellory, which had been adopted by the other German courts and the Senates of the Free Cities in their official communications.[57] His inborn gift of realistic expression stood him in good stead in moulding it into a fit instrument to express the meaning of the Greek original. "Translation," he says in his "Table Talk," "is a special grace and gift of God."[58] His German New Testament, from which Melanchthon expected to profit more than from all the commentaries of the learned,[59] is a striking monument of this gift. Even so, he spent many a weary hour in struggling to adapt his common medium to his purpose, and was fain to supplement it from his intimate knowledge of the popular Saxon, *i.e.*, Low German speech. "Now I realise," he wrote to Amsdorf on the 13th January, "what it means to be an interpreter and why it has hitherto been attempted by no one who considered only his own reputation."[60] He felt unequal to the task of translating the Old Testament without the assistance of his colleagues, and suggested that a secret lodging should be prepared for him at Wittenberg, where they might work together at the task of giving to Germany a worthy translation which all Christians could read with edification, and which would be a real improvement on the Vulgate. It is, he adds, a great and worthy work which demands the labour of all, in view of its public utility and its religious importance.[61]

## IV. THE RADICAL MOVEMENT AT WITTENBERG

The Elector had not only enjoined the Town Council of Wittenberg to punish the authors of the disturbances in the beginning of December. He had, in reply to the petition of the University of the 12th of the month, directed

---

[57] "Tischreden," iv. 57.        [59] "Corp. Ref.," i. 563.

[58] *Ibid.*, iv. 571.        [60] Enders, iii. 271.

[61] *Ibid.*, iii. 271. An estimate of Luther's translation will be given later in connection with the complete translation of the Bible.

that no innovations should be made in the service of the Mass without due deliberation and unanimous consent.[62] Undeterred by these injunctions and emboldened by the growing demand of the citizens [63] for a practical reformation, Carlstadt, in the course of a sermon which as archdeacon he delivered in All Saints on the 22nd, intimated that he would dispense the communion in both kinds on the 1st January 1522. Anticipating the Elector's intervention, he carried out his purpose on Christmas Day. After explaining to his hearers that not confession and fasting, as hitherto, but a firm faith was alone necessary for participation in the sacred rite,[64] he read the introductory part of the service of the Mass, and then, omitting the sacrificial passages and the elevation of the host, invited the people to partake of the bread and wine in the words of the original institution, " Take, eat, etc." The daring thing in this celebration, which he performed without priestly garments, was not merely the giving of both kinds to the communicant, but the invitation to take from the altar with his own hands the elements which the priest alone had hitherto been permitted to handle.[65]

The sensation aroused by this daring contravention of use and wont was heightened by another unseemly demonstration on the previous night against the Mass in both the parish church and All Saints, which was also reported in detail to the Elector by the Chapter.[66] Despite the official request to refrain from this innovation,[67] he repeated the innovation on New Year's Day, on the following Sunday, the 5th January, and on Epiphany Day, and

[62] " Corp. Ref.," i. 504 f. ; Nik. Müller, 117 f., 15th and 19th Dec.

[63] The active movement led by Carlstadt and Zwilling had the support of a party among the citizens who had already, on the 17th Dec., presented to the Town Council a number of articles in favour of a radical reform of the religious and social life of the community.

[64] See the account of the sermon in Barge, i. 359-361.

[65] See the letter of the Chapter of All Saints to the Elector, 29th Dec., in which this enormity is emphasised. Barge, ii. 558-559; cf. " Corp. Ref.," i. 512 ; Nik. Müller, 131 f. ; Ulscenius to Capito, " Z.K.G.," v. 330. See also the contemporary account in ibid., xxii. 125.

[66] See its Report in Barge, ii. 559 ; Nik. Müller, 133-134.

[67] " Corp. Ref.," i. 612-613, 26th Dec. ; Nik. Müller, 125-126.

the increasing number of communicants showed that, at Wittenberg at least, the people, if not the Government, were ready to welcome it.   His example was followed by Zwilling who, after a series of violent sermons against the Mass in the parish church at Eilenburg, dispensed the communion in both kinds on New Year's Day in the castle chapel under the patronage of Hans von Taubenheim and other electoral officials.[68]   Here again, unfortunately, the rowdy element, roused by the reckless eloquence of the fiery preacher, showed its indignation at the opposition of the local priest by smashing the windows of the parsonage. In Lochau and several other places, on the other hand, the priests took the lead in introducing the evangelical celebration.[69]

Other innovations rapidly followed.   Many ceased to go to confession or to fast on Friday.   On the 19th January Carlstadt publicly espoused Anna von Mochau, the daughter of a poor nobleman resident in a neighbouring village, in the exercise of his Christian liberty and as an example to the priesthood, as he informed the Elector.[70]   Justus Jonas, the Provost of All Saints, and others erelong followed suit.[71] A number of the Franciscan monks left their monastery and took to shoemaking or other trades in order to earn their living and support their wives.[72]   On the 11th January, the day after the conclusion of the Chapter of the Order, the Augustinians, under Zwilling's leadership, startled the citizens by removing the altars from the monastery chapel, smashing the images, burning the pictures of the saints, and thereafter distributing to the people the communion in both kinds.[73]   This dramatic proceeding started the demand for the clearance of the churches of these " emblems of idolatry," which was vigorously abetted by Carlstadt in the pulpit

---

[68] See the contemporary accounts in " Z.K.G.," v. 327-329, and xxii. 125-126.

[69] " Z.K.G.," xxii. 122-123.

[70] *Ibid.*, v. 331 (Ulscenius to Capito); *cf. ibid.*, xxii. 125; "Corp. Ref.," i. 538.

[71] *Ibid.*, v. 332; xxii. 121.

[72] *Ibid.*, xxii. 121.

[73] *Ibid.*, v. 332; Nik. Müller, 169, 212.

and in a philippic against images.[74] Zwilling also fanned the radical spirit by his fiery sermons on the subject and took occasion to rebuke Jonas and Amsdorf from the pulpit for their lack of zeal in the good cause.[75] Carlstadt, it appears, would, like Zwingli, have gone the length of eliminating instrumental music as well as images from the churches.[76] Amsdorf, Aurogallus, and Melanchthon were shocked by these iconoclastic excesses and thought of leaving Wittenberg.[77]

By this time the agitation had impressed the Town Council, which had so far striven to carry out the Elector's negative policy, with the necessity of averting the threatened anarchy by making concessions to the active reformers. To this end the new Burgomaster, Dr Beyer, who had acted as the Elector's representative in the earlier stage of the movement, entered into negotiations with the University. The result of the united deliberations of Council and professors, in which Melanchthon took a very active part,[78] was an ordinance regulating the social as well as the religious life of the community on evangelical lines [79] (24th-25th January). Its aim is not only to regulate public worship in accordance with the Gospel, but to bring the spirit of the Gospel into communal life. It accordingly directs that the communion should be celebrated in accordance with the institution of Christ. Such specified parts of the traditional service as are contrary to this institution are to be omitted ;

[74] Von der Anbetung der Bilder. A summary of it is given by Barge, i. 386 f. The dedication is dated 27th Jan.

[75] " Z.K.G.," v. 331.                    [76] Barge, i. 490-491.

[77] " Z.K.G.," v. 331 ; Nik. Müller, 172-173.

[78] Ibid., v. 331. Habentur cotidie concilia hic a præposito (Jonas, Provost of All Saints), Karolstadio, Philippo, reliquoque clero et magistratu de mutandis plurium rebus. Philippus ardentissime rem agit.

[79] Ain lobliche ordnung der Furstlichen Stat Wittenberg. Richter, " Die Evangelischen Kirchenordnungen des 16ten Jahrhunderts," ii. 484-485 (1871) ; " Corp. Ref.," i. 540-541. Beyer's summary, dated 25th Jan., which adds some details. Sehling, " Die Evangelischen Kirchenordnungen des 16ten Jahrhunderts," i. 697-698 (1902). See also " Z.K.G.," xxii. 122. Clemen gives the oldest version, which he discovered in the Zwickau Lib. in " Theol. Stud. und Kritiken," 1897, 820-821.

the others are only retained " for the sake of those weak
in the faith." After sermon and consecration by the priest
in the vernacular, the communicant may—not must, as
Carlstadt and Zwilling would have directed—take in his
hand the bread and the cup and partake thereof, thus
evidently following the precedent set by Carlstadt in his
celebration on Christmas Day. To avoid idolatry the altars,
beyond the number of three, shall " in time " [80] be removed
from the parish church. Ecclesiastical revenues and the
vessels of the church are transferred to a common fund
to be administered by the Town Council for the benefit of
the poor—certain benefices, which are only to fall to this
fund on the death of the incumbent, excepted. Compensation for those revenues immediately transferred is to be
paid to the priests at the rate of six gulden annually. All
begging, whether by monks, students, or others, is henceforth
forbidden, and the monks in particular shall work for their
living. Fraternities, *i.e.*, social and religious associations,
twenty-one in number, are abolished and their income is also
made over to the common fund. Loans shall be made from
this fund to poor craftsmen out of work, without any charge
for interest. Orphans and poor children, especially young
girls, shall be supported out of it, and in case it does not
suffice for such objects, the citizens shall contribute. The
sons of poor parents who show sufficient ability shall be
assisted to remain at school in order to provide efficient
preachers of the Gospel and properly equipped servants of the
State. Those not of sufficient ability to serve the commonweal in this capacity shall be trained as craftsmen. To
prevent extortion, citizens in need of loans shall receive such
out of the common fund at 4 per cent., instead of 5 or 6
charged by private lenders. Prostitution is forbidden.
Women of ill-fame must marry or leave the town, and
keepers of brothels are liable to severe penalties.[81]

[80] So in Beyer's summary.
[81] According to Barge a special ordinance was drawn up regulating
in detail the administration of the common fund. It is given by Barge,
ii. 559-561. The question is whether this ordinance was not already
passed in Nov. 1521 at the instigation of Luther (this has been inferred
from a letter of Ulscenius to Capito, 30th Nov. 1521, given by Hartfelder

The ordinance is interesting and important as the first attempt of the civic authority to introduce an evangelical form of worship, to mould social and economic conditions, and exercise a strict supervision of public morality in conformity with the Gospel, and to secularise ecclesiastical revenues for the common benefit. It has been decried as visionary and puritanic as well as revolutionary by German historians who see in it merely the fanatic radicalism of Carlstadt and Zwilling.[82] Carlstadt and Zwilling doubtless contributed to its inception, and the regulation of public worship certainly reflects the hand of Carlstadt.[83] But its composition was the result of the co-operation of the Council and the University, of Beyer, Melanchthon, Jonas, and others, as well as Carlstadt, and it is a mistake to see in it the fruit merely of irresponsible fanaticism. On the contrary, granting the necessity of inaugurating the change from the old order to the new, it is in the circumstances a moderate and enlightened solution of a very difficult problem. The secularisation of ecclesiastical revenues was, indeed, a daring procedure. But it was not entirely new and it proceeds on the principle of applying these revenues for the common benefit, including education as well as poor relief. It leaves

in " Melanchthoniana Pædagogica," 120) who had already concerned himself with the subject in the " Address to the Nobility," or whether it was the result of the more general ordinance of 24th to 25th Jan. 1522. Barge maintains the latter view, " Theologische Studien und Kritiken," 1913, 461 f., and " Historische Vierteljahrschrift," 1908, 193 f. Karl Müller, " Historische Zeitschrift," vol. xcvi. 471 f., and "Luther und Karlstadt," 31 f. (1907), and Köhler, "Gött. Gelehrte Anzeige," 1912, 524 f., maintain the former view. Winckelmann, "Hist. Viertel Jahrschrift," 1914, 205 f., also maintains this view, but thinks that the ordinance was not carried out and was, in any case, displaced by the larger one of Jan. 1522.

[82] See, for instance, Kolde, " Luther," ii. 36; Hausrath, " Luther," i. 528; Köstlin-Kawerau, " Luther," i. 483.

[83] Barge would ascribe its provisions mainly to Carlstadt, without adequate justification, however, i. 385. Karl Müller ("Luther und Karlstadt," 56 f.) shows that the ordinance was, in part at least, an attempt to put in practice Luther's teaching in the sermon on Usury and the " Address to the Nobility." Melanchthon also took an active part in its composition in the hope apparently of regularising and moderating the movement. *Ibid.*, 62 f.

benefices in the possession of the incumbents during their lifetime and it allows compensation for the loss of income from confiscated sources. The inhibition of begging on economic grounds needs no apology, and the attempt to reduce excessive interest on loans is economically defensible. To put down public prostitution may be " puritanic." But Luther himself had strongly advocated this course in the " Address to the Nobility," and it is amply justified on the ground of the public welfare and morality as well as Christian duty. To denounce as Antichristian the Mass and image worship and yet refrain indefinitely from abolishing these abuses was neither logical nor advisable, if the Reformation was to be something more than a theological controversy within the schools. Moreover, whilst communion in both kinds is made obligatory, the taking of the bread and the cup in the hand of the communicant is, contrary to the demand of Carlstadt, left optional. The removal of the images is, according to the report of Beyer, not to be precipitately carried out. Whilst all this is revolutionary enough, the revolution is carried out in the interest of order and the commonweal, and not merely at the dictate of irresponsible fanatics. Carlstadt himself, in fact, though preaching and writing in favour of a radical policy, did not approve of popular violence, and had no desire to foment it, though he was not disposed to take his orders in matters of religion from the Government.[84] " For my person I assert that I have followed the Scriptures, and I appeal for confirmation to the unsuspected evidence of my hearers. . . . Therefore I will remain strictly on the foundation of God's Word and shall not allow myself to be led astray by what others teach. Woe is me if I preach not the Gospel."

Its authors had, however, not reckoned with the fact of the antagonism of the Elector who had from the outset,

[84] Letter of 4th Feb. to the Electoral Minister, von Einsiedel, who had written a sharp reproof of his preaching. " Corp. Ref.," i. 544-547 ; Barge, " Aktenstücke Zur Wittenberger Bewegung," 13-15 (1912); N. Müller, " Die Wittenberger Bewegung," 180 f. (1911). K. Müller (" Luther und Karlstadt," 68 f.) contests Carlstadt's disclaimer of inciting the people to violence and Barge's assertion to this effect, i. 407.

from political reasons, discouraged and opposed what he regarded as a precipitate departure from the existing order. In addition to his innate dislike of revolution, his fear of provoking the resentment of the Imperial Regency (Reichsregiment) at Nürnberg predisposed him against such a far-reaching measure. He had warmly professed his readiness to further the cause of the Gospel and his profession seems to have been sincere. But the wary politician instinctively sought the path of least resistance in furthering the movement, and this path seemed to lie in the direction of retarding rather than hurrying change in the existing order. Individual initiative like that of Carlstadt and Zwilling against his declared will was both distasteful to his sense of order and likely to involve him in grave conflict with the central Government. And on the back of the news of Carlstadt's daring innovation in the service of the Mass on Christmas Day, came letters from Melanchthon, informing him of the arrival at Wittenberg of certain disciples of Thomas Münzer—Stübner, Storch, and another whose name is not given—who had been driven from Zwickau as disturbers of the peace. Of these " prophets " Stübner was a former student of Wittenberg University and a friend of Melanchthon ; Storch and his companion were weavers and illiterates.[85] Melanchthon was at first impressed by their knowledge of the Scriptures, their claim to direct inspiration by the Spirit, and their pretension to foretell the future by means of visions. He feared to condemn them lest he might extinguish the Spirit and was greatly perturbed over their arguments against infant baptism, especially as they appealed to Luther's teaching in support of their claims.[86] On reflection he expressed himself, in a report to the Elector on the 1st January 1522, as more sceptical about their claims to inspiration, and suggested that the matter should be referred to the judgment of Luther.[87]

---

[85] " Corp. Ref.," i. 513. Huc advolarunt tres viri, duo lanifices, literarum rudes, literatus tertius est.

[86] See his letters to the Elector and to Spalatin, 27th Dec. 1521. " Corp. Ref.," i. 513-515.

[87] *Ibid.*, i. 533-534. Amsdorf also sent a report of a similar tenor. *Ibid.*, i. 534-535.

The matter-of-fact Elector had already been informed
from Zwickau about the doings of these "prophets," [88]
and on the 2nd January sent von Einsiedel and Spalatin
to explain to Melanchthon and Amsdorf what he thought of
them. In his view they were religious anarchists and
fomenters of sedition, with whose vagaries it was not
necessary to trouble Luther, though to his credit he was
not disposed to use force against them.[89]   Their presence
at Wittenberg seems, however, to have contributed to deepen
his suspicion and dislike of Carlstadt and Zwilling who, in
his eyes, were hardly less obnoxious revolutionaries.   In
reality there is no evidence that either Carlstadt or Zwilling,
unlike Melanchthon, was seriously impressed by their
claims to supernatural enlightenment.[90]   Their influence on
the Wittenberg movement seems to have been practically
negligible, and the passing excitement they created subsided
with their departure shortly after.   Certain it is that there
is no trace of even a spasmodic influence on the practical
provisions of the ordinance.

What moved the Elector to challenge once more the
policy of the innovators was not only the dislike of revolution, but the knowledge that the Imperial Regency had
resolved to suppress the movement.   At the instigation of
Duke George of Saxony it emphatically condemned the
innovations in the worship and the usages of the Church
(particularly the revolt against the celibacy of the clergy
and the obligation of monastic vows) as detrimental to
religion and ecclesiastical order, and requested the princes
to prohibit them within their territories under threat of
severe punishment, and to instruct the people by means of
skilful preachers to observe the old order until a Reichstag
or a Council should authoritatively determine the question.
In particular, the authors or adherents of these innovations
are to be visited with exemplary punishment if they persist

[88] Letter of Hausmann to the Elector from Zwickau, 18th Dec. 1521,
" Z.K.G.," v. 323-325.
[89] " Corp. Ref.," i. 535-538.
[90] See Barge, i. 402-405.   Against the conventional view of a large
number of German historians.

in maintaining them.[91] In this emergency there was only one of two alternatives open to the Elector—either to risk an open conflict with the central Government, or to take energetic measures against the innovators at Wittenberg and elsewhere. Old and ailing, he seems to have been no longer equal to the strain of the diplomatic fencing which he had practised so successfully in defence of Luther against the Pope and the Emperor. He was besides alienated by the independent initiative of Carlstadt and Zwilling. He therefore chose the latter alternative in spite of the fact that his representative at Nürnberg, von Planitz, had strenuously opposed the proposals of Duke George. As a preliminary, Einsiedel attempted to silence the radical preachers at Wittenberg.[92] Carlstadt, as we have seen, answered with a spirited refusal, and Melanchthon, who was requested to abet this demand, replied that he was powerless to stem the tide of Reformation and hinted that it was time to show a more active sympathy with the movement.[93] On the back of these letters came the tidings that the people, anticipating the promised action of the Town Council, had burst into the parish church, torn down the images and pictures, and smashed and burned them.[94] Though the Council arrested and punished a number of the rioters, the incident brought upon the innovators a sharp condemnation of the revolutionary measures which had given occasion to such disorder.[95] In this communication the Elector, whilst not absolutely inhibiting the ordinance, enlarged on the danger of truckling

[91] Barge, "Aktenstücke," 3-6; Walch, xv. 4616-4619. For the discussion at Nürnberg on this mandate see "Reichstagsakten," iii. 20-21.
[92] "Corp. Ref.," i. 543-544; Barge, "Aktenstücke," 11-13. Letters to Melanchthon to bring Zwilling to desist from his aggressive sermons, and direct to Carlstadt to refrain from such preaching, 3rd Feb. Einsiedel seems to have acted on his own initiative in this matter. Barge, "Hist.Vierteljahrschrift" (1914), 7-8.
[93] Barge, "Aktenstücke," 16-17; "Corp. Ref.," i. 544-546. Ich kann aber das Wasser nicht halten, wäre von nöthen dass man zu solichen Sachen die der Seelen Heil betreffen, ernstlicher thäte.
[94] "Corp. Ref.," i. 550, 553, probable date 5th or 6th Feb.
[95] Ibid., i. 549-552; Barge, "Aktenstücke," 25-30; Nik. Müller, 190 f., 13th Feb.

to revolution at the instigation of the radical preachers, repeated his former caveat against precipitate action, and demanded to be informed why they had acted in this matter against his declared will. In reply, the University Commission accepted responsibility for the ordinance drawn up in co-operation with the Town Council in the interest of the public welfare, and while expressing disapproval of the violent removal of the images, laid the blame on the obstructive tactics of the opponents of the Reformation [96] (the Romanist section of the Chapter of All Saints). In a supplementary statement, however, which was evidently inspired by the pliant Melanchthon, the Commission resiles to a considerable extent from this spirited vindication of its action, and makes concessions in a conservative direction in regard to the communion service.[97] In the interview between its members and Einsiedel at Eilenburg on the 13th February, Carlstadt went the length of promising to cease preaching, and the more moderate Amsdorf undertook to exhort the people from the pulpit of the parish church to observe moderation, whilst Zwilling contributed to ease the situation by retiring in the meantime from Wittenberg.[98]

With this compromise the Elector was by no means satisfied, and on the 17th February sent from Lochau an emphatic condemnation of the religious innovations and their authors, and a decisive expression of his will that the old order should be restored, pending a general and authoritative decision on the question.[99] He based his demand on the imperial mandate of the 20th January and the intimation of the Bishop of Meissen of his determination to execute it in his diocese, which included part of the electoral territory.[100]

[96] " Corp. Ref.," i. 552-553; Barge, " Aktenstücke," 30-32; Nik. Müller, 194 f. The editor of the " Corp. Ref." wrongly ascribes the first part of this document to the Town Council.

[97] " Corp. Ref.," i. 554-555. Barge, " Aktenstücke," 33-34; Nik. Müller, 201.

[98] " Corp. Ref.," i. 556-558; Barge, " Aktenstücke," 41 f.

[99] " Corp. Ref.," i. 558-559; Barge, " Aktenstücke," 44-46; Nik. Müller, 206-208.

[100] The bishop's intimation was dispatched to the Elector on the 7th Feb. It is given by Barge, " Aktenstücke," 19-21, and, together with the mandate, explains his decision to prohibit outright the innovations

It might be the prudent course to adopt. But this kind of tactic would hardly have produced the Reformation, especially as Melanchthon, Justus Jonas, and Amsdorf in the face of this *impasse* were at the end of their resources and also of their courage. They were not made of the stuff of resolute leadership, and Melanchthon, in particular, in the absence of Luther's backing, had recently shown a lack of firmness of resolution and purpose. He had, for instance, undoubtedly been impressed by Stübner's arguments on behalf of a subjective revelation, and then at the Elector's nod had agreed to discard the prophets. He had also at Einsiedel's request undertaken to reprimand Zwilling,[1] though he had some days before written a eulogy of him to his friend Hector Pomer at Nürnberg.[2] He had all along felt the lack of Luther's presence and pined for his return. Whilst Carlstadt would have stood by the ordinance, his only expedient was to shift the responsibility for a decision of the question on to Luther's shoulders. Hence the message sent on the 20th February to the Wartburg urging his return to Wittenberg.

at Wittenberg. The passage in which the Elector gives the reason for his decision is lacking in the version of his missive to Einsiedel in the " Corp. Ref.," i. 558-559. The full text is given by Barge, " Aktenstücke," 44-46, and Nik. Müller, " Die Wittenberger Bewegung," 206-208. K. Müller (" Luther und Karlstadt," 76 f.) contests the view that Frederick acted from apprehension of the central Government, and ascribes his action to his conservative instinct and his conventional method of evading responsibility in such matters. It does appear, however, from the concluding passage of his missive that the Elector was really anxious on the score of the intervention of the central Government.

[1] " Corp. Ref.," i. 546.          [2] *Ibid.*, i. 542.

# CHAPTER III

# LUTHER'S RETURN FROM THE WARTBURG

## I. LUTHER AND THE ELECTOR

LUTHER had been following with a lively interest the progress of the movement at Wittenberg since his return to the Wartburg about the middle of December. He rejoiced at the news of Carlstadt's marriage, and in a letter to Amsdorf on the 13th January had intimated his intention of bringing him a present on his return after Easter.[1] He must have known of the celebration of the communion in both kinds on Christmas Day when he wrote in this friendly tone concerning him, and though he mentions his intention to return in a letter to Melanchthon of the same date, the reason adduced is not the innovations in worship, not even the advent of the prophets, but the furthering of his translation of the New Testament.[2] Some days later (17th January) he refers, indeed, in a letter to Spalatin to the innovations at Eilenburg and Wittenberg as a reason for putting an end to his enforced exile, and says that the matter demands his return either to Wittenberg or some other place. But he does not explicitly condemn them, and is concerned rather to disarm the Elector's opposition to his purpose.[3] He does not take the prophets very seriously,[4] and in the letters to Amsdorf and Melanchthon of the 13th January advises them to try the spirits. He expresses scepticism about their professed revelations, and reminds the anxious Melanchthon of the advice of Gamaliel. God sends no one without a call through human agency, or without accompanying signs. The prophets of old received and proved their vocation in

---

[1] Enders, iii. 270-271.  [3] *Ibid.*, iii. 286.
[2] *Ibid.*, iii. 277.  [4] *Ibid.*, iii. 286. Neque enim me movent.

this manner. Subjective revelations by means of dreams and visions and direct inspiration are not to be credited without substantial attestation of this kind, even if these prophets claim to have been caught up to the third heaven. Nor is he impressed by their insistence on adult baptism on the ground that infants cannot exercise personal faith. God accepts the faith of the parents on their behalf (*fides aliena*) and is able to inspire faith even in the infant mind. More convincing is the argument that Christ received the little children, and we should follow His example. Moreover, the presumption is that " what is not against Scripture is for the Scripture and the Scripture for it." [5] Satan is certainly at the bottom of the movement.[6] Whilst he thus rejects their pretensions and reasonings, he would not use force against them. It would ill become the followers of the Gospel to resort to persecution, and he charges Spalatin to see that the Elector does not resort to it.[7]

During the next five weeks there is a blank in his correspondence, and at the end of this interval there is a marked change in his tone in reference to the Wittenberg movement. He has evidently received the letter of his colleagues urging his return and revealing their utter impotence to cope with the situation in the face of the Elector's drastic intervention. He has evidently been informed of the danger to his cause that threatens from Nürnberg and of the trepidation that reigns in the electoral court, as well as the prevailing helplessness and confusion at Wittenberg. His first impulse [8] was to dash off a note to the Elector in his bluffest style without the usual deferential preamble. With an ironic reference to the Elector's zeal as a collector of relics, he tells him that God has sent him a whole cross with nails, spears, and scourge to boot. He sardonically wishes him good luck with this new acquisition to his

---

[5] Enders, iii. 276. Quod ergo non est contra Scripturam pro Scriptura est et Scriptura pro eo.

[6] *Ibid.*, iii. 271-277.

[7] *Ibid.*, iii. 286.

[8] The so-called letter to the Wittenbergers towards the end of Feb., noted by Enders, is really the sketch of a sermon which he proposed to deliver and which he made after his return. " Werke," x. 74 f.

collection and begs him not to let himself be frightened
thereat, but to act prudently and wisely rather than in
accordance with mere diplomatic reason and the outward
appearance of things (a hit at the Elector's predilection for
politic measures). Whoever will have the Word of God
must be prepared to find not only Annas and Caiaphas
raging, but Judas among the Apostles and Satan among
the children of God. Judas evidently stands for Carlstadt
and his associates, whose reforms are inspired by Satan.
High time, therefore, for him to be at Wittenberg in order
to frustrate these satanic wiles. He knows Satan's tricks
too well to be afraid of him. " God willing I will straightway be there." [9]

The letter, he tells us, was written in haste, and the
judgment strikes the reader as equally hasty. It was
evidently based on one-sided information about the reform
movement and coloured by his obsession of the devil's impish
doings, which the solitude of the Wartburg had intensified.
These reforms were the logical outcome of his own principles
though he had himself refrained from drawing the inevitable
practical conclusion and had warned others against doing
so. At the same time, he had frequently in his works incited
to revolt against the papal ecclesiastical system and had
evidently discovered nothing in the movement at Wittenberg
up to the middle of January to suggest the agency of Satan.
Nor had he taken the ebullition of popular feeling against
the old order there seriously. Even the ordinance of the
24th January had been initiated by the public authority
in accordance with his declared principle, and was therefore
not liable to the objection of being the fruit of irresponsible
revolutionary violence. Its provisions relative to the
practical reform of religious and social life (the simplification
of the Mass, usury, prostitution, poor relief, education)
were in keeping with his teaching.

What seems to have suggested the agency of Satan in his
reforming capacity was the active antagonism of the Elector,
under the influence of the Nürnberg mandate of 20th
January, and the failure of his Wittenberg colleagues to

[9] " Werke," 53, 103-104 (Erlang. ed.).

maintain the ordinance in the face of this antagonism. Their lack of resource and nerve had certainly produced a situation that called for his intervention. But while the crisis might appear serious enough, it hardly justified him in so hastily prejudging their work as satanic, or denouncing Carlstadt as the Judas of the Reformation. Carlstadt had only acted on the principle of his own letter to Spalatin in the middle of December, in which he put the pointed question whether they were to go on perpetually disputing on the Word of God and always abstaining from putting it in practice.

The Elector was, however, very nervous on the score of his declared determination to intervene personally. In his reply, which took the form of an instruction to John Oswald, his bailiff at Eisenach, he explained the situation at Wittenberg from his point of view—the prevailing dis-union and anarchy which the innovations had produced, the diminution of the number of students, the intervention of the Council of Regency and of the Bishop of Meissen as its mandatory. Whilst asking Luther to advise him in this emergency, he adduces the difficulties and dangers to which his resolution to return in the face of the papal and imperial ban will expose both himself and him. If, how-ever, he could be sure that it was the will of God that he should take upon him this cross, he is prepared to do so. Only things are in such a state of chaos at Wittenberg that he is unable to see God's hand in these ongoings or run the risk of grave complications for such a cause. Perhaps Luther would do better to exercise patience for a time and submit the case in writing to the forthcoming Diet.[10] The missive is very characteristic of the wary politician who would fain prompt Luther to use his influence to put down the radical movement at Wittenberg and thus obviate the threatened intervention of the central Government and its mandatory, the Bishop of Meissen, whilst transferring to him the responsibility for the decision whether to return or not.[11]

[10] Enders, iii. 292-295.
[11] Kawerau in the " Deutsche Literaturzeitung," xiv. 1584 f. (1893), interprets the Elector's letter as a camouflaged invitation to Luther to return and deal with the situation. He incorporated this interpretation,

When this missive reached Luther, he had already made his preparations for his departure on the following day. It did not alter his determination to start on the morrow, and he had reached Borna on the way to Wittenberg before he found time to answer it on the 5th March. The answer is one of the most characteristic revelations of his dynamic personality, and brings out in striking relief the contrast between the calculating but worried politician and the fearless and resolute reformer, who believes himself to be commissioned and directed by God and moulds his course in accordance with this conviction and no other. He starts in an apologetic tone, for the Elector had evidently felt the sting of his ironic reference to his mania for relic collecting and his predilection for diplomatic calculation. He had not intended to depreciate his distinguished gifts as a ruler, whom he esteemed above all other princes, but only to comfort him in the midst of the trouble which the ill-conceived measures of the misguided innovators had caused him " to the great dishonour of the Gospel." All the ill done him hitherto by his enemies is as nothing compared to this distortion of the Gospel, which cannot be excused before God or the world and for which he will be held responsible. Clearly the hand of the devil is in this game. But the Elector need not worry himself about him or his cause. He has received the Gospel, not from man but from heaven alone through the Lord Jesus Christ. He had offered to appear at the bar of the Diet of Worms not because he had any doubt about the truth, but only that by his humility he might draw others to it. Similarly he had allowed himself for reasons of expediency to be buried in the Wartburg. The devil knows only too well that he

which Berger adopts ("Luther," i. 431), in his edition of Moeller's "History of the Christian Church," iii. 37 (Eng. trans.), but subsequently dropped it in "Luther's Rückkehr," 44. Bezold, on the other hand, contests this interpretation and concludes that the letter was rather meant to discourage Luther's return and was not a mere roundabout way of prompting him to do so, "Z.K.G.," xx. 202 f. The letter seems to me to warrant the interpretation I have given in the text. It really leaves to Luther the decision whether he shall return or not and does not forbid his return.

had not been actuated by fear in adopting this expedient.
Had he not defied him when he determined to enter Worms
even if there were as many devils within it as tiles on the
roofs ?   And now that he is trying on his old game through
Duke George, shall he lose confidence in the Father of
Mercies who has made us, through the Gospel, lords over the
devil and death and over Duke George's fury as well ?
Verily not.  For if necessity should call him to go to
Leipzig instead of Wittenberg, he would ride into it even if
it rained for nine days Duke Georges, and every one of
them were more furious than this one.  He is going to
Wittenberg under a higher protection than that of the
Elector.  He does not desire his protection, and if he
depended on such protection he would not go at all.   In
this matter the secular power can neither counsel nor help.
God alone can provide without all human care and co-
operation.  He who believes most will, therefore, have the
most protection.  Since he observes that the Elector is
still all too weak in faith, he can by no means regard him
as the man to protect or save him.  The Elector esteems
that he has done too little in this matter.  Luther respectfully assures him that he has done too much and should do
nothing at all.  For God will have this affair left in His own
hands and in no one else's.  If the Elector has not this
faith, Luther has it and must leave him to worry in his
unbelief.  And since he refuses to follow his direction,
he need have no responsibility for what happens to him.
Let him obey the imperial authority as is his duty.  Resistance to it is resistance to God, who has established it.  He
trusts, however, that the imperial Government will act
with reason and recognise the divine hand in this cause.
But if not, and it seeks to seize him, let the Elector permit it
freely to do so.   Christ has not taught Luther to be a
Christian at another's expense.  If, however, it is so bereft
of reason as to command the Elector to arrest him, he will
then tell him what his duty is.  Happily it is a different
man from Duke George with whom he has to do, though,
through his lack of faith, he has not yet seen the glory of
God.[12]

[12] " Werke," 53, 104-109 (Erlang. ed.).

The letter reveals Luther in his true character as the prophet to whom God is everything, man, even an Elector, is nothing, when it boots to vindicate what he conceives to be God's will. The Elector was, however, by no means minded to leave the political aspect of the matter out of account. These heroics could hardly be adduced in a diplomatic explanation to the Imperial Regency of the reappearance on the scene of the redoubtable outlaw, for which the Elector would be asked to account. Luther must, therefore, be persuaded to drop his prophet's mantle for the nonce and give a version of his action which the Elector could use for diplomatic purposes. In a missive to Schurf he accordingly requested that he should furnish him with such a declaration of the reason of his return, without his permission, as he could show to his fellow-princes (Duke George and the members of the Regency at Nürnberg) in his own exoneration,[13] and as far as possible that of Luther himself. Luther had perforce, therefore, to exchange the rôle of the prophet for that of the diplomatist, and in a letter to the Elector, written on the 7th March as of his own accord, acknowledges that he had returned without his " will and permission." In so doing he had not acted in contempt of the authority of the Emperor or any other, for although human authority is not to be obeyed when it ordains anything against God, it is as a rule to be honoured and not despised. Though Christ did not justify Pilate's judgment, He did not gainsay it. He had returned for three reasons : He had received a call from the Church at Wittenberg and was bound in conscience to respond to it. Satan had made an inroad into his fold and the situation, which could not be remedied by letter, demanded his personal intervention. Moreover, Germany was standing on the brink of a great uprising. The people are apprehending the Gospel in a fleshly sense and the tendency is all the more dangerous, inasmuch as the powers that be, instead of striving to mitigate this danger, are intensifying it by their efforts to extinguish the Gospel. It was, therefore, imperative that he should seek, in co-operation with his friends,

---

[13] Enders, iii. 297-298.  Instruction to Schurf, 7th March.

to counteract their insensate policy of force. " For your Electoral Grace should know and be assured of this, that it is altogether decreed otherwise in heaven than at Nürnberg, and those who unhappily presume that they have swallowed the Gospel will yet discover that they have not even learned to say the ' Benedicite.' " The Elector is lord only over material things and the body. Christ is the lord of the soul, and in this sphere he must needs do His will who has sent him and raised him up for this purpose. He hopes that Christ will prevail over his enemies and will protect him. But if not, His will be done. The Elector need have no fear of incurring any danger or detriment on his account.[14]

He evidently felt that this essay in diplomacy was hardly up to the Elector's standard, and in a postscript he expresses his readiness to alter the terms of it in accordance with any changes the Elector may suggest, though he intimates that this is the last time that he will pay such a tribute to political expediency. The suggested amendments [15] proved to be so material that in the final version of the letter, bearing date 12th March, the prophet almost disappears behind the plausible diplomatist. The Elector's decided opposition to his return is more categorically asserted, and he now refers to the Emperor as " his most gracious lord " instead of the formal " imperial majesty." The rather contemptuous reference to the Imperial Regency is suppressed, the Elector's forgiveness is asked for his disobedience to his express will, and an undertaking is given to refrain with God's help from all unseemly and insulting accusations.[16] The missive is meekness itself compared with the high-spirited effusion of the 5th March. It was wrung from him, as he wrote to Spalatin, by consideration of the Elector's infirmity, and the reference to the Emperor as his most gracious lord was very much against the grain, since all the world knew that he was his direst enemy and would only ridicule this manifest pretence. The only salve for his conscience was that he was merely using the conventional language of courtly address.

---

[14] " Werke," 53, 109-112 (Erlang. ed.).
[15] See the Elector's letter to Schurf, Enders, iii. 303-304.
[16] " Werke," 52, 114-118 (Erlang. ed.).

But he has had enough of this sort of subterfuge (*fucus*), and no more of this make-believe is to be expected from him.[17]

Neither the Elector nor Luther comes heroically out of this diplomatic business. The situation was undoubtedly a difficult one for the Elector who, as patron of the Reformation, had to face the possibility of forfeiting title and territory for the sake of the Gospel, and had to consider every step in the light of this possibility. Even so, the hesitation to take risks in such a cause, which at heart he seems really to have embraced, displays him too much in the light of the victim of an excessive and rather helpless prudence. As for Luther, the spirit of Worms, which had blazed up in the letter of 5th March, has almost evaporated in the effusion of a week later. And yet it is the self-same Luther that had once more set out on a hazardous journey to do the will of God in the face of the opposition of man and devil, regardless of the difficulties and dangers of the enterprise. It is assuredly not a case of loss of nerve in the face of the opposition, or mere truckling to political expediency at the expense of the cause of the Gospel. Whilst going so far as to invite the ridicule of public opinion in his desire to safeguard the timorous Elector, he has not the slightest intention of belying his convictions or betraying this cause by surrendering either at the behest of the Imperial Regency. Even in the letter of 12th March he makes it clear enough that he means to stand fast, without the protection of any human patron, for what he deems the cause of God against its enemies at Nürnberg or elsewhere. The diplomatic attempt to save the Elector is not an attempt to save himself. He is not afraid to stand alone for the Gospel even if he must equivocate somewhat for the Elector's sake.

The glimpse we get of him at Erfurt and Jena during the journey in his now familiar disguise as Knight George reveals no trace of trepidation or irresolution. In the inn at Erfurt, according to Ratzeberger, he listens to the tirade across the table of an ignorant parson against the great heretic, and calmly begs him to tell him what this execrable Luther has taught. The parson, more exercised in ranting than in

---

[17] Enders, iii. 305-306.

learning, being unable to specify one of the 100 heresies which, he says, are to be found in Luther's writings, the knight remarks that, though not a scholar, he had learned to read and write and, having dipped into some of these writings, had found that one of these 100 errors consisted in his appeal to Scripture and especially to Paul. In the inn at Jena two bedraggled students from Switzerland on their way to Wittenberg seek shelter from the pouring rain and a night's lodging. The friendly knight reading a book at one of the tables offers them a drink and enters into conversation with them. Recognising by their accent their Swiss origin, he tells them that they will find at Wittenberg fellow-countrymen in the jurist Schurf and his brother, the professor of medicine. He talks to them about Melanchthon and the other Wittenberg professors, and asks news of Erasmus at Basle, where they have studied. One of them picks up the book, and finding that it is a Hebrew Psalter, avers that he would willingly give one of his fingers to be able to read it. The knight replies that he shares their desire and exercises himself daily in this language. The innkeeper confides to one of the students, Kessler by name, that the knight is none other than Luther himself. Kessler concludes that he is pulling his leg and his companion is of opinion that he has misunderstood the word Luther for Hutten, to whom the appearance of the strange knight would better apply. The knight leaves them under this illusion. Anon two merchants enter the inn, one of them carrying a book, which turns out to be Dr Luther's *Postille*. Whereupon the knight remarks that he also will soon get a copy. The conversation at the meal, to which the knight invites the two students at his own charge, shifts to the assembled princes at Nürnberg, who, instead of discussing the religious condition of Germany, waste their time in tournaments and other diversions. " And these are our Christian princes," concluded the knight, adding that he hoped the rising generation would improve upon their elders as the fruit of the new evangelical teaching. Luther, remarked one of the merchants, must be either an angel from heaven or the devil from hell. In any case, he would willingly give his last ten gulden for the privilege

of making his confession to him. At the close of the meal
the students thank him for his generosity and gave him to
understand that he is Hutten. The innkeeper boldly opines
that he is Luther. " The students," jocularly returned the
stranger, " hold that I am Hutten, you that I am Luther.
Before long I shall be taken for Marculf " (a well-known
creation of the popular humour). The knight ended the
colloquy by asking the students to clink glasses with him
in a bumper of wine. Rising from the table he shook
hands with them and asked them to carry his personal greeting to Dr Schurf· at Wittenberg. " Say only," was the reply
to the question whom they should say had sent his greeting,
" he who shall come sends his greeting. He will soon
understand what these words mean." [18]

## II. Sermons in Behalf of Moderation

On the 6th March he rode into Wittenberg in the midst
of a cavalcade of horsemen who had joined him near the
town,[19] and dismounted unrecognised in the dwelling of Justus
Jonas. On the following Sunday, the 8th, he appeared in
the pulpit of the parish church to preach the first of a
consecutive series of eight sermons adapted to the situation,
besides a number of daily Lenten sermons on the Ten
Commandments

These sermons show Luther at his best as a preacher.
They are models of persuasive reasoning and reveal the
striving to calm excitement and restore harmony. He
addresses his hearers as his " dear friends " and eschews
recrimination, though he speaks his mind freely and mingles
on occasion reproof with exhortation. One of his hearers,
the student Burerius, writes enthusiastically of his kindly
and cheerful manner, his rich and sonorous voice, his
melting eloquence. If one hears him once, one wants to
hear him again and again, so lasting is the impression he
makes on the minds of his hearers, so powerful the appeal
of his personal piety in whatever he speaks, teaches, or

[18] Kessler's " Sabbata," 76 f.
[19] " Z.K.G.," v. 332. Letter of Burerius to Beatus Rhenanus.

does, although his enemies represent him so differently.[20]
Schurf in his account to the Elector is equally appreciative.[21]

Faith, he explains in the first of these sermons, is the
essential for salvation from sin, and this essential of the
Gospel has been effectively preached in his absence. But
faith must be paired with love, and here his hearers have
been led astray. The kingdom of God consists not in words,
but in deeds. Love teaches patience and self-denial for the
sake of others. We may not do what we have a right to
do without considering whether it is serviceable to our
brother. Paul says, " All things are lawful for me, but
not all things are expedient." Some are strong in faith,
others weak, and the strong must have respect to the weak
in the matter of these innovations. The cause in itself is
good, but it has been more hastily promoted than he would
have sanctioned had he been present. He claims the right
to a say in this matter, since he was the first to begin the
work of God among them, and he complains that he has not
been consulted in regard to these changes. " I have not
been so far away that you could not have informed me
beforehand by letter." They have overlooked the fact that
the responsibility for all that has occurred will be saddled
on him. In this respect they have not acted in the right
spirit, though they have shown a great knowledge of the
Scriptures. The Mass in the sense of an offering is undoubtedly an abuse which ought to be abolished. Private
Masses should also cease. But this is to be done by preaching and working, not by force, for no one can change the
heart or mind of another except God alone. Force can only
make hypocrites or mechanical Christians. Persuasion is
the only effective instrument in religion and the individual
must be left to judge for himself.[22] Preach the Word and
leave the result to God, is Luther's remedy. By continuing
to preach, the Word will ultimately triumph. With those
who adopt other methods he will not co-operate. " *Summa
Summarum*—I will preach the Word, will declare it, will
write it. But I will never force or press anyone with

[20] " Z.K.G.," v. 333.
[21] Enders, iii. 299-302.
[22] Sermon I., " Werke," x., Pt. III., 1 f.

violence, for faith can only be willingly, unconstrainedly nourished. Take an example from me. I opposed indulgences and all the practices of the papists. But not with force. I have urged God's Word alone, preached and written and done nothing else, and the Word has accomplished so much, whilst I slept or drank a glass of Wittenberg beer with Philip and Amsdorf, that the Papacy has been rendered more impotent than any prince or emperor has ever succeeded in making it. I have done nothing; the Word everything. If I had so wished I might have deluged Germany with blood; yea, I might have started such a game at Worms that the Emperor himself would not have been secure. I have only let the Word act. Had I done otherwise, I would only have done the devil's work for him. Let them follow the example of Paul who, in his conflict over the Mosaic law, was content with vindicating his own freedom, and let them not take an example from the papists who have mocked and oppressed us with thousands of laws." [23]

The abolition of the Mass is certainly defensible on scriptural grounds. But it has not been done in an orderly manner, or without offence to others. Moreover, it has been done without the consent of the Government (*die Obersten, die Obirkeit, i.e.*, the Elector) and cannot, therefore, be of God. As far as the opposition of the papists is concerned, he would not have hesitated. But it is incumbent on them to forbear such changes for the sake of the weak brethren and to distinguish between what is commanded and what is left free in the Scriptures. Some things we may do or not as long as faith is not endangered. But our liberty in these things must always be conditioned by our obligation to our neighbour.[24]

Among the things that are left to the individual conscience are celibacy, the monastic life, abstinence from meat on Fridays, the presence of images and pictures in churches, communion in both kinds, confession. To make hard and fast rules in regard to such matters, with which he proceeds to deal in detail in the following sermons, is against God's

[23] Sermon II.                    [24] *Ibid.*, III.

ordinance.   Personally, he would wish all monks and nuns to leave their monasteries and marry, and thus make an end of monkery.   But the decision must rest with the individual, who must act with a clear conscience before God and not merely follow the example of others.   He would prefer to have no images and pictures in the churches.   But he denies that it is forbidden to make images in the Old Testament. It is only forbidden to worship them.   The patriarchs had their altars.   Moses himself fashioned a brazen serpent, and even in the Holy of Holies there were two cherubim. If the people were really to worship these pictures and images they ought undoubtedly to be destroyed.   But he questions this assumption, and thinks that it is sufficient in this case also to preach against this practice, which he is fain to confess is a serious abuse, as Paul did at Athens, without violently laying hands on these emblems of idolatry. Though wine and women, gold and silver bring many to ruin, they are not, therefore, to be destroyed.   Images are neither good nor bad in themselves, and as long as it is possible to make a good use of them they may remain as far as he is concerned.   Fasting should not be obligatory. Every one should be free to eat flesh instead of fish on Fridays, if his health requires it, or if he deems it necessary to protest against papal tyranny and vindicate his freedom.   On the other hand, it is incumbent on the strong to reckon with the infirmity, the prejudices of the weak in such matters in order to win them to the use of their freedom, and on this ground to restrict their own liberty.   Thus St Paul acted towards the Judaisers when he circumcised Timothy, though he rightly refused to circumcise Titus in protest against their attempt to constrain him.[25]

In regard to the communion, the words, " Take, eat " are not to be understood as if the communicant can only communicate worthily by taking the bread and wine in his own hands.   To understand these words literally and force on others a mere form of this kind is the height of folly, and he feels so strongly on this point that he threatens to leave Wittenberg if this sort of folly is persisted in.   Not

[25] Sermons III. and IV.

that the touching of the bread and wine by the communicant is sinful. But it is not well to cause widespread offence by departing for such reasons from the old usage, which only allows the priest to handle the elements, and for which he seems to have an innate reverence. Whilst recognising communion in both kinds as the original institution, it is not to be forcibly introduced nor to be regarded as a *sine qua non.* Here, too, they are to beware of magnifying a mere form into an essential. Though he has approved of the introduction of such communion, he cannot endure this hasty zeal which has made it an ordinance binding on all, especially as it has been accompanied by much lightmindedness and hypocrisy. For it is esteemed to be an essential mark of a good Christian to take the elements in both hands and communicate in both kinds, and then go home and get drunk.[26] Since the essential for participation in the Sacrament is faith in Christ, the Saviour from sin, it is foolish to turn it into an ordinance obligatory on all, as the Pope has done. Nay, without this indispensable faith, which few attain, it is far better to abstain, instead of running helter-skelter to partake without the appropriate spirit of fear and humility and the longing for the comfort which it imparts.[27] The fruit of this communion is love, and love is the grand test of the Christian spirit which he finds is lacking in all these proceedings in his absence. They have, indeed, the true Gospel and the pure Word of God. But they have failed to bring forth its fruit because they have been too much engrossed in self, too much swayed by self-will instead of self-denial.[28] Confession of sin on the part of one Christian to another is a New Testament practice, which he would fain see revived in the Christian community, and is not to be neglected, though he denies the right of the Pope to exact confession to the priest. He has found in his own experience in his spiritual conflict how helpful and comforting it is thus to seek instruction and relief in the midst of the trials of the spiritual life. " For I— none better—know how much comfort and strength it has brought me, who have often and sorely fought with the

---

[26] Sermon V.         [27] *Ibid.*, VI.         [28] *Ibid.*, VII.

devil. I would long ago have been throttled by the devil but for this refuge of the soul. . . . You have no idea what a terrible thing it is to face and overcome the devil. But I know what it means to eat salt with Satan. I know him only too well and he knows me. If you knew him as I do you would not so lightly give up confession and absolution." It is on this practical ground that he presses for its retention, whilst admitting that there is full absolution in the Gospel and ample consolation in baptism and the Lord's Supper apart from this practice.

The sermons thus reflect the radical-conservative attitude of his writings in which, while attacking doctrines, institutions, and usages, he had shown himself disposed to pay tribute to religious expediency and limit the application of his principles, if individual liberty to hold and enunciate them were allowed. His doctrinal radicalism had in the last resort been curbed by his conservative temperament when it came to the practical question of discarding the old for the new. He shares, moreover, the Elector's fear of revolution and his inborn reverence for the civil authority, though he certainly does not speak merely as the mouthpiece of the Elector's policy. There can be no doubt that in these sermons he is voicing his own convictions in emphasising expediency and moderation, limiting individual initiative, and reserving this right for the civil authority. Equally characteristic is his insistence on liberty in things not essential to faith. In opposition to the intolerance of the radical party, he appears as the advocate of religious toleration, though he is not prepared to yield an inch to the uncompromising enemies of the Gospel. He believes in the power of enlightened public opinion and patient self-restraint for the sake of others to vindicate the Gospel, and ultimately overcome prejudice against it or lack of faith in it. There is certainly force in the warning against the tendency to substitute for the tyranny of the Pope the literalism and the legalism which lay stress on the letter rather than the spirit of the Word, and would magnify certain forms at the expense of the liberty of the Gospel.

On the other hand, there is a trace of soreness (jealousy would probably be too strong a word) over the predominance

of Carlstadt during his absence and a decided tendency to
assert his claim to sole leadership.   He is not content
solely to argue on the question of the communion.   He is
not prepared to make allowance for honest difference of
opinion on this subject, and threatens to leave Wittenberg
unless his will prevails.   He is not quite fair in assuming
that the movement is the outcome of irresponsible fanaticism
in opposition to constituted authority, and inclines too much
to regard excesses which were only incidental, and which
he himself had not taken very seriously on his furtive visit
to Wittenberg, as its main characteristic.   He overlooked
the fact that the ordinance was the combined work of
the University and the Town Council.   He makes no
attempt to consider the document on its own merits as a
deliberate attempt to organise a new order in place of the
old.   He ignores the fact that it had the sanction of the
local authority, even if it lacked that of the Elector.   He
regards it as the fruit of mere violence and indiscriminate
zeal, while the fact seems to be that it did not include the
demands of the extreme radical party.   He forgets that the
antagonism of the Romanist party, represented by the
majority of the canons of All Saints, had also some share in
fanning the popular excitement.   He is rather too prone
to demand sacrifice in favour of the weak brethren without
asking himself whether, among these weak brethren, there
were not a few antagonists of the evangelical cause.   He
is hardly fair to Carlstadt who was not disposed to yield
so much as he to religious expediency and who, if narrower
in his conception of the Gospel, had a keener sense of the
necessity of adopting and applying an active policy in the
interest of a practical Reformation.   Moreover, there was
room for difference of opinion on some of the points at
issue, and he does show a tendency to treat rather lightly
the obligation to restore the original institution of the
communion and the need for drastic action against the
popular superstition, undoubtedly associated with images
and pictures and other conventional religious observances.
One feels that he is rather evading the issue, which sooner
or later he will be called on to face, in discouraging both
individual and communal action and relying solely on the

Word to affect and vindicate a practical Reformation. Would the Reformation, on the principle of merely preaching the Word, have had much chance of maintaining itself against the adherents of the old order, who, at the instigation of Duke George and other active enemies, were taking steps to repress it and with whose demands the Elector was fain to comply? It is not the case, as Barge contends, that Luther was, albeit unwillingly, lending himself to the tactics of his enemies.[29] He was not acting a prescribed part in the pulpit of the parish church, but giving expression to his own convictions and trying to grapple with the *impasse* which the Elector's intervention and the lack of nerve on the part of his colleagues had produced. Defiance of the Romanists who would reassert their tyranny breathes throughout those sermons. But whether in doing so he did not adopt a too negative attitude in view of the vexatious tactics of the enemy is a different question. From this point of view one may fairly conclude that he would have been wiser to adopt a more constructive and militant attitude and thus give a definite practical lead, which many of the weaker brethren would, probably, under his influence, have followed. Moreover, he shows a rather pronounced tendency in these sermons to make himself the measure of the movement and to take too little account of the convictions of others, more logical and less conservative than he. One wonders whether he will be able to carry the spirit of forbearance, which he inculcates so admirably, the length of compromising, for the sake of the weak brethren, on matters of doctrine as well as practice? On the questions of the Real Presence, baptism, free-will, for instance.

Meanwhile, this compromise took the form of a modification of the ordinance, heavily weighted on the side of concessions to the adherents of the old usages. Whilst private Masses were disallowed, the Latin Mass was restored with the exception of the sacrificial passages. Pictures and

---

[29] Boehmer energetically rebuts Barge's version of Luther's intervention, though in rather a one-sided fashion. "Luther im Lichte der neueren Forschung," 129 f. See also K. Müller, "Luther und Karlstadt," 88 f.

images in as far as they had not been destroyed were replaced in the churches, and confession and fasting resumed at the discretion of the individual. Communion in both kinds was conceded, but only privately, to those who might desire it, whilst the provisions of the ordinance respecting prostitution, the poor, and begging were allowed to remain in force.

With this makeshift Luther had succeeded both in satisfying the Elector and rallying his colleagues, with the exception of Carlstadt, in support of the principle of religious expediency. His success in handling the situation was certainly a striking testimony to the power of the Word, in the form of these sermons, in exorcising party spirit as far as Wittenberg was concerned. Melanchthon staunchly abetted his policy,[30] and Schurf in a letter to the Elector voiced the general satisfaction that Luther had led his flock back to the truth, from which it had strayed under the influence of the now obnoxious preachers, " to the great joy of both learned and unlearned." [31] Capito, who had come to Wittenberg to hear him, became a confirmed adherent in spite of the strain which the correspondence on " the Idol at Halle " had temporarily begotten.[32] Zwilling professed penitence and was received into favour.[33] Only Carlstadt remained obdurate and was forbidden to preach.[34] Luther's victory thus at the same time brought the first rift in the reforming ranks, which was unfortunately widened by the confiscation of the book [35] in which Carlstadt sought relief for his wounded feelings in an attack on the " tyrants," among whom he evidently reckoned his great fellow-reformer, though he did not mention him by name. This philippic was directed against the Romanist, Dungersheim von Ochsenfart. But Luther indirectly came in for a share of the animadversion of the angry author, and Luther was of opinion that he was actuated by jealousy and the striving to assert his own authority at the expense of his.[36] Most of his modern biographers have too readily shared his judgment.

[30] " Corp. Ref.," i. 566.
[31] Enders, iii. 307.
[32] Ibid., iii. 307.
[33] Ibid., iii. 315.
[34] Ibid., iii. 315.
[35] " Corp. Ref.," i. 570.
[36] Ibid., iii. 326.

Carlstadt deserves at least the credit of maintaining and developing his views single-handed in his own rather opinionated fashion.

Although Luther had conceived a very unfavourable opinion of the Zwickau prophets from the reports Melanchthon had sent to the Wartburg, he reluctantly consented to grant them an interview,[37] and along with Melanchthon received Stübner, Kellner (Cellarius), and another, whose name is not given, early in April. Like Stübner, Kellner had had a university education at Tübingen and Wittenberg and was intimate with Melanchthon. Both professed to be in possession of a spiritual illumination independent of the Scripture, and were eager to convert Luther to this higher revelation, directly inspired by the Spirit. Kellner accordingly opened the interview in very flattering terms. Luther's vocation, he declared, was superior to that of the Apostles. Luther declined to be thus flattered at the expense of the Apostles, and proceeded to admonish them in a friendly tone against being wiser than the Scriptures and bade them beware of the wiles and lies of Satan. Whereupon Kellner burst into a furious tirade, during which Luther was unable to get in a single word. "Go your way and do as you list," he curtly remarked when the storm of vituperation had subsided. Stübner was more composed, though equally opinionated, and expostulated in an enigmatic and high-sounding jargon on the new revelation. Luther, he said, needed to be emancipated from the religious grossness in which he was still entangled (grobigkeit). He was still not in the condition of "immobility" (Unbeweglichkeit) in which the Spirit made known the mind of God to the individual soul. Asked to explain this jargon, he said that it could only be understood by those apt to receive his teaching. In proof of his inspiration he claimed to be able to tell at first sight what was in men's minds. As a test of his power of thought reading, Luther asked him to read his thoughts. "You are reflecting in your mind," came the assured reply, "that

---

[37] "Corp. Ref.," iii. 328, to Spalatin, 12th April. Prophetas istos novos passus sum.

my teaching is true." As a matter of fact, the question
had suggested itself to him. But at once the words of
Zechariah flashed into his mind, "the Lord rebuke thee,
Satan," and thus put on his guard against this devil's trick,
he stoutly refused to accept any revelation beyond Scripture
unless it were substantiated by a miracle. It was a crude
method of testing truth. Luther's limited conception of
inspiration left little enough room for the progressive
manifestation of truth in accordance with individual experience and enlightenment, though in theory he did assume
the possibility of such a revelation. He refused to admit
that these visionaries might possibly have discovered aspects
of the truth which he might have missed. To him the idea
of a subjective or a progressive revelation, apart from a
special miracle in attestation of it, was only one more devil's
wile, and Stübner's didactic jargon was certainly not fitted
to convince him of their claim to have superseded the
revealed Word. In conclusion, Stübner assured him that
the miracles he demanded would erelong be forthcoming.
" My God," retorted Luther, " will forbid your God to work
miracles." " God Himself," defiantly returned Stübner,
" shall not deprive me of my doctrine." The heated colloquy
thus ended at daggers drawn, and the prophets decamped
to Kemberg, from which they sent him a letter exhorting
him to think better of the matter. " And so," adds Luther,
" good-bye, dear Marcus." [38] In the following September
he had a visit from Storch, who was accompanied by another
cultured convert, Dr Westerburg, a Cologne jurist. Storch
was more concerned with the question of adult baptism
than with that of a new revelation, in which he differed
from Stübner. But neither his views on baptism nor his
personal character made a favourable impression. Of
Westerburg, on the other hand, Luther formed a high
opinion as an enthusiastic though impressionable seeker
after truth.[39]

He had, however, by no means heard the last word on

[38] Enders, iii. 328, 331; " Tischreden," ii. 306-307; iii. 13-16
(Weimar ed.).
[39] *Ibid.*, iii. 350; iv. 2.

the subject, and Stübner's boast of coming miracles was erelong to verify itself in the startling development of this subjective aspect of the Reformation movement, which Luther vainly strove to stem by his appeal to the written Word.

# CHAPTER IV

## LUTHER AT WITTENBERG

### I. Progress as Practical Reformer

LUTHER strove to win adherents outside Wittenberg for his
policy of moderation in letters to Hausmann, Duke John
Frederick, Spalatin, Lang, Link, John Hess, Güttel, and
others.[1] Very remarkable is the constant appeal in these
letters for liberty of conscience in matters of belief and
usage. In this respect Luther has emancipated himself in
a remarkable degree from the mediæval conception of an
enforced uniformity in the service of religion. His own
experience of the Roman system had given him an insight
into the true spirit of the Gospel, all the more striking in
view of his dogmatic temperament and prophetic fervour.
He is still at this stage the thoroughgoing advocate of
toleration and a large-minded charity towards opponents
whether within or outside the reform movement. There are
golden passages in these letters which, in urging the policy
of moderation, nobly express this reaction against the
despotic mediæval spirit. " See to it," he writes to
Hausmann at Zwickau in the spirit of the eight sermons,
" that you permit no innovations to be made by public
decree and oppressive methods. By the Word alone these
usages are to be impugned and overthrown, which our people
at Wittenberg have attempted to do by force and violence.
I indeed condemn the Mass as a sacrifice and a good work.
But I desire to lay hands on no one or to compel the unwilling and the unbelieving by force. I condemn by the
Word alone. He who believes let him believe and follow
his faith. He who does not believe, let him not believe and

---

[1] Enders, iii. 311 f.; " Werke," 53, 118-119 (Erlangen ed.).

be left alone. No one is to be compelled to faith or to those things which are of faith. He is to be drawn to the Word in order that, believing freely, he may come of his own accord. I condemn images, but by the Word ; not directing that they may be burned, but that confidence may not be placed in them, as has hitherto been the case, and still is. They will fall of themselves if the people, properly instructed, come to know that these things are nothing in the sight of God. Thus I condemn the papal laws concerning confession, communion, prayers, fasting, but only by the Word in order that I may set free the consciences of men. Where these are liberated, where these are freed, they can observe these things on account of the weak, or not observe them among those who are strong in the faith. And thus charity will reign in regard to these external works and laws." [2]

In order to commend his policy to a wider circle, he sent the gist of his eight sermons to the press under the title, " On the Partaking of the Sacrament in Both Forms," which appeared shortly after the middle of April.[3] This plea for moderation and toleration does not, however, justify indifference to the Gospel on the part of believers. There must, he insists in conclusion, be no betrayal of Christ in the face of the enemies of the Gospel. If, in order to evade persecution, the believer adduces the pretext that he is no Lutheran, but an adherent of the Gospel and the Holy Church, this is assuredly to deny Christ. It matters not, indeed, what either Luther or the Pope thinks of the Gospel, since neither has died for sinners as Christ has done. Christ alone is lord and master. It matters not whether Luther, Claus, or George preaches Christ. The person of the preacher is nothing ; his teaching is the essential thing. But if the believer is convinced that Luther has proclaimed the true evangelical teaching, he is bound to maintain it against its persecutors, whilst following Christ's example in loving his enemies and eschewing all thought of revenge.[4]

[2] Enders, iii. 312.

[3] *Ibid.*, iii. 319, 325, 330, 342 ; " Werke," 53, 119 (Erlangen ed.). It is given in " Werke," x., Pt. II., 11 f. (Weimar ed.).

[4] " Werke," x., Pt. II., 39-41.

In behalf of this policy he undertook a mission to a number of towns in Saxony at the end of April and the beginning of May, and preached at Borna, Altenburg, Zwickau, Eilenburg, and Torgau. The mission was also designed as an offset to the visitation of Saxony by the Bishop of Meissen, in accordance with the anti-Lutheran mandate of the Imperial Regency at Nürnberg. He even ventured to pass through the territory of Duke George on the return journey from Zwickau to Borna, though he took the precaution to doff his monk's habit and travel by night.[5]

At Altenburg he was brought face to face with the practical difficulty of carrying out his policy of forbearance towards conservative brethren. In the middle of April the Town Council had applied to him for an evangelical preacher for the parish church of St Bartholomew.[6] He recommended the appointment of the repentant Zwilling, whom he now warmly befriended.[7] The Council readily accepted the nomination. But the Provost and Canons of Our Lady on the Mount would not hear of the appointment of the renegade monk and insisted on their right to appoint to the benefice. Instead of waiving his nomination in accordance with his own principle of reckoning with the scruples of others, Luther, on his visit to Altenburg on the 28th April, drew up a memorandum to be submitted to the Elector, in which he maintained the right of the Council, as embodying the public authority, to choose an evangelical preacher in spite of the opposition of the enemies of the Gospel. The Provost and Canons, he urged, are not true pastors, but wolves in sheep's clothing. They have forfeited their right to their privileges and dues by their infidelity to the Gospel, and it is the right and duty of the Council, yea of every Christian, to resist their pretensions on the principle, which Carlstadt had adduced in defence of the Wittenberg innovations, that it is incumbent to obey God rather than man. Hence the alternative to the

---

[5] Notices of the Visitation in Enders, iii. 346 f.

[6] *Ibid.*, iii. 333-334.

[7] "Werke," 53, 131-132 (Erlangen ed.).

Provost and Canons either to forego their privileges and dues, or to preach the pure Gospel alone as the condition of retaining them.[8]  In a letter to the Elector he not only vindicated the right of the Council, on scriptural and public grounds, to change the religious order of things, but urged him as a Christian prince to enforce it throughout his dominions in spite of the opposition of recalcitrant clergy.[9]  Though the Elector was not disposed to favour the obnoxious Zwilling,[10] he agreed to Luther's demand that he should himself provide an acceptable substitute and, in spite of the renewed clerical opposition, on the 28th June appointed the evangelical Link, who subsequently resigned his office as Vicar-General of the Augustinian Order and introduced communion in both kinds at Altenburg.[11]

Luther was thus driven by the logic of the situation to make use of other expedients than the preaching of the Word in furthering the Gospel.  This preaching inevitably led to division and party spirit which sooner or later made compromise toleration on Lutheran lines impracticable. At Erfurt, for instance, the adherents of the old and the new order were at bitter enmity.  The former found an unbending champion in Usingen, Luther's old teacher, who had years before become a member of the Augustinian Order ;  the latter in Lang, who in April had renounced his office as Prior, and in stating his reasons for so doing had roundly and rashly denounced all priors as asses and ignoramuses.  His example was followed by many of his brethren who inveighed from the pulpits of a number of the Erfurt churches against the old usages in the spirit of a Carlstadt and Zwilling, and gained a large following among the citizens.  Luther was very dubious about the wisdom of these aggressive proceedings and the wholesale withdrawal of the monks.  It appeared to him, he wrote to Lang, that many of the monks were leaving the monasteries for no

[8] Enders, iii. 347-349.

[9] " Werke," 53, 134-136 (Erlangen ed.) ; cf. Enders, iii. 351, where he urges the same policy in reference to the church at Eilenburg, and offers the choice of one of two suitable preachers.

[10] Enders, iii. 354.

[11] Ibid., iii. 354-355, 370-374, 379, 381, 434-435.

other reason than that for which they had entered them, viz., for the sake of the belly and carnal liberty.[12] Whilst fearing that the result would be a repetition of the disorders which he had suppressed at Wittenberg, he declined Lang's invitation to visit Erfurt on the ground of the danger of the journey in the case of one who was under the imperial ban. He promised to write a public missive instead, and ultimately, on the 10th July, dispatched an "Epistle to the Church at Erfurt."[13] He chose as his theme the invocation of saints, one of the burning questions which was being discussed in both the pulpits and the press. Whilst he has ceased to attribute real validity to the intercession of the saints and emphasises the sufficiency of confiding in Christ alone, he will allow the weak brethren to pray to the saints if they choose. He repeats his caveat against compelling others to accept the Gospel and admonishes in characteristic fashion the extreme preachers to moderate their zeal and eschew mere popularity. His appeal fell on deaf ears. The opinionated Usingen would not yield an inch. "Age," wrote Luther to Lang, quoting the vernacular proverb, "avails not against folly."[14] In October he felt safe enough in the ever-increasing number of his adherents to journey to Erfurt in the company of Melanchthon and Agricola. He was enthusiastically acclaimed and feasted[15] during his stay of a couple of days (20th to 22nd October), and preached several evangelical sermons appropriate to the situation.[16] On the return journey he spent a week at Weimar, and at the request of Duke John and his son, John Frederick, preached another series of evangelical sermons in the presence of the court and the people.[17]

His mission to Erfurt did not, however, succeed in establishing a feasible compromise. Usingen, whose name he parodied into Unsingen (Nonsense), continued on the war-path,[18] and the two parties remained at daggers' ends. Nor

[12] Enders, iii. 323-324.  [14] Enders, iii. 403.

[13] "Werke," x., Pt. II., 164 f.  [15] "Corp. Ref.," i. 579.

[16] Ibid., i. 579. The sermons are given in "Werke," x., Pt. III., 352 f.

[17] "Werke," x., Pt. III., 371 f.

[18] Enders, iv. 27.

did the policy of mutual forbearance ultimately prove a success at Wittenberg itself, where the Chapter of All Saints continued to sing Masses for the dead and to retain the old order intact. Luther himself bore with increasing impatience the incongruity of suffering this " Bethaven," or house of sin, as he called it, in the citadel of the evangelical movement, and already, in a letter to Spalatin in July 1522, urged that the Elector should forcibly intervene and apply its revenues for the furtherance of the Gospel.[19] He repeated his demand in the following December,[20] and on the 2nd January 1523 roundly declared that this forbearance with the scruples of the papists had become a scandal and a stumbling-block to the progress of the Gospel. He still professes to respect the principle of liberty and would not compel anyone to faith and piety. But their Masses and their relic worship being, he rather questionably argues, equivalent to spiritual fornication, it is the bounden duty of the prince to abolish these Masses and deprive the Chapter of its revenues, and thus make a beginning with the work of reform.[21]

The Elector was not disposed thus forcibly to intervene in the interest of the Gospel. He had a partiality for the foundation which his forbears had endowed and for the collection of relics which he had spent so lavishly in augmenting from about 5,000 to 18,000 articles. As a politician, he had, moreover, to walk warily in the matter in view of the forthcoming meeting of the Diet at Nürnberg, and for this reason he took up the same conservative attitude towards Luther's demand as he had shown towards those of the advanced reformers during his absence in the Wartburg. A two-years' duel between him and the conservative members of the Chapter on the one hand, and Luther on the other, ensued before he at last gave way at the end of 1524. During this interval, Luther practically played the part of Carlstadt over again in his insistence on the repression of the scandal of this " idolatry." In the face of the Elector's opposition and with the support of Jonas, the Provost of

---

[19] Enders, iii. 417.     [20] *Ibid.*, iv. 46-47.
[21] *Ibid.*, iv. 54. Ut fieret exordium aliquod rerum novandarum.

the Chapter, he appealed to the canons themselves to undertake the work of reform.[22] The canons referred the question to the Elector. Whereupon Luther emphasised the obligation of conscience and asked what the Elector had to do with a matter of conscience, in which it behoved them to obey God rather than man.[23] He submitted to them a scheme of reform [24] which was supported by Jonas in a missive to the Elector,[25] but which the Elector summarily rejected.[26] Though the opposition in the Chapter had by this time dwindled to what Luther calls "three or four pigs and bellyservers," the Elector remained impervious to further representations, and fully a year elapsed before Luther at last determined to force a decision in an ultimatum to the Chapter to suppress the obnoxious services, under threat of forcible measures in case of refusal.[27] In response to this appeal the Elector reminded him of his principle of relying on the Word of God alone to bring about such a reform.[28] For Luther, however, the principle, which he had applied against Carlstadt and the advanced reformers two and a half years earlier, was now out of date, and in spite of the Elector's protest [29] he proceeded to enforce his ultimatum. On the 27th November he preached a violent sermon on the abomination of the Mass and called on all princes and public authorities to put down the evil thing [30] if they would escape the wrath of God. He was supported in his demand by the Town Council and the University,[31] and by the people who broke the windows of the obnoxious Dean of the Chapter. Some days later the opposition gave

[22] Enders, iv. 89; "Werke," 53, 178-180 (Erlangen ed.), 1st March and 11th July 1523.

[23] "Werke," 53, 179.

[24] Enders, iv. 210-213, 19th Aug.

[25] "Corp. Ref.," i. 628-638, 24th Aug.; Kawerau, "Jonasbriefe," 86.

[26] "Corp. Ref.," i. 641, 4th Oct.

[27] "Werke," 53, 269-270 (Erlangen ed.), 17th Nov. 1524.

[28] Enders, v. 55, 24th Nov.

[29] Burkhardt, "Luther's Briefe," 76.

[30] "Werke," xv. 764 f. This sermon is the basis of his philippic "Vom Misbrauch der Stillmesse," which he published early in 1525. "Werke," xviii. 22 f.

[31] Walch, xix. 1453-1457.

way, the Dean informing the Elector that he could no longer maintain the Mass. " We have at last compelled the canons to agree to abolish the Mass," wrote Luther to Amsdorf on the 2nd December.[32] Shortly after the Dean offered the Wittenberg monastery, of which he and the Prior, Brisger, were now the only occupants, to the Elector, who accepted the gift and, in return, presented it, along with the garden, to Luther as a dwelling-house.[33]

Meanwhile he had been approximating more and more to the position of the advanced reformers in respect of worship and usages. By the beginning of 1523 he had come to the conclusion that the time had come for a more radical reform of the service of the Mass in the parish church. He was now prepared freely to concede communion in both kinds in deference to the demands of those to whom the current service was an offence. They had, he wrote to Spalatin on the 14th January, practised indulgence towards the weak brethren long enough. There are hardly any such left, and it is now time to give free scope to the Gospel and make use of their liberty in this matter, in deference to the insistent and general demand for this reform.[34] On the 23rd March he took in hand the further reform of worship by introducing daily services for edification in the parish church, in place of the daily Masses which had been discontinued since his return from the Wartburg. The evangelical character of this tentative reform is reflected in the " Order of Worship," which he shortly after drew up for the church at Leisnig.[35] He finds three great abuses in the worship of the church. God's Word is neglected. Many fables and

[32] Enders, v. 80.

[33] " Werke," 53, 278-279 (Erlangen ed.) ; Enders, v. 86.

[34] Enders, iv. 63. Utramque speciem libere dandam et accipiendam deinceps censeo. Satis enim hactenus infirmis indultum est, et ubique res ista jam Cantata et nota, cum ferme assueti sint majora ferre. Tempus est ut evangelio locus fiat, et ferme jam non infirmi, sed potius pertinaces qui rei tam notæ et cantatæ usu offenduntur. Itaque libertate utamur in hac causa.

[35] Von Ordenung des Gottisdiensts inn der Gemeine, " Werke," xii. 35 f. ; cf. xi. 61-62, which informs us that at the end of his sermon on the 11th March he announced his intention of introducing daily service. The Order is also given in Sehling, i. 2-3 (1902).

lies have crept into it and it has been regarded as a means
of meriting grace and salvation, to the detriment of faith.
For the reform of these abuses it is essential that in every
assembly for worship the Gospel should be preached. Where
this is lacking, it were better that the people should abstain
from attending. The essential thing is the instruction of
the people in God's Word. To this end, therefore, the
congregation is invited to assemble morning and evening to
hear a portion of the Old and New Testament read and
expounded in accordance with the Apostolic practice (1 Cor.
i. 27). The whole Bible is thus to be systematically read
and expounded in these daily services, which shall be
concluded with prayer and praise as the pastor shall select
from the liturgy, and the people thereby become versed in
the Scriptures. No constraint is, however, to be used.
The people are to be exhorted to come freely to these
services, not merely as a matter of obligation or merit, as
under the old system, but only for the glory of God and the
common good. They are to last no longer, as a rule, than
an hour, in order that those present may not be fatigued
and burdened, as in the monasteries and churches, with
wearisome and long-drawn out devotions (asses' work,
*eselsarbeit*, is the term he applies to them). On Sundays,
when Mass and Vespers are still to be sung and the Sacrament
of the Lord's Supper celebrated in accordance for the most
part with the liturgy, the reading and preaching of the
Word also form the main essential of the services. The
celebration of Saints' Days, with the exception of that of
the Virgin Mary, is abolished, though edifying passages
from the lives of the saints may be read on Sundays after the
Gospel of the day. "Other changes may be made in due
time. But the end should be that the Word should have
full sway and the service be no longer a mere droning and
drawling as has hitherto been the case. That Mary should
sit at Christ's feet and hear His Word is the better part.
His Word is eternal; the rest must pass away, however
much it may trouble Martha." [36]

Among these eventual changes was the reform of the

---

[36] "Werke," xii. 37 ; Sehling, i. 3.

Mass.   During the summer of 1523 he was contemplating the introduction of this reform, and was repeatedly urged by Hausmann and others to undertake it.[37]   Pressure of work prevented him from carrying out his purpose till the autumn, when he at length found time to realise it in the " Formula Missæ," or Service of the Mass, which he drew up for the parish church at Wittenberg and printed for the guidance of Hausmann and other reformers.   On the 13th November he wrote to Hausmann that the new form would very soon be in operation at Wittenberg,[38] and on the 4th December sent him a printed copy of the new Order,[39] which he dedicated to him.   The Order being designed for other churches as well as that of Wittenberg, he disclaims any desire to make precipitate changes, as in the case of the radical innovators, and still professes to respect the scruples of weak brethren.   He retains, in fact, a large portion of the old service, and whilst discarding what he deems objectionable, leaves room for difference of view or practice, and is ready to welcome suggested improvements from others.   At the same time, he does not hesitate to assert that the celebration of the Lord's Supper, as instituted by Christ, has been so deformed by human invention, that nothing but the name remains.   The additions of the Fathers, who added certain Psalms and portions of the Gospels and Epistles and the Kyrie Eleison, were altogether laudable. Nor can any objection be taken to the addition of the Gloria, the Hallelujah, the Nicene Creed, the Sanctus, the Agnus Dei, etc.   But the later additions, which he ascribes to the ambition of power and the mercenary spirit of the priesthood, and in which the Mass is conceived as a sacrifice and a priestly monopoly (*monopolium sacerdotale*), he condemns and utterly rejects

With this general preface he proceeds to deal in detail with the introductory part of the Mass, which led up to the second part in which the actual communion takes place. Whilst retaining the greater portion of the liturgy relative to part one, he leaves to the minister or bishop (for so he

---

[37] Enders, iv. 215, 253, 254-255, 259-260, Aug.-Nov.
[38] *Ibid.*, iv. 259.          [39] *Ibid.*, iv. 261.

designates the celebrant in substitution for the term priest)
considerable discretion to omit or abridge.  The celebrant
should avoid prolixity, which engenders tedium, and simplify
the liturgy as far as possible in order not to weary the
congregation.[40]  He would prefer to introduce passages
from the Gospels and Epistles which emphasise faith in the
evangelical sense, though in the meantime the celebrant
may use the stated passages and supply this lack of evangelical teaching in the sermon, which may be given at the
beginning of the service or after the repetition of the Creed.
Personally, he would prefer that it should be given at the
beginning of the service, since the sermon is an invitation
to faith in the Gospel, the Mass the actual appropriation of
the Gospel by the believer at the Lord's Table.  It is at this
point that he makes the most radical change in the service,
in which the priest performs the supreme mystery of transforming the elements into the body and blood of Christ and
offers them for the sins of the people.  This part he suppresses
as " an abomination and idolatry," and whilst retaining
portions of the liturgy, proceeds to celebrate the rite in
accordance with the words of institution.  He would have
these words, which the priest, in order to emphasise the
mystery of transubstantiation, repeated in a whisper,
recited in a clear voice in order that they might be heard
by the whole congregation.  He would also, in deference to
the weak brethren, elevate the elements, though not for the
purpose of worshipping them.  Thereafter follows, with
the appropriate liturgy, the communion in both kinds,
first by the minister and then by the people.

This order is, however, not to be received in the sense
of a law to be followed to the letter.  Diversity of rites
has prevailed in the Church from early times, and Christians
are free to change and amend them as they may deem
advisable.  " For although we cannot do without external
rites, just as we cannot do without food and drink, these
things do not commend us to God, but faith and charity.
In these, therefore, the word of Paul is to prevail, ' The
kingdom of God consists not in meat and drink, but in

[40] " Werke," xii. 210; Sehling, i. 5.

righteousness, peace, and joy in the Holy Ghost.' "[41] Similarly in the matter of vestments, candles, vessels, music, incense, etc., freedom is allowable, though he disallows the pomp and splendour of ceremonial with which the celebration has been invested. Private Mass is incompatible with the conception of the Supper as a fellowship or communion, and is, therefore, disallowed. While confession before communion is no longer obligatory, those who desire to communicate shall make known their desire to the minister, who shall satisfy himself by examination of their knowledge and life that they are worthy to partake. Notorious sinners, such as adulterers and fornicators, are to be debarred from participation unless they give manifest proofs of repentance. Communion in both kinds, in accordance with the primitive institution and practice, is the only form to be observed, and he will not agree to refer the question to the decision of a Council. He would introduce hymns in the vernacular, and looks forward to the time when the whole Mass shall be said in the language of the people and piously inspired poets shall enrich the reformed Church with a vernacular hymnology. Meanwhile, let them make use of such hymns, too few in number, as are already available. For instance, " Gott sei gelobet," " Nun bitten wir den Heiligen Geist," " Ein Kindelin so lobelich," which should be sung not merely by the choir, but by the people. He himself was erelong to supply this dearth of sacred songs in the vernacular. The religious muse had already in the course of this year inspired him to celebrate in verse the martyrdom in the Netherlands of the first two victims of the evangelical faith, on the 1st of February 1523, in the poem beginning, " Ein neues lied wir heben an." Before the year was at an end he had given proof of his own gift as a hymn writer in " Nu freut Euch lieben Christen Gemein," "Ach Gott vom Himmel sieh darein," " Aus tiefer noth schrei ich zu Dir." He wrote to Spalatin and others encouraging them to turn a number of the Psalms into verse for the use of the people in worship.[42]

In the meantime Luther left the baptismal service

[41] " Werke," xii. 214; Sehling, i. 7.     [42] Enders, iv. 273.

largely unchanged and contented himself with translating it into German, and himself using the vernacular and commending its use to others.[43]     But he shared the current conception of baptism as an act of regeneration, and felt that its celebration in an unintelligible language tended to obscure its significance and render it a more or less formal ceremony on the part of the parents.     Moreover, he believed that faith is generated in the infant at baptism in virtue of the prayers of priest and parents.     He, therefore, added an exhortation in which he impressed on them the necessity and the efficacy of personal faith and earnest participation in these prayers. The mere external and symbolic parts of the rite (the exorcism of the infant by the priest, etc.) were, by comparison, of the least importance and altogether without profit to the infant, apart from the new birth wrought by God's grace in this sacrament.     From this point of view he rates the rite very high as the means whereby God regenerates the soul, delivers it from the power of the devil, sin, and death, and makes it the heir of eternal life.     Though he would fain simplify the ceremonial part of it, he leaves it in the meantime practically intact in deference to the scruples of the weak.[44]

In issuing the reformed service of the Mass, Luther assumes the right of the churches to make such changes in virtue of their inherent powers.     This right he had already sought to vindicate at the instance of the church at Leisnig in an important document dealing with the organisation of the Christian community.     In this document, which he issued in the spring of 1523,[45] he elaborates the thesis that, on the ground of Scripture, " the Christian congregation or community has the right and power to judge of doctrine

[43] Das Tauf Büchlein Verdeutscht, "Werke," xii. 42 f.; Sehling, i. 18 f. (1523).   The translation appears to have been used shortly after the " Order of Service."

[44] A shorter form of the baptismal service in the vernacular, dated by Walch 1523, in which more material changes were made, is also ascribed to Luther. Kawerau adduces weighty arguments against its ascription to Luther, who, it seems safer to conclude, only made such changes in the revision of 1526.

[45] He announced his intention to do so in a letter of 29th Jan., in response to the request of the Leisnig church. Enders, iv. 69-71.

and appoint and depose its teachers." [46]  What constitutes
for Luther the Christian community is the preaching of the
pure Gospel.  His model is the primitive community which
the preaching of the Gospel called into existence, and of
which it was the directing force.  It is not and cannot be
constituted by mere ecclesiastical law, since it is a spiritual
association to which temporal or human law does not apply.
" For the soul of man is an eternal thing, above all that is
temporal.  Therefore it can only be constituted and ruled
by the divine Word." [47]  With this fundamental and
radical contention he rejects the historic constitution of the
Church, with its developed hierarchy and ecclesiastical
ordinances, as a human organisation which is incompatible
with the spiritual character of the Christian association
or society.  He finds the warrant for this conception in
John x. and other passages from the Gospels and Epistles.
Christ is the shepherd of the flock which hears His voice
and follows Him and refuses to follow the stranger.  Therewith He gave to the flock the power to judge whether the
teaching is in accord with His voice or not.  The voice of
the Pope, bishops, councils, with their man-made laws and
ordinances, has no validity against this fundamental principle
which involves a radical revolution of the ecclesiastical
constitution.

Since the preaching of the Gospel is an essential of this
community, and the bishops, under the present unchristian
régime, do not and will not provide preachers of the Gospel,
the community itself has the right and duty to provide such.
Every Christian, in fact, in virtue of the priesthood of all
believers, is entitled and commissioned to proclaim and
spread the Gospel, especially in places where there are no
true believers, without any call or commission from others.
Thus did Stephen, Philip the Evangelist, and Apollos, for
instance, proclaim the Word in the Apostolic Age without
any call from the Apostles.  Even where a community of
believers exists, the individual believer is entitled to edify
or correct his brethren, if necessary, as long as he does
so decently and in order.  How much more has the whole

[46] " Werke," xi. 408 f.          [47] Ibid., xi. 409.

community the right to choose one to preach the Word in place of the others. But did not Paul and Barnabas and other Apostles appoint presbyters in the churches founded by them? Certainly, and if the bishops were really concerned for the Gospel, they might also be allowed to do so. But in these days the worldly minded bishops are wolves in sheep's clothing, enemies of the Gospel, who are fitted only to drive asses and lead dogs. Even if they were worthy of their office, they would have no right to appoint preachers without the will and choice of the community. For neither Paul, nor any other Apostle, appointed a presbyter or deacon without the choice of the community. And in these evil times, when the bishops so glaringly belie the Gospel and neglect and despise the highest function in the Church—the preaching of the Word—the community can and ought to do without their confirmation.[48]

As in doctrine, so in organisation, Luther thus has recourse to the Word and seeks to revive the primitive community in place of the mediæval hierarchic Church. For this Church he substitutes the spiritual democracy of the New Testament in his attempt to vindicate and organise the everspreading evangelical movement which he has started. He does so without concerning himself with the rights and claims of the ecclesiastical or the civil power. He boldly sets out to establish outside the Church and within, but independent of, the State, a sovereign, self-governing, religious community on thoroughly democratic lines, in virtue of the Word and the spiritual priesthood of believers. Truly a far-reaching and momentous project, which he developed in the autumn of the same year in a work addressed to the Bohemian Christians which, in response to their request, appeared in November.[49]

He not only maintained the right of the Christian community to exercise its inherent powers as a religious association. He invested it with the right to appropriate the ecclesiastical revenues for the common good. Under his guidance and with the co-operation of the Town Council and

---

[48] " Werke," xi. 411-416.
[49] *Ibid.*, xii. 169 f. De instituendis Ministris Ecclesiæ.

a local nobleman, Seb. von Kötteritz, the community at Leisnig, to which he had paid a visit in September 1522,[50] drew up, in January 1523, an ordinance on the lines of that adopted at Wittenberg under Carlstadt's auspices.[51]   In this document all ecclesiastical property and revenues are made over to a common chest for the support of the evangelical clergy, the poor, education, etc.   Luther added a preface in defence of the appropriation of ecclesiastical endowments for these purposes.   This appropriation, he contends, is justifiable on the ground of the misuse of these endowments in the service of error and superstition.   But whilst depriving the priests and the monks of these revenues and devoting them to the public good, he would not force anyone to accept the new order, and would provide mainten- ance for the priests and monks who adhere to the old order, and assist those who decide to devote themselves to a secular occupation.   He would also assign a portion to the poor descendants of pious founders on the ground that it is not or should not have been their intention to deprive their relatives of subsistence.   At the same time, he warns against the greed and selfishness of those who are out to enrich themselves by laying hands on this property.   The warning was by no means superfluous.   The Town Council and the church at Leisnig were erelong at variance over the question of its disposal, and Luther fears that his equitable plan will stand a poor chance of realisation at the hands of those who are on the outlook for a share of the spoil.   " For greed is a disobedient, unbelieving rascal." [52]

## II. Renewed Polemic from Wittenberg

These changes naturally intensified the antagonism of the adherents of the old order and involved him in renewed controversy with opponents old and new.   This polemic is lacking in the originality of the earlier period in which he evolved his distinctive teaching in conflict with the scholastic

[50] Enders, iv. 8 ; cf. 69.
[51] " Werke," xii. 11 f.   Ordenung eyns gemeynen Kastens.
[52] Ibid., xii. 12.

theology, the Papacy, and the institutions of the Church. In general, he merely reiterates and maintains this teaching as the developing situation demands. In these later controversial writings the prophet tends to disappear in the protagonist of the ever-widening movement which the prophet has called into being. He has little to add to his prophetic message, except by way of expansion or vindication. There is, however, no diminution in the pugnative, self-assertive spirit of the earlier writings. His confidence in himself and his cause has, in fact, become intensified since the Diet of Worms and the long vigil in the Wartburg. He is no longer fighting with his back to the wall. He now faces his opponents as the leader of an ever-widening, militant movement, and while professing to rely on the Word to assert and vindicate itself, is ever on the alert to parry or strike a blow in its behalf. His return from the Wartburg is that of the victor, not the vanquished, eager to face the foe once more in open conflict, sure of ultimate victory, though an outlaw in the midst of enemies, bereft of all protection, except that of heaven.[53] " We believe," he wrote to Link within a fortnight after his return, " that Christ, the Son of God, is the Lord of life and death. Who, therefore, is he that we should fear. We have the first fruits of victory. We triumph over the papal tyranny which hitherto has oppressed kings and princes. How much more shall we conquer and spurn the princes themselves. He does not lie who has said, ' Thou hast put all things under His feet.' " He foresees, indeed, that a struggle between the friends and foes of the Gospel is inevitable. The war of the pen, he fears, will erelong be followed by the war of the sword. Satan will not rest till he has deluged the whole of Germany in its own blood.[54] If the princes go on deferring to that stupid brain of Duke George, there will surely come an upheaval which will destroy rulers and magistrates and will at the same time involve the whole clergy. " The populace is everywhere in agitation. It has eyes to see. It neither will nor can be suppressed by force. It is the Lord who works these things and hides His threats

[53] Enders, iii. 313-314.          [54] *Ibid.*, iii. 314.

and these forthcoming dangers from the eyes of princes. Yea, through their blunders and violence He will bring these things to pass, so that I seem to see Germany wading in blood." [55] For himself, though deploring these dread portents, he was never so fearless and confident in the triumph of his cause.

He began this active campaign from Wittenberg against the enemy by issuing his " Caveat against Human Teaching." [56] In this tract he develops afresh his fundamental principle that only what is taught in the Word of God is authoritative and obligatory, and that what has been subsequently added by men has no validity and is to be considered as mere human invention. It is, therefore, to be rejected as contrary to the Word. At the outset he quotes Deuteronomy iv. 2 : " Ye shall not add unto the Word which I command you, neither shall ye diminish aught from it." But his appeal is not to Moses, but to Christ and the Apostles, from whom he quotes a series of passages in support of his thesis and argues from them, with no little force, against the vast accretion of teaching, ordinance, and usage which has been imposed on the Church. It is of no avail to adduce against his thesis what Gregory, or Bernard, or Francis, or any Pope has taught. Nor does it invalidate his contention to appeal to the authority of the Church itself, or quote Augustine that he would not have believed the Gospel but for its authority. Augustine in other passages ascribed the supreme authority to Scripture alone, and to assume that he ascribed an equal authority to the Church is to misinterpret his words. In any case, Augustine, who frequently erred, has no monopoly of infallibility. Christ is the supreme doctor of the Church. " Neither be ye called masters, for one is your Master, even Christ." The relative sayings of Christ are supported by

[55] Enders, iii. 316.

[56] Von Menschenlehre zu meiden, " Werke," x., Pt. II., 72 f. He was busy writing it on the 24th May 1522, as he informed Spalatin, and promised to send him the MS. next day, Enders, iii. 369. It was printed by the end of the month, *ibid.*, iii. 383. He later added a supplement, " Antwort auf Sprüche," apparently after writing his work against Henry VIII. See " Werke," x., Pt. II., 61-62.

numerous passages from Paul's Epistles. The points particularly dealt with refer to fasting, abstinence from meat
and drink on certain days, the monastic conception of the
Christian life, and penitential works as a means of attaining
salvation. All this ecclesiastical accretion is an unwarrantable and unscriptural invention which has translated the
Gospel into a burdensome legalism, oppressive to the
conscience and subversive of Christian liberty. Moreover,
it substitutes for the Gospel the old system of work righteousness which the Gospel displaced, and for which the Gospel
substituted salvation by reliance on God's grace through
faith, not on human merits, which cannot bring the assurance
of salvation. It is because this oppressive and unwarranted
system is a mere human invention and is incompatible with
the original teaching of Christ and the Apostles that he
rejects it, though he is prepared to admit additions of man
that are not contrary to the Gospel.

He followed it up with the philippic " Against the Falsely
Called Spiritual Estate of the Pope and the Bishops." [57]  It
seems to have been written under the irritation produced
by the perusal of Henry VIII.'s book against him. It is a
furious blast of denunciation and defiance, the most choleric
and violent that had yet come from his pen. Since the
hierarchy has paid no heed to his repeated appeals for
reform, has, indeed, done its worst to destroy him and
his cause, he proclaims at the outset war to a finish against
it. He has wasted forbearance and humility on these
murderers and blasphemers. After his experience of
them at Worms and elsewhere, he will never again recognise
their jurisdiction or submit to their judgment. Compromise
or quarter is henceforth out of the question. They shall

---

[57] Wider den falsch genannten Geistlichen Stand des Papsts und der
Bischöfe, " Werke," x., Pt. II., 105 f. This is, as the editors have
pointed out, a revision and an enlargement of the tract which he had
written against the Archbishop of Maintz and the indulgence at Halle,
but which he refrained from publishing at the instance of Spalatin.
He now (July 1522) changed it into a philippic against the Pope and the
bishops in general, and in spite of Spalatin's remonstrances (Enders,
iii. 435) sent it to the press immediately after. He was already working
at it in the beginning of July. Enders, iii. 426.

never have peace as long as he lives.   Even if they kill him,
they shall much less have peace, for in the words of Hosea,
he will be to them a bear in the way and a lion in their path.
He is aggressively dogmatic as well as defiant.   No one who
refuses to accept his teaching can be saved.   It is God's,
not his.[58]   His method of attack is to expose their iniquities
in the light of Scripture and the actual state of things.   He
had a strong case from both points of view.   As a body,
the hierarchy was very unlike the New Testament ministry
and it was undeniably corrupt.   It was largely a refuge,
a career for the sons of princes and nobles, and Luther
characteristically and repeatedly uses the phrase, " Ecclesiastical Junkers."   Its members were feudal magnates as
well as churchmen and exercised the rights and privileges
of such.   They were a secularised caste, participating in
worldly pursuits and pleasures, living in state and luxury,
and in too many cases tainted with the vices of the age,
in spite of their profession of celibacy and the pretence
of exercising a purely spiritual function.   Luther recognises
that there were some worthy men among them who would
fain reform the Church and took their spiritual duties
seriously.   But as a class he represents them as a worldly
minded and oppressive set of hirelings who merely wear the
mask (*larva*) of bishops.   They are usurpers, not true bishops
of the New Testament type.   He has no difficulty in bringing
out the contrast between this secularised, feudalised episco-
pate and the Christian ministry of early times.   He quotes
passages from Paul's Epistles, the Acts of the Apostles, and
other sources which delineate the early ministry, and bids
them look at themselves in this mirror.   He can see no
vestige of a likeness between the two, and exhausts his rich
vocabulary of expletives in damning them as murderers
of souls and ministers of Satan.   In as far as he confines
himself to the New Testament passages relative to the
ministerial office, he makes out a strong case for his contention.   But he spoils it, for the modern reader at least, by
the violence and virulence of his language, though one
must not forget that he is confronting men who were in too

[58] " Werke," x., Pt. II., 105-107.

many cases gravely unworthy of their profession and who were only too eager to send him to the stake. Moreover, he devotes too many pages to quoting and labouring irrelevant passages from Paul and 2 Peter, in which they are made to testify against the Roman hierarchy of his own time. He would have been more effective if he had confined himself to the actual facts of the case, instead of burdening the reader with these arbitrary divagations on irrelevant texts. He certainly shocks the taste of the modern reader by the grossness of the language in which, in reference to the evil effects of celibacy, he speaks of the operation of physiological laws in matters of sex. Even though it is perfectly evident that he does so from moral motives and that this freedom of speech was a characteristic of his time, it does show a lack of the sense of fitness to transfer this popular liberty of expression to the printed page.

He undoubtedly tends, too, to consider the case in the light of his own dogmatic convictions on faith and works which the bishops have refused to accept, and which they persist, at the Pope's behest, in spurning as heresy. They must, therefore, perforce be enemies of God, wolves in sheep's clothing. Under the influence of this theological obsession, there is in the philippic a lack of reasoned restraint and a tendency to exaggerate the evils he condemns, as when he says that all religious foundations in which the inmates strive to attain salvation by monastic works are much worse than houses of prostitution and murder dens.[59] He is thus apt to paint the picture all black under the influence of his theological prepossessions, and generalise *a priori* without duly examining the facts in order to substantiate his conclusions. But, then, Luther is no historian, but a religious reformer with an extraordinary gift of explosive language, writing under strong provocation and bent on the overthrow of a régime which he regards as both unchristian and antichristian. The philippic was a fiery cross summoning to the death struggle with the Antichrist in Germany as well as at Rome. At the same time, it is no mere case of swearing at large, though he is too apt to rave and revile. He assumes

[59] "Werke," x., Pt. II., 148.

that the facts are so notorious that it is superfluous to particularise. They are, he repeatedly says, common knowledge, too well known to need proof, and may be left to speak for themselves. What he does is to drive them home and to found on them a demand for a trenchant reformation at the hands of the people. Away with the ungodly brood of usurpers of Christ's spiritual kingdom, is his slogan. It is more than time that this sham, and the scandal of this make-believe Christianity, which seeks to combine God and the devil, were swept away. He clamantly demands an uprising against them as tyrants and soul murderers who live on the sweat and toil of the people, and who, whilst enforcing celibacy, license concubines and prostitution at so much per head, are generally a disgrace to their profession, and, in their pursuit of power and gear, deem it beneath them to preach the Gospel and study the Bible. Not that the people shall hurl them down from their usurped seats by force and the sword. They are simply to renounce their jurisdiction, withdraw their obedience, and their régime will fall of itself. To this end he assumes the function of Pope and sends forth his own Bull of Reformation.[60] In this Bull he would abolish the hierarchy root and branch and substitute for it the bishops or presbyters of the local Christian community in the New Testament Church. Each congregation should have one or more pastors or overseers, who preach the Word and tend the flock. Even Irenæus, Cyprian, Ambrose, Augustine were bishops of a single city, not feudal lords of large ecclesiastical dioceses. " Let this be Doctor Luther's Bull, which gives God's grace as a reward to all who hold and follow it. Amen." [61]

On the heels of this bellicose effusion came the equally drastic reply to Henry VIII.'s "Defence of the Seven Sacraments against Martin Luther." [62] King Henry had some learning, could write Latin that evoked the praise of

---

[60] " Werke," x., Pt. II., 148 f.

[61] *Ibid.*, x., Pt. II., 144.

[62] " Assertio Septem Sacramentorum adversus Martinum Lutherum," 1521. I have used the edition of 1523. There is an English translation by T. W., 1687.

Erasmus, and was the patron of liberal studies.  With this
culture he at this period combined a conservative adhesion
to the mediæval faith and the Church as constituted under
its papal head, for he had not yet developed into the ruthless
antagonist of the Papacy, the most aggressive champion of
national independence of Rome.  On the appearance of the
" Babylonic Captivity " in England in 1521, he threw himself into the breach in defence of the papal authority and the
Seven Sacraments.  He had, in fact, been meditating an
attack on the arch-heretic a couple of years before the
publication of the " Captivity " in 1520,[63] and his perusal
of it sent him at once to his desk to carry out his purpose.
It was printed in July 1521, with a dedication to the Pope,
and copies were forwarded to John Clerk, his representative
at Rome, for presentation to Leo X.  This Clerk did on the
2nd October in an oration loaded with abuse of Luther.
The Pope expressed his admiration in the most flattering
terms, and as a reward conferred on the royal author the title
of Defender of the Faith.  On its merits it by no means
deserved this special distinction.  It shows considerable
dialectic ability, and some familiarity with the stock arguments of the theologians in defence of the teaching of the
Church, culled from the theological textbooks.  It discovers
some weak points in Luther's armour.  But it does little
more than reiterate the argument that the Church and the
Fathers have held such and such a doctrine, and that what
they have believed and maintained is true, and is, therefore,
obligatory on all.  Though expressing a wish that Luther
may repent and return to the fold, it hopes that he may
yet be burned if he persists in his errors.  Its tone is
vituperative and contemptuous   Luther is inspired by the
devil, a hideous monster, an incurably scabbed sheep, a
man of corrupt and putrid heart, a hissing serpent.  He
makes faith nothing but the cloak of a wicked life, and so
forth.  We may take as a sample of Henry's estimate of
him the turgid sentence in which, towards the conclusion,
he sums up his feelings.   " Alas, the worst wolf of hell has
surprised him, devoured and gulphed him down into the

---

[63] Brewer, " Reign of Henry VIII.," i. 601.

lowest part of his belly where, half alive and dying in death, he belches forth out of the filthy mouth of that hellish wolf those vile barkings against the chief pastor who has called him back and deplored his perdition, which the ears of the whole flock detest, abominate, and abhor." To the reader there is a certain humour, in view of his own subsequent attitude towards the Pope, in King Henry's complaint that Luther, having first ascribed a certain power to the Pope, afterwards denies it, and thus contradicts himself.

Luther, who first mentions the royal effusion in a letter to Lang on the 26th June 1522, might well have afforded to ignore it on its own merits. To judge from the tone of his reference to it, he does not at first seem to have taken the matter seriously. But the prestige of the writer, the publicity which the dedication and presentation to the Pope conferred on it, its widespread perusal seemed to demand a reply. Moreover, he saw in it a covert attempt on the part of his enemies to discredit him and his teaching, and erroneously ascribes its real authorship to Edward Lee, Henry's chaplain and future Archbishop of York.[64] The appearance of a German translation by Emser in the summer of 1522 finally decided him to set to work on a reply in the vernacular, which appeared in the beginning of August, and one in Latin, which he published in September.[65] In answer to the charge of inconsistency and self-contradiction, he maintains that his fundamental teaching on faith and works, etc., has been the same throughout, and appeals to his published works in support of his contention. In regard to the papal power and ecclesiastical institutions, he admits that his views have undergone development in the course of controversy. He has only gradually discovered the falsehood of the whole papal and ecclesiastical system in the light of the closer study of Scripture, to which the conflict with his opponents has led

[64] Enders, iii. 403, 426, and in the introduction to his reply.

[65] Antwort Deutsch auf Könnig Heinrich's Buch ; Contra Henricum Regem Angliæ, " Werke," x., Pt. II., 180 f., and see editorial introduction, 175 f. The Latin work is dedicated to Count Schlick, an ardent adherent of the evangelical movement on the border of Bohemia. The contents of both are pretty much alike, though the latter is not a mere version of the former.

him. For this reason he is ready to admit that his earlier works contain admissions and concessions which he has since been led to condemn and revoke.[66] But to change one's opinion in the light of further knowledge does not fairly lay one open to the charge of self-contradiction unless, having changed an opinion, one refuses to acknowledge the change and persists in maintaining it.

King Henry's defence of the papal power and the sacraments, he rightly points out, rests merely on the reiterated assumption that what has been asserted and believed by the doctors of the Church is bound to be true and must, therefore, be accepted by all. He quotes in reply the proverb, "Whatever has been wrong for a hundred years was never right for one year," and retorts that, on this principle, the Turks and the Jews could argue with equal or greater force in proof of the truth of their religion. Nay, if age guarantees a belief or a practice, the devil himself would have the best right on earth, since he is over 5,000 years old! The Fathers themselves have erred, and even if they had not, they had no power to impose new articles of faith. King Henry labours under the delusion that it is sufficient to quote a passage from Ambrose or Augustine or Aquinas to make a doctrine an article of faith. The Scripture alone is the supreme, the exclusive authority on such matters, and he reiterates his claim that since his teaching is founded on this supreme authority, and not on mere human opinion, it is God's, not his, even if a thousand Augustines and a thousand King Henrys maintain the contrary. In defending the traditional doctrine of the sacraments, he has merely dished up the teaching of Aquinas on transubstantiation, etc., at second hand, on the pretence that it is the teaching of Christ and Paul. "You papists," he defiantly concludes, "shall never accomplish your purpose, do what you will. The Gospel which I, Martin Luther, preach, shall prevail over Pope, bishop, parson, monks, kings, princes, devil, death, and all that is not Christ and in Christ. Against it nothing shall avail." [67]

[66] " Werke," x., Pt. II., 229-233.
[67] Ibid., x., Pt. II., 262.

In thus rebutting in detail the royal attack, Luther shows his superiority in dialectic skill, theological learning, and passionate conviction.   He rallies and ridicules his antagonist with a supreme command of sarcasm and humour.   Unfortunately he was unable to withstand the temptation to cover him with abuse as well.   He had received no little provocation to call names.   King Henry, he complains, has applied to him more insulting terms than he himself had used of his opponents in all his books put together, and in his wrath he pays him back with compound interest. He is not only a theological charlatan and a servile flatterer of the Pope.   In wilfully misrepresenting his teaching, he is a liar, and what is worse, he makes God and His Word liars. He is an unmitigated fool, and has amply proved the truth of the proverb, that there are no greater fools than kings and princes.   He must have been drunk or dreaming when he wrote such rubbish.   But then what else can be expected when an ass takes to reading the Psalter.   It is not surprising that he should take to defending the usurpation of the Papacy, that Babylonian whore, seeing that he himself owes his crown to murder and tyranny, and imagines that he can silence Luther by scolding like a foul-mouthed harlot.

Unfortunately, Luther, in this choleric mood, was unable to see that he was doing his cause little service by imitating and even outdoing the King in the use of scurrilous language, and that he would have done better had he adopted a more dignified tone and stopped short at raillery and ridicule. In this mood he cares not a straw whether his opponent wears a doctor's cap or a king's crown.   A fool is for him a fool, whether he sits in a professor's chair, or even that of St Peter, or on the throne of England, or the ducal throne of Saxony at Dresden.   He is only the more obnoxious as the figurehead of the great pack of fools who cannot see the truth beyond the mountain of lies and shams which they have heaped in front of it.   On his own confession many, even of his friends, were aghast at his violence.[68]   To one of those who desired an explanation, he replied (forgetting that he himself was very provocative at times) that he had had more

[68] Enders, iv. 1, 27.

than enough of these personal and libellous attacks, and that he was determined henceforth not to mince words with these slanderers and liars. Christ and the Apostles were not always mild, and it is high time to shut the mouths of these Pharisees who only revile the more the more gently they are treated.[69]   On his side King Henry, also forgetting his own offences against decent controversy, complained in letters to the Elector, his brother, and Duke George of the scurrilities of the unconscionable monk. The Elector regretted the cause of his chagrin, but, as usual, professed his inability to intervene, and referred him to a future Council. Duke George was more accommodating, and brought the matter to the notice of the Imperial Regency, whilst, besides Emser, Murner, Dietenberger, and Cochlaeus in Germany, Fisher, Bishop of Rochester, and Sir Thomas More in England, came to the rescue with counterblasts in the same unparliamentary style.[70]

Whilst Luther seems to have paid no attention to these effusions, Cochlaeus (Johann Dobneck) succeeded in drawing him into a skirmish in defence of his doctrine of justification, which he had rudely attacked in a work on " Sacramental Grace," published towards the end of 1522. The work was forwarded to Luther by his friend, the Frankfurt humanist, W. Nesen. Like Eck, Cochlaeus, who was incumbent of St Mary's at Frankfurt, was eager to distinguish himself as the champion of orthodoxy with an eye to certain coveted benefices. As a humanist he had at first been disposed to favour the Lutheran cause, but had veered round to the opposite camp and, as we have noted, had sought to make a reputation at the Diet of Worms as the abettor of Aleander's policy.[71]   To this end he had challenged Luther to a disputa-

[69] " Werke," 53, 149-151 (Erlangen ed.).

[70] The anonymous effusion, professing to be written by W. Rosse, is included in More's works, though More's authorship has been questioned on what Mr Brewer thinks insufficient grounds. " Reign of Henry VIII.," 608-609.

[71] In his " Commentaria de Actis et Scriptis Mart. Lutheri," 39 (1549), he says that he went to Worms out of pure zeal for the faith. He was, however, regarded by Luther and his friends as a scheming busybody and self-seeker, and their judgment seems not to have been unfounded.

tion on the absurd condition that he should first renounce
his safe conduct, and he now boasted that Luther had
declined his challenge.  It was this boast that drew from the
Reformer a reply in the form of an open letter to Nesen,
which appeared in February 1523.[72]   In this spirited philippic
he ridicules the would-be victor who had succeeded only in
making a laughing-stock of himself at Worms, and, glancing
at the Latinised name Cochlaeus, asks how a poor snail,
which draws in its horns at the slightest danger, could ever
think of such a thing as a disputation.  He then proceeds
to vindicate his doctrine of justification by faith alone for
the benefit of those whom Cochlaeus tries to mislead.  He
treats him as a type of those sophistic theologians who do
not understand Paul and, while making use of the Apostolic
language, wrest and misinterpret it in accordance with their
own assumptions and vicious dialectic.  In his impatience
with " these blockheads," he is unable to keep himself within
the limit of ridicule, and breaks into vituperation and
contemptuous invective.  Cochlaeus retorted in similar
fashion [73] within a few weeks in a violent diatribe to which
Luther deigned no response.  Henceforth he became one
of his most pertinacious adversaries, and ultimately in 1549
took his revenge in a history of Luther and his movement
which contained calumny as well as misrepresentation, and
became a quarry for his Roman Catholic detractors to
excavate from that day to this.[74]

Luther's attack on celibacy inevitably provoked a counter-
attack, and involved him in controversy over this burning
question.  The Franciscan, Caspar Sasger, or Schatzgeyer,
set the ball a-rolling with a " Reply," which appeared in
the autumn of 1522, and in which he ascribed the " De
Votis Monasticis " to the inspiration of Satan.  It also
affords him clear proof that its author was bent on ridding
himself of the obligation of chastity which he was unable

[72] Adversus armatum virum Cochleum, " Werke," xi. 295 f.

[73] " Adversus Cucullatum Minotaurum Wittenbergensem," ed. by
I. Schweizer, " Corpus Catholicorum," iii. (1920).

[74] " Commentaria "; see also Kolde, " Cochlaeus," in Herzog-
Hauck, " Encylopädie "; Köhler, " Das Katholische Lutherbild der
Gegenwart " (1922).

to observe.[75]    Luther was too busy at the time [76] to refute
these assumptions which the good monk's brethren ascribed
to the Holy Spirit, and contented himself with submitting
the book to his friend and disciple, John Brissmann, another
Franciscan, who had taken his doctor's degree at Wittenberg
some months previously, and whose " Responsa " appeared
in March 1523.  He merely added an epistle by way of
preface,[77] in which he controverted Sasger's contention that
what is not contrary to Scripture is in accord with Scripture,
and that, therefore, monasticism is scriptural.[78]  Nor did he
deem it worth while to reply to the ponderous effusion which
John Schmidt or Faber, the vicar of the Bishop of Constance,
published at Rome in August 1522, and which Duke George
of Saxony reprinted at Leipzig in April 1523.  Whilst Faber's
work was a general attack on Luther's teaching, it contained
a defence of priestly celibacy.[79]  In this case he deputed the
task of answering for him to Justus Jonas on the ground
that, being recently married, he was more concerned and
better fitted to justify the blessings of priestly matrimony
than he.  As for this tiresome compiler of quotations from
the Fathers and Councils, he had written nothing that he
had not already confuted.[80]  With this contemptuous preface
Faber, who was eager to gain the fame of a reply from Luther
himself, had to be content, and Jonas did not fail to remind
him of his personal responsibility as episcopal vicar of
Constance for the scandal of priestly concubinage in the
diocese.[81]  The reminder was certainly anything but flattering to his self-esteem or gratifying to his keen desire to acquire
notoriety at Luther's expense.

[75] " Werke," viii. 567. On Schatzgeyer, who had shortly before
entered the arena against the Lutherans in a comparatively moderate
work, " Scrutinium Divinæ Scripturæ," ed. by Schmidt, see " Corpus
Catholicorum," v. (1922).

[76] Enders, iv. 105.  Ego occupatior sim quam ut ipse respondeam.

[77] Ibid., iv. 104 f. ;  " Werke," xi. 284 f.

[78] " Werke," xi. 286-287.  Sasger duly replied with an " Examen "
of Brissmann's work, to which neither he nor Luther seems to have
paid any attention.  Of the polemics of the Dominican Dietenberger
and the Sorbonne doctor Clichthoven he took no notice.  Both works
appeared in 1524.  " Werke," viii. 568-569.

[79] Ibid., xii. 82.          [80] Ibid., xii. 85.          [81] Ibid., xii. 83.

Luther himself, however, could not escape the task of dealing with the question, which had a social as well as a religious aspect, and was exciting a widespread practical interest. His work on " Monastic Vows " had given an impulse to the emancipation movement which, in the words of Justus Jonas, was depopulating so many monasteries. Requests for help and guidance poured in from monks and nuns who, from conscientious scruples or other motives, were bent on freeing themselves from the monastic yoke. The baneful practice of destining children of both sexes to the religious life—particularly on the part of parents of the higher classes—as a means of subsistence, apart from any religious vocation or inclination for the celibate state, tended to sap the morals of many of the members of the monastic Orders. Moreover, the evangelical movement had gained not a few adherents in the monasteries, though Luther was fain to confess that religious considerations were by no means the exclusive factor in producing an increasing alienation from the monastic system. In the face of the growing revolt against it, he was erelong brought up against the necessity of taking active steps to assist its victims to regain their freedom, especially in the case of nuns whose parents or relatives hesitated or declined to intervene in response to their appeals. It was on this ground that he felt bound to protect a number of nuns whom, at his instigation, Leonard Koppe of Torgau and two accomplices had succeeded in withdrawing from the convent at Nimbschen, near Grimma, in the beginning of April 1523. They were mostly members of noble families, and some of them, including the sister of Staupitz and Catherine von Bora, whose parents resided in the territory of Duke George and were, therefore, unwilling to run the risk of harbouring them, were conducted by Koppe to Wittenberg. In the circumstances Luther did not hesitate to give them a temporary asylum in the Wittenberg monastery until he could communicate with their relatives and provide for their future welfare. He wrote to Spalatin, begging the Elector's assistance for their provisional maintenance on the ground of the slender resources at his disposal.[82] It seemed a

[82] Enders, iv. 126-128.

compromising as well as a daring defiance of public propriety thus to befriend a party of runaway nuns, and his action was certainly open to misapprehension, and, from the current ecclesiastical standpoint, animadversion. But he did not allow himself to be swayed by such considerations, and wrote a public letter to Koppe accepting responsibility for his action,[83] repelling the insinuation of dishonourable motives, and defending it as a justifiable deliverance from priestly tyranny and an example and encouragement to noble parents to free their children from this immoral and irreligious bondage. These young women have acted from conscientious motives in seeking deliverance from a condition into which they had entered without due consideration or voluntary choice, and after requesting their parents to release them. But the scandal of it ! " Scandal here, or scandal there," retorts Luther, " necessity breaks iron and cares nothing for scandal." [84]

Nor was this example without due effect in encouraging the emancipation movement. Two months later sixteen nuns escaped from the convent at Widerstet, and five of them were taken under the protection of Count Albrecht of Mansfeld. To the Counts of Mansfeld he dedicated the story of another fugitive who had escaped from the convent of Neu Helfta at Eisleben.[85] In this document Florentina von Oberweimar tells how in her sixth year she was placed in the convent by her parents ; how at the age of eleven she was consecrated to the life of virginity without her consent and due knowledge ; how in her fourteenth year she discerned her unfitness for this vocation and vainly represented to the abbess her desire for freedom ; how she was nevertheless formally received into the Order as a professed nun by command of the abbess and against her will ; how she became acquainted with Luther's evangelical teaching and wrote to him for instruction and counsel ; how she was betrayed by some of her fellow-nuns and was subjected to

[83] " Werke," xi. 394 f.   Ursach und Antwort das jungfrauen Klöster göttlich verlassen mögen, April 1523.
[84] *Ibid.*, xi. 400.
[85] Ein Geschicht wie Gott einer Klosterjungfrau ausgeholfen hat, March 1524, " Werke," xv. 86 f.

a lengthy process of harsh treatment by the abbess, including, besides severe and humiliating penance, imprisonment in a cold cell ; how she communicated to her relative, Caspar von Watzdorf, her miserable condition, was again betrayed, cruelly beaten by the abbess and four other nuns, put in irons for twenty-four hours, and again imprisoned ; and how she managed to escape through the negligence of an attendant in leaving the door of her cell unlocked.  " From this and many other cases," concludes Luther in the introductory epistle, " the world can see what a devilish thing this monkery and nunnery is, in which they think to drive and compel people to God with harshness and blows.  God will have no such enforced service." [86]  He calls on the Counts of Mansfeld and other princes to remember the saying, " No one cometh to me except the Father draw him," and to see that freedom is allowed and exercised in the monasteries within their territories.

Whilst he treated the polemics of a Sasger and a Faber with contempt, he was compelled by such experiences to appeal to public opinion on the question.  Hence the series of controversial tracts [87] in the vernacular on the married versus the celibate state, in which he deals very freely with the sex question.  One is struck and sometimes shocked by the freedom with which he discusses this delicate theme.  In his day people evidently spoke and even wrote on sexual matters with far less reserve or refinement than the cultured Christian of to-day is accustomed to observe, and Luther, writing in the common tongue, does not hesitate to enter into details which a modern reader, who dislikes vulgarity, would prefer to assume rather than describe. What appears to us gross or prurient does not seem to have been so regarded in the sixteenth century, though a writer of a more severe taste, like Calvin, would have shown a more delicate touch in dealing with matters of this kind.  In Luther's case, at all events, the tone is drastically naïve

---

[86] " Werke," xv. 87.

[87] Vom ehelichen Leben, 1522, " Werke," x., Pt. II., 275 f. ; Das Siebente Kapitel St Pauli zu den Corinthern ausgelegt, 1523, *ibid.*, xii. 92 f. ; Das Eltern die Kinder zur Ehe nicht zwingen noch hindern, 1524, *ibid.*, xv. 163 f.

rather than intentionally coarse. At the same time, there was in him a vulgar grain which is rather unpleasantly reflected in his style, especially in the more violent and popular of his controversial works. It does grate at times on a delicate ear, and he himself is fain to apologise for inflicting these details on the reader. He would rather have left the subject alone if the exigencies of the time had not forced him to grapple with it. He condemns, too, the flippant and sensual spirit in which the sexual question is treated in certain humanist circles, which denounce marriage as a conventional tyranny and shamelessly advocate free love. But he cannot evade the necessity of exposing the evils of a system which he regards as both false in itself and detrimental to morality and religion. The low conception of marriage as incompatible with the perfection of the religious life, from which clerical celibacy sprang and which it tended to foster, is to some extent reflected in his own rather one-sided view of it as a necessity of the flesh, though he does not fail to emphasise the married state as a high vocation in reaction both from the sensualist writers of the time and from the false, unchristian, and unnatural asceticism imposed by the Church on the clergy. His object is, in fact, to raise the standard of social morality and ensure pure Christian living against both these tendencies, which he regards as alike false and reprehensible on moral and religious grounds. At the same time, he is apt to dwell too much on the animal side of human nature, to overlook at times or relegate to the background the more spiritual aspect of wedlock in the union of two souls from other motives than the gratification of the sensual instinct, of human love as the expression of the finer emotions which may and do have their part in this relation. In a word, in his revulsion from and conflict with the unhealthy and unnatural elements in the celibate system, he allows his naturalism at times to blur his vision of the nobler side of manhood and womanhood.

For him marriage is the law of God which is reflected in the natural impulse to the cohabitation of man and woman. It is a physical necessity in virtue of the constitution of the human body by the Creator. Every human being is by divine ordinance subject to this law, and to ignore it is pure foolery, which is bound to result in sins of the flesh.[88] No vow is valid against this law of Nature, which is also the law of God. " Increase and multiply " is the divine fiat, and the attempt to counteract this divinely implanted impulse inevitably leads to fornication. There are, indeed, exceptions to this law, as Christ has pointed out (Matt. xix. 12). Impotence, for instance, in which case he would allow the married woman to seek satisfaction by agreement with her husband, though in case of common bodily infirmity both parties are patiently and dutifully to bear the cross. There are also exceptional cases in which by the special gift of God the body is so constituted that a man or woman may feel no inclination for marriage and may freely devote themselves to a purely spiritual life, as Paul commands (1 Cor. vii.). But these exceptions are few and they do not warrant the segregation of men and women, without due consideration of this fact, in monasteries and convents under a man-made and artificial obligation to observe the celibate state, which militates against the divinely ordained law of human nature. Though he inclines at times to over- emphasise the sexual side of marriage as a physiological necessity to the obscuring of the more ideal aspect of it, the married state is not to be conceived as incompatible with the higher spiritual life, and it is false to assume with St Jerome that the celibate state is superior to the married state in God's sight.[89] While as a monk he himself is to a certain extent influenced by the traditional monastic concep- tion of the married state as a means of carnal gratification, he would evidently have taken the side of Jovinian in his opposition to this conception, as championed by Jerome and his fellow-monks in the fourth century. As ordained by God, it is a high as well as a legitimate and natural vocation to be fulfilled in a Christian spirit, and not to be spurned because of its conjugal obligations and its cares and trials, or in preference for licentious living and unnatural lust, as described by Paul in the first chapter of Romans and

[88] Vom ehelichen Leben, " Werke," x., Pt. II., 276-277.
[89] " Werke," xii. 99.

vaunted by the apostles of free love.  God has ordained and
sanctified these natural functions, though the sexual impulse is not exercised without sin, in virtue of the fall.  He
has not created woman to be the slave of man's lust.  Both
husband and wife are to carry into and exercise in the
married state the spirit of service and obedience to God.
Following Paul, he insists on the necessity of self-control
and abstinence in the interest of the spiritual life, though he
objects to formal ecclesiastical regulation in such a matter.[90]
In begetting children, rearing them in the fear of God, and
training them in the Gospel, they are performing the highest
service.  They are the true bishops and apostles of their
children.  There is no greater, nobler power on earth than
that in the hands of parents.[91]  In fulfilling this vocation
they are exemplifying the more ideal side of the marriage
relation which the monastic conception ignores and rejects
in the interest of a false, unchristian, impossible, and
essentially hypocritical celibacy.  It is, moreover, the only,
the indispensable safeguard from fornication, impurity,
which celibacy cannot guarantee.  In its evil effects in this
respect the practice of the celibate life is, in fact, the strongest
argument for the necessity and the moral efficacy of marriage.
It practically imposes the licensing of concubinage and
frustrates its professed object, " for there is no more unchaste
class than those professing chastity, as daily experience
teaches." [92]  It is a silly and futile device which causes
terrible misery of conscience among the clergy.[93]  Without
a pure heart there can be no chastity.  It is, too, utterly
reprehensible in as far as it is embraced merely as a refuge
from the duties and cares of married life.  There is far
more spiritual benefit to be derived from the discipline
which gives scope for the exercise of faith and self-denial,
than from the immunity from the battle and burden of
common life which celibacy ensures.  It is, in fact, in his
eyes a fundamental objection to it that it tends to displace
faith and foster religious formalism, belief in works, though
it is not necessarily incompatible with the life of faith.[94]

[90] "Werke," xii. 103.                    [93] Ibid., xii. 99.
[91] Ibid., x., Pt. II., 301.              [94] Ibid., xii. 107-108.
[92] Ibid., xii. 93, 109, 112.

Moreover, on purely economic grounds, the married is vastly superior to the unmarried state. The father of a family must toil for his livelihood and contribute his share to the common benefit. The celibate lives in and for himself. " He is a lazy rascal who shuns work and lives on the labour of others." [95]

At the same time, while emphasising the necessity of marriage as the indispensable safeguard against fornication, he would, like Paul, leave all free to marry or not, and commends the unmarried state where the gift of chastity exists. He would, further, reform the common law relative to the degree of relationship within which marriage is inadmissible, since it forbids what Scripture allows and its provisions can be easily overridden for a money payment.[96] He would allow marriage with non-Christians, i.e., Jews and Turks, in accordance with the declaration of Paul and Peter, who recognised the union of a Christian man or woman with a heathen as valid. In the case of the refusal of cohabitation by the wife, he holds that the husband is justified in repudiating the wife and taking another, and vice versa, and he would sanction separation on the ground of incompatibility of temper, but without subsequent marriage.[97] He favours early marriage as the surest means of preventing youthful excess, and would limit the power of parents to force children to marry at their behest and will, and thus diminish the danger of unhappy unions.[98]

[95] "Werke," xii. 108.
[96] Ibid., x., Pt. II., 280 f.
[97] Ibid., x., Pt. II., 290-291.
[98] Ibid., xv. 163 f.

# CHAPTER V

# THE EMPIRE AND LUTHER

## I. THE SPREAD OF THE MOVEMENT

LUTHER'S literary activity as the champion of an evangelical Reformation during the three years, 1521-24, had made a powerful impression in Germany. The long series of controversial tracts or treatises in Latin and German is apt to surfeit the modern reader who plods through them in search of the distinctive ideas which he enunciated or reiterated during this period in defiance of the imperial ban, the counter-attacks and calumnies of embittered opponents, new and old, and the head-shaking of hesitating or wondering sympathisers. But these successive attacks on conventional ideas and institutions had a power of appeal which to that age was elemental. Luther's study at the Wartburg and at Wittenberg is the centre of a spiritual cataclysm that shatters the old, in the effort to create a new order. One after another old beliefs, usages, laws, which have been the religious palladium of centuries, crash under the blows of this terrible iconoclast. His only weapon is the spoken, written, and printed word, the pulpit and the press, the sermon, the epistle, the treatise, the pamphlet. A voice and a pen—this is all. But there is more power in this voice and this pen to shake and mould the world than in all the Bulls of a pope or the armed strength of emperor and kings. What Luther speaks or prints is far more potent for millions within and even without his native Germany than papal Bull or imperial Edict, backed as they are by the prestige of the Roman See and the material power of the Holy Roman Empire. The testimony of Valdès, the Emperor's secretary, is conclusive on this point. " I see that the minds of the Germans are generally exasperated against the Roman See, and they do not seem to attach great importance to the Emperor's edicts, for since their publication Lutheran books are sold with impunity at every step and corner of the streets and in the market-places." [1]  His writings were as eagerly awaited and as widely circulated as the most popular novel of our day.  First editions were exhausted as soon as they left the press, and were followed by others as fast as the printing presses could turn them out.[2]  The business of printing them was so lucrative that they were reproduced without his permission, and he found it necessary to address to the printers a remonstrance against the unauthorised versions of them put in circulation.[3]  He had created a public opinion which was insatiable in its demand for more and ever more of this theological pabulum, which may have for us at times only an antiquarian interest.

Its bulk was swelled by the increasing contributions of his abettors in the press, which the Edict of Worms was equally impotent to prevent.  The Edict was, in fact, followed by a notable increase of the very writings it was designed to suppress.  Between the years 1518 and 1523 the output of theological controversial literature, to which Luther himself contributed the lion's share, was increased sevenfold, and Ranke hazards the estimate that four-fifths of it were on Luther's side.[4]  It largely monopolised the German press, whilst Cochlaeus complains that anti-Lutheran writers could only with difficulty find a publisher for what the booksellers at the Frankfurt Fair and elsewhere derided as barbarous and trivial stuff.[5]  Among the middle class in the Free Imperial Cities, in particular, these books found enthusiastic readers, while the democratic note of the " new Gospel " and its denunciation of Roman tyranny found a

---

[1] Quoted by Lindsay, " History of the Reformation," i. 299.

[2] See the numerous editions of his works given in the bibliographical introductions in the Weimar edition of his " Werke."

[3] Enders, iv. 153, 269.

[4] " Deutsche Geschichte im Zeitalter der Reformation," ii. 79-80. II. 62 of the new edition of the German Academy, 1925, by Marcks, Meinecke, and Her. Oncken.

[5] " Commentaria," 58-59.

ready response on the part of the lower classes.[6]  By discarding more and more the language of the learned for that of the common man, Luther and his collaborators widened the appeal of this Gospel to the masses. The great controversy thereby bursts the limits of the schools, within which it had at first been confined, and is carried into the cottage, the tavern, the market-place. Very significant in this respect is the appearance of the popular pamphlet written, mostly in dialogue form, in the vernacular for the common man. These publicists skilfully brought the Lutheran theology within the comprehension of the peasant who becomes a theologian, takes the side of Luther against his opponents, and puts the parson and the monk to the rout with quotations from the Bible and Dr Martin. The common man becomes keenly conscious alike of his own worth and the corruption and oppression of the Church, which fleeces him and keeps him in grinding poverty by its exactions for the benefit of a worthless, lazy, unscriptural set of parasites, who batten on the commonwealth. Among the most effective and widely circulated of these effusions were " Karsthans " (Jack Mattock), " Neukarsthans," " The Old God and the New," and the numerous series of pamphlets issued by the ex-Franciscan, Eberlin von Günzburg. " Karsthans " was directed against Murner, who had himself indulged in this popular polemic against the evils rampant in the Church and society before he became one of the keenest of Luther's opponents.[7]  On the ground of Scripture and in the interest of the commonweal, he will disestablish Pope and prelate, and will only recognise the lordship of Christ over the Church, proclaims Dr Luther's doctrine of the priesthood of believers, and finishes the discussion by calling for his flail wherewith to vent his wrath on Murner's detestable head.

[6] " Commentaria," 57-58.
[7] It is given by Böcking, " Hutteni Opera," iv. 620 f.  On Murner see Kawerau, " Th. Murner und die Kirche des Mittelalters," and " Th. Murner und die Deutsche Reformation " (Niemeyer, Halle, 1890-1891). Burckhardt ascribes " Karsthans " to Joachim von Watt.  " Flugschriften aus der Reformationszeit," iv. 1 f.  See also art., " Murner," Herzog-Hauck, " Encyclopädie."

In "Neukarsthans," which appears to have emanated (September 1521) from Sickingen's circle (was the author Oecolampadius or Bucer?), the doughty knight of the Ebernburg has turned a pious evangelical.[8] He spends the winter evenings with Hutten and other friends reading the Scriptures and Luther's works, and sets forth for the benefit of his peasant visitor the main points of Dr Martin's teaching, especially on its practical side. The supreme test of the true theology and the true Church is the New Testament, which Sickingen quotes profusely. The Church in its papal, hierarchical form is as like that of Christ and the Apostles as night is to day. Clergy and monks ought to be deprived of their ill-gotten and ill-used wealth. The hour of their undoing is about to strike. High time, bursts out Hans, to go for them with our flails and mattocks! Sickingen counsels patience meanwhile, and says that it ought to be done justly in the interest of the truth, not out of envy and greed. Hans agrees, though he regrets that through their lying and deceit he has so long been ignorant of the truth. Now he will buy Luther's books and get some one to read them to him. The thing cannot last much longer, remarks Sickingen, since the common man has learned more from the New Testament and Dr Martin's writings than all the parsons who have preached and studied for ten or fifteen years. The New Testament is the great teacher of the common man, who is of Luther's opinion that the real heretics are the Pope, the theologians, and parsons who have twisted the Word of God to suit their own self-seeking. There never was a time when people were more eager to hear the preaching of the Gospel. The new Gospel age has dawned. The laity has realised its rights and means to enforce them against this oppressive régime of usurpers and hirelings who buy their livings from the Pope. "We are all the Church and no one more than another." [9]

Under the author's tuition Hans is, on the whole, self-

---

[8] It is given by Böcking, "Hutt. Opera," iv. 651 f. W. Köhler concludes that the author was Hutten ("Zeitschrift für Deutsche Philologie," 1898). Böcking ascribes it to Oecolampadius. Kalkoff gives reasons for assigning it to Bucer ("Hutten und die Reformation," 537 f.).

[9] "Hutt. Opera," iv. 664.

restrained, though choleric. The impulse to go for the
parson and the monk with his flail is kept in check in deference, apparently, to Luther's "Exhortation against Revolt
and Tumult." Eberlin is far less prudent and tolerant in
the fiery appeal for a radical and violent Reformation which
he voiced in a series of pamphlets in 1521 and the following
year, though under the influence of Luther and Melanchthon
he subsequently struck a more moderate note.[10]  This radical
tendency also found expression in the Thirty Articles,
printed along with the "Neukarsthans," in which Junker
Helfrich, Knight Harry, and Jack Mattock renounce the
régime of Antichrist, devote themselves body and goods to
bring about such a drastic Reformation, and swear undying
hostility to all Dr Luther's enemies.[11]

Meanwhile the movement was spreading far and near
in virtue of its inherent power. Luther himself, as we have
noted, had no definite plan for the propagation of his teaching
and the organisation of its adherents. Hitherto he had
laboured to influence public opinion by means of the press,
the lecture, the sermon, and a vast correspondence. He
trusted to the power of the Word to establish a new order,
and the Word was doubtless powerfully working towards this
end. The publication, after revision with the assistance of
Melanchthon, of his translation of the New Testament on
the 21st September 1522,[12] was a factor of the first importance
in hastening its realisation. But in spite of his professed
reliance on the missionary power of the Word, the greatest
force in the spread of the movement was the personality and
the manifold activity of Luther himself. Though inferior
to Calvin as an organiser, his correspondence [13] during this

[10] See the collection of his popular pamphlets edited by Enders
in the "Flugschriften," 1898, 1900, 1902. On Eberlin see the works of
Reggenbach (1874), Radlkofer (1887), Julius Werner (1895), and the
art. by Kolde in Herzog-Hauck. Also Bezold, "Geschichte der
Deutschen Reformation," 357 f.

[11] Given by Böcking, "Opera Hutteni," iv. 680-681. These violent
articles are ascribed by Kalkoff to the printer, Johann Schott of Strassburg.
Hutten's "Vagantenzeit und Untergang," 310-311.

[12] Enders, iv. 4-5.

[13] See the latter part of Vol. III. and the whole of Vols. IV. and V.
of his "Briefwechsel."

formative period proves that he was by no means so indifferent to the necessity of active, constructive effort as
his profession of reliance on the Word alone seems to imply
and his critics have often assumed. His activity as a
propagandist was not confined to the controversial tract or
treatise in which he maintained an incessant warfare against
the enemy, or defended his position against the enemy's
counter-attacks. He is ever immersed in the task of
winning adherents, encouraging and guiding the efforts of a
growing band of fellow-workers whom his teaching has
inspired with an Apostolic fervour. He addresses missive
after missive to individuals, to churches, to Town Councils,
or other governing bodies. He takes the lead in constituting
churches on an evangelical basis and instituting a reformed
order of worship. He responds to constant appeals for help
and advice and befriends the refugees from the monasteries
or the ranks of the secular clergy who flock to Wittenberg,
and for whom he strives to find maintenance and a vocation.
He provides evangelical preachers for the churches that
apply to him from far and near. He appeals to the civil
authorities or to the Elector and other magnates on behalf
of persecuted brethren, and writes letters of comfort and
encouragement to the communities in Germany and the
Netherlands which are suffering for the faith. Through
Spalatin he constantly strives to influence the Elector to
adopt a more energetic policy on behalf of the Gospel,
whilst disclaiming any desire to compromise him in his cause
with the Emperor and the Regency. He complains again
and again that he is overwhelmed by his enormous correspondence in the effort to help and direct and encourage
what has become a national and even an international
movement.[14]

In addition to his own titanic activity, the movement
owed much to the co-operation of his colleagues at Wittenberg and to the scholars and theologians who became its
leaders in other universities and centres of enlightenment—
at Erfurt, Nürnberg, Basle, Strassburg, and elsewhere.
Foremost among these collaborators stood Melanchthon

---

[14] See, for instance, Enders, iv. 304, 328, etc.

who conferred on it the prestige of his rare humanist scholarship and systematised in his " Loci Communes " (December 1521) the fundamental doctrines and principles which Luther had enunciated and developed in his didactic and controversial writings in rather haphazard fashion. Based on his study of the Epistle to the Romans, on which he had lectured to his students during the session 1519-20, and divested of the conventional scholastic speculation, it conveyed to the theological student, and, in Spalatin's German translation, to the layman as well, a clear and succinct comprehension of the Gospel of God's grace according to Paul, and thus rendered a timely service to the Lutheran cause both as an exposition and a vindication of the new against the old theology. Its influence in furthering this cause was both profound and far-reaching. Within four years it passed through seventeen editions, besides several editions of Spalatin's translation.[15]

Equally potent was the influence of the students whom the fame of the Reformer had attracted to Wittenberg in increasing numbers during the previous half-dozen years. From Wittenberg went forth many an ardent young disciple to carry the Master's teaching over the length and breadth of the empire and to other lands as well. It had, too, gained many adherents among both the regular and secular clergy, and in these clerical recruits it found ready made a band of aggressive preachers. Very remarkable is the fact that a large proportion of them came from the monastic Orders. His doctrine of justification by faith found the readiest response among those who, like himself, had learned by experience to doubt the religious efficacy of the burdensome formalism of the monastic life. His own Order of the Augustinians furnished many enthusiastic recruits, such as Wencelaus Link, its Vicar-General, John Lang, the prior of the Erfurt monastery, Kaspar Güttel, prior of Eisleben, Gabriel Zwilling, its most popular preacher, the Netherlander, Jacob Probst, prior of Antwerp, and his successor, Heinrich Moller, otherwise known as Henry of Zutphen. From his own Order came, too, the first martyrs

<hr>

[15] For the origin and gradual shaping of the work, see Ellinger, " Melanchthon," 123 f. (1902).

of the Gospel in two young monks, who, in the summer of 1523, endured the flames for their evangelical convictions and whose heroism drew from Luther the first of his popular religious poems and an inspiring missive to the Christians of Holland, Flanders, and Brabant.[16]  The other Orders also contributed not a few missionary recruits. From the Franciscans came Eberlin, Brissmann, Myconius, Pellican, and Kempe ; from the Dominicans, Bucer and Blarer ; from others, Oecolampadius, Urbanus Rhegius, Otto Braunfels, Frosch. Equally remarkable the number of recruits from the secular clergy who preached the new Gospel and, where the pulpits of the parish churches were denied them, took to preaching in the open air—the church-yards or the market-places, under the protection, in some cases, of their armed parishioners. Laymen even took a part in this evangelistic work where the priests were hostile. " The Gospel," wrote Luther to Gerbel in May 1524, " takes its course ever farther and more widely, the more they try to prevent it." [17]

Unfortunately these clerical recruits were not always a credit or a benefit to the movement, and Luther at times was fain to confess that purely spiritual motives were far from being at the back of this secession from the old system. Too many of the emancipated monks " have given occasion to the adversary to blaspheme," through whom " Satan has cast an evil odour on the fragrance of our teaching," and who have embraced the Gospel " for the sake of the belly, the freedom of the flesh." [18]  The same is true of too many of the nuns and the secular priests, and his testimony is confirmed by that of Eberlin, Johann Hess, and others. The transition from the cloister to evangelical freedom too often meant, as Erasmus said, " freedom to live as they please." Such converts were, as Grisar remarks,[19] only too worthy products of the system that had nurtured them. Some of those who became preachers were ignorant ranters who repeated parrot-like Luther's teaching on faith and works, and whose shallow vehemence was but the thin veil of their lack of real knowledge and real moral earnestness.

---

[16] " Werke," xii. 73.

[17] Enders, iv. 334.

[18] *Ibid.*, iii. 323-324.

[19] " Luther," ii. 127-128.

Without a due sense of the limitations and obligations of freedom, which Luther as a rule emphasised, they were totally unfitted to be its true exponents.

In contrast to this discreditable element stands the able and cultured band of preachers to whom the proclamation of the Gospel is a divinely imposed vocation and to whose activity, next to that of Luther and his immediate associates, the astounding progress of the movement during the years 1521-24 was mainly due. As the result of this spontaneous and ever-widening missionary effort, it takes shape in the establishment of reformed congregations all over the empire, especially in the free cities of the south and the north. The process is everywhere more or less identical. The parish priest, an emancipated monk, an ardent layman, begins preaching the new Gospel and inveighs against the old doctrines and usages. The people usually welcome his message and become ardent partisans, in spite of the opposition of bishop and clergy.[20] This opposition excites the popular spirit which here and there breaks into tumult, as at Erfurt in 1521, Miltenberg in 1523, Augsburg in 1524, Stralsund in the same year. The popular restiveness necessitates the intervention of the civil authority, and this intervention, especially in the free cities, is usually on the side of the Reformers. The recurring friction between the civic and the ecclesiastical authorities, the hatred of a corrupt clergy, the keen impatience of ecclesiastical abuses which injuriously affect the material interest of the burghers, the influence (though only to a limited extent) of Hussite and Waldensian sectaries,[21] the spread of the new culture, of which Nürnberg and Augsburg were centres—all these factors predisposed the cities to welcome the evangelical preachers. Hence the remarkable results of the preaching

[20] For this early preaching in the cities, see the relative notices in Luther's " Briefwechsel," iii., iv., v. ; Ranke, " Deutsche Geschichte," ii. 65 f.; 1925 edition, ii. 51 f.; Bezold, " Geschichte der Deutschen Reformation," 381 f. ; Köstlin-Kawerau, i. 610 f.

[21] In the introduction to the Kirchenpostille of 1522, Luther refers to the existence of a Hussite congregation at Sangershausen, near Eisleben, by which, according to his enemies, he had been early corrupted. " Werke," x., Pt. I., 6-7.

of Zell, Bucer, and Capito at Strassburg, Blarer at Constance, Eberlin and Kettenbach at Ulm, Urbanus Rhegius and Frosch at Augsburg, Johann Hess at Breslau, Theobald Pellican at Nördlingen, Johann Brenz at Schwabischhall, Erhard Schnepf at Wimpffen, Michael Stiefel at Eislingen, Mirisch and Amsdorf at Magdeburg, Kempe at Hamburg, Henry of Zutphen and Jacob Probst at Bremen. In the far north-east, where the Teutonic knights held sway, the Bishop of Samland espoused the cause of Luther, who sent Brissmann and Paul Speratus to evangelise at his episcopal seat of Königsberg and elsewhere in Prussia. From Riga came a request for help in the extension of the Gospel in Livonia,[22] which was eager to renounce the kingdom of Antichrist, and erelong turned almost wholly Lutheran.[23] Albrecht of Brandenburg, Grandmaster of the Teutonic Order, himself ultimately accepted Luther's advice to marry and transform Prussia into a secular duchy,[24] though the main motive seems to have been personal and political rather than religious.[25] Thus within little more than three years after the proclamation of the imperial ban, the evangelical movement had found corporate expression in a large number of reformed congregations in the more important centres of civic and industrial life from the Lake of Constance to the Baltic.

Among the princely class there was as yet, on the other hand, little active and open response to the appeal of the new Gospel. The cautious old Elector continued for political reasons to follow the policy of official neutrality in the face of the Edict of Worms. His brother John and his nephew John Frederick were far more responsive,[26] though not free to contravene too openly the Elector's policy. Duke Henry of Mecklenburg asked for an evangelist,[27] and so did Duke Magnus of Saxe-Lauenburg,[28] whilst the Margrave George

[22] Enders, iv. 11-12. Luther's reply in " Werke," xii. 147 f.
[23] Ibid., iv. 270 ; cf. 296.
[24] Ibid., iv. 359.
[25] See the negotiations with Luther, Enders, iv. 40, 158, 285 f., 359, and Luther's own missive to the Teutonic Order, " Werke," xii. 228 f.
[26] See, for instance, Enders, iv. 356-357.
[27] Ibid., iv. 340.          [28] Ibid., iv. 145

of Brandenburg-Ansbach sent a request for instruction on the sacramental question and expressed his goodwill.[29] Duke Henry of Brunswick was also reported to be favourable, but the report erelong turned out to be fallacious. The same thing happened in the case of Duke Charles of Savoy, whilst Duke Karl of Münsterberg, though at first assuring Luther of his adhesion, erelong became an ardent opponent.[30]

Not a few of the higher nobility appear, in Luther's correspondence, as declared patrons of his cause, among them Counts Ludwig von Stollberg, George von Wertheim, Sebastian von Passun, Henry von Schwarzburg, Edzard von Ost Friesland, Albert von Mansfeld, Barth. von Stahremberg.[31] Whilst, under the influence of Hutten and Sickingen, a large number of the lesser nobility were professedly Lutheran, mainly from class and political motives, some of them, like Johann von Schwarzenberg and Hartmuth von Cronberg, were whole-hearted and active converts.[32] After the promulgation of the Edict of Worms, Cronberg gave up his imperial pension of 200 gulden,[33] and devoted himself to the task of vindicating Luther in a series of aggressive missives to the Emperor, the Pope, the Imperial Regency, and others.[34] Luther wrote him a warm appreciation in March 1522, in which he thanked God that he had found a disciple who, unlike too many others, not merely professed the Word of Christ, but had whole-heartedly received and actively championed it.[35] In Argula von Grumbach he found a feminine protagonist who wrote a spirited defence of his teaching to the University of Ingolstadt and to Duke William of Bavaria on behalf of a young Magister indicted for heresy.[36]

[29] Enders, iv. 58.       [30] *Ibid.*, iii. 408-410.

[31] "Werke," 52, 132 (Erlangen ed.); Enders, iii. 433; iv. 2 and 160; iv. 26; iv. 40; iv. 168; v. 10.

[32] For Schwarzenberg see Luther's letter to him, "Werke," 53, 151-155.

[33] Enders, iii. 149.

[34] Kuck, "Die Schriften Hartmuth's von Cronberg," in Niemeyer's "Neudrücke," Nos. 154-156 (1899); Walch, xv. 1955 f.

[35] "Werke," x., Pt. II., 53 f.

[36] Enders, iii. 397; iv. 279, 293-294. See also "Werke," xv. 110 f., for Luther's own denunciation of the intolerance of the university.

## II. THE TWO DIETS OF NÜRNBERG (1522-24)

Against this ever-widening movement the Pope and the Emperor were powerless to enforce the Edict of Worms. Luther's comparative moderation in opposing the radical party at Wittenberg after his return from the Wartburg had tended to conciliate the Imperial Regency and gained him the goodwill of the majority of the Diet, which assembled at Nürnberg in November 1522 and continued its session till the beginning of March 1523.[37]   To this Diet the new Pope, Hadrian VI., deputed Chieregati, Bishop of Tiramo, as Nuncio to offer the reform of practical abuses in return for the active repression of heresy.   Before his unexpected election as the successor of Leo X., Hadrian had been the tutor of Charles V. and professor of the scholastic theology at Louvain, Inquisitor-General and joint-administrator, with Cardinal Ximenes, of Spain, and latterly Vicar of the kingdom during the young Emperor's absence in Germany. As Inquisitor he had shown an inflexible zeal against heresy and an active sympathy with Ximenes' policy of practical reform, though, as a purely scholastic divine, he did not share the cardinal's enlightened interest in humanism.[38] This policy he ardently espoused as Pope in an energetic though vain effort to put down the corruption rampant in the Roman Curia and to effect a drastic practical reformation of the Church at large.   In an Instruction to the Nuncio, which was submitted to the Diet, he exposed and deplored with commendable frankness the prevailing degeneration of the Curia and the hierarchy, and promised an effective remedy.   But there must be no compromise with the heretic and his followers.   Luther has spread heresy and sedition throughout Germany, has striven, like Mahomet, to corrupt the minds and manners of the people, incited the princes to seize ecclesiastical property and stirred up civil war, has undermined all constituted authority, secular as well as ecclesiastical, on the pretext of vindicating evangelical

[37] " Deutsche Reichstagsakten," iii. 383 f.

[38] For Hadrian's career before he became Pope and the history of his short pontificate, see Pastor's " History of the Popes," ix. 34 f.

liberty, has attacked the faith of their fathers, condemned
them as heretics and consigned them to hell. Hadrian
denies that he has been condemned unheard, and, in
any case, in matters of faith no discussion is permissible.
In such matters he avers, in words that Luther himself
might have used, the Apostles, not the dialecticians are to
decide.   But for Hadrian the faith is not merely what the
Apostles have taught, but what in addition the Fathers and
Councils have decreed as articles of faith, and it was just this
that Luther had so strenuously denied.   He must, therefore,
share the fate of Hus if he will not renounce his heresy, and
the Edict of Worms must be promptly put in force against
him and his followers.[39]

In his exposure of the inveterate evils in the Curia and
the Church, the Pope had gone far to justify Luther's revolt,
and the majority of the Diet did not lose the opportunity
of reminding the Nuncio of the fact.   Moreover, he overlooked the fact that public opinion in Germany had advanced
a long way since Hus's day, and was in no mood to accept
the deliverance of even a reforming Pope as to what constituted heresy.   The evangelical preachers at Nürnberg
did not hesitate to proclaim this heresy from the pulpit,
despite the Nuncio's demand for their repression, and the
Town Council stoutly refused to arrest and imprison them,
and intimated its determination to defend them if need
be.[40]   The rising of Sickingen and the lesser nobility, professedly in the cause of Luther, emphasised in addition the
extreme risk of attempting to enforce the Edict.   In spite,
therefore, of the Nuncio's eloquence and the efforts of a
small minority, led by the Archduke Ferdinand, the Elector
Joachim of Brandenburg, and Duke George of Saxony,
the majority of the Diet resolved to refer the papal demands
to a couple of Committees.[41]   On the strength of their report,
which reveals the influence of Luther's friend, Johann von
Schwarzenberg, the Diet declared its inability to comply
with the demand (5th February 1523).   Whilst professing

[39] See the Instruction in " Reichstagsakten," iii. 393 f. ; *cf.* the
papal Brief directly addressed to the Diet, *ibid.*, iii. 399 f.
[40] *Ibid.*, iii. 410 f.                    [41] *Ibid.*, iii. 419 f.

reverence for the Pope and the Emperor, they were not
prepared to execute the Edict against Luther and his
followers.   In view of the strength of the Lutheran movement, any attempt to do so would be regarded as an attempt
to crush evangelical truth and strengthen the corruption
and abuses rampant in the Curia and the Church, of which
they submitted a formidable statement,[42] and without the
reform of which there could be no hope of peace or the
extirpation of the Lutheran heresy.   To this end, as well as
for the purpose of dealing with this heresy, they demanded
the convocation within a year of a free Christian Council
in some German city in which the laity should have a voice.
They would use their influence with the Elector of Saxony
to prevail on Luther and his followers to abstain meanwhile
from writing or publishing any controversial books in
Saxony.   Whilst refusing the demand of the Nuncio for
the punishment of the Lutheran preachers at Nürnberg,
they would endeavour that all preachers should abstain
from controversial preaching and limit themselves to the
preaching of the pure Gospel as contained in Scripture and
received by the Christian Church, on pain of fit punishment
for disobedience by the ecclesiastical authorities, on condition
that there should be no attempt to hinder and suppress the
preaching of evangelical truth.   They further undertook to
maintain a strict supervision of the press throughout the
empire, and authorised the punishment of married priests
and renegade monks and nuns by the ecclesiastical courts.[43]
This deliverance was issued by the Imperial Regency as a
mandate on the 6th March.[44]

This decision virtually amounted to a suspension of the
Edict of Worms and left the Lutheran movement to develop
meantime unhindered by any effective organised opposition.
It plainly revealed the conviction that it was too powerful
to be crushed at the Pope's fiat, and that any attempt by
either the Emperor or the Diet to do so would only lead to
a national uprising against Rome.   At the same time, it
made no secret of the fact that, in the view of the majority
of the Diet, the reform of practical abuses was more important

[42] " Reichstagsakten," iii. 645 f.          [44] Ibid., iii. 447.
[43] Ibid., iii. 435.

than the overthrow of Luther and his cause. " The doctrine of Luther," wrote the Archduke Ferdinand to his brother Charles on 27th January 1523, " has taken such deep root throughout the whole empire, that to-day among every 1,000 persons there is not one who is not to some extent touched by it." [45]

To Luther the refusal of the Diet to do the Pope's bidding was very gratifying.[46] The mandate embodying it was in due course forwarded by the Elector. In reply, whilst expressing his willingness to refrain from further controversy pending the assembly of a free Council, exonerating the Elector from all responsibility for his views, and disclaiming any intention to excite revolt by his writings, he could not undertake to keep silence under the attacks of a Faber and an Emser, and would not admit that the mandate deprived him of the right to defend evangelical truth.[47] In a communication to the Imperial Regency at the beginning of July he subjected the mandate itself to some criticisms, and whilst warmly recognising its moderate spirit, protested against the unfavourable interpretation put upon it by his opponents. He strongly objected to the tendency to identify the preaching of the Gospel in accordance with Scripture, as received by the Christian Church, with the teaching of the Roman Church, Aquinas, Scotus, and others of the schoolmen. " Preach the Gospel as Christ Himself has directed, and not as the scholastic theologians have devised," is for him the only safe standard to follow. He cannot, therefore, accept the nominees of the hierarchy as the arbiters of true Gospel preaching. Nor can he agree to desist from translating and printing the Word of God in the vernacular, nor, in view of the grave evils of the celibate life, approve

[45] " Reichstagsakten," iii. 911.

[46] Enders, iv. 96. Wittembergæ habemus decreta Nurmbergæ per imperii Proceres edita ad legationes papæ, mire libera et placentia, excusa autem habemus et latina et vernacula. He refers not to the mandate of the Regency embodying the decision of the Diet, which he had not yet received, but to the report of the Committees on which the decision was based.

[47] Letter to the Elector, " Werke," 53, 164-167 (Erlangen ed.), 29th March.

of any other punishment for married priests and emancipated monks and nuns than excommunication.[48]

Towards Pope Hadrian himself he is far less restrained. The papal Nuncio had brought a number of Briefs to Nürnberg, and one of these addressed to the Town Council of Bamberg came into his hands. In this missive the Pope denounced him and his teaching in very bitter and defamatory style. Luther responded by translating it into German, with short sarcastic notes, and addressing a brief letter to the reader in which he in turn spoke his mind freely about this obscurantist and sophistic product of Louvain University who wore the tiara, reminding him that the truth which the popes had so long suppressed by force would no longer be stifled by such abuse and impotent ravings.[49]

Less defensible was the concoction in which, jointly with Melanchthon, he exercised his ingenuity in expounding the significance of certain portents, which naturally in that superstitious age called for a providential interpretation, and applying them to the Papacy and its satellites. Two monstrosities were at his disposal. One, evidently of the modern sea-serpent type, with the head of an ass, the breasts and stomach of a woman, etc., had, it was believed, been fished out of the Tiber in 1496. Another, also in semi-human form, with a calf's head and something that looked like a monk's cowl, had been born in Freiberg in Saxony. An astronomer had seen in the Freiberg monster a presage of Luther.[50] To Luther, on the other hand, it was a representation of the monastic orders and a clear indication of the divine wrath against the papal-monastic deformation of Christianity. Similarly, Melanchthon saw in the Tiber monster an embodiment of the Pope, and the result of their joint lucubration was the " Interpretation of the Pope-Ass found at Rome and the Monks Calf at Freiberg." [51] The ass's head on a human body, gravely expounds

---

[48] " Werke," xii. 63 f.  Wider die Verkehrer und Fälscher kaiser-lichsmandats.

[49] *Ibid.*, xi. 342 f. ;  Walch, xv. 2652 f.

[50] Enders, iv. 57-58, 67.

[51] " Werke," xi. 375 f., March 1523 ;  *cf.* Enders, iv. 64.

Melanchthon, signifies the human foundation of the Papacy
on which the Pope's power rests. "For as an ass's head ill
fits a human body, so little fitting is it that the Pope should
be head of the Church." And so forth in detailed fashion
in regard to the other features of this monstrosity. Luther
is equally ingenious and equally outrageous in expounding
the distinctive features of the other monster as a providential
indication of the abominations of the Roman Antichrist
and his satellites, the monks. It was really too grotesque
a persiflage of the Papacy as represented by a man of the
high character and reforming though narrow zeal of a
Hadrian at all events. But it suited the taste of the age,
if it did not reflect credit on that of either Luther or
Melanchthon, and the concoction instantly leaped into
many editions. At the same time, it should not be forgotten
that the worst revilers of the memory of this exemplary
Pope were the brood of self-seekers who haunted the Curia.[52]

Hadrian's successor, the papal Vice-Chancellor, Giulio di
Medici, who took the title of Clement VII., renewed the
attempt to enforce the Edict of Worms, through his Legate,
Cardinal Campeggio, at a second Diet which assembled
in the same city [53] in the following January-April 1524. It
met with little real success. Public opinion was too hostile
to Rome to admit of any organised and effective effort
to crush the Lutheran movement. It is significant of the
attitude of the people that, on his official entry into Augsburg,
the citizens jeered at the Legate's benediction,[54] and that
he was fain to dispense with this formality on his arrival
at Nürnberg itself and straightway ride to his lodging.[55]
In spite of his presence the sacrament was celebrated in
both kinds by the evangelical preachers to nearly 4,000
participants, among them being several members of the
Imperial Regency, whilst even the Emperor's sister, Isabella,
the ex-Queen of Denmark, partook in the same manner

---

[52] See, for the attitude of its members, Pastor, "Hist. of the Popes,"
ix. 222 f.

[53] Lindsay mistakenly makes the Diet meet at Spires, "Hist. of
the Reformation," i. 322.

[54] "Reichstagsakten," iv. 137-138.

[55] *Ibid.*, iv. 142.

in the castle chapel.[56] The majority of the Estates, indeed, in spite of the opposition of the representatives of the cities, formally undertook to observe and fulfil the Edict " as far as it was possible," and to repress objectionable literature. But they renewed the demand for a free General Council in Germany and decreed that, pending its convocation, a national German assembly should convene in November at Spires to discuss what was acceptable and what was objectionable in Luther's teaching, and draw up a statement on the subject to be submitted to the Council. Meanwhile, the Gospel should be preached without controversy in accordance with the interpretation of the doctors acknowledged by the Church (18th April).[57] While approving their declared intention to enforce the Edict, Campeggio objected to the proposed General Council and the preliminary national assembly, without succeeding in altering the Diet's resolution.[58] The Pope shared the Legate's objection, and at his instigation the Emperor issued an Edict on the 15th July requiring the Estates to put in force that of Worms, condemning their interference with the prerogative of the Pope in the matter of a Council, peremptorily forbidding the proposed assembly at Spires, and denouncing Luther as a greater enemy of the faith than Mahomet.[59]

It was, however, too late in the day to attempt to repress what had become a national movement by the absolute fiat of the Pope, or the Emperor, or even the Diet. Luther had become too potent a force to be treated with the contempt and the obloquy which those in the seats of the mighty still thought good enough for a foolhardy and rebellious monk. The Emperor was, in fact, too deeply immersed in the toils of international complications to do more than issue impotent commands and threats. In any case, Luther was as little disposed as ever to take his orders in the cause of the Gospel from Pope, Emperor, or Diet.

[56] Ranke, " Deutsche Geschichte," ii. 139-140; ii. 105-106 (1925 ed.); Bezold, " Geschichte der Deutschen Reformation," 439.
[57] " Reichstagsakten," iv. 603-605, in German. A Latin version is given by Balan, " Monumenta Reformationis Lutheranæ," 320 f.
[58] Balan, 332.
[59] Walch, xv. 2705 f.

He was, in fact, at first not very anxious about the doings of the Diet. He knew the ways of Satan too well, he said, to worry over them.[60] The actual decision, which in reality did not mean very much, seemed, however, in comparison with that of March 1523, to be a serious blow to the Gospel, and he gave unstinted vent to his wrath in a scathing criticism.[61] He angrily points out at the outset the inconsistency of the mandate of " these drunken and mad notables " who have agreed to carry out the Edict of Worms against an outlawed heretic, and yet propose to consider and decide at Spires what is good and bad in his teaching. With daring defiance and prophetic fervour he then arraigns the blindness, the presumption, the stupidity of these misguided notables, and finishes with an angry outburst against the Emperor and other rulers. " Well, then, we Germans must remain Germans and Pope's asses. It is no use complaining, teaching, praying, and entreating. Even our daily experience of extortion and oppression has no effect. Now, my dear princes and gentlemen, you make haste to deliver my poor person to death, and when you have succeeded you imagine that you will have triumphed. If, however, you had ears to hear, I would tell you something that would startle you. How would it be if Luther's life has so much value in God's sight that, even if he were gone, not one of you would any longer be sure of his life and authority, and that his death would be the undoing of every one of you ? Go, then, merrily on ; throttle and burn. I will not give way if God wills it. Here I am. But I ask you in friendly fashion to beware lest when you have put me to death, you do not call me to life again and have to put me to death a second time. God has not granted me to have to deal with reasonable men, but with German beasts who would tear me in pieces like wolves and bears. I will at all events remind every one who believes that there is a God to refrain from putting in force this mandate. Although God has given me the grace not to fear death,

---

[60] Enders, iv. 295.

[61] " Werke," xv. 254 f. Zwei uneinige und Widerwärtige Gebote den Luther betreffend, Aug. 1524. He first gives the Edict of Worms and then the mandate based on the decision of the Diet of Nürnberg.

as I formerly did, and will help me to die willingly, they shall not bring it about before God wills it, rage and curse as much as they please. For He, who has into the third year preserved me against their will and beyond all my expectation, can keep me in safety still longer, although I have no great desire to live. And even if they kill me, it will be such a death as neither they nor their children will overcome. Of this I give them due warning. But what does it help. God has blinded and hardened them. Nevertheless, I beseech you all, dear lords and gentlemen, gracious and ungracious, for God's sake to have God before your eyes and handle this matter in a different fashion. A great calamity is at your door. God's wrath has begun to move and you shall not escape if you persist in so acting. What will ye, my dear lords ? God is too clever for you. He will soon make fools of you. He is also too mighty and will erelong destroy you. Have a little fear of His wisdom and ask yourselves whether He has not put such thoughts and lack of grace in your hearts in order that you may experience what He is wont to do with great lords like Pharaoh. One part of His song is, ' God has cast down the mighty from their seats.' *Deposuit potentes de sede.*" [62]

As for that poor mortal " maggot sack," the Emperor, who imagines himself to be the true supreme protector of the Christian faith, does not the Scripture say that Christian faith is a rock, a divine force stronger than the devil, death, and every other power ? And such a force shall need the protection of a creature of death whom the scab or the smallpox can to-morrow throw on a sick bed ! God help us ! What a senseless world we live in ! So with Henry VIII., the King of Hungary, and all other would-be defenders of the Christian faith. Let all pious Christians join with him in commiserating such mad, foolish, senseless, raging, insane fools ! [63]

This is a sample of how Luther in his wrath can stand up to his foes, even those of them who wear an imperial or a royal crown. He smites them with that terrible pen of his with the blast of God's wrath, before which all their armed

---

[62] " Werke," xv. 254-255.        [63] *Ibid.*, xv. 278.

omnipotence is only next door to death. Though the apostrophe in his rough Saxon to the Emperor is rather shocking to a delicate ear, one can hardly help thinking of "Imperial Cæsar dead and turned to clay," or wondering whether William Shakespeare might not have borrowed something from Martin Luther.

If Campeggio failed to persuade the Diet to adopt a more aggressive policy against the evangelical movement, he succeeded in sowing the seeds of a reaction against it. At his instigation the Archduke Ferdinand, the Dukes of Bavaria, the Archbishop of Salzburg, and a number of other South German bishops convened under his auspices [64] at Regensburg at the end of June 1524 to consider and decide on expedients for the defence of the Church and the reform of ecclesiastical abuses.[65] The zeal of the Archduke and the Bavarian Dukes was quickened by the concession of a tax on the ecclesiastical revenues of their respective territories.[66] The fruit of the conference was the outbreak of persecution in Austria and Bavaria,[67] whilst the Pope urged the Emperor to deprive the Saxon Elector of his dignity, and place the Lutheran cities under the ban.[68] The meeting at Regensburg proved, in fact, the beginning of the disruption of Germany into two organised religious parties. A reformed national Church on evangelical lines was henceforth an impossibility. Nothing came either of the national assembly at Spires or the General Council. The Emperor, at the instigation of Ferdinand, negatived the former project, whilst a number of the cities, in a convention at Spires in July and at Ulm in December, undertook to render mutual assistance against any attempt to put in force the Edict of Worms.[69]

[64] Balan, " Monumenta," 328, 361 f.
[65] Ranke, " Deutsche Geschichte," ii. 145 f.; ii. 120 f. (1925 ed.); Janssen, " Hist. of the German People," iv. 44-47, Eng. trans.
[66] Enders, v. 14.
[67] Ranke, ii. 170-174; ii. 129 f. (1925 ed.).
[68] Bezold, " Geschichte der Deutschen Reformation," 442-443.
[69] Ranke, ii. 175; ii. 133 (1925 ed.); Bezold, 442; Janssen, iv. 58-60.

# CHAPTER VI

## LUTHER AND THE REVOLUTIONARY MOVEMENT

### I. Luther, Hutten, and Sickingen

THE rapid growth of the Lutheran movement during the years 1521-24 was not due solely to the preaching of the Word. Luther's revolt against the Papacy on national as well as religious grounds was fitted to appeal to national sentiment. National sentiment might not be very strong in an empire which was rather a confederation of petty states than an organic unit, and in which the central Government, in virtue of the growth of the princely power, was notoriously ineffective. "The Holy Roman Empire of the German nation" was, in the words of Voltaire, neither Holy, nor Roman, nor Empire. The national State in the modern sense was, even beyond the borders of Germany, only in the making. In theory the empire embodied, in fact, the conception of the universal not the national State. It was the political counterpart of the universal Church, and was thus ill-fitted to develop a strong national consciousness. But it had been associated with Germany and its history for over 700 years, and was invested with a prestige that contributed to preserve the sense of a common nationality from the Vosges to the Vistula, from the Baltic to the Alps. Even if this sense of a common nationality was weakened by the particularism, the dissension to which the mediæval constitution gave scope, the empire was sufficiently homogeneous to respond to an appeal against an alien ecclesiastical régime, which was generally felt to be detrimental to the commonweal. The corruption and extortion of Rome constituted a grievance affecting the general welfare, which had found expression in the "Gravamina of the German Nation," and for which redress had been demanded in

Diet after Diet. In view of the material evils which more or less affected all classes, Luther's arraignment of the Papacy had excited throughout the empire a keen and sympathetic interest,[1] which the purely theological element in the indictment would hardly have aroused. The majority of the Estates at the Diet of Worms, for instance, whilst professing acquiescence in the papal condemnation of his teaching, had very significantly reserved the errors and evils of a more practical character, the redress of which they agreed with the national Reformer in demanding. The princes and the nobility, high and low, might be ready enough to profit from these abuses in providing Church preferment for their needy dependents. They none the less resented the greed and corruption of the Roman Curia, which drained so large a portion of German wealth Rome-wards in the form of papal dues and exactions. Their resentment was shared by even the clerical order, which was also the victim of Roman rapacity. In as far as the Lutheran movement gave expression to this resentment, it struck a truly national chord. In the face of this fact it erelong appeared that the Emperor and the small papal minority had gained only a Pyrrhic victory at Worms. The national opposition to an alien and oppressive régime had rendered the Edict practically a dead letter. It was really a work of supererogation to incarcerate Luther in the Wartburg. To enforce the Edict would have been to conjure a civil war, if not a revolution.

As it was, the anti-Roman spirit was erelong to find vent in an appeal to force to bring about a new order of things in the State, the Church, and Society. Among a section of the lesser nobility, the poorer element in the town population, and the mass of the peasants, in South Germany in particular, there was deep-rooted discontent with the old order. Hence the existence of a widespread movement on behalf of political and social as well as ecclesiastical reform. In Franconia and the Middle Rhine region the lesser nobility resented the growing power of the territorial magnates, ecclesiastical and

---

[1] On the participation of all classes in the demand for the reform of ecclesiastical abuses for which the Papacy was responsible, see Below, " Ursachen der Reformation," 35 f.

secular, and envied the prosperity of the middle class of the towns which had acquired affluence and political influence as the result of a thriving industry and commerce. They were a lawless, degenerate survival of the feudal age which cherished the pride and arrogance of the feudal caste without the power which, in palmier days, they had exercised under the old feudal system. They arrogated to themselves the right to maintain a predatory warfare on the commerce of the cities. They held in contempt the higher clergy, on whose wealth, to which their ancestors had materially contributed, they cast longing eyes.[2] In the towns the working class, whether organised in the artisan gilds or not, was seething with discontent and striving to better its lot in antagonism to the upper class, which usually absorbed the municipal government and exercised it largely in its own interest. Among the peasantry the movement on behalf of social emancipation, which had periodically found expression in spasmodic risings during the previous half century, had been quickened by Luther's evangelical teaching and was ripe for a final reckoning with the feudal social system.

Characteristic of this complex revolutionary tendency was the anti-papal and anti-clerical spirit which saw in a radical, practical reformation of the Church an indispensable condition of the redress of both social and political grievances. In this sense the movement was pro-Lutheran and assumed a more or less religious aspect. *Nolens volens* Luther had become the prophet of a social and political as well as a religious revolution. Without sharing the revolutionary aspiration as far as it concerned the redress of political and social grievances, he had foreseen the coming cataclysm and had again and again warned the ruling classes of its imminence.

The cause of the nobility found its literary champion in Ulrich von Hutten, its would-be vindicator in Franz von Sickingen. Hutten had anticipated Luther as a national

---

[2] Below minimises their degeneration (" Ursachen der Reformation," 62-64), and it seems that it cannot be maintained of the lower nobility as a class. See also Lenz's criticism of Lamprecht's " Deutsche Geschichte," " Historische Zeitschrift," 1896, 406-408. At the same time, as Kalkoff points out (" Hutten und die Reformation," 126 f.), the evil was more widespread than Below and Lenz assert.

reformer in a series of effusions in dialogue and verse between 1517 and 1520, in which he had exposed and denounced the corruption and tyranny of the Pope and the hierarchy, and demanded a radical reformation. The main motive of his reform programme was political, not religious. The impulse to a purely national reformation came from a humanist not a religious source. Hutten will vindicate the imperial sovereignty and the national independence from an alien ecclesiastical jurisdiction and will make an end of the rampant abuses in the Church in the interest of the commonweal, and more particularly, if not professedly, of his own order of the lesser nobility. His programme of ecclesiastical reform was not new. It does little more than re-echo the demands which had found expression through the press and the Diet, and Luther owed little, if anything, to his inspiration in his championship of these demands. It owed its vogue to the patriotic verve, the literary felicity with which he played his part as a reforming publicist, at first in the language of the humanists and later in the vernacular. It also owed something to the religious note which, under Luther's influence, he ultimately blended with his appeal for reform on national lines. If his influence on Luther has been greatly overrated, there can be no doubt about Luther's influence on him in this respect. After the Leipzig Disputation he saw in Luther the leader of a national revolt against Rome and adapted his appeal accordingly. In his " Complaint and Admonition against the Power of the Pope " (1520), he ranges himself alongside the Wittenberg Reformer, and even Hus against the Pope and the hierarchy,[3] and professes the Lutheran conception of the Church and the supreme authority of the Word. In the " Exhortation to the Free and Imperial Cities " (1522), he appears as the defender of his cause against the princes.[4] But this profession of zeal for the Gospel according to Luther was little more than skin deep, and his ill-regulated life as a humanist of the adventurer type was hardly fitted to make him a credit to the evangelical movement. We miss in his flamboyant polemic against Rome and the hierarchy the note of passionate and perfervid

---

[3] " Opera," iii. 506-507, 517.          [4] Ibid., iii. 536.

religious conviction which made Luther the prophet of a new epoch in religion. He adopts the current evangelical phraseology. In reality he is interested only in the political aspect of the Lutheran movement as a means of vindicating the national freedom from Rome and, at the same time, furthering the interest of his own class. As a publicist, he was quick to see and take advantage of its political implications as he conceived them, and to render it the lip service of the politician. In any case, the recourse to violent methods in order to attain the end in view was incompatible with Luther's conception of a reform by means of the Word, and his problematic, impulsive, and reckless polemic did not tend to inspire confidence in his capacity as a leader in the cause of even national reform. He is the type of the aristocratic hotspur, the militant *Reichsritter* as well as the enthusiastic votary of the new culture. He will, indeed, reform both Church and State by means of the constituted secular authority, as Luther was also prepared to do. In the " Complaint and Admonition " he calls on the Emperor and the Estates to take in hand the cause of the oppressed Fatherland and the truth of God in the war against Roman superstition and error, ecclesiastical corruption and exaction.[5] If reform can be achieved by peaceful means, good and well. But if not, force must be used, even unto bloodshed, against the whole clerical order as the common enemy. Nothing less than an armed rising against the Pope, the clergy, and the monks will avail,[6] though he would exempt the more reputable clerics from violence, and if the Emperor and the Estates will not unite in this crusade, the nobility and the towns shall not hesitate to strike for God, the Fatherland, and the truth.

> " Now's the time to take in hand
>   The cause of freedom at God's command." [7]

> " Now then, ye pious Germans, now,
>   Much armour have we and much horse,
>   Halberds enough and also swords.
>   Should friendly warning not avail,
>   To these will we then have resort." [8]

---

[5] "Opera," iii. 504-505, 522-523.  [7] *Ibid.*, iii. 506.
[6] *Ibid.*, iii. 523.  [8] *Ibid.*, iii. 525.

This, in the last resort, is the method of the robber-knight in the guise of the national reformer. It was not the method that appealed to Luther, who flatly refused to identify his cause with this revolutionary violence. Though he had used very incendiary language in his reply to Prierias and in the "Address to the Nobility," he had never contemplated an irresponsible rising, and had summarily rejected the idea of a war against the clergy in his letter to Spalatin in January 1521. His conception of a national Reformation was one undertaken by the Diet, acting deliberately in the general interest in virtue of its constitutional powers and its obligation, as a Christian institution, to repress evil and maintain the common good. Otherwise, the Word of God, not the sword of the *Reichsritter*, is the only weapon he will use in behalf of the Gospel.

Moreover, Hutten's summons to a war against the Church was, in part at least, motived by class interest. He is the enemy not only of Rome but of the territorial magnate. In the "Exhortation to the Free and Imperial Cities" the crusade on behalf of a national Reformation becomes a revolt of the towns, in alliance with the nobility, against the princes, secular and ecclesiastical, who are a set of tyrants and usurpers of the rights of the nobles and burghers.

> "The poor nobility they devour,
>     The towns of freedom to deprive,
>   They daily strive with all their power." [9]

From these tyrants and usurpers and their artful jurist advisers, justice cannot be had. They make the Imperial Regency their catspaw, appropriate the powers of the Emperor, and strive to crush Dr Luther and the Gospel. The only remedy lies in the union of the knights and the towns to vindicate the old rights and liberties and stem this unconstitutional princely usurpation at their expense. There was no little force, from the constitutional point of view, in this indictment of the growing power of the territorial magnates and of the misuse of their power for their own aggrandisement. As we have seen, Luther, as well as Hutten, is found on occasion denouncing their misgovern-

[9] "Opera," iii. 529.

ment.  But the idea of a union of the lesser nobility and the towns for this purpose was, in view of their inveterate antagonism, too visionary to be taken seriously.  The towns had suffered too much from the predatory lawlessness of the robber-knight to see in this class the vindicators of their constitutional rights and their interests against the princes.  Moreover, Luther was too conscious of his indebtedness to the territorial magnate, in the person of the Elector of Saxony, to countenance such a fantastic scheme, even if Hutten was ready to except the " pious princes " from its operation.[10]  Besides, the régime of the territorial magnate, however self-seeking, was at least a check on the egoism and lawlessness of the class to which Hutten belonged. It stood for law and order within the princely territory, if it tended to weaken the central imperial Government and the empire as an international force.[11]

The leader behind whom the nobility and the towns should range themselves against the princes and in behalf of Luther and ecclesiastical reform was Franz von Sickingen. Like Hutten himself, and with still less reason, Sickingen has been idealised by his modern admirers into the ardent champion of German nationalism against its enemies, both internal and external.  Facts do not tend to confirm this idealist acceptation of the man and his aspirations. He is primarily the type of the freebooting *Reichsritter* on the grand scale — a combination of the robber-knight and the military adventurer who, by a series of successful military exploits, had acquired affluence and invested his name with a widespread prestige.  By the time that Luther had begun his crusade against Antichrist he had, in fact,

---

[10] " Opera," iii. 529.

[11] The older conception of Hutten as a national hero and a co-worker with Luther in the cause of religious reform, which found classic expression in the work of Strauss (1858, revised ed., 1871) and in vol. vii. of Strauss's works, edited by Zeller (1877), has been greatly modified by more recent research.  Though this conception found supporters in Szamatolski, " Hutten's Deutsche Schriften," " Quellen und Forschungen zur Sprach und Culturgeschichte," Heft 67 (1891), and others, it has been subjected to a trenchant examination and criticism by Kalkoff, " Ulrich v. Hutten und die Reformation " (1920), and Hutten's " Vagantenzeit und Untergang " (1925).

become a force to be reckoned with in the imperial and princely chancellories, and even in those of foreign rulers. But his exploits as a German *condottiere* constitute a rather meagre foundation for the hero worship that later transformed him into a statesman of far-reaching vision, a leader in the cause of national regeneration and religious independence of Rome. Seen through the critical microscope of recent research, he does not seem to have risen much, if at all, above the level of the enterprising military adventurer who might shine in a freebooting raid, but had no real military capacity, let alone political genius. Certain it is that he proved a failure as the leader of the campaign on the Meuse against France, with which the Emperor entrusted him in the summer of 1521, and that the last of his raids against the Elector-Archbishop of Trier in the following year proved a fiasco and brought his meteoric career to a sudden and tragic conclusion.[12]

Through Hutten, Sickingen had been made acquainted with Luther's struggle with Rome, and in June 1520 he had offered him a refuge in the Ebernburg.[13] Luther had no desire to exchange the patronage of the Elector of Saxony for that of the redoubtable *condottiere*. But at the Elector's instigation he wrote him a couple of letters (29th June, 31st August) requesting him to use his influence with the Emperor in his behalf.[14] The request was seconded by Spalatin's personal intercession (November 1520), and Sickingen, who was then at Cologne in attendance on the Emperor, readily undertook to present his " Erbieten " and accompanying letter to the young monarch, whose favour he had earned by a loan of 20,000 gulden.[15] In April 1521 he attempted to deflect him from his resolution to enter Worms by the renewed offer of a refuge in the Ebernburg. The offer, as we have seen, was merely a

---

[12] The more idealist conception of Sickingen as a national hero is represented by Ulmann, " Franz von Sickingen " (1872). The more critical attitude is taken by Boos, " Franz v. Sickingen und die Stadt Worms," " Zeitschrift für die Geschichte des Oberrheins," Neue Folge, iii. (1888), and especially by Kalkoff in his two recent works on Hutten.

[13] Enders, ii. 410.

[14] *Ibid.*, ii. 426, 471.                    [15] Ulmann, 163.

manœuvre on the part of Luther's enemies to prevent him from appearing before the Diet, and Luther was shrewd enough not to fall into the trap. He does not, however, appear to have suspected the good faith of his would-be protector, and on the 1st June he dedicated to him from his " Patmos " in the Wartburg his work on " Confession," in recognition of the great comfort and help he had experienced at his hands.[16] He addresses him, moreover, as his " special lord and patron." In view of his career as a lawless marauder the designation can hardly be said to have been well chosen. In his feud against Worms, for instance, he had applied without stint in the neighbouring region the barbarous method of forcing a capitulation by every species of outrage and wanton cruelty. Luther must have known of the rough deeds of the ferocious filibuster whom he addresses so respectfully and appreciatively, and even if such ferocity was an all too common feature of the brutal warfare of the period, it does seem a stretch of Christian charity to recognise in the lawless freebooter a patron of the Gospel, even though he was now the commissioned leader of a mercenary army against the Emperor's enemy. It may be said in exculpation of this myopic view that to the solitary seer in the Wartburg, oppressed by the impotence of exile, the strong man of the Ebernburg who, under Hutten's tutelage, was glibly professing allegiance to the Word of God as interpreted by Dr Luther, might at least be destined to be the agent of God's judgments against the enemies of the Gospel—" the ecclesiastical junkers and tyrants " who are striving to crush him and the truth of God, and who in their blindness are courting their own destruction. This is the contingency which Luther foreshadows in the dedicatory letter if these blind tyrants, who have rejected all his pleas and efforts for a reformation by discussion and reason, continue in their infatuated policy of suppressing the truth by force. They are heading straightway for disaster, and if they will not betimes change their mad course, some one else will teach them their folly, " not like Luther by letters and words, but by deeds."

[16] " Werke," viii. 138-140.

He does not say that this is his method, which is expressly
that of proclaiming the truth.  He had, in fact, promptly
rejected Hutten's plan of an anti-clerical war, and there is
no reason to suppose that he was deliberately inciting
Sickingen to undertake such a war.  The dedication is, in
truth, directed rather to the enemies of the Gospel than to
Sickingen.  It is sent forth as a warning to beware of the
consequences of the policy of persecution on behalf of a
doomed system of corruption and falsehood, which will
infallibly lead to violence and revolution.

In view of the growing restiveness which he had observed
during his furtive journey to and from Wittenberg in December
1521, Luther deemed it advisable to restrain the aggressive
revolutionary spirit which the reform movement, under the
influence of Hutten and other professed adherents, was
tending to develop.  Hence the emphasis in the " Exhortation against Tumult and Revolt " on the obligation
of all Christians to leave the reform of religion to the secular
power and the operation of the Word.  This caveat against
revolutionary violence entirely failed to deflect the hotspur
Hutten, against whom, according to Kalkoff,[17] it was
particularly directed, from his plan of a league of the
nobility and the towns against prince and priest.

After the failure of the expedition on the Meuse, Sickingen
was in a mood to try his fortune in any desperate adventure
on his own accord.  An assembly of the Upper Rhenish
nobility at Landau on the 13th August 1522 elected him
Captain-General of their league to vindicate the rights and
privileges of their order.[18]  Though the towns stood aloof

[17] Kalkoff assumes that in writing the " Exhortation " he had in mind
the " Neukarsthans " with its appended thirty articles, in which Luther
saw the hand of Hutten (Hutten's " Vagantenzeit," 310).  If so, he
was mistaken.  The author of the " Neukarsthans " was, according to
Kalkoff, Bucer, not Hutten, and represents Sickingen as counselling
Karsthans to observe moderation and justice in carrying out the proposed
Reformation.  This rather militates against Kalkoff's assumption that
the " Exhortation " was primarily a counterblast to the " Neukarsthans,"
rather than to the unrest among the peasants, though the thirty articles
appended to it by the Strassburg printer, Schott, were certainly violent
enough and might well excite Luther's apprehension, if he had read them.

[18] Ulmann, 250 f.

from this combination in spite of Hutten's specious appeal to their self-interest, Sickingen took advantage of the situation to carry out a predatory raid against the Archbishop-Elector of Trier, against whom he had a personal grievance, and whose territory offered a rich booty.   Hence the declaration of war which he hurled from the Ebernburg against him as an enemy of God, the Emperor, and the empire.[19]   The archbishop's delinquency as an enemy of God seems to refer to his treatment of Luther at Worms.   In reality the motive of the expedition was the freebooting instinct of the robber-knight, and the attempt of Kettenbach, Hartmuth von Cronberg, and other zealous Lutherans to magnify it into a crusade " against the unchristian yoke of the priesthood on behalf of evangelical freedom," as Kettenbach phrased it in his manifesto in Sickingen's name, is purely an idealising distortion of the reality.   With Luther and his cause the expedition had precious little to do, except in the make-believe of such visionary partisans, whom Luther himself had denounced beforehand.[20]   Instead of inaugurating a revolution, the raid speedily proved a fiasco.   Richard von Greiffenklau defended the walls of Trier against the raiders so stoutly that Sickingen was fain to retire baffled in the middle of September, to be in turn besieged in his castle of Landstuhl by the archbishop and his allies, the Elector Palatine and the Landgrave of Hesse, and mortally wounded (30th April 1523) whilst standing in the breach of its walls with his face to the foe.   His premature death, the flight of Hutten to Switzerland, and the expedition of the Suabian League against the Franconian nobility gave the quietus to a movement which, even if it had succeeded, would not have inaugurated the millennium in Church and State.   " Even at that time," judges Ranke, " it was perceived that if the power of the princes was overthrown and the constitution

---

[19] Ulmann, 283-284.

[20] Kettenbach's manifesto was, in fact, composed after Sickingen's death, Kalkoff, " Vagantenzeit," 320 f.   The older accounts of Ranke, Bezold, and others are written too much under the influence of the assumption that Sickingen was the evangelical champion that these enthusiasts represent.   They should be compared with Kalkoff's critical treatment of the subject.

of the empire broken up, nothing was to be expected but an exclusive, violent, and, at the same time, self-conflicting rule of the nobles."[21]   In the case of poor Hutten the abortive rising had certainly not been a success.  He, too, shortly afterwards ended his stormy career at the age of thirty-four, the victim of an ill-regulated life and an ill-conceived political programme, which he had neither the means nor the capacity to bring to fruition.  " He left," pathetically says Zwingli, who befriended him in his forlorn condition, " nothing of any value.  He had neither books, nor furniture, nothing but a pen."[22]

" This affair will have a very bad ending," wrote Luther on hearing the news of Sickingen's adventure.[23]   " God is a just but a wonderful judge," was his comment on hearing of his death.[24]   His opponents regarded him as Luther's ally, and Luther himself as the instigator of his attack on a great ecclesiastical potentate.  " That devil of a monk and Franz von Sickingen are one and the same thing," wrote Duke George's representative at Nürnberg.[25]   " The anti-emperor has fallen ;  the anti-pope must soon follow," boasted the Romanists.[26]   Both the implication and the prognostication were unfounded.  Whilst warning his enemies of the danger to themselves of the policy of persecution, and telling them that they will deserve the fate they are courting, Luther had plainly enough condemned the propagation of his cause by lawless force six months before Sickingen started his rash enterprise.  True, he himself in his angry moods had used very fiery language in denunciation of the prelates in his philippic against the falsely named Order of Bishops (July 1522).  It is, he urged, the duty of every Christian to maintain God's Word and ordinance and to sacrifice body, life, goods, honour, and friends, and all things to overthrow the devil's order, or if they cannot do so, to shun and flee from it.  All who thus

[21] " Deutsche Geschichte," ii. 76; ii. 83 (1925 ed.).

[22] See Mackinnon's " History of Modern Liberty," ii. 67.

[23] Enders, iv. 40.                    [24] *Ibid.*, iv. 143.

[25] " Deutsche Reichstagsakten," iii. 880; Gess, " Akten und Briefe zur Kirchenpolitik Herzog Georgs," i. 401 (1905).

[26] Ulmann, 386.

strive to overthrow the bishop's ungodly rule are God's children and true Christians, whereas all who support it and are willingly subject to it are the devil's servants and strive against God's ordinance and law.[27] This does sound like an incitement to violence. But this explosion was not in reality so revolutionary as it sounds, and was not meant to incite the people to rise in arms against the bishops and the clergy. It was the excited prelude to his Bull of Reformation which contemplates no more than the exercise of the right of the Christian congregation in every town to elect an evangelical preacher on the Pauline model, and forswear obedience to the episcopal rule which is striving to crush the Gospel to the destruction of souls.[28] It was certainly not intended to be an apology for the lawless enterprise of Sickingen. At the same time, it must be admitted that Luther did not always weigh the possible implication of such violent language, or realise the effect of such an outburst in an atmosphere charged with the electricity of political and social as well as religious revolution.

It was in the midst of this upheaval that he sent forth the work in which he discussed the civil power and its claim to the allegiance of the subject.[29] It was the systematic presentation of the thoughts contained in a couple of sermons preached at Weimar in October 1522,[30] and was dedicated to the Elector's brother, Duke John. His attitude to the question is conditioned by that of the princes towards the evangelical movement, and he disclaims any desire to intrude into the purely political sphere. He writes as a theologian, not as a political philosopher, and tends to evaluate the government of the rulers according as they are friendly or hostile to the Gospel as he interprets it. He had, he reminds them, appealed to them in the " Address to the Nobility " to take up the cause of Reformation. The outcome of this appeal, in which he had recognised their right to undertake this task, had been the Edict of Worms

[27] " Werke," x., Pt. II., 139-140.    [28] *Ibid.*, x., Pt. II., 144.
[29] Von Weltlicher Obirkeit, wie weit man ihr Gehorsam Schuldig sei,  March 1523, " Werke," xi. 245 f.
[30] Enders, iv. 22.

against him and his adherents, which was based on the
assumption that they were entitled to lord it over the faith
and conscience of their subjects, and that their subjects were
bound to obey their decisions in spiritual things.[31]　This
assumption he now emphatically denies, and he, who had
not feared to brave the Pope, cares not if he excites their
wrath in plainly telling them so.　The civil power is, indeed,
divinely ordained.　Princes rule by divine right and their
subjects are bound to render obedience to their absolute
rule in things secular.　Luther is no democrat like Zwingli,
and leaves no room for individual self-assertion under the
political constitution which he adduces from the Bible.
If all the members of the State were true Christians, the
sword of the ruler would be superfluous, since all would
mould their actions in accordance with the divine will, and
injustice and wrong would not exist.　But as society, in
which the true Christians form but a mere fraction, is actually
constituted, the civil power is essential for the prevention
of anarchy and the punishment of evildoers.　This being
so, the Gospel does not free the Christian from subjection
to it, as the extremists proclaim in the name of evangelical
freedom.　At the same time, there is a limit to its jurisdiction,
and here Luther becomes the prophet of spiritual, if not of
political liberty, in reaction from the mediæval conception
of the subjection of the individual mind and conscience
to priestly domination operating through the State.　The
civil power has no right to intrude into the spiritual sphere,
were it even only as the agent of this priestly domination.
There is an absolute distinction between the spiritual and
the material which the civil power may not ignore.　Its
jurisdiction extends only to material and external things.
It has no jurisdiction whatsoever over the soul, no right to
command and enforce its authority in matters of faith.
To do so is to encroach on God's prerogative and the
function of the Word, through which alone He rules the soul.
The prince, therefore, has no right to enforce the decisions
of the Church, the Fathers, or Councils, at the behest of an
ecclesiastical authority which has distorted the faith and

---

[31] " Werke," xi. 246.

which is not the Church according to God's Word, but the apostle of the devil. For the individual soul God's Word alone is the only standard of truth and obligation. Moreover, faith cannot be engendered by force. God alone can evoke and nurture it in the soul. At most, force can secure only an external conformity and foster hypocrisy. Hence the proverb, "Thought is duty free." It is, therefore, as futile as it is contrary to Christ's teaching. "Heresy can never be warded off by force. . . . It can only be overcome by God's Word. You may burn every Jew and heretic in the world. You will not convert or overcome a single one thereby." [32] The princes, ecclesiastical and secular, who will not see this are a set of blind fools and tyrants, oppressors of the bodies and souls of their subjects, who are steering straight for destruction, and whose misgovernment is ripe for the judgment of God. Against these tyrants he boldly maintains the right of the subject not to obey their tyrannical decrees. He does not say that the subject may actually resist. It is the duty of the Christian to suffer wrong and violence, not to repel it. But he shall not yield a hairsbreadth to their tyranny over soul and conscience in things spiritual, and must be prepared to suffer gladly under it in the conviction that the tyrants will erelong find their judge. Meanwhile he tells these tyrants in very drastic terms what he thinks of them. "From the beginning of the world a wise prince has been a rare bird, a pious one still rarer. They are usually the greatest fools, the worst scoundrels on earth." [33] Whilst he inculcates passive resistance and assigns their punishment to God, he warns them of the blind folly of presuming too much on the long-suffering of the common man, whom their misgovernment is surely driving to desperation. He reminds them of the text, *Effundit contemptum super principes*. "There are few princes whom the people do not regard as fools and scoundrels. This comes of their proving themselves to be such. The common man is becoming intelligent and holds them in contempt. He will not and cannot suffer your tyranny and arbitrary rule indefinitely. Make your account with this fact, my dear

[32] " Werke," xi. 268-269.        [33] *Ibid.,* xi. 267-268.

princes and lords. God will no longer put up with your
tyranny. The world is no longer the world of the old days,
when you could hunt and harass the people like game." [34]
Though the prince rules by divine right, this does not imply
that he is entitled to rule as he pleases. They may only
use the sword in the service of justice, and should temper
force by law and reason, which is the highest law. They
shall model their government on the will of God, not merely
on the jurists and their law books, and rule for the common
good, in accordance with Christian duty, not for their own
aggrandisement. Whilst the princes shall show due
obedience to the Emperor as their overlord and be prepared
to suffer injustice at his hands, they are entitled to defend
themselves and their subjects from the aggression of other
princes, and in such a contingency their subjects are bound
to follow them in war. But if they wage war in an unjust
cause, their subjects are not bound to obey and aid them.
No one can be forced to act against the right, and in this case
they are bound to obey God, not man.[35] Though he
recognises the right of war, he urges the application of the
principle of arbitration and the Golden Rule as a surer means
of attaining a just decision and preventing disputes.[36]

## II. LUTHER AND SOCIAL REFORM

Luther's warning to the princes to beware of the effect
of their misgovernment on the common man erelong proved
to be only too well founded. Within little more than a
year the empire was in the throes of a revolution against
the feudal political and social system, on which the princely
régime was based. It was only the climax of a series of
violent attempts which had periodically occurred in Germany
during the previous half century. This pre-Reformation
revolutionary movement was social and political, not
specifically religious, though it more or less contained a
religious element. It was primarily a movement on behalf
of the emancipation of the masses from the feudal social
system, coupled with the aspiration for a more democratic

[34] " Werke," xi. 270.    [35] Ibid., xi. 277.    [36] Ibid., xi. 279.

order in the State in place of the feudal constitution, which conferred power and privilege on the higher classes. The striving of the peasants for emancipation from feudal services and dues was to some extent influenced by the growing tendency on the part of the landowners to subvert the old customary law by the application of the principles of the Roman law, in support of the absolute right of the local lord over the land and its tillers. Whilst the peasant was striving to secure the abolition or the modification of his servile or semi-servile status, his lord was attempting by means of this expedient to counter this striving and thereby aggravate and perpetuate his bondage. Similarly, within the industrial cities there was active discontent on the part of the working class with the régime of the master gilds on the score of wages and hours of labour, and the preponderant influence of the members of these gilds on the municipal government. Moreover, the revolutionary spirit was intensified by the economic development which in the late mediæval age in Germany, in virtue of a thriving industry and commerce, was tending to raise prices and monopolise wealth in the hands of the merchant class, especially the great trading companies, to the detriment of the masses in town and country.[37]

[37] The phrase " Rising of the Peasants " is, strictly speaking, insufficient as a designation of the insurrection of 1524-25, in view of this wider discontent which coalesced in the movement. The social and economic conditions which produced the Rising have been expounded, discussed, and summarised in a long series of works from that of Ranke onwards. See the later works of Janssen, Lamprecht, Bezold, Kautsky, Lenz, von Below, Schönlank, Blos, Schmoller, etc. One of the most illuminating and judicial reviews of the subject is given in the recent work of Stolze, " Der Bauernkrieg und die Reformation," 11 f. (1926). The latest elaborate work on the pre-Reformation movement is that of Rosenkrantz, " Der Bundschuh, die Erhebungen des südwest deutschen Bauernstandes," 1493-1517 (1927). In English the subject is treated by Bax, " German Society at the Close of the Middle Ages "; Schapiro, " Social Reform and the Reformation " (1909); and in my " History of Modern Liberty," i. (1906). Recent research has tended to modify in some respects the views of Lamprecht and his school. See the criticisms of Lenz, " Historische Zeitschrift " (1896), 385 f.; von Below, " Ursachen der Reformation," 57 f., and his review of Käser's book in " Historische Zeitschrift " (1902), 100-103.

Very noteworthy is the antagonism to the Church as a
feudal institution in this pre-Reformation revolutionary
movement.  Roman Catholic historians are quite mistaken
in their attempt to minimise or ignore the anti-ecclesiastical
element in this movement, and to ascribe that of 1524-25
largely or solely to Luther's influence.  The anti-clerical
feature is discernible long before Luther's advent, and it is
highly probable that, even if he had not started the evangelical Reformation, the revolutionary challenge in behalf of
" the Justice of God " (*Gerechtigkeit Gottes*), as opposed to
the existing oppressive and unjust social order and legal
system, would nevertheless have sounded over a large part
of the empire.  " The idea of a great revolution had, during
the previous fifty years, become a fixed idea—revolution of
society, revolution of the Church, for the two usually went
hand in hand, though the peasant was, of course, more
immediately concerned with the amelioration of his miserable
lot.  Ominous prophecies, elaborate schemes of this great
transformation had passed from lip to lip, nay, had been
written down like any party programme of the present
day.  A deliverer should appear (for long it was the
resurrected Frederick II. who should put his hand to
the task of a radical reform of empire and society), and the
outline of his work was ready to his hand.  Such an outline
is ' The Reformation of Kaiser Sigismund,' to whom, when
the great Frederick came not, the popular expectation had
eagerly but vainly turned.  Another, ' The Reformation of
Kaiser Frederick,' had pinned the popular faith to Frederick
III., and then the hopes that the third Frederick disappointed
had sought their realisation in his son, the chivalrous
Maximilian.  But the peasants were doomed to discover
again and again that, in spite of the favourable omens which
the astrologers read in the movements of the planets, each
prospective reformer on the imperial throne would not or
could not rise to the height of his humanitarian mission.
The peasant, it was patent, must help himself, must be his
own benefactor, and to this end must unite in a great Bund
or union, and secure by his own brawny arm the Reformation
which kaiser, prelate, prince refused to grant." [38]

[38] Mackinnon, " History of Modern Liberty," i. 170-171.

During the five years preceding that in which Luther nailed up his theses against indulgences, there were, in fact, repeated local attempts to inaugurate this social transformation—in Würtemberg, Alsace, Baden, and other regions of South Germany.

At the same time, it is obvious that the religious movement started by Luther could hardly fail to quicken the revolutionary spirit, however little he might intend to sweep away the dominant political and social order by force, and however much he might strive to dissociate the evangelical movement from this spirit. He himself had appealed in the " Address to the Nobility " to constituted authority to take in hand the pressing task of social reform. He did not lose sight of the subject in the course of his absorbing polemic against his theological opponents, and there can be no doubt that he was genuinely interested in the social betterment of the people, though he did not regard it as his specific mission as a religious reformer to concern himself with social, economic, and political reform, and professed his unfitness to intrude into this sphere. In the very summer of 1524 in which the revolution broke out, he attacked the new commercial system in his tractate on " Commerce and Usury." [39] He does so more from the theological and moral standpoint than in accordance with the new economic outlook. In this respect his political economy is rather antiquated, and while he shows a remarkable knowledge of the business methods and transactions of his time, he has not grasped the economic principles which were operating the transformation from the mediæval to the modern commercial and financial system. What, as a Christian moralist, he sees and condemns in this system is the tendency to concentrate undue wealth in the hands of individuals and trading associations. This tendency he ascribes purely to the greed of the merchant class in which " there are few who would rather be poor with God than rich with the devil." [40] The new commercial system is, therefore, both unchristian and detrimental to the commonweal, and he goes so far as

[39] Von Kaufshandlung und Wucher, in which he incorporated his sermon on Wucher of 1520. " Werke," xv. 293 f.

[40] *Ibid.*, xv. 293.

to denounce the import trade with foreign countries like England, Portugal, India, which drains Germany of its gold for the benefit of the merchants and impoverishes the people, and by raising prices diminishes its capacity to buy the necessaries of life.  He shares the idea that the wealth of a country consists in money, and that its prosperity depends on keeping its money within its own borders.  The new commercialism, he insists, has transformed the merchant class into a set of extortioners and usurers and is incompatible with Christian altruism, which seeks the good not of self but of others.  The rascally merchant, whose striving is to sell his wares at as high a price as possible, lives by the plunder of his neighbour, lends his ill-gotten wealth at a high interest, which he would limit to the Mosaic standard, sells his goods on credit, gets thereby the property of his neighbour into his clutches, buys up certain articles in order to monopolise the sale of them, and thus secures an undue profit.  The whole system is steeped in trickery, is, in fact, pure swindling, which makes these swindlers richer than emperors and kings.  No one ought to have the right or the power to charge more than a fair price. Those who do so are thieves and robbers, and it is the duty of kings and princes to take drastic measures against these plunderers.  The appeal to the Christian conscience being ineffectual, the secular princes would, he thinks, act quite rightly in seizing the goods of these financiers and rings and driving them out of the country.[41]  Unfortunately, kings and princes are mostly hand and glove with these thieves and robbers.  They hang a thief who steals a gulden and traffic with those who rob all the world.  Hence the proverb, " Great thieves hang the small ones."

All this is, of course, one-sided and lacking in scientific insight as a diagnosis of the economic development of the time.[42]  But it did bring into relief some of the objectionable features of the new system and, as the dis-

[41] " Werke," xv. 307.

[42] See the Introduction to the tractate in *ibid.*, xv. 279 f., and the special reviews of Schmoller, Wiskemann, Roscher, Uhlhorn, Kluckholm, Nathusius, etc.  A summary of the tractate is given by Waring, " The Political Theories of Martin Luther," 213 f. (1910).

cussions and demands in the Diets at Nürnberg show, it appealed to a widespread public opinion which, if equally incapable of understanding the economic forces at work in undermining the old system, was none the less resentful and restive on this account. Whilst Luther seeks a remedy, not in revolution, but in an appeal to conscience and constituted authority (the Diet and the local governments), he does not mince words in denouncing the system and its abettors. The evil has become intolerable, and in flaming language he proclaims the judgment of God on it and them. God is at hand with His scourge. What if the people takes the divine scourge into its own hands and starts the revolution which Luther would certainly not consciously encourage, far less sanction? He assuredly cannot be accused of subservience to the rich middle class of the towns in the interest of the evangelical movement, though this movement found material support in this class.

In his attack on Rome he had also at times made use of very revolutionary language. This attack, even within the limits he had set himself, was revolutionary enough, and the principles of the new theology undoubtedly contained democratic implications. The watchword of his religious teaching was liberty—liberty for the individual Christian from the religious trammels of the past, from the domination of Rome, and the Roman ecclesiastical system. His doctrine of the priesthood of all believers involved the equal rights of all Christians as such, the ideal of a spiritual democracy. His conception of the autonomous religious community freely recognised the right of its members to a controlling voice in its government. In the early stage of the evangelical movement it seemed, in view of these democratic implications of his religious teaching, as if he were destined to be the leader of a larger Reformation than he himself wot of, or was really fitted to achieve. The people might well see in him the long-looked for champion of the new order in the State and society as well as in the Church, which the popular seers had foretold and the popular agitator had vainly attempted to realise. Again and again he had protested against the oppression of the common man, pleaded for a more equitable system of government, and warned prince and prelate of the retribution which their misgovernment invited. It was, however, as the theologian and the religious leader that he trenched on this wider sphere. As a theologian and a religious reformer he sharply differentiated between the spiritual and the temporal, the things of the soul and the things of the world. Whilst he would Christianise the State, and recognised its ethical function, he exempted the individual soul in its relation to God from its domination. Civil government has to do with the body, not the soul, and the things of the body are of immeasurably less consequence than the salvation of the soul, which is the thing that really matters. Outside the religious sphere the Christian is called on to suffer, to submit to his lot in an evil world, as part of God's discipline, without demur. There is no necessary connection between religious and social and political reform.


## III. The Radical Party and Social Reform

In this respect Luther did not really understand the tendency of the religious movement he inaugurated, and erelong the movement threatened to go farther and faster than he contemplated—to develop a more radical, subjective, and democratic character. The result was the disruption of the Reformation party, and this disruption is of great significance for the connection of the social Revolution with the religious Reformation. While, on the one hand, it tended to set Luther against the revolutionary spirit with which his radical opponents sympathised, and to which he was otherwise by principle and predilection opposed, it provided, on the other, a link between the religious and the social movement. Carlstadt not only preached a more radical religious Reformation than commended itself to Luther. He had far more sympathy with the democratic aspirations of the masses, though he was not an advocate of revolutionary violence and had refused to make common cause with extremists like Münzer.[43] Similarly, reforming preachers like Strauss at Eisenach, Schappler at Memmingen,

---

[43] Barge, ii. 14-16, 114-117.

Jacob Wehe at Leipheim, Hubmaier at Waldshut, Waibel at Kempten, inveighed against the oppression of the masses and actively abetted their demands for redress. Many of the emancipated monks took the same side and preached the necessity of a social as well as a religious Reformation. Only the extreme left wing of this more advanced section of the reform party went the length of advocating a blood-red revolution and the forcible inauguration of the kingdom of God. This extreme left had started into existence with the prophets of Zwickau, whom Luther had repudiated from the first. Its leading spirit was Thomas Münzer, who had been expelled from Zwickau in the spring of 1521, and had actively pursued his vocation in various places as the divinely commissioned emissary of the Holy Spirit.[44] He was no mere fanatical windbag who, like the ordinary religious ranter, claimed for presumptuous ignorance a monopoly of divine wisdom. Like Stübner he had had the benefit of a university education at Leipzig and Frankfurt, and like Luther himself, whose acquaintance he made at the Leipzig Disputation and who in 1520 recommended him for a pastoral charge at Zwickau,[45] he had been an earnest seeker after truth in his own independent fashion.[46] At Zwickau he still appears as his disciple, and started preaching against the monks and priestly ecclesiastical usages and dogmas— at first with the approval of the Town Council and the applause of the townsfolk.[47] From this beginning he quickly

[44] On Münzer, see Seidemann, " Thomas Münzer " (1842); Enders, " Flugschriften," x. (Niemeyer); Förstemann, " Neues Urkundenbuch zur Geschichte der evangelischen Kirchenreformation " (1842); Kolde, art. " Münzer " in Herzog-Hauck, " Encyclopädie " (1903); Nathusius, " Christlich-Sociale Ideen der Reformationszeit " (1897). The latest works on Münzer are those of Ernst Bloch, " Th. Münzer, Theologe der Revolution " (1922); Zimmermann, " Thomas Münzer," a moderate and careful biography (1925); Hohl, " Luther und die Schwärmer, Gesammelte Aufsätze " (1927), a detailed exposition of his teaching; Boehmer, " Studien zu Th. Müntzer " (1922), a valuable critical review; Walter, " Thomas Münzer et les Luttes Sociales " (1927).
[45] Enders, ii. 404.
[46] On his remarkable learning and keenness for study, see Boehmer, " Studien zu Thomas Müntzer," 15-17.
[47] See his letter to Luther, Enders, ii. 435-438, 13th July 1520.

developed into the stormy petrel of the evangelical movement and alienated the Lutherans of the town as well as
the orthodox clergy by his aggressive diatribes on behalf of
a purely spiritual religion. "A man born for schism and
heresies," wrote Egranus, the reforming priest of St Mary's,
who was an enthusiastic disciple of Erasmus, and whose *locum
tenens* he had been before being transferred to the parish
of St Catherine.[48] From the same aggrieved source we
learn that, with the aid of laymen like the master weaver,
Nicolas Storch, and Stübner, he had gathered round him
a zealous following which professed to be the true spiritual
Church, and appealed to the inner Word as a higher authority
than the Scriptures.[49] Like Luther, he had studied Tauler
and the mediæval mystics and assimilated their teaching
on the inner light and the direct inspiration of the Spirit,
who makes use of laymen, in preference to the clergy, as His
mouthpiece. He now discarded the Lutheran doctrine of
the supreme authority of the written Word for that of the
direct inspiration of the believer in communion with God.
With this direct revelation by means of dreams and ecstatic
visions he combined the sectarian tendency to see in his
faction the elect people of God, from which all unbelievers
are to be excluded, by force if need be. His aggressive
spiritualism became so subversive of public order that the
Town Council determined to take proceedings against him
in April 1521. Rather than face the ordeal, he fled from
Zwickau and, along with Stübner, betook himself to Prague
in the hope of finding in the land of John Hus and the
Taborites a more fertile soil for his subjective message.
On the 26th May he proclaimed himself in a public manifesto
the prophet of the living Word which God inspires in the
heart of the elect, and which is not confined to the Scripture,
but, as in the prophets of old, continues to illuminate the
pious soul throughout the ages. To this living Word the
Church and the Biblical theologians (Luther and his colleagues are meant, though not named) have been impervious,
and the time has come to revive it in the new Church of the

---

[48] Enders, iii. 395. Egranus to Luther, June 1522.

[49] *Ibid.*, iii. 395. Qui neque amicorum consiliis, neque scripturarum
autoritatibus obsequatur, sed suo innixus spiritui meras factiones excitat.

elect which, since the days of the Apostles and their disciples, has been corrupted by the spiritual adultery of the clerical order.[50] The project of the new prophet was nipped in the bud by the Town Council, which placed him under police supervision. Thus baffled, though not disillusioned, he left Bohemia, and during the next two years wandered about Thuringia in search of a new sphere. In the course of these wanderings he seems to have visited Wittenberg [51] and consorted with Carlstadt, if not with Luther. Ultimately he turned up at Alstedt, near Eisleben, in the spring of 1523, and was installed by the Town Council as preacher in the Church of St John. Here he introduced a reformed order of worship in the vernacular on scriptural and evangelical lines, in spite of his depreciation of the written Word.[52] It is a remarkable production from both the literary and the devotional point of view. Had he confined himself to the religious sphere, he might have rendered material service to the Reformation as the exponent of a less dogmatic and more experimental Christianity than Luther evolved. In a conciliatory letter to the Reformer on the 9th July, in answer to one written apparently in a friendly spirit (Luther's letter has not been preserved), he emphasises the conformity of the will to that of the crucified Christ through suffering and conflict, and the testimony of his indwelling spirit as the test of truth and true piety. Whilst rating highly scriptural revelation, with which all revelation must be in conformity, he recognises the fact of a continued revelation in communion with the living God, disclaims responsibility for the opinions or professions of the prophets, maintains an independent attitude, and complains of the calumnies of Egranus and other enemies. He claims the right, on the ground of John xvi. 13, " When the spirit of truth is come he shall guide you into all truth," to believe in a personal

[50] The manifesto is given by Zimmermann, " Thomas Münzer," 58 f., and by Walter, " Th. Münzer," 342 f.; Walter differs from Zimmermann in dating it 1st Nov. 1521, " Th. Münzer," 80.

[51] Luther (" Werke," xv. 214) speaks of Münzer's visiting Wittenberg, and implies that he had had an interview with him, which Münzer subsequently denied.

[52] The three liturgies composed by him are given by Sehling, i. 472 f.

revelation, and evidently will not tie himself down to a dogmatic Biblicism, though he adopts a deferential tone towards Luther personally.[53] There was more reason and even more religion in his contention than the Reformer and his fellow-theologians were able or fitted to perceive. On Luther it made the worst possible impression. " Münzer," he wrote to Spalatin on the 3rd August 1523, " must be either mad or drunk." [54] The idea of a progressive revelation in accordance with the intellectual development and the religious experience of the believer was, nevertheless, not in itself either irreligious or unevangelical. The danger lay in the tendency, in ill-balanced minds like Münzer and the prophets, to self-deception and extravagant fancy, especially if it took the form of a fantastic and fanatic apocalyptic. Luther's test of a fresh revelation was, as we have seen, a miracle or other incontestable proof of divine authentication. Dreams and ecstatic visions were not for him necessarily reliable credentials of divine illumination. The miracle test is a narrow and artificial one, as a Savonarola had found to his cost. In any case, revelation, whether new or old, must be in accord with the rational and moral nature of man, especially if it would insist in intruding itself into the social and political as well as the purely spiritual sphere. It is only too evident from the sequel of his stormy and tragic activity that, in preaching the repression of the wicked by the sword and the violent reconstruction of the Church and society, Münzer was all too prone to substitute his own fanatic fancies for the Decalogue and the ethical teaching of the New Testament as the standard of right and wrong. Whilst insisting, and doubtless sincerely insisting, that the individual Christian life should be the concrete expression of the indwelling Christ, he did appeal to the lower passions of the masses and incite them to indiscriminate violence and outrage against " the ungodly," as the indispensable preliminary of the establishment of the new Church, the kingdom of God's elect on earth.

The apologetic and moderate tone of the letter to Luther evidently did not express the real spirit of the man or the

[53] Enders, iv. 169-172.     [54] Ibid., iv. 201 ; cf. 359.

whole content of his teaching. There can be no doubt that, as the two effusions [55] which he issued from the press early in 1524 show, he was conscious of a deep rift between his teaching and that of the Wittenberg Reformer, though he had learned much from him as well as from his own independent reflection. Whilst Luther recognised no supreme authority in religion outside the written Word, Münzer found this authority in the inner Word by which God continues to inspire the individual believer, as in the case of the prophets of old. Revelation is not confined to the past, but continues in the immanent Word uttering itself in the elect soul attuned to God. In virtue of this immanent revelation the peasant may know more of God than the most learned theologian, though it is necessary to guard against deception. For Luther justifying faith, operated by the Spirit through the written Word, or promise of God in the Gospel, is the sole ground and medium of salvation. For Münzer the faith that saves is the fruit of the direct revelation of God in the soul, not a mere second-hand apprehension of the teaching of Scripture. The Scripture is, indeed, "a testimony to faith." But it is not the source or the inspiration of saving faith which is due solely to the direct working of the Spirit in the troubled heart that waits for the divine voice within to deliver it from the misery and despair of an accusing conscience. Moreover, such a "borrowed faith" as Luther proclaims as the sole requisite of justification, to the exclusion of works, tends to make the way of salvation too easy and leads the believer, in self-deception and self-gratification, to shun the way of the Cross. By stressing the Augustinian doctrine of the impotence of the will, Luther deadens the moral sense and kills individual initiative. Again, for Luther the Church is the invisible communion of the saints, and the use of force in the interest of this spiritual communion is absolutely inadmissible. For Münzer it is the visible community of the elect, strictly separated from and aggressively antagonistic to the world, and the reign of the saints on earth which it

[55] " Protestation oder Empietung Tome Müntzer's," 1524 (copy in Edinburgh University Collection of Reformation pamphlets), and " Von dem getichten Glawben," 1524.

is the object of this community to realise can only be established by the repression or the destruction of the wicked.
In addition, infant baptism, which Luther would retain as
a divine ordinance, is emphatically rejected as a qualifica-
tion for membership of the elect community, though
Münzer does not advocate adult baptism, like some of his
fellow-prophets, and only insists that children should
only be baptized after instruction in the true faith as he
interprets it.

In view of this radical divergence in important respects
from Luther's teaching, the specious tone of the letter of
the 9th July 1523 is, to say the least, misleading. In spite
of some affinities, it is evident that the Reformer of Alstedt
had, in his revulsion from the mediæval Church, far outrun
the Reformer of Wittenberg in his programme of a new order
in Church and State, founded on the democratic régime of
the elect people of God. At Alstedt he set himself to
foment and organise a thoroughgoing revolution of both,
and in so doing not only denounced Luther's teaching, but proclaimed the gospel of violence by which alone the apocalyptic
kingdom of God could be established on earth. This gospel
he did not hesitate to preach in the presence of the Elector
himself and his brother, Duke John, in the castle of Alstedt,
on the 13th July 1524, in a sermon in which he inveighed
against the Biblical theologians (Luther and his colleagues)
and summoned the Saxon princes to draw the sword on behalf
of the true faith against its ungodly enemies in Church and
State. " The ungodly have no right to live farther than the
elect shall accord them." [56]

This violent sermon, to which the Elector and his brother
listened with remarkable tolerance, brought Luther into the
arena with a " Missive to the Princes on the Revolutionary
Spirit." [57] For Luther, Münzer is clearly one of those false
prophets whom Satan has inspired to distort the Gospel,

[56] Summaries of the sermon are given by Zimmermann (" Münzer,"
105 f.) and Walter (" Münzer," 126-127), from the version of it which
Münzer published.

[57] " Werke," xv. 210 f. Ein Brief an die Fürsten zu Sachsen von
dem aufruhrischen Geist. Spalatin had sent the sermon to Luther,
Enders, iv. 371.

and who, like the Pope, have given rise to sects and heresies throughout the centuries. He utterly rejects a superior spiritual illumination which preaches the use of the sword in the service of reform, the establishment of the kingdom of God on earth by murderous violence. Did not Christ say in the presence of Pilate, " My kingdom is not of this world " ? The spirit that inspires these fanatic visionaries to burn chapels, as at Mallenbach, is not of God, but of the devil. The test of the possession of the Holy Spirit is not spiritual arrogance and mob violence, but love, joy, peace, long-suffering, meekness, as Paul teaches, and the keeping of God's commandments. At the same time, he would not deny them the right of their opinions. Let them preach, argue, agitate without stint on behalf of the truth. The truth will know how to take care of itself. Controversy, conflict of wits in matters theological are inevitable, nay indispensable. " Let them, therefore, preach as much as they like and against whom they please. Sects there ever will be, for the Word of God must take the field and fight. . . . Allow opposing minds to draw and hit out on each other. If some should be misled, well, this is the way of war. Where there is strife, battle, some must fall and suffer wounds in the mêlée. He that fights best will gain the crown." [58] Luther is still the champion of the free exchange of opinion in the cause of truth, and Münzer certainly did not owe to him his doctrine of an armed crusade on behalf of his apocalyptic kingdom of God. His appeal to force in the repression of error is merely that of the mediæval Church applied from a different angle and for a different end. But for Luther there is a limit beyond which tolerance may not go. If the disputants will not be content to fight with arguments on behalf of their opinions and will needs have recourse to blows, then the princes must intervene and forbid them their dominions, whether they are Lutherans or non-Lutherans. " For we, who concern ourselves with the Word of God, may not strive with our fists. We are engaged in a spiritual strife, the object of which is to wrest heart and soul from the dominion of the devil. To preach

[58] " Werke," xv. 218-219.

and suffer is our office, not to strike blows and defend ourselves by force. Christ and His Apostles did not burn
churches and throw down images. They won hearts by
means of God's Word, and thereby the temples and images
fell of themselves." [59]

In consequence of this missive and the excesses committed
by his adherents, Münzer was summoned to a hearing at
Weimar on the 1st August 1524. A week later he deemed
it prudent to forestall a second inquisition by slipping out of
Alstedt and betaking himself to the free imperial city of
Mühlhausen, where the ex-monk Pfeiffer was preaching the
revolutionary crusade. Luther again intervened with a
warning to the Town Council,[60] which contributed to bring
about the banishment of both in the end of September.
Thence Münzer betook himself to Nürnberg and south-west
Germany, preaching and writing against Luther in the most
violent terms as he went.[61] His agitation in behalf of his
fanatic gospel found little favour with the more moderate
preachers of a social Reformation in South Germany, and
it was only in Thuringia, after his return to Mühlhausen at
the beginning of 1525, that he ultimately succeeded in
impressing to a certain extent [62] his fanaticism on the local
revolutionary movement.


## IV. THE RISING OF THE PEASANTS

This movement began in June 1524 at Stühlingen in the
south-west corner of the Black Forest in the rising of the
peasants of the Count of Lupfen, in protest against the command of the countess to gather strawberries and snail shells in
harvest time. This particular grievance appears to have been

---

[59] " Werke," xv. 219.        [60] *Ibid.*, xv. 238 f.

[61] Particularly in his " Schutzrede und Antwort auf das Geistlose und
sanft liebende Fleisch zu Wittenberg." Given by Enders, No. 118 of
Niemeyer's " Neudrucke," and in his " Ausgetrückte emplossung des
falschen Glaubens." A summary of both is given by Walter, " Th.
Münzer," 350 f.

[62] As Zimmermann has shown, his influence on the movement, even
in Thuringia, has been considerably overestimated.

merely the pretext for a revolt against the whole agrarian system, and in a number of articles the peasants proceeded to arraign this system. They complain of the seizure by the lord of the common lands, his exclusive use of the forests and streams, forced labour, which interferes with the proper cultivation of the peasant's holding, and other servile burdens, the strict preservation of game which destroys the crops, the arbitrary administration of justice, etc. From these articles it appears that the peasant is the victim of intolerable oppression and injustice which he is determined forcibly to amend or end, and for this purpose the people of the Hegau and Kletgau in August 1524 band themselves together over 1,000 strong under the agitator and ex-lands-knecht, Hans Müller of Bulgenbach, and march to Waldshut, which Hubmaier had won for the Reformation, and which was in revolt against the Austrian Government. The Wald-shutters welcomed the rustic band as brothers in a common cause, though the peasants were apparently not adherents of the religious Reformation, and the articles are concerned with the rectification of purely social abuses. The association of the two movements is, however, symptomatic of the trend towards the Christian Brotherhood into which the rising, as it widened its area, was to develop in South Germany. Equally significant the alliance of the agrarian with the discontented element in the towns, which was also to become a distinctive feature of the movement.

From this small beginning it spread during the autumn and winter of 1524-25 by means of agitation and organisation over the whole of Upper Swabia and Würtemberg, as far east as Memmingen and Kempten. The effort of the Swabian League to temporise by means of negotiation failed, and even the repulse of the exiled Duke of Würtemberg, who sought to turn the movement to account in an attempt to recover his duchy, did not overawe the insurrectionary spirit. Duke Ulrich was compelled to halt in his march on Stuttgart against the forces of the League by the desertion of his Swiss mercenaries and seek refuge in his castle of Hohentwiel (March 1525). The insurrection nevertheless continued to extend. George Truchsess, Count of Waldburg, the League's general, might rout a peasant band here and there, which ran away at the first shot, and negotiate with others.   The attempt to localise the outbreak was hopeless, and the forces of the League were helpless to cope with the ever-swelling numbers of the insurgents.   The war in Italy had drained the country of troops, and after the victory of Pavia large numbers of the returning landsknechts would not fight against the peasant class, to which they belonged, or joined their ranks.   Moreover, it was no longer a question of rebellion in Swabia.   By the spring of 1525 the revolution had spread north, east, west—northwards into Franconia, the Odenwald, the Neckerwald, Hesse, the Rheingau, Thuringia, Saxony, Brunswick ;  westwards from the Black Forest and Baden into Alsace-Lorraine, Treves ;  eastwards into Salzburg, the Tyrol, Carinthia, Styria.   The proletariat in the towns as well as the peasants in the country were seized by the revolutionary contagion.   Two-thirds of the empire were ablaze with revolution.   Verily, Luther's denunciation of the judgment of God against the princes and the magnates had been fulfilled with a terrible swiftness.

It is difficult to generalise a movement so widespread as this.   We might call it a social revolution based on the " divine justice " (the popular phrase) as revealed in the Bible, and this description applies at least to some of the peasant programmes, especially to the most famous of them, the Twelve Articles adopted by the peasants of Upper Swabia at Memmingen in March 1525 and very widely accepted. Their authorship is unknown, but both Schappeler and Hubmaier were credited with having a hand in them.[63] The influence of the religious Reformation is unmistakable in the appeal to the Word of God, " the New Gospel," as the arbiter of social justice, and in the consciousness of the rights of the individual Christian.   The disclaimer of any intention to overthrow all authority—secular and spiritual —and establish a pure anarchy, which is a slander of their

[63] See the contemporary testimonies in Boehmer, " Urkunden zur Geschichte des Bauernkrieges," Kleine Texte, Nos. 50-51, 11-16 (1910). See also the summary of the discussion on the question in Schapiro, " Social Reform and the Reformation," 132 f. ;  W. Mau, " Balt. Hubmaier," 49 f. (1912) ;  Karl Sachsse, " B. Hubmaier als Theologe," 106-109 (1914) ;  Stolze, " Bauernkrieg und Reformation," 82.

Antichristian adversaries, is also in keeping with the profession of the more moderate democratic preachers of the type of a Schappeler. The Gospel, the peasants insist, is no cause of rebellion, since it teaches only love, peace, patience, and unity, and the aim of the articles is to ensure " that men should hear the Gospel and live in accordance therewith." They are meant, in a word, to establish the ideal of a Christian Brotherhood in place of an intolerable social order. To this end the first article demands for the community, in accordance with certain scriptural passages, the right to choose its pastor, who shall preach the Gospel without any addition of man, and, in case of unseemly life, to displace him. They are willing, according to the second article, to pay the great tithe of corn, which has the sanction of the Old Testament, for the support of the preacher of the pure Gospel and of the poor, and to devote any residue to the public service, in case of war, in lieu of a general tax. The small tithe (of a head of cattle) they will on no account pay to any lord, spiritual or temporal, " since God has created the beast for the free use of man." (More texts.) The third article declares their determination to submit no longer to villainage, which is incompatible with the Gospel. They do not disclaim obedience to lawful authority, but as Christians they are free, and free they will be. (More scriptural references.) Further, by the fourth article, they are entitled, according to the Word of God, to their share of game and fish, for God hath given a right to all men to the fowls of the air and the fish in the water. Anyone who cannot prove the purchase of " a water " must restore it to the community, and the excessive preservation of game by the lord must cease. (See Gen. i., Cor. x., etc.) Similarly in regard to the woods, the fifth article declares them forfeited to the people in the case of lords who have not purchased them. In the sixth article they insist on the diminution of the oppressive services demanded by the lords (see Rom. x.), and in the seventh, the lord shall observe the ancient agreements with the peasants, shall not oppress them, and shall not require them to render service at an unseasonable time, and even then shall pay them a fair price for this labour. (References to Luke's Gospel and the Epistle to the Thessalonians.) The eighth demands a fair rent for their holdings (Matt. x.) ; the ninth protests against unjust punishments, which contravene the ancient written law (four texts quoted) ; the tenth against the usurpation of the common lands, which they will take back in all cases where they have not been honestly purchased. The eleventh denounces the death due (heriot) as an unmerciful oppression of widows and orphans, and demands its entire abolition. (More texts.) Finally, they agree to resile from any of these articles that may be found contrary to God's Word.[64]

The moderate, persuasive tone of these articles is surprising. The peasants will not use force except in the last resort and against glaring abuses, which were really indefensible from the Christian standpoint. They are ready to reason and compromise in a brotherly spirit. Brotherly love and the Gospel are to decide in all contentious matters. Arbitration in a Christian spirit is the method they would fain apply. The method is admirable. But it was one which the privileged party was not minded to adopt where vested interests clashed with demands based on ideal justice, Christian equity, and in organising to enforce these demands, if need be, the peasants were taking the only course that could bring about their practical realisation. Unfortunately, in view of the bitter spirit begotten by oppression and the antagonism of the dominant class to a revolution based on professedly Christian principles, there was little chance that the Christian spirit of the articles would effectively avail to restrain the rising flood of popular passion, now that it had come to an actual trial of strength between the two parties. It would simply be a struggle conducted with all the expedients of pillage and plunder of mediæval warfare.

Moreover, the Christian spirit is by no means so marked in other revolutionary programmes. They are less scriptural and more aggressive in tone and mingle political demands with the redress of social grievances. The peasants of Alsace-Lorraine, for instance, demand the preaching of the true Gospel. But they also insist on their rights as men and will simply take back the common lands without discussion. They have political as well as social aspirations. They are ready to own allegiance to the Emperor, but they will not recognise any other authority that is not in accord with the people's will. The men of Tyrol, as voiced by Michael Gaismeyr, similarly demand, in addition to the pure Gospel and the right to elect their pastors, the establishment of popular government under the central authority of the Archduke Ferdinand, the secularisation of ecclesiastical property, the abolition of feudal institutions, secular and ecclesiastical, and equal law and justice without distinction of class. In a subsequent programme (June 1526) these demands are amplified in a more radical direction, including the uprooting of all godless persons who oppress the people and hinder the general welfare. In other programmes all hereditary authority is abolished, and the idea of a republic based on the sovereignty of the people, along with complete social equality and the right to deprive and depose all rulers and superiors, finds decisive expression.[65] In contrast to such passionate appeals on behalf of the sovereignty of the people is the statesmanlike programme of imperial reform on the basis of existing institutions, formulated by Hipler and Weigant, who adapted the so-called " Reformation of Kaiser Frederick III." to this end, and strove to organise and direct the revolution by means of a central committee at Heilbronn. It is couched in the spirit of the Twelve Articles. But it is more constructive and its scope is much wider. Whilst it demands the secularisation of ecclesiastical property for the common good, it allows compensation for loss incurred thereby. Here, too, the community shall choose and support its pastor, who shall concern himself solely with his spiritual functions. The old social hierarchy of princes, counts, knights, squires, burghers, and peasants shall remain. But the higher classes shall cease to oppress the people and act towards them in a Christian spirit, shall lose their feudal jurisdiction, and become imperial officials, administrators of the central imperial authority. All leagues within the empire shall cease, and equal law and justice be meted out in accordance with natural right. To this end a

[65] See " History of Modern Liberty," ii. 83 f.

series of courts, from the Supreme Imperial Court (*Reichs-kammergericht*) downwards to the Court of the Rural Commune, shall be established, and each class shall have its share in the administration of justice. From these courts doctors of the Roman law shall be excluded and be relegated to the lecture rooms of the universities. Taxes, tolls, and other oppressive exactions shall cease. The Emperor only shall be entitled to levy a general tax every ten years, and the oppressive monopolist companies be abolished. Finally, all classes in this reformed empire are to live in brotherly love and conform to the law of God and nature as well as the law of the land.

Finally, there is the theocratic revolution which Münzer was striving to realise in Thuringia from his centre at Mühlhausen. Its root idea is a fantastic communism [66] to be established by the sword. Its redeeming feature is the undoubted sympathy with the common man which animates it, but which could only end in the establishment of the worst form of tyranny—that of the so-called theocracy of the elect, the kingdom of God based on fanaticism and force.

In most of these programmes the influence of the religious Reformation is unmistakable. The Lutheran movement had evidently taken a far-reaching grip of the people in Southern and Central Germany. The appeal to " the Gospel " as the standard of religious, political, and social institutions, which makes itself so generally heard, is clearly a reflection of the response of the common man over a large part of the empire to his religious message. In this message the common man has evidently seen the dawn of a new era in Church, in State, and in society. For him the Reformation is not merely a new theology and a reformed Church in accordance therewith. It involved a new social system in the spirit of " the Gospel," as Luther had rediscovered it, and warranted him in applying, if need be, by force the right of revolt against an unchristian régime, which was a principle of mediæval political thought, if not of Luther himself. The

---

[66] Certain of his utterances in his sermons and letters are susceptible of a communist interpretation. Walter questions this interpretation and concludes that he had not definitely worked out a communist reconstruction of society, " Th. Münzer," 359 f.

use of the term in these programmes may not necessarily always denote the Gospel in the evangelical sense, or invariably imply that those who appealed to the Gospel on behalf of " the justice of God " were confirmed followers of Luther. The general antagonism to the secularised Church, which long before his appearance had characterised the pre-Reformation revolutionary movement, is sufficient to remind us that such antagonism was not necessarily an indication of adherence to the evangelical movement. The common man had appealed to the Gospel as the arbiter of social justice before Luther's advent, and this appeal could quite well consort with adherence to the Gospel in the traditional sense. Moreover, the specific reforms based on the Gospel were largely a reflection of those which are found in the Reformation programmes of the fifteenth century. The peasant Rising was undoubtedly inspired by mundane as well as religious motives, and the generally accepted view is that the former were primary, the latter only secondary. At the same time, it is evident that the appeal to the Gospel, especially in the Twelve Articles, which, with local variations, were very widely accepted as the common aspiration of the peasant bands, was inspired by Luther's teaching, as interpreted by the more advanced preachers. It is not without significance in this connection that the insurgents submitted these Articles for his judgment, in the belief that they embodied the practical implications of his teaching. Moreover, there is ground for the conclusion that the Rising was an attempt to frustrate the reaction against this teaching which the South German princes, secular and ecclesiastical, had united at Ratisbon to bring about in their respective territories, and which was already finding expression in the persecution of the evangelical preachers and the adherents of Luther in Austria and Bavaria. Recent writers like Stolze [67] find, in fact, the main explanation of the actual insurrectionary outbreak on a large scale in the widespread determination of the common man to seize the opportunity of the war between the Emperor and Francis I. to defend and vindicate a movement with which he identified his own

[67] " Bauernkrieg und Reformation," 46 f. (1926).

cause, and in the triumph of which he saw the realisation of his own aspirations. The reasoning which leads to this conclusion may not always be convincing, especially in cases where direct evidence is lacking. The striving for social and political reformation was too deep-seated, too well founded on the grievances of the common man against the oppressive feudal system in Church and State to be a mere appendage of the defence of the religious Reformation. Nevertheless the evangelical influence was a very real factor in the moulding of the insurrectionary movement. The appeal to the Gospel in the Twelve Articles was no mere tag of the party and class programme, but a serious attempt to achieve a new social and religious order in the spirit of the new teaching, and is by no means to be identified with the crude fanaticism of a Münzer, whose influence was very limited, and who cannot fairly be taken as the type of the responsible peasant leader.

Arbitration in the spirit of the Twelve Articles proving visionary, the movement in the spring and summer of 1525 took the form of a trial of strength between the opposing forces. The peasant bands conducted the revolutionary campaign in accordance with the predatory warfare of the time. In those days burning and plundering were accounted fair tactics even in ordinary warfare. Not only had the robber knight set them a bad example. Kings and their generals, and even high Church dignitaries at times, had committed ravage and arson in wartime all through the Middle Ages as a matter of course. That the peasant bands should do likewise is not, therefore, surprising in view of the military practice of the age. If emperor, kings, princes, and lords systematically indulged in this brutal practice in regular warfare, it is hardly to be expected that the peasants would observe a higher standard in their irregular operations, though it certainly is not obvious that their mode of operations could be made to tally with the divine justice based on the Gospel which they professed to vindicate. Specially noteworthy is the violence directed against the property of ecclesiastical lords, against which the attack was, in fact, in the first instance levelled. The peasant bands sacked monasteries and even churches before directing their fury against the castles of the lords who actively opposed the movement or refused to yield their demands. They smashed images and relics, burned Mass books and the tomes of the schoolmen, and even spilled the sacramental wine, as emblems of Antichrist. They thus drastically gave vent not only to their instinct for plunder, but to their contempt for a feudalised and secularised Church which had fatally neglected the real moral education of the people, whilst tempting its covetousness by its overgrown wealth, too often scandalously misapplied. Hatred of the Church and its degenerate hierarchy is, in fact, a notable feature of the Rising.

On the whole, however, apart from the actual fighting, there was comparatively little wanton bloodshed.[68] In this respect the German Rising of 1525 compares favourably with the French Jacquerie of 1358 or the Rising of the English peasants in 1381, for instance. The Weinsberg tragedy was exceptional. The butchery of Count Helfenstein and nearly a score of knights in the presence of the countess, a natural daughter of the Emperor Maximilian, was the work of the cutthroat Jäcklein Rohrbach, and was perpetrated against the orders of his superior, George Metzler. It was a ruffianly deed. But its perpetrators had been exasperated by the slaughter of one of the peasant bands under the walls of Weinsberg and other outrages on the part of the count. As a rule the peasants were content to make the lords who fell into their hands swear the Articles and enrol themselves in the Brotherhood. They were quite willing to accept their superiors as their enforced allies and even as leaders, and among the chiefs of these rustic bands (*Haufen*) were men of knightly rank like Florian Geyer of Franconia, Stephan Menzingen of Swabia, and Götz von Berlichingen, who filled the part of generalissimo of the united peasant bands at Heilbronn.[69]

[68] On this point see Stolze, " Bauernkrieg und Reformation," 91-92. Even in Thuringia under the auspices of the fanatic Münzer, murder was rarely perpetrated. Walter, " Th. Münzer," 288.

[69] Mackinnon, " History of Modern Liberty," ii. 91-92.

## V. LUTHER AND THE RISING

Among those who were horrified by the doings of the peasants was Luther.   In August 1524 he had, by direction of the Elector and Duke John, undertaken a visitation of Thuringia for the purpose of counteracting the activity of Münzer and of Carlstadt, who had left Wittenberg in the previous year and established himself as preacher at Orlamunde, had renewed his crusade in favour of a more radical reformation, and cleared the parish church of images and altars.   Carlstadt had, moreover, by this time discarded the Lutheran doctrines of the Lord's Supper and Baptism, and approximated Münzer's view of individual spiritual illumination, whilst rejecting his appeal to the sword.   At an interview with Luther at Jena on the 22nd August, he rebutted his charge of complicity with Münzer's rabid gospel and formally accepted Luther's challenge to a theological duel by means of the press on the points at issue between them.[70]   In the course of a warm discussion at Orlamunde on the 24th, his adherents argued against the Reformer with no little force in defence of their action in removing the images.[71] The discussion ended in a rupture over this burning question, and this rupture led to the expulsion from Saxony of Carlstadt (18th September) who, like Münzer, betook himself to South Germany, denouncing Luther by the way,[72] and is ultimately found taking an active part on the popular side at Rothenburg on the Tauber.   Luther henceforth regarded him, with more prejudice than reason, as the incarnation of Satan. " Carlstadt," wrote he to Spalatin, on the 13th September, " is at last given over to a reprobate mind, so that I despair of his return. . . . He is more hostile to me and ours than any opponent I have yet met.   There is not a single devil that has not taken possession of him." [73]   In response to a number of tracts against his doctrine of the Lord's Supper, which this embodiment of all the devils issued from Basle

---

[70] " Werke," xv. 334 f.

[71] *Ibid.*, xv. 341 f. ; *cf.* the notices of this discussion given by Luther in his philippic, Wider die himmlischen Propheten, " Werke," xviii. 83-84, *passim*.

[72] See Enders, v. 39, 42, 82, 153.        [73] *Ibid.*, v. 23 ; *cf.* 102.

in December, he hurled his most violent philippic, "Against the Heavenly Prophets, concerning Images and the Sacrament," [74] in January 1525.

In this embittered mood the fact that the more advanced reformers were joining Carlstadt in playing an active part on the democratic side doubtless contributed to prejudice him [75] against the cause of the peasants, who sought his judgment on the Twelve Articles.[76] This judgment he gave in "An Exhortation to Peace in Response to the Twelve Articles of the Peasants in Swabia" [77] (April 1525). He expresses his satisfaction that they are willing, according to the twelfth article, to receive instruction and be guided by the Word, and whilst apprehensive of coming catastrophe, still hopes for a peaceful accommodation. To this end he addresses himself to both parties. His attitude is conditioned to a certain extent by the fact that many of the princes— spiritual and temporal—were opposed to the Reformation and were already (after the second Diet at Nürnberg) striving to repress it in accordance with the Edict of Worms, and that the radical preachers, whom he detested, were identifying themselves with the revolutionary movement. Hence the pointed denunciation of the tyranny of the princes and lords, and of the false teaching of these preachers in support of a social as well as a religious revolution. He lays the responsibility for the rising on the princes and lords, and especially on "the blind bishops and mad priests and monks" who rage against the Gospel. Moreover, they harass and harry the common man to such a degree that he neither can nor may longer endure it. Now the sword is at their throats, and their blind confidence and pride will only break their own necks in spite of repeated warnings. "I have often enough proclaimed it to you, Beware of the text, *Effundit contemptum super principes.*" [78] This is what they have been striving for, and this the signs and wonders in heaven and on earth have been foretelling. It is the day of the wrath of God. He it is who so works that the people will no longer bear their fury. They must change their ways

[74] "Werke," xviii. 62 f.
[75] See, for instance, Enders, v. 153.
[76] Boehmer, "Urkunden," 22-24.
[77] "Werke," xviii. 279 f.
[78] *Ibid.*, xviii. 294.

and cede to God's Word, if not willingly, then in virtue of
force and ruin. " It is not the peasants, dear sirs, that
stand against you, but God Himself to punish your
madness." [79] Some have said that they will root out
Luther's teaching. Let them have a care lest they become
the prophets of their own undoing. This, say they further,
is the fruit of his teaching, forgetful that he has preached
against revolt and exhorted to obedience to their tyrannical
and oppressive government. They confound his teaching
with that of " the murder prophets," who have been busy
among the people and whom he has opposed might and
main. He does not desire merely to inspire them with fear
of the peasants. They are to fear God, whose judgment is
come upon them. He himself might see in all this a just
retribution for their opposition to his work and take pleasure
in their tribulation, and even by taking the side of the
peasants augment it. Instead of so doing, he will endeavour
to give them good counsel. Let them eschew wrath and
harsh methods, and reason with the peasants as with a drunk
or an erring man. Some of their demands are reasonable
even if they are acting only from self-interest. They have
a right to the preaching of the Gospel, and no government is
entitled to prescribe what anyone shall believe, whether it is
gospel or lies. It has as little right to oppress the people
in body or in soul in order that the upper classes may welter
in luxury and excess.

He then turns to the peasants. Princes and lords, he
admits, by their attitude towards the Gospel and their
oppression of the people, well deserve to be overthrown
by God. They have no excuse. If the peasants are acting
with a good conscience, God will stand by them, and even
if for a time they suffer defeat and death, they will gain
the victory in the end. A good conscience before God is
the main thing. Let them especially beware of listening
to the spirits and preachers whom Satan has inspired under
the guise of the Gospel, and of taking God's Name in vain
in professing to establish God's justice by violence. Let
them remember the Word of Christ that they that take the
sword shall perish by the sword, and the saying of Paul

---

[79] " Werke," xviii. 295.

who inculcates obedience to the powers that be. To rise in rebellion and seek the forcible redress of grievances is, therefore, contrary to God's ordinance. It is no justification of rebellion to adduce their wicked oppression. To punish such belongs not to the individual by divine and natural right. To commit injustice in the attempt to obtain justice is to wrong God's Word. For anyone forcibly to seek to right his wrongs is to open the door to anarchy and murder. This is not permissible to those who profess the Name of Christ, whatever the false prophets say. Vengeance is mine, saith the Lord, who commands obedience to wicked as well as good princes. Christ teaches us to suffer, not to withstand injustice. " Suffering, suffering, cross, cross—this is the Christian's right and no other." [80] To adduce natural right in justification of the forcible redress of worldly grievances is contradictory of this gospel of suffering. Let them trust in God, as he himself has done, and behold what God has accomplished for him, despite Pope and Emperor and all other tyrants. Let them pray, exercise patience, and eschew force. Any other attitude is utterly contrary to the Gospel, which has nothing to do with temporal things. Even the demand for the preaching of the Gospel is not to be enforced against the will of the powers that be. The only remedy is to remove to another place, where the Gospel is rightly preached, as Christ teaches. From the Christian standpoint the peasants have, therefore, no case. Even the demand for the abolition of serfdom has no warrant in the Gospel. Serfdom is quite compatible with spiritual freedom. Did not Abraham and the patriarchs practise slavery, and did not St Paul exhort slaves to be obedient to their masters ? He refuses to allow that Christianity has anything to do with the contentions of either side. The whole movement is purely a worldly matter. There are faults on both sides, and he concludes by advising a friendly accommodation, befitting worldly affairs, on the ground of mutual concessions. Otherwise Germany will be overwhelmed with destruction and misery. If both parties refuse to listen to this advice, he disclaims all responsibility for the terrible consequences.

This advice was eminently sound if only in view of the

[80] " Werke," xviii. 310.

lamentable issue of the appeal to force.  It cannot be said,
however, that the train of reasoning that preceded it was
fitted to convince the peasants of the inadmissibility of this
appeal.  He places the responsibility for the rising on the
intolerable tyranny of the princes and lords.  He admits
that the position of the peasants is unbearable, and that
such a rising was inevitable.  He states the case for them
and then runs away from it, telling them that, unbearable as
their lot might be, they have no right as Christians to rebel
in order to remedy it, because Christianity teaches obedience
to constituted authority, no matter how tyrannical it may
be, because it is a religion of suffering, because it has nothing
to do with worldly things.  This was simply to strengthen
the iniquitous régime of the princes by admitting their
right to oppress their subjects without fear of active opposition on their part.  He forgets, moreover, that the teaching
of Christ and the Apostles in this respect applied to a society
that was non-Christian, and that while it might be the
duty of the primitive Christian to obey and suffer at the
hands of such a society, it by no means followed that it was
equally a duty to do so in one that was professedly Christian.
The peasants might forcibly retort that the oppression by
one section of Christians, in a Christian State, of the mass
of their fellow-Christians was absolutely at variance with
Christianity, and that it was their Christian duty to put a
summary end to it, not abet it by submission and suffering.
He had not hesitated, in the "Address to the Nobility,"
for instance, to recognise this duty in reference to the reform
of the abuses in the Church, and even incited to revolutionary
methods against the oppressive papal régime.  If, in a
Christian State, Christianity inculcated only submission to
scandalous social abuses, it was merely bolstering up and
perpetuating injustice and wrong and stultifying and
nullifying the Gospel.  Luther was becoming too prone to
be the slave of the Word, to interpret it without due judgment or discrimination.  To threaten the princes with the
wrath of God was all very well, but such a threat would have
no effect in remedying the peasants' grievances, and they
might well argue that God had chosen them, as he practically
admitted, to be the effective agents of His wrath.  Equally

inept, from the standpoint of the downtrodden peasant, the
contention that Christianity has nothing to do with the
worldly lot of the Christian. To calmly assert that it is
immaterial in a Christian society whether the Christian is
a serf or a free man, whether the laws and institutions
under which he lives are good or bad, whether he and his
family are ground in the dust in order that a privileged class,
which professes to be Christian, may live in selfish ease and
luxury, showed a lack of understanding of human nature and
what is permissible in a Christian State. Moreover, whilst
his denunciation of the princes was too much coloured by his
resentment at their antagonism to his religious teaching,
his animus against the more advanced preachers was in
itself sufficient to prejudice the peasants against him. He
writes on the assumption that all these preachers are of the
type of a Münzer, and that, at all events, every reformer
who differs from him and champions a reformation in the
larger Christian sense is an enemy of the Gospel. In reality
the preachers who helped to mould the Twelve Articles
were not fanatical revolutionaries of the Münzer type, and
their sympathy with the people was not likely to appear to
the peasantry in the light of the heinous offence that it was
to Luther. Nor was it likely that these peasants would
discard their guidance in deference to one who had the
bad taste to tell them that, because Abraham and the
patriarchs had slaves, they had no reason to seek emancipation from their servile or semi-servile status.

The " Exhortation " accordingly proved a failure as an
attempt to forestall the further progress of the movement.
The peasants ignored Luther in their preference for the
preachers of the right of rebellion, and Luther waxed furious.
The pillage of castles and monasteries was bad enough.
The Weinsberg tragedy and the fanatic vapourings of
Münzer, who was spreading the revolutionary fever in the
Thuringian region, in spite of his efforts [81] to preserve the
peasants of this region from the contagion, led him to see in

[81] He published, with a preface and a conclusion, the Articles of
Agreement between the Swabian peasants and Truchsess, which held out
the prospect of a peaceful conclusion of the conflict (22nd April 1525),
" Werke," xviii. 336 f.

it the work of the devil pure and simple.  Hence the deplorable effusion, " Against the Robber and Murdering Bands
of the Peasants." [82]  The peasants have been false to the
Gospel they profess to follow, and are doing the devil's work
under the inspiration of " the arch-devil that rules at
Mühlhausen."  This was to a certain extent true enough.
But he errs in taking Münzer as a type of the peasant leader,
and in his savage mood overlooks the fact that the devil's
work was not all on one side.  He errs, too, in ascribing
wholesale a bloodthirsty character to the movement.  He
now sees in the peasants a set of wanton murderers, while the
fact is that murder was the exception, not the rule.  He not
only reiterates his doctrine of unconditional obedience.  He
commands every one who can to throttle a rebellious man
without further ado, as one would hasten to extinguish a
conflagration by every possible means.  It is the devil in
person that is raging in the land.  " Therefore strike,
throttle, stab, secretly or openly, whoever can, and remember
that there is nothing more poisonous, more hurtful, more
devilish than a rebellious man." [83]  These are fine Christians
who appeal to the first chapters of Genesis in proof that all
are created equal, with an equal right to all things.  In the
New Testament, Moses is of no account.  The Gospel teaches
obedience to Cæsar, and baptism makes not the body or
property but only the soul free.  " I believe there is no
longer a single devil in hell.  They have all taken possession
of the peasants."  Such devils the princes are entitled
without further parley to strike down.  He adds, indeed,
that the Christian princes, humbling themselves before God
on account of their sins and in deference to the Gospel may
attempt to recall the peasants to their duty.  But in case of
refusal the only remedy is the sword, and they must wield the
sword without mercy.  In his previous effusion princes and
lords were a set of scoundrels for the most part.  Now,
they are all God's ministers and if they fall in the cause
they are martyrs ; whereas whoever is killed on the peasants'
side will burn for ever in hell.[84]  These are wonderful times

[82] " Werke," xviii. 344 f.  Beginning of May 1525.
[83] " Werke," xviii. 358.
[84] Eyn ewiger hellebrand ist.

when a prince can gain heaven by bloodshed better than by praying. He interjects a few words in favour of mercy to those who have been forced or led astray by others. But he ends by repeating the savage summons to strike, stab, throttle who can.

This savage conclusion is its own judgment, and the judgment certainly goes against Luther as a Christian theologian. In this wild outburst he outdoes even Münzer as the apostle of irresponsible violence. His realistic belief in Antichrist and the devil, his mistaken assumption that the whole movement was dominated by the spirit of a Münzer, his honest but indiscriminating revulsion from the theory of force in the redress of grievances may explain, but cannot excuse, the furious spirit of this incitement of the brutal instincts of the feudal class against the mass. Luther has clearly lost his head, if not his courage, in the face of a situation which was indeed terrible enough, but which his wild effusion, by giving scope to the spirit of vengeance, could only make still more terrible. No wonder that it excited protests on the part of some of his followers, such as the Mansfeld Councillor Rühel and Hausmann, the pastor of Zwickau. In view of these criticisms, he felt compelled to write a defence in a circular letter to the Chancellor of Mansfeld, Caspar Müller, and attempted to intervene in letters and sermons on the side of mercy. He expresses, too, indignation at the cruelty with which the princes are treating the peasants after they have won the victory. But he would not retract a single word of his pamphlet or apologise for it as the offspring of momentary passion. " A rebel is not worthy to receive a reasonable answer, for he will not accept it. With the fist one must answer such foul-mouthed fellows, so that the blood spurts from their noses. . . . Their ears must be opened with musket balls so that their heads fly into the air." [85]  " As the ass will have blows so the mass will only be ruled by force," [86] is his fixed conviction.

[85] Ein Sendbrief von dem harten Büchlein wider die Bauern, " Werke," xviii. 386; cf. his letters to Rühel, " Werke," 53, 291 f. 306 (Erlangen ed.);  and to Amsdorf, Enders, v. 182-183.

[86] Ibid., xviii. 394.

Luther's thirst for the blood of the insurgents was destined to receive an early quenching. The princes were preparing to take a terrible vengeance in the spirit of their theological mentor. The peasants, though inspiring terror far and near by the pillage of castles and monasteries, had wasted their strength and their opportunity in these outbursts of violence. The movement was widespread, but it was not cohesive. The hundreds of thousands in the field were split into many bands, which engaged in local raids and sieges, but did not co-operate in any general plan of operations. There does not, in fact, seem to have been a general plan, for the Committee at Heilbron never got into proper working order, and had no firm grip on the movement. This lack of cohesion gave their enemies the opportunity of attacking in detail the ill-led and ill-disciplined peasant armies which could not be taught to obey orders, and were given to drinking and feasting whenever a chance offered. These bands, it must be remembered, attracted the scum as well as the more reputable element of the population. "The peasants were always drunk," we are told, "and would not be ruled by any man." [87] Moreover, the moderate party, which was in favour of compromise, did not pull with the extremists, who insisted on the complete concession of the Articles. Thus in the early summer of 1525 the movement was suppressed with much slaughter in Franconia, and in the south and west in spite of an occasional peasant success here and there. In the north the fanatic adherents of Münzer were broken and dispersed at Frankenhausen on the 15th May by the forces of the Landgrave Philip of Hesse, Duke George of Saxony, and Duke Henry of Brunswick, and their leader captured, tortured, and beheaded. In the east, where the struggle lasted into 1526, the Tyrolese mountaineers were at length forced to submit, and their leader, Gaismeyr, was driven to seek refuge in Italy.

Over a large part of the insurgent area defeat was followed by a terrible retribution, which was called bringing the rebels to justice. A brutal revenge is the more fitting term to apply to it in those regions at least where such savage

---

[87] "History of Modern Liberty," ii. 96.

reactionaries as the Duke of Lorraine and the Margrave Casimir of Ansbach gave free rein to their brutality in wholesale hanging, decapitating, massacring, maiming, and devastation.   In this orgy of vengeance such rulers forgot their own sins and shortcomings as rulers and trustees of the commonweal.   Among the few who showed moderation and humanity, the Landgrave Philip of Baden and the Elector of the Palatinate deserve honourable mention, and ultimately it began to dawn even on the more savage of these princely repressors that a limit must be put to this orgy of revenge, if only on the ground of self-interest.   " If all our peasants are done to death in this manner," wrote the Margrave George to his brother Casimir, " where shall we find others to grow our food ?   It really behoves us to consider the matter wisely." [88]   Thus the gruesome drama came at last to an end.   But what an ending for the common man !   Over 100,000 at the lowest computation had lost their lives during the Rising and the retribution that followed it,[89] and many thousands more sought safety in flight across the Swiss border.   The peasant sank back into his servile condition and the boon of emancipation was relegated to the far distant days of the French Revolution.   Only to a limited extent had he succeeded, as in Baden, in obtaining any amelioration of his lot.   In general the Rising resulted in the aggravation of his oppression.   For this result he had himself, in no small measure, to blame.   By his violence and love of plunder, his lack of discipline, his bibulousness, his inexperience in tactics, his proneness to panic in the face of the trained soldier, he had lost what was in the main a good cause and failed to vindicate claims, most of which a more enlightened age has come to regard as rights.

The suppression of the Rising had an unfortunate effect on the evangelical movement.   The hope that this movement would become the means of effecting a far-reaching social reformation was blasted.   The preachers who had worked for this larger reformation were crushed in the general crash.   In those regions where the anti-Lutheran princes triumphed, the ruffianly repression of the peasants sealed

[88] Janssen, iv. 348 (Eng. trans.).          [89] Ibid., iv. 347.

at the same time the fate of the religious Reformation itself. In a large part of the south Roman Catholicism shared in the victory of the princes and lords, and thus Luther in championing their cause against the people with such reckless violence was in reality working into the hands of his enemies. The hope of winning the whole empire was thereby wrecked, and even if the movement continued to make headway in the north, which had largely been exempt from the revolutionary fever, it was not so much because of its democratic appeal as of the play of princely self-interest to which Luther had, if unwittingly, thirled it. Lutheranism ceased to be a popular creed for the time being at least.[90] The people denounced him as " the flatterer of the princes," [91] and threatened to take his life. " All the lords, parsons, and peasants are against me and threaten me with death," he wrote to Rühel on the 15th June.[92]  Their ill-will, he adds, does not trouble him, and he certainly made no attempt to disarm it.  The Rising had shattered his trust in the masses, and he continued to reiterate his dogma that force is the only remedy in dealing with discontented subjects.  Even long afterwards, when the passion begotten by the struggle had had time to subside, he is found defending in his dogged fashion the obnoxious philippic against the peasants.  " It was I, Martin Luther, who slew all the peasants during the Rising, for I commanded them to be slaughtered.  All their blood is on my head.  But I throw the responsibility on our Lord God, who instructed me to give this order." [93] He doubtless acted from a kind of bovine conviction, and not from any desire to gain the favour of the ruling class. His previous denunciations of the princes and their misgovernment convincingly show that he was not actuated

[90] Von Below questions the generally accepted view of the adverse effects of the repression of the rising on the Lutheran movement (" Ursachen," 55-56, 59-60) against Karl Müller, " Kirchengeschichte," ii. 325-326; Hermelink, " Reformation und Gegen Reformation," 89; and others. Stolze, " Bauernkrieg und Reformation," 119 f., also questions the accepted view; whilst Ritter, another recent writer (" Luther," 123-124 (1925)), supports the adverse conclusion.

[91] Enders, v. 182, adulator principum.

[92] " Werke," 53, 314; cf. 305 (Erlangen ed.).

[93] Ibid., 59, 284 (Erlangen ed.).

by such a motive. He was in principle up to this period opposed to the use of force in behalf of religious or any other reform, and to him religious reform was the thing that mainly mattered. Moreover, the revolution threatened to engulf his cause in the general chaos which it was tending to bring about, and on the rejection of his own wise proposal of arbitration he might well see in a victory for constituted authority the only guarantee of the preservation of law and order. Even so, his sudden change from the rôle of the wise arbiter to that of the raving partisan, who advocates the wholesale slaughter of the insurgents and the restoration of the old system, irrespective of Christian equity, shows a lack of anything like statesmanship, let alone Christian self-restraint. His influence over public opinion was such that he might at least have moderated the havoc and fury of princely retaliation. At all events, he himself assumed that a word from him would have gone far to turn the scale the other way. Even if nothing he could have said or done would have prevented the tragic collapse of the popular cause, it was not his province to proclaim so dogmatically the political nullity of the common man in a professedly Christian State, as an axiom of the movement of which he was the leader, and inculcate unquestioning obedience to the absolute ruler, however oppressive his rule. Unfortunately, under the influence of the revolutionary scare, the Reformation in Germany, as directed by him, henceforth contributed to strengthen the régime of the absolute ruler, whether elector, duke, landgrave, or other petty potentate, instead of developing into the larger and more democratic movement of which it had at first seemed to be the promise, and to which his theological teaching had undoubtedly given an impulse. Luther, Melanchthon, Bucer swam with the political current that was bearing the absolute ruler to port in Germany, France, Spain. In the political sphere they have no wide vision. They preach the doctrine of divine right pure and simple. They dethrone an absolute pope only to put in his place the absolute prince. Passive resistance may be permissible in matters of conscience. The Christian subject may not deny God at the prince's command. But he may not actively resist. Even this modicum of right was denied by Bucer, who insists that subjects must obey the commands of the prince even when contrary to God's Word.[94]

[94] See "History of Modern Liberty," ii. 103. For Melanchthon's views see his "Refutation of the Twelve Articles" which he wrote for the enlightenment of the Elector of the Palatinate. "Corp. Ref.," xx. 641-643; cf. Janssen, iv. 364-367; Ellinger, "Melanchthon," 211-212; Richard, "Melanchthon," 149-152. The literature on the subject of the Rising is voluminous. The older work of Zimmermann (1856) has been edited by Blos (1891). A valuable collection of documents is given by Baumann, "Akten zur Geschichte des Bauernkriegs" (1877) and "Quellen zur Geschichte des Bauernkriegs in Oberschwaben" (1876). More recent are the works of Stolze, "Der Deutsche Bauernkrieg" (1907) and "Bauernkrieg und Reformation" (1926); Götze, "Die Artikel der Bauern," "Hist. Vierteljahrschrift" (1901); Jaeger, "Die Politischen Ideen Luther's," "Preuss. Jahrbücher" (1903); Zimmermann, "Thomas Münzer" (1925), to mention only these out of a large number of recent monographs. A luminous account is that of Von Bezold, "Geschichte der Deutschen Reformation." Janssen, "Hist. of the German People," iii. and iv., is fuller, but prejudiced; and Ranke, "Deutsche Geschichte," is also one-sided. Schapiro, "Social Reform and the Reformation" (1909), and Waring, "Political Theories of Luther" (1910), who rather feebly attempts a complete vindication of Luther, are the most recent reviews in English. The work of Bax, "The Peasants' War in Germany" (1899), is a popular account on the side of the insurgents. So is that of Friedrich Engels, translated into English by Olgin (1927). Other accounts in English are given in my "History of Modern Liberty" (1906) and in Oman's short survey in the "English Historical Review" (1890).

# CHAPTER VII

# THE CONFLICT WITH ERASMUS

## I. LUTHER AND EDUCATION

LUTHER'S warfare with the extremists included the sphere of culture as well as of religion and politics. The emphasis on the supreme value of the Word as the norm of truth and on the right of the Christian community to judge of doctrine, the exaltation of faith and the depreciation of reason as the medium of a knowledge of the divine, the antagonism to the scholastic theology, the denunciation of the scholastic educational method, tended to foster in ignorant and ill-balanced minds a contempt for all culture —the new as well as the old. The prophets saw in individual illumination by the Spirit the infallible guarantee of truth, and refused to attribute this exclusive prerogative to the Word. Carlstadt, learned doctor though he was, turned to the ordinary layman for the true interpretation of Scripture texts.[1] In this he was not necessarily so eccentric as his fellow-theologians were disposed to assume. Spiritual intuition is no monopoly of learned doctors, whether Roman Catholic or evangelical. Genuine religious experience in the case of a weaver or a shoemaker may teach even the most erudite scholar whose learning lacks the intuition which experienced truth alone can give. The critics of Carlstadt and even Münzer are apt to forget that in the New Testament community edification was the right of every member who had something to say for the common enlightenment, not the sole prerogative of apostle, prophet, or presbyter. On the other hand, Carlstadt carried his predilection for this laic, New Testament type of religion beyond the limit of

[1] Barge, i. 416-417.

good sense in renouncing the practice of promoting candidates to theological degrees, on the ground of the equality of all Christians, and the command in Matt. xxiii. 8 to call no man master.[2]   The religious excitement of the time was tending, like strong drink, to go to the heads even of learned professors, not to speak of ordinary Christians, whilst many of the emancipated monks, who had been ignorant obscurantists before becoming evangelical preachers, were compromising Luther's doctrine of the supreme value and authority of the Word by their superficial diatribes against the new learning as well as the old scholasticism.   At Erfurt, for instance, these hotheads carried the war against their scholastic opponents the length of depreciating the study of the classics and proclaiming that, for an understanding of the Scriptures, a knowledge of Latin and Greek was superfluous.[3]   At Nürnberg, Basle, Strassburg, and elsewhere this new obscurantism found expression in sermons or pamphlets, to the distress of Melanchthon, Eobanus Hessus, and other apostles of the new culture, who had espoused the cause of Luther.   Melanchthon was fain to confess in his " Encomium Eloquentiæ" that this depreciation of classical studies was spreading like an infectious disease, not only among the preachers, but among professors of law and medicine.[4]   " Good God," wrote he to Hessus in April 1523, " how preposterously do those theologise who wish to show their wisdom solely by their contempt of these good things ! What is this error but a new species of sophistry ? "[5] Similarly, Eobanus expressed his strong disapprobation of this obscurantist tendency in a Latin elegy addressed to Luther under the title of " Captiva."[6]

Nor were these apprehensions merely the Jeremiads of opinionated humanists who were inclined to see in the study of the classics the exclusive medium of a liberal education.   They were substantiated by the growing lack of interest in the higher education reflected in the general decline of the number of students attending the secondary

[2] Barge, ii. 12.

[3] " Werke," xv. 10.

[4] " Corp. Ref.," xi. 50 f.

[5] Ibid., i. 613.

[6] Printed by Secerius at Hagenau, 1523, under the title of " Ecclesiæ Afflictæ Epistola ad Lutherum," Enders, iv. 120.

schools and the universities during this period. During the five years 1521-25 the number of those matriculating at Wittenberg University sank from 245 in the former year [7] to 171 in the latter. This decline is, in fact, apparent in all the German universities, and in some of them it was more marked than at Wittenberg. In the case of Leipzig, for instance, the number sank from 339 to 102, of Cologne from 251 to 120, of Freiburg from 171 to 22. In 1526 only 9 students matriculated at Rostock, compared with 118 in 1521, whilst teaching at Greifswald was suspended between 1524 and 1539 for lack of students.[8]

The shrinkage plainly shows that the humanist movement, which had contributed to fill the class-rooms during the previous two decades, had passed its zenith and had given place to a reaction under the influence of the evangelical Reformation. There can be no question that the religious excitement which manifested itself in student riots at Wittenberg and Erfurt took, in part at least, the form of a superficial tendency to divorce religion from culture, under the mistaken belief that the votaries of the new Gospel could afford to dispense not only with the old theology and philosophy but with a literary education.[9] Ulscenius, for instance, writes to Capito in January 1522 that a number of the students had left the University of Wittenberg as the result of this reaction,[10] whilst the Elector in a message to Luther at the Wartburg shortly after anxiously noted the same fact.[11] At the same time, this reaction against the new culture was not peculiar

---

[7] Compared with 579 in 1520.

[8] Eilenburg, " Über die Frequenz der deutschen Universitäten in früherer Zeit," "Jahrbücher für Nationalöconomie," Bd. 13 (1877); Barge, i. 419-420.

[9] For details see Albrecht, " Studien zu Luther's Schrift, An die Ratherren," "Theologische Studien und Kritiken" (1897), 782 f. Paulsen is mistaken in reckoning among these obscurantists John Lang, " Geschichte des gelehrten Unterrichts," i. 190. Lang, in fact, preached a sermon in May 1523 against these fanatic preachers, which was published in the same year, and which Luther had probably read before issuing his own famous address to the municipalities on " School Reform " in the following year. See Albrecht, " Studien," 737 f.

[10] " Z.K.G.," v. 331.

[11] " Corp. Ref.," i. 560.

to Wittenberg or Erfurt. It was by no means due merely to the obscurantist influence of a Carlstadt or the ex-monks who, as preachers, espoused the cause of Luther with more zeal than wisdom. Its factors were economic as well as religious. Begging, for instance, had hitherto been recognised as a legitimate means of subsistence for students, even in the case of those who belonged to well-to-do families, as well as for the monastic Orders. As the reform ordinances at Wittenberg and elsewhere show, one of the effects of the evangelical movement was to discredit the practice and create a more healthy self-respect in the rising generation, as against this demeaning form of charity. The prospect of securing a living, in the form of an ecclesiastical prebend, as the result of a university education had, further, lost its attraction for those who had forsworn the Pope and all his works. In any case the secularisation of ecclesiastical property threatened to dry up this source of income for the needy scholar. Moreover, the changing economic conditions of the age were tending to foster a more material and practical view of life. An expanding commerce was offering a more alluring prospect for the enterprising youth, who, as Bucer deplores, were more concerned with the quest of wealth than the things of the spirit. " Nobody," he complains, " will learn anything nowadays except what brings in money. All the world is running after those trades and occupations which give least work to do and bring the most gain, without any concern for their neighbour or for honest and good report. The study of the arts and sciences is set aside for the barest kinds of manual work. . . . All the clever heads which have been endowed by God with capacity for the nobler studies are engrossed by commerce." [12] " Things have become so deplorable in the last few years," complains the writer of the " Clag eines einfältigen Klosterbruders," "that no Christian mother can any more send her children to the schools, which either have been abolished or are despised ; so all the young folk are turned into tradespeople, and the children of the poor, who are especially God-forsaken, become petty craftsmen in towns and villages

[12] Janssen, iv. 162-163.

without much knowledge of these trades. Most of them become small shopkeepers, pedlars, hawkers, all of which varieties abound in excess." [13]

That Luther should take the opposite side from the extremists on the culture question was a foregone conclusion. Though not a professed humanist, he had in his student days found both pleasure and profit in reading the Latin classics. When he entered the Augustinian monastery at Erfurt he had carried his Virgil in his pocket. Under the influence of Lang, Spalatin, and other humanist friends, he had gradually learned to prize the study of the ancient languages as an indispensable adjunct of the interpretation of the sources of Christianity, and had, for this reason, availed himself of the scholarship of Lefèvre, and especially of Erasmus, in his early exegetical work as professor of Holy Writ. He had submitted to the drudgery of learning Hebrew and Greek in order the better to fit himself for this vocation. His translation of the Bible from the original languages is a monument of his practical interest in the new culture, without which it would not have been possible, as well as of his ability to mould the vernacular idiom into a fitting medium to convey to the common man the sense of the sacred writings. The study of these languages was an integral part of the sketch of educational reform contained in the " Address to the Nobility." It is not surprising, therefore, that, in reply to Eobanus Hessus, he emphatically rebutted the obscurantist vapourings of the shallow and ignorant advocates of the divorce of religion from culture, and that in his later negotiations with the Bohemians he adduced, among other objections to their theological teaching, their neglect of the ancient languages in the education of their priests.[14] He himself, indeed, had proclaimed the capacity of the individual believer to attain, under the guidance of the Spirit, a knowledge of the way of salvation, and even preach Christ, from a perusal of the German Bible. But, as a rule, he recognised and emphasised the value of an adequate linguistic and literary training for the preacher as well as

---

[13] Janssen, iv. 163.

[14] In his treatise, " Von Anbeten des Sacraments," written for the instruction of the Bohemians, " Werke," xi. 455-456 (April 1523).

the theologian.[15] " Do not give way to your apprehension," he wrote to Eobanus on the 23rd March 1523, " lest we Germans become more barbarous than ever we were by reason of the decline of letters through our theology. I am persuaded that, without a skilled training in literary studies, no true theology can establish and maintain itself, seeing that in times past it has invariably fallen miserably and lain prostrate with the decline and fall of learning. On the other hand, it is indubitable that there never has been a signal revelation of divine truth unless first the way has been prepared for it, as by a John the Baptist, by the revival and pursuit of the study of languages and literature. Assuredly there is nothing I should less wish to happen than that our youth should neglect poetry and rhetoric (humanist studies). My ardent vow is that there should be as many poets and rhetoricians as possible, because I see clearly that by no other methods is it possible to train men for the apt understanding, the right and felicitous treatment of sacred things. Wherefore I beg that you may incite the youth of Erfurt to give themselves strenuously to this study. I am often impatient that in this age of enlightenment time will not permit me to devote myself to poetry and rhetoric, though I formerly bought a Homer in order that I might become a Greek." [16] " I beg you," he wrote to Strauss at Eisenach a year later (April 1524), " to do your utmost in the cause of the training of youth. For I am convinced that the neglect of education will bring the greatest ruin to the Gospel. This matter is the most important of all." [17]

His sense of the value of a Christian education and of the pressing need of educational reform, in the interest of the State as well as the Church, found more elaborate expression in the famous "Appeal to the Municipalities of Germany" early in 1524. The "Appeal" is a monument of the enlightened interest in education which the Reformation, as inspired by

---

[15] See, for instance, "Werke," xi. 455-456. On Luther and humanism see the monographs of Schmidt, " Luther's Bekanntschaft mit den Classikern," and Evers, " Das Verhältnis Luther's zu den Humanisten " (1895).

[16] Enders, iv. 119-120.          [17] *Ibid.*, iv. 328.

Luther, Melanchthon, Zwingli, and other reformers, in spite of the obscurantism of the extremists, fostered not only in Germany, but in all the lands in which the reformed displaced the mediæval Church. It reflects, too, the influence of Melanchthon, the *Præceptor Germaniæ*, to whose humanist learning Luther, and Germany along with him, owed so much, and who had begun his career as Professor of Greek at Wittenberg with an inaugural discourse on " The Improvement of the Studies of Youth." [18] This plea in behalf of the new, in opposition to the scholastic culture, and of the imperative necessity, in the case of theology, of the study of Greek and Hebrew for the true understanding of sacred literature, made a powerful impression on Luther, though its spirit was that of Erasmus rather than of the militant leader of the evangelical movement. " When we go to the sources we are led to Christ." In the six years that had intervened between its delivery in August 1518 and the "Appeal to the Municipalities," Luther's appreciation of the value of classical studies had deepened as the result of his intercourse and collaboration with the brilliant young scholar, who, on his part, had developed into the active champion of evangelical as well as educational reform.

Although he has been for three years under the ban of the Pope and the Emperor and an outlaw in the eyes of men, no human authority will prevent him from fulfilling his God-appointed mission to proclaim the truth. Accordingly he begs the German municipal authorities at the outset [19] to receive his message on the subject as the voice of Christ. He acknowledges that the evangelical movement has had an adverse effect on education. Now that the monastic and clerical career is falling into disrepute as the result of the preaching of the Gospel, parents are naturally

[18] Ellinger, " Melanchthon," 88 f.

[19] An die Ratherren aller städte Deutsches Lands, " Werke," xv. 27 f., with valuable introduction by O. Albrecht. See also his " Studien zu Luther's Schrift an die Ratherren," " Theolog. Studien " (1897), 687 f. ; Paulsen, " Geschichte des gelehrten Unterrichts," 197 f. ; and " German Education, Past and Present," 53 f., Eng. trans. by Lorenz (1908). Paulsen is rather unsympathetic, and underrates Luther's significance as an educational reformer, in contrast to the more purely humanist reformers.

enough asking what is the good of educating their children in accordance with use and wont. Hitherto, he naïvely explains, the devil was only too pleased to see the children brought up in the error and falsehood of the monastic and collegiate schools. But now that he is in danger of losing their souls through the spread of the Gospel, he has changed has tactics and descants on the futility of all education. Ignorance and contempt of all knowledge will serve his purpose equally well. In reality, the lack of a sound education is a worse enemy of the commonweal than the Turk, and if we give a single gulden for the defence of the empire, we ought to give a hundred to educate even one boy to become a right Christian man, in view of the value of such an educated man to the country. Let the town authorities, therefore, take to heart the importance of the education of youth on which its highest well-being depends. If they spend money in fortifying and improving the town, why should they grudge spending in providing schoolmasters for the purpose of securing this supreme object ? The individual citizen as well as the public authority has his responsibility in this matter. If people formerly gave so readily for indulgences, masses, pilgrimages, and other rubbish, should they not be ready to devote a part of this wasted expenditure to a sound training of the rising generation ? In giving the Gospel to the present age, God has provided a multitude of men educated in the new learning and gifted with the requisite knowledge and skill to impart such a training. The present age is the year of jubilee for Germany. Formerly we spent long years of drudgery in the schools and learned neither Latin nor German properly. The whole school instruction, he says, in his exaggerated manner, produced only asses and blockheads and tended to the corruption rather than the edification of youth. Rather than revive this pernicious system, against which he has evidently been biased by his changed religious standpoint, he would prefer no education at all ! But now that God has blessed Germany in such full measure with the pure Gospel, let it take advantage of the opportunity and beware of missing it. To neglect the education of youth is no less a crime than to deflower a virgin, as the scholastic proverb has it. There is no greater danger to the common good than an uneducated and ill-disciplined youth, and as parents, as a rule, are unfitted or too busy to attend to the education of their children, the schoolmaster is indispensable. Hence the imperative duty of the public authority to provide schools and teachers in the common interest. Nor should it be content merely to establish elementary schools for the instruction of pupils in German and the Bible. It is in the interest of both Church and State to foster the study of the classic languages as the best instruments of the higher education, for the lack of which Germans are decried in foreign lands (Italy is specially meant) as barbarians. By neglecting these studies in the schools they will only too well merit such supercilious gibes.

In the first place, for the understanding of the Gospel, the study of Latin, Greek, and Hebrew and other *Artes Liberales* is essential. The Gospel was revealed in these languages, and to the widespread use of Latin and Greek in the ancient world its diffusion was due. In this modern age God has similarly brought about their revival, just before the rediscovery of the primitive Gospel, in order that it might thereby be better understood and the reign of Antichrist disclosed and overthrown. For this reason He allowed the Turks to conquer Greece and thus bring about, through fugitive Greeks, a wider knowledge of the language of the New Testament. Let there be no mistake about it. Without a knowledge of these languages Germany will not long retain the Gospel. They are the scabbard wherein the sword of the Spirit is sheathed, the shrine in which this treasure is laid. Not only will it lose the Gospel; it will fall back into the old wretched educational system which, for Luther, stands for barbarism in both religion and education. Without a knowledge of them there can be no real knowledge of the Word and no higher education worthy of the name. With their decline in the ancient world true Christianity began to fall and came under the power of the Pope. On the other hand, their revival has brought about such an enlightenment and has accomplished such great things that all the world must acknowledge that we now possess the Gospel in as pure and true a form as the Apostles had it, and much more purely than in the days of St Jerome and Augustine.[20]   St Bernard, whom he prizes above all doctors, old and new, as a spiritual teacher, often fails, for this reason, to catch the true sense of the sacred text—a failing which is sometimes predicable of his own exegesis.   But have not many Fathers taught Christianity and attained to honour without these languages ?   True.   On the other hand, how many errors disfigure the exegetical writings of Augustine, Hilary, and other Fathers who were ignorant of the original languages of Scripture !   Whilst a preacher may preach Christ with edification, though he may be unable to read the Scriptures in the originals, he cannot expound or maintain their teaching against the heretics without this indispensable knowledge.   Luther here speaks from his own experience as professor of Sacred Writ.   This experience had both revealed to him his own deficiencies as an exegete and driven him to the serious study of both Greek and Hebrew. He has travelled a long way from his early dependence on Augustine and other Fathers, and has learned not only to assign supreme authority to the Scriptures alone, but to interpret them independently and to criticise unhesitatingly even their patristic interpreters.   In complaining of the obscurity of Scripture the schoolmen were, he forcibly points out, reproving their own ignorance of these languages, and it is useless to try to make up for this ignorance by quoting from the Fathers and reading the scholastic commentaries.   " As the sun is to the shadow, so is a knowledge of the originals to all the commentaries of the Fathers." [21] What folly, then, to neglect or depreciate the study of them. For this reason he cannot approve of " the Waldensians " (the Bohemian Brethren) who despise this study.

In the second place, this study is essential in the interest of the State as well as the Church.   Apart from religion, such a training is, on purely utilitarian grounds, of the utmost importance for the State.   " It is a sufficient reason for establishing the best possible schools for boys and girls that the State, for its own advantage, needs well educated men and women for the better government of land and

---

[20] " Werke," xv. 39.                    [21] *Ibid.*, xv. 41.

people, and the proper upbringing of children in the home." [22]
In view of the inestimable benefit to the State to be derived
from this education, he would radically change the old
educational method in a practical direction. He would,
therefore, discard the tyrannical memorising drill of this
system and make the task of learning a joy and a recreation
for the pupils. He calls to mind the useless drudgery of his
own schooldays at Mansfeld, Magdeburg, and Eisenach,
and of his student days at Erfurt. The recollection seems
to be rather overcoloured by his subsequent religious
experience, which inclines him to see only error and evil
in everything connected with the old system, as applied
under the brutal inspiration of the rod. " The schools were
no better than hell and purgatory, in which we were martyred
with the grinding of tenses and cases and nevertheless learned
nothing at all, in spite of the blows, trembling, terror, and
misery we suffered at the hands of our brutal schoolmasters.
. . . How much I regret that we did not read more of the
poets and the historians, and that nobody thought of teaching
us these. Instead of such study, I was compelled to read
the devil's rubbish—the scholastic philosophers and sophists
with such cost, labour, and detriment, from which I have
had trouble enough to rid myself." [23] Happily, by God's
grace, a more rational, practical, and humane method bids
fair to introduce a new era in education under the influence
of the great religious transformation of which he has been the
instrument.

Not that he demands the higher education for all. But
he would place a sound elementary education, combined
with practical training in some useful craft, within the reach
of every boy and girl, and even make it compulsory. For
the training of talented boys for the service of Church and
State he would provide suitable instruction in secondary
schools. To the same end he would establish libraries in
the towns and fill them with useful books, instead of the
scholastic rubbish which he regards as so much lumber.
He would exclude from these collections the textbooks of
canon law and the scholastic theology and philosophy,

---

[22] " Werke," xv. 44.        [23] Ibid., xv. 46.

and in place of this " filth " install the Bible in the original languages and in German and other translations, along with the best ancient commentaries, the classic authors, both pagan and Christian, and approved books in law, medicine, and all the arts and sciences.   He would add the best histories and chronicles in any language, particularly those relating to German national history, which are indispensable for a proper understanding of the past, the ways of God as revealed in the doings of men.

The " Address " is a remarkable performance.   It has been described as " the Charter of the German gymnasia," [24] or high schools.   Whilst formally it does not answer to this description, it is so far appropriate inasmuch as it tends in its own way to stress classical study, combined with religious, historical, and scientific instruction, as the fundamental principle of a sound secondary education.   In this respect it is a worthy example of the interest in education characteristic of the Reformed Churches, of which Luther was the inspirer in Germany, Zwingli and Calvin in Switzerland, and John Knox in Scotland.   In Ranke's judgment it is as significant in its own sphere as the " Address to the German Nobility."   Contemporaries like Erasmus and Cochlaeus, who lay the blame on Luther's shoulders for the decline of the schools and universities, have certainly no warrant for their accusations in this fervid appeal.   It alone suffices to rebut the sweeping Erasmian dictum, " Wherever Lutheranism prevails, there the destruction of letters takes place."   By 1524 Erasmus was becoming more and more incapable of discriminating between the good and the bad in the Lutheran movement.   He represents it far too much in the light of its extreme wing, as represented by the obscurantist preachers, from whom Luther in this appeal expressly dissociates himself.   He forgets, too, that humanism itself, as far at least as it tended to stress intellectual culture at the expense of the practical and spiritual side of education and to isolate itself from the life of the people, could have learned more from it in this respect than

---

[24] Schmid, " Encyclopädie des gesch. Erziehungs und Unterrichtswesens," art. " Luther."

it deigned to acknowledge. Moreover, as Hartfelder has pointed out, the complaint of lack of interest in classic study in the young generation was voiced by humanists like Glareanus, Wimpheling, Rudolf Agricola, long before the advent of Luther. The fact is that Luther, though primarily a religious reformer, had several years before combined educational with religious reform in the reform programme addressed to the nobility. It redounds to his credit that he realised the need for fanning the rather jaded zeal of the municipal authorities which, with the development of industry and trade in the later mediæval period, had founded and fostered these schools, but which were in danger of neglecting them and devoting secularised ecclesiastical property to other ends. The "Appeal" is assuredly no mere afterthought, suggested merely by the necessity of saving the Reformation from disaster and himself from the consequences of his own reckless religious anarchism, as Paulsen, who merely reflects Cochlaeus, assumes.[25] Along with Bugenhagen he took steps to revive and reorganise the Wittenberg school, which had been closed during his absence in the Wartburg, and in response to his "Appeal" a beginning was made with the work of establishing reformed schools at Magdeburg, Nordhausen, Halberstadt, Gotha, Eisleben, and Nürnberg within a year of its publication.[26]

It was not without reason that Melanchthon in the preface to the Latin translation by Obsopæus warmly commended it to the academic youth of Germany.[27] Though Luther's motive in penning it was mainly the interest of the evangelical movement, he does not overlook the material well-being of the nation or the value of education as a good in itself. He strove to advance thereby the national interest and to raise the national reputation in the

[25] He calls it a "Notschrei der durch die Thatsache des plötzlichen und allgemeinen Niedergangs des Unterrichtswesens seit dem Anfang der Kirchenrevolution ausgepresst ist," i. 197. Was, then, the sketch of educational reform already outlined in the "Address to the Nobility" in 1520 a Notschrei or cry of despair ? In view of this fact Paulsen's assertion that Luther's esteem for education "was very moderate indeed " ("German Education," 48) is rather astounding.

[26] Albrecht, "Studien," 772-773.

[27] "Corp. Ref.," i. 66 f.

face of the charge of barbarism and grossness with which the Italians besmirched it, and which, though exaggerated, he regards as sufficiently well founded.   At the same time the supreme end of education is for him the furthering of the Gospel as revealed in the Word, and the building up of Christian character as the indispensable and the incomparable foundation of the higher moral and spiritual life.

## II. LUTHER AND ERASMUS

As has been previously noted, humanists of the type of Hutten, after being contemptuous or indifferent towards the Wittenberg movement, suddenly discovered in Luther an ally in the war against the old culture.   With the Leipzig Disputation and the growing boldness of his challenge to Rome, this militant monk became for Crotus, Hutten, and other stalwarts of humanism the morning star on the horizon of the new age.   What attracted them was not the new Gospel of justification by faith, to which they paid little more than lip service, but the antagonism to the Papacy, the hierarchy, and the scholastic theology and philosophy, and the plea for liberty of thought and conscience as against the Roman autocracy, to which the Wittenberg professor was giving such resounding expression.   Others, like Lang, Melanchthon, Eobanus Hessus, Bucer, Oecolampadius, were from the outset, or became, adherents on religious as well as intellectual grounds.   Luther, in fact, became the magnet of an increasing circle of young scholars who whole-heartedly acknowledged him as their master in theology, whilst owning allegiance to Erasmus in the sphere of culture.   Even when in due course the time came to choose between adherence to the militant reformer or the prince of scholars, the members of this circle did not shrink from adopting the former alternative.   Erasmus thereby lost the unquestioned intellectual dictatorship which he had exercised for nearly two decades.   Though no professed humanist, Luther had deprived him of his supremacy over the republic of letters. Truly a striking testimony to the strength of his personality, the dynamic of his religious genius.

The crisis came in 1521-22 when, in spite of condemnation and outlawry, he persisted in and even widened his attack on Antichrist and the institutions of the Church. It was this development, in which the older disciples of Erasmus saw the spectre of religious revolution and chaos, that led to the parting of the ways. Without the profound conviction, based on personal religious experience, and the indomitable will power of the irrepressible outlaw, Mutian, Crotus, Zasius, Pirkheimer, and others shrank before this spectre, whilst Reuchlin disowned his grandnephew, Melanchthon, who refused to abandon Luther.[28] The attitude of Erasmus himself was a foregone conclusion. It was difficult for one whose intellectual development, temperament, and religious experience were so different from those of Luther fully to understand or appreciate the man and the movement, and Luther, as we have seen, was early aware of the fundamental difference between their theological standpoints. For some years, indeed, after Luther's emergence as a religious reformer, his attitude was on the whole sympathetic, if non-committal. Both were at one in their warfare against the scholastic theology and the obscurantism of the schools, in their appeal from the schoolmen to the sources of Christianity, in their recoil from the conventional religion, in their demand for a comprehensive reform of ecclesiastical abuses. So much had they in common that the opponents of Luther were also the opponents of Erasmus, and regarded them as fellow-workers in the same cause. The great humanist, they held, was the inspirer of the great heretic. They even believed him to be the author of some of Luther's writings. " Erasmus," it was said, " laid the egg that Luther hatched." There was a certain amount of truth in the saying. Erasmus by his critical labours paved the way to a truer knowledge of the original sources, particularly the New Testament writings, from which the evangelical reformers drew their inspiration, though his edition of the New Testament is, of course, very imperfect judged by the standard of modern critical scholarship.[29] In " The Method of True Theology,"

[28] Geiger, " Johann Reuchlin," 466.

[29] Drummond, " Erasmus," i. 315-316, 345-346 (1873); Binns, " Erasmus, the Reformer," 75-76 (1923); cf. P. Smith, " Erasmus," 163 f. (1923).

prefaced to it and afterwards published separately in enlarged form (*Ratio veræ Theologiæ*), he anticipated Luther in insisting on the importance of a knowledge of the original languages for the understanding of the Scriptures, and in exalting such direct knowledge above the scholastic theology, of which the Apostles and the Fathers knew nothing and were, indeed, the antagonists.[30]   He emphasised the supreme authority of Scripture and would even test the Apostles' Creed by it,[31] if he also recognises the validity of ecclesiastical tradition.   For him, as for his friend Colet, belief in the Scripture and the Apostles' Creed is sufficient, and he refuses to submerge the mind in scholastic speculation.   He would, in fact, displace the scholastic by a scriptural theology, and would accord liberty of opinion in theological speculation. He shares Luther's denial of the right to impose such speculations as articles of faith and his protest against the excessive ecclesiastical regulation of the Christian life.   The Church has become Judaic in this respect, and with Paul, as well as Luther, he would restore the liberty of the Gospel, and holds that such regulation is not obligatory because it is not voluntary.[32]   He directs the shafts of his satire especially against the monks and the monastic life, which he regards as a deformation of the Gospel,[33] and though he does not, like Luther, carry his aversion the length of demanding the abolition of monasticism, his exposure of its evils is equally scathing.   In his onslaught on this and other abuses he undoubtedly prepared the way for Luther, though he later found it convenient to ignore his responsibility in this matter. In virtue of his tendency to criticise and ridicule the conventional religion and theology, he has, in fact, been regarded as the precursor of the modern freethinker, the Voltaire of the sixteenth century, the ancestor of the age of enlightenment, as the eighteenth century has been called.   The

[30] Drummond, i. 326.
[31] Pineau, "Érasme, sa Pensée Religieuse," 260-261 (1923). See also Lindeboom, " Onderzoek naar zijne Theologie " (1909); Renaudet, " Érasme, sa Pensée Religieuse et son Action," 6 f. (1927).
[32] *Ibid.*, 234-235.
[33] *Ibid.*, 221 ; Ernst, "Die Frommigkeit des Erasmus," "Theol. Stud. und Krit." (1919), 72.

inference is rather far-fetched, if only in view of the fact that
a precursor of Voltaire would hardly have spent the greater
part of a laborious life in producing critical editions of the
New Testament and the Fathers for the purpose of contribut-
ing to the knowledge of early Christianity, in place of the
current ecclesiastical and scholastic development of it, and
thereby restoring and strengthening the Church and the
religious life. Whilst attacked and decried by his
obscurantist opponents and even accused by the Sorbonne
of heresy, he was hailed by his admirers, with exaggeration
no doubt, as the prince of theologians, and was a sincere
believer in the Christianity of the New Testament and the
Fathers, if not in its later scholastic and ecclesiastical
development. Moreover, it is rather hazardous to see or
seek in German humanism, as represented by Erasmus, an
anticipation of modern freethought.[34] It is in general too
much limited by its subservience to the mediæval principle
of authority to anticipate a Bayle or a Voltaire, and there
is a danger in such judgments in unduly " modernising "
Erasmus. Ritter, in fact, contends, as against Dilthey,
Troeltsch, and Wernle, that Erasmus, in spite of his critical
and reactionary attitude towards the Church and its
institutions and theology, did not essentially go beyond
the standpoint of mediæval piety.[35] At the same time,
there is undoubtedly a modern note in the tendency freely,
if tentatively, to apply the critical, rational method to the
interpretation of the New Testament and the dogmas and
institutions of the Church, which he owed to Laurentius
Valla, and to conceive of Christianity in the larger spirit
of a Ficino, Pico,[36] and the Italian Platonists who sought
to reconcile Christ and Plato.

It thus appears that there was a good deal in common

[34] See Ritter, " Die Geschichtliche Bedeutung des Deutschen Humanismus," "Hist. Zeitschrift" (1923), 416. " In der Geschichte der
Wissenschaft (von der Theologie sei hier zunächst abgesehen) bedeutet
der Humanismus noch nicht der Anfang des modernen Denkens ";
cf. 446-448.
[35] Ibid., 442-445.
[36] For the influence of Pico on Erasmus see Pusino, " Der Ein-
fluss Picos auf Erasmus," "Z.K.G." (1928), 75 f.; and ibid. (1925),

between the standpoints of the two reformers. Up to a point, they were undoubtedly allies in the same cause, and to this extent there is plausibility in the assumption of their opponents that, in the matter of what they deemed heresy, Luther was simply the *alter ego* of Erasmus. Nevertheless, the assumption was substantially baseless. A fundamental difference lies in the fact that Erasmus came to his reforming standpoint primarily from the humanist and only secondarily from the religious approach. His progress as a reformer was mainly on the line of critical, rational thought. "Erasmus," judges Mestwerdt in his recent book on the early religious and intellectual *milieu* in which he grew up, "is neither exclusively nor predominantly a religious character. Much rather is the religious motive only one among many." [37] Luther, on the other hand, was led to his reforming standpoint almost exclusively by way of the religious approach. For him the religious motive is the dominating one, the humanist only of secondary importance. His activity as a reformer was due first and foremost to his personal religious experience —to the struggle to find a gracious God in the face of the overwhelming sense of human sin and the divine righteousness, from which he had ultimately found deliverance in his distinctive apprehension of the Pauline doctrine of justification by faith. Erasmus, on the contrary, had known nothing of this convulsive conflict with the problem of human sin and divine righteousness. He had grown to manhood in the religious atmosphere of the "Devotio Moderna," as represented by the Brethren of the Common Life or Lot,[38] which, while fostering a living personal piety in contrast to the ecclesiastical type (the *Devotio Antiqua*), and striving to reform the degenerate Church, kept essentially

540-451. Pusino would assign to Pico the main influence in shaping his ideas, as the "Enchiridion" shows, and to Colet the inspiration to advocate a thorough practical reform of the Church. See also Renaudet, "Préreforme et Humanisme à Paris" (1916).

[37] "Die Anfänge des Erasmus, Humanismus und 'Devotio Moderna,'" 10 (1917). This gifted young scholar fell in the war, and the work, which was published after his death, was thus unfinished.

[38] According to Prof. Whitney "Lot" is the more correct term. Art. on Erasmus in the "English Hist. Review," 1920, in which he also emphasises the debt of Erasmus to the Brethren.

within the limit of the traditional orthodoxy.[39] This " devotion," coupled with his early religious training, became, according to Mestwerdt, the dominating influence in moulding his career as the greatest of contemporary scholars and the protagonist of a practical reformation. Mestwerdt tends, however, to exaggerate this influence, and Pusino, whilst admitting its predominance in his earlier period, argues with no little force that there is little trace of it in his later years, and that his distinctive position as a reformer was mainly fashioned in the humanist mould.[40]

The historians have differed as to the character of this reformation in view of his somewhat enigmatic personality. There is, indeed, great difficulty in exactly fixing his position as a religious reformer. Though he could be militant and trenchant enough as a critic of manifest evils, he was characteristically cautious and evasive when it came to anything like a crisis for himself and his cause. Very unlike Luther, he hesitated to declare himself decisively in such a contingency, by reason of his innate prudence and fear of consequences. When Luther would say, "Perish the consequences," Erasmus was disposed to ask, "What will be the consequences?" Whereas Luther, for example, stands up to the Sorbonne doctors, who accuse him of heresy and blasphemy, and pays them back in their own coin with compound interest, Erasmus is prone to be apologetic and evasive. Hence, in part at least, the divergence in judging his attitude to the Church and determining his religious position. Neither Roman Catholic nor Protestant writers are agreed on the

[39] Devotio moderna and Devotio antiqua are not to be identified with the Via moderna and the Via antiqua as technically applied to the controversy in the schools in the fifteenth century. These latter phrases denote the distinction in method and matter between the Neo-Thomist and the Occamist schools of theology and philosophy. The distinctive contentions of these parties have been recently expounded by Ritter, " Studien zur Spätscholastik," ii. (1922), in which the author controverts Hermelink's theses (in " Religiöse Reformbestrebungen des Deutschen Humanismus," 1907) that German humanism was an indigenous product and that it grew out of and was closely allied with the pre-Reformation reforming movement within the Church. It is a masterly exposition and discussion of the late scholasticism.

[40] " Z.K.G. " (1925), 625.

question.   Whilst among Roman Catholics Nève regards him as a consistent adherent of the Roman Church,[41] Janssen denies him this privilege.[42]   The Protestant Hermelink contends that his thought does not outstrip the Roman Catholic standpoint,[43] whilst other Protestant writers assign him a middle position between the two, or assert his independence of both.   The fact seems to be that while his personal religion was mainly shaped in the mould of the prevalent piety of the Netherlands reforming circle within the limit of the Church, he was a sort of free-lance in theology in the spirit of a Valla, a Pico, and a Ficino, who, in spite of their free and large-minded humanist standpoint, could accommodate their criticism or their Platonism to the conventional orthodoxy. It is, indeed, very characteristic of Erasmus that he could with remarkable liberality apply on occasion the Pauline axiom to be all things to all men, though hardly in the Pauline spirit.   He was ready to pay a large tribute to opinion, and M. Pineau concludes that he would heartily have subscribed to the saying of Montaigne, " The wise man should retire within himself from the crowd and preserve his soul in liberty to judge freely of things.   As to the external world he ought to follow entirely the received fashions and forms." [44]   This is perhaps too opportunist a dictum to apply to him in view of his strenuous and even militant attack on conventional religion.   At the same time, it might be almost paralleled from some of his own admissions in the face of compromising and dangerous situations, and it must be remembered that, in satirising and criticising ecclesiastical institutions or dogmas, he was expressing not merely his own but a widespread public opinion.   What is lacking in him, compared with Luther, is just the power of passionate religious conviction, coupled with a dominating will power, which underlies and inspires both thought and action and expresses itself in imperative assertion.

In this respect also there could be no real fellowship

[41] " La Renaissance des Lettres en Belgique " (1890).

[42] " History of the German People," iii. 8 f.

[43] " Die Religiösen Reformbestrebungen des deutschen Humanismus," 32 (1907).

[44] " Érasme," preface.

between the impassioned and insistent monk and enigmatic and rather opportunist scholar. Luther could not understand or appreciate a man who was too prone to express certain ideas and then, if need be, recede from them, and whose " greatest audacities are tempered by restrictions," to use the words of Pineau.[45] Luther and his friends were, however, apt too hastily to see in him only the dissembler and the egoist. The self played, indeed, its characteristic part in shaping his life. But his egotism was by no means the thing that conditioned his attitude towards the Lutheran movement. He believed in culture as a good in itself. He believed, further, in its power to effect gradually the amendment of the Church and society and raise both to a higher plane. He relied on the informed reason, rather than on the impassioned soul, for the enlightenment and betterment of humanity. His mind was free alike from mysticism and religious enthusiasm and was inclined to scepticism rather than to dogmatism, whether scholastic or Lutheran. To Luther his rationalism was Antichristian, his plea for a rational faith an offence against the Gospel. He himself could appeal to reason on occasion and exercise it critically even the Scriptures, but on the Occamist understanding that reason was strictly subordinate to faith ; whereas Erasmus would go the length of including Plato, Cicero, Socrates among the saints. He refuses to believe, with Augustine and Luther, that the virtues of these pagans are only splendid vices. The great company of the faithful is not confined to the Roman calendar. Above all, his failure to appreciate the Lutheran distinction between faith and works, or subscribe to the dogma of the unmitigated corruption of human nature and the total impotence of the will, was in itself an insuperable barrier to anything like a feasible alliance between them. His conception of Christianity was not conditioned by any such haunting sense of original and actual sin. It is rather that of the Sermon on the Mount than of the Epistles to the Romans and Galatians. For him it consists in the knowledge of the divine will in Christ, which is the norm and the inspiration of the Christian life.

[45] " Érasme," 244.

His view of it is the moralist rather than the distinctively Pauline one. For both, theology is the formulation of the religious life, not of abstract dogma. But then the experience of Erasmus differs materially from that of Luther, who was incapable of seeing that any other formulation of it could possibly be right. "The human," wrote Luther to Lang early in March 1517, "avails more with Erasmus than the divine." [46] There is too much of free will and too little of God's grace in him.

Moreover, like most of the humanists he had a nervous dread of the people, of anything likely to excite "tumult," revolution. He lives apart from the common people. His appeal is confined to the cultured class. He does not, like Luther or Hutten, appeal to the masses in the common tongue,[47] though it should not be forgotten that he wished the Bible to be given to the people in the vernacular. As a cosmopolitan he was a stranger to the national sentiment which, even in Luther, contributed to nurture the militant antagonism to Rome. To a man of Luther's bellicose temperament this nervous dread of tumult, in the face of the imperative necessity of appealing to the popular intelligence as well as the cultured intellect, was nothing but an evidence of moral weakness, culpable indifference. In addition to irreconcilability on dogmatic grounds, this was the thing that ultimately turned the scale of Erasmus's judgment against the Wittenberg Reformer, in spite of the fact that he himself had gone far to undermine some of the institutions and dogmas of the Church. Reform, yes; revolution, never, is his characteristic position. He will only countenance a gradual amendment of what is amiss in the Church and in theology. Luther, on the other hand, though temperamentally so conservative, will end, if he cannot amend, and will in any case only amend on his own conditions. In other words, if the Roman Antichrist will not give way on the issue of a radical reformation of doctrine as well as institutions, he will renounce his authority and will be the instrument in God's hand of his overthrow,

[46] Enders, i. 88.

[47] "Erasmus," says Mestwerdt, "zeigt sich als würdiger Schuler fast aller Humanisten wenn er die Masse zu verachten lehrt," 208.

or die in the attempt. For Erasmus this alternative is a sheer impossibility. If it comes to this he would, he said, play the part of Peter over again. He preferred the more comfortable belief that reason, in virtue of the diffusion of true knowledge, the exercise of good sense, will ultimately prevail in the warfare with corruption and error. A problematic as well as a comfortable belief. For Erasmus, as for Burke, change can only be the work of time. But what if the fullness of time had come, when the issue was not merely to amend but to deliver the Church from the papal absolutism and the corruption and oppression for which it stood? Nothing short of a revolution could accomplish this, however desirable it might be to change things by force of argument and criticism. For this mission only a Luther could suffice, and an Erasmus could at most only contribute to pave the way for it. He was totally unfit to face Nemesis, much less to be the instrument of it. This heroic, elemental rôle is reserved for the prophet, not for the critic and the scholar.[48]

As we have seen, Luther had become aware of the fundamental difference between his theological standpoint and that of Erasmus as early as 1516. Erasmus preferred Jerome and Origen to Augustine. Luther's preference was for Augustine and Paul whom, he thought, Erasmus misinterpreted. At the same time, he admired his learning and acknowledged his merits as a reforming scholar. Whilst dissenting from his theology, he refrained from publicly criticising it in order not to appear to abet the enemies of the great humanist and, in the letter to Lang in March 1517, spoke of him as " Our Erasmus." [49] He himself at this stage of his career had too many enemies to make one of Erasmus, and under Melanchthon's influence he sent him a letter in

[48] In his Hulsean lectures on " Erasmus the Reformer," Mr Binns champions the Erasmian conception of reform. He seems to me to be over-sanguine. Moreover, in his admiration for Erasmus, he is rather unfair to Luther. His one-sided lecture on the great Reformer is evidently not based on a first-hand knowledge of his writings, as in the case of his study of Erasmus. It consists of a series of generalisations based on second-hand sources.

[49] Enders, i. 88. Richter, "Erasmus und seine Stellung zu Luther," 8, erroneously says the letter was written to Spalatin.

March 1519, in which he begged him to recognise him as a little brother in Christ.[50] On his side, Erasmus, in letters to Lang and others, had approved generally of the theses against indulgences and of his manful efforts to vindicate them against his opponents, whilst deprecating aggressive theological controversy and expressing his own neutrality. To Luther himself he adopted the same tone in a rather non-committal though kindly reply to his letter, and did him the material service of strongly commending him to the protection of the Elector of Saxony (14th April 1519).[51] Six months later he intervened in his behalf in a remarkable missive to the Archbishop of Maintz, in which he vigorously denounced the odious and shortsighted policy of persecution adopted towards him by the theologians of Louvain and elsewhere, who were also his own enemies. " Men who above all others it beseems to practise meekness seem to thirst for nothing else but human blood, so eager are they that Luther should be seized and destroyed. Their conduct is worthy of the butcher, not the theologian. If they wish to show themselves great theologians, let them convert the Jews, let them bring the pagans to Christ, let them amend the morals of Christendom which are more corrupt than those of the Turks. How can it be right that he should be dragged to punishment who at first merely proposed for discussion certain questions on which the schoolmen have always disputed and even doubted ? Why should he be punished who wishes to be taught, who is willing to submit himself to the judgment of the Holy See, and has agreed to refer his cause to that of the universities ? But if he will not trust himself in the hands of those who wish rather to destroy than justify him, this ought certainly not to appear strange. . . . In former times a heretic was heard with due respect and absolved if he gave satisfaction. If, on conviction, he persisted in his errors, the extreme penalty was that he was not admitted to catholic and ecclesiastical communion.

[50] Enders, i. 490. In the preface to the " Commentary on Galatians " he refers to him as Erasmo, viro in Theologia summo et invidiæ quoque victore. " Werke," ii. 449, Sept. 1519.

[51] Allen, " Erasmi Epistolæ," iii., 14th April 1519 ; Kalkoff, " Erasmus, Luther, und Friedrich der Weise," 36 f.

Now the crime of heresy is deemed much more serious, and yet for any light cause forthwith they shout 'Heresy,' 'Heresy.' Formerly he was esteemed a heretic who dissented from the Gospels and the articles of faith, or from those doctrines which were held to be of equal authority. Nowadays, if anyone differs from Thomas Aquinas, he is decried as a heretic ; nay, he is a heretic if he demurs to any disputatious effusion which some sophist yesterday fabricated in the schools. Whatever they don't like, whatever they don't understand is heresy. To know Greek is heresy. To speak grammatically is heresy. Whatever they do not do themselves is heresy. I confess that it is a grave crime to vitiate the faith. But every subject ought not to be turned into a question of faith. And those who treat of matters of faith ought to be free from any species of ambition, greed, hatred, or revenge." [52]

He even ventured in an apologetic letter to the Pope [53] (13th September 1520) to asperse the reprehensible methods of his opponents and, though disowning all complicity with Luther's views, spoke approvingly of his gifts and discriminated between his good and bad qualities. Even after the papal condemnation he suggested to the Elector Frederick the reference of his case to a commission of learned men and exerted himself to win the imperial ministers for his plan.[54]

Whilst thus actively befriending him against his opponents, who were also his own, and working behind the scenes to further his cause even after the papal condemnation, he was not prepared to follow him in his breach with Rome. As between Wittenberg and Rome there could be for him no question of neutrality. The dread of revolution, his inability to see eye to eye with him in theology, the shrinking also from personal risk, decided him to remain within the fold of Peter. "If it comes to revolution (ad extremum tumultum) and the state of the Church totters from both sides, I will meanwhile remain firmly fixed on the

---

[52] Allen, "Erasmi Epistolæ," iii. 99 f. The whole letter is translated by Drummond, "Erasmus," ii. 32 f. See also Froude, "Life and Letters of Erasmus," 252-257.

[53] Ibid., iii. 344-346.  [54] Richter, 22.

rock of Peter until it shall become clear where the Church is. And so wherever there is evangelical peace, there will Erasmus be." [55]  "I would certainly rather have Luther corrected than destroyed," he assured the humanist secretary of the Prince of Nassau on the 13th March 1521, "but I shall not oppose if they roast or boil him. The fall of one man is a small matter, but I am very much concerned for the public tranquillity." [56]  "Not all have sufficient strength to face martyrdom," he wrote to Pace after Luther's heroic stand at Worms, "I fear I should act the part of Peter over again. I follow the Pope and the Emperor when they decide well, because it is pious to do so; I bear their bad decisions, because it is safe to do so." [57]  His opportunism compares ill with Luther's heroism. Theology apart, Luther is morally greatly superior to his timid, if critical, well-wisher who, compared to him, is only an armchair reformer and would never have left his armchair to defy the Pope and face the Emperor and the Diet in defence of his convictions.

Whilst ready, if need be, to leave Luther to his fate, he continued on occasion to protest against the outcry of the obscurantist zealots, who were anti-Erasmian as well as anti-Lutheran, and even to arraign the greed and tyranny of the Roman Curia and the oppression of Christian liberty by ecclesiastical ordinances.[58] He emphasised the folly and futility of seeking to suppress religious conviction by force. The love of the people for Luther was not so dead as his enemies imagined, he informed the President of the Grand Council at Malines. At Basle he hears that there are more than 100,000 men (in Germany) who hate the Roman See and approve of Luther.[59] He wrote to Duke George of Saxony and others in a similar strain against the policy of persecution. The Pope's Bull and the Emperor's Edict have only made matters worse.[60] He refrained, too,

[55] Allen, iv. 442.

[56] *Ibid.*, iv. 453; *cf.* 458. Froude wrongly dates the letter 19th Nov. 1521. "Erasmus," 300.

[57] *Ibid.*, iv. 541, 5th July 1521.

[58] *Ibid.*, v. 44. Letter to La Mota, Bishop of Palencia, 21st April 1522.

[59] *Ibid.*, v. 83, 14th July 1522.

[60] *Ibid.*, v. 126-128, Sept. 1522.

from entering the lists against the great heretic in spite of repeated and urgent requests from Duke George, the new Pope Hadrian VI., the King of England, and others, to write against him. He declined on the score of his health and his age the invitation of the Pope to come to Rome. He refused to write against Luther on the ground that what authority he formerly wielded availed not with either party, and that whatever he might write would find acceptance with neither. Of one thing he is certain. Force can be no remedy in a business of this kind. It will only tend to slaughter. Formerly it might prove serviceable against the Wiclifites in England, though even there heresy was scotched rather than killed. In Germany, where there is a multitude of contending rulers, the thing is impossible. Let the Pope, therefore, go to the root of the evil and before all begin the work of healing by drastic reform. Let him proclaim an amnesty to the erring. If God daily forgives the sinner, why should not His vicar? He might with advantage control the press, and the magistrates could effectively deal with sedition. He could show the world that grievances justly complained of will be redressed. He could restore liberty, to which the people have a just claim, without any real injury to religion. And he ends by suggesting the convention of what was evidently meant to be an international assembly of good men, though he breaks off in the middle of the sentence and leaves the reader to divine that he still contemplates the submission of the Lutheran controversy to an impartial arbitration tribunal.[61]

At the same time, the persistence with which his enemies aspersed his orthodoxy and identified his position with that of Luther, the fear that unless he declared himself against the heretic the ecclesiastical authorities would proceed against him as an accomplice,[62] the reiterated appeals from his patrons in high places were forcing him to face the alternative of publicly and definitely declaring himself for or against the heresiarch. The decision to choose the latter alternative owed something to the bitter attack of the

[61] Allen, v. 257-261, 23rd March 1523.
[62] Kalkoff, "Die Stellung der Deutschen Humanisten zur Reformation," "Z.K.G.," 1928, 218 f.

fugitive Hutten who, in passing through Basle, had solicited and been refused an interview and avenged himself by publicly denouncing him in July 1523 as a turncoat and a coward. Hutten had some reason, apart from the personal one, for pointing out the inconsistency between his former trenchant attack on the Church and his present conservative attitude, though it by no means necessarily followed, as he contended, that it was due to cowardice and bribery.[63] Erasmus repelled those charges in a lengthy vindication of his career as a reforming scholar and publicist, in which he maintains that he had not changed his attitude either towards the Church or towards Luther.[64]

He had by this time determined, though with reluctance, on an encounter with Luther himself. On the day after the publication of the " Spongia " he informed Henry VIII. that he was preparing an assault on the new dogmas.[65] This seemed to him the only expedient for disproving the oft-repeated reproach of being a secret Lutheran. So far he had received no direct provocation from Luther himself, who disapproved of Hutten's violent polemic in his behalf as well as of Erasmus's bitter rejoinder.[66] Luther was, however, becoming impatient of what he deemed his lack of straightforwardness and his pinpricks. He would far rather, he wrote to Spalatin on the 15th May 1522, have to deal with an Eck, who openly attacked his enemy, than with this shifty temporiser who played the part, now of friend, now of enemy.[67] Whilst admiring his scholarship, he had no great opinion of his ability as a theologian, and though had no desire to provoke his enmity, he would not hesitate to take up the challenge if attacked. Erasmus will find in him a very different antagonist from Lefèvre, whom he boasts of having vanquished.[68] He was becoming more and

---

[63] " Expostulatio," " Hutteni Opera," ii. 180 f.

[64] " Spongia Erasmi adversus Asperinges Hutteni," Sept. 1523.

[65] Allen, v. 330. Molior aliquid adversus nova dogmata, 4th Sept.

[66] Enders, iv. 234.

[67] Ibid., iii. 360. Melior est Eccius eo qui aperta fronte hostem profitetur. Hunc autem tergiversantem et subdolum, tum amicum, tum hostem detestor.

[68] Ibid., iii. 376. Letter to Borner, 28th May 1522.

more convinced that Erasmus was a mere trimmer in religion. "What Erasmus holds or feigns to believe in spiritual things," he wrote to Oecolampadius a year later (20th June 1523), "both his early and his recent books abundantly testify. Although I feel his pricks here and there, nevertheless because he publicly pretends not to be an enemy, I also make-believe that I do not perceive his craftiness, although others see through him more than he reckons. He has performed the work for which he was destined. He has furthered the study of the classics and recalled men from impious sophistry. Perhaps like Moses he will die in the land of Moab, for to the higher pursuit of spiritual things he cannot lead. I could wish that he would refrain from writing of Holy Scripture, because he is not equal to this work, and only misleads his readers and hinders their advance in scriptural knowledge. He has done enough in exposing the evil. To show the good and lead men to the promised land is beyond his capacity." [69]

These letters came into Erasmus's hands and made him angry with the writer. "I only wish," he wrote to Zwingli on the 31st August, "that he were the Joshua who is to lead us all into the promised land, and I should be glad to learn from you what are the spiritual things he speaks of. For myself I seem to have taught almost all that Luther teaches, except that I do not do this so savagely and that I have kept clear of certain enigmatic and paradoxical dogmas." [70] "This outburst is the prelude to war," he angrily wrote to Faber three months later. [71]

The attempts of Zwingli and other friends to prevent the impending rupture were futile. In issuing a new edition of his "Commentary on Galatians," Luther suppressed the appreciative references to Erasmus. To Pellican he retorted that though he was sorry that his letters had been treacherously handed to Erasmus, he had learned to stand alone against the world and cared not for either his patronage or his enmity, since he does not truly understand Christianity. "Let him learn to know Christ and bid farewell to human

[69] Enders, iv. 164.  [71] *Ibid.*, v. 349, 21st Nov. 1523.
[70] Allen, v. 329-330.

prudence. May the Lord illumine him and make another man of him. I bear him no ill-will, but I truly pity him." [72] Six months later he told him directly, in a tone very different from that of the humble epistle of March 1519, to refrain from further concerning himself with him and his cause. The letter is that of a superior to an inferior both morally and spiritually. He bore him no grudge for siding with his enemies, the papists, in writing books in which he had bitterly attacked him in order to gain their favour or mitigate their fury against himself. God had not given him the fortitude to join with him in the battle with these monsters, and he would not dream of asking him to attempt what was quite beyond his powers. "We have chosen rather to bear your weakness and venerate the gift which God has given you. For the whole world cannot deny that the progress and flourishing state of letters, which tends to the true interpretation of the Bible, is a magnificent and excellent gift for which we ought to render thanks to God. I have never desired that you should give up or neglect your true vocation by concerning yourself with a business for which you have neither aptitude nor courage, and which is entirely outside your sphere." Only he warns him not, by continuing to asperse his method of conducting his cause and his teaching, to make it necessary for him to join issue with him. He sympathises with him in the sufferings which the zealots have caused him, and admits that he himself has written too bitterly against his opponents, though, considering the provocation he has received, he thinks that he has shown no little forbearance and clemency. He has hitherto refrained from attacking him in spite of his persistence in rejecting or misrepresenting his teaching, and will continue to do so as long as he does not come out into the open against him. His cause is now happily beyond the power of an Erasmus to harm, and he begs him to recognise the fact and abstain from his biting and bitter rhetoric and become simply a spectator of his tragedy. Mutual forbearance is the only fitting attitude. What a miserable spectacle it would be if they should start to destroy each

[72] Enders, iv. 234-235.

other, as it is most certain that neither really wishes ill to piety.[73]

In reply, Erasmus rebutted the assumption that he had done nothing for the Gospel, for which he had effected more than many who boasted the name of Evangelical. What to Luther was weakness was to him a matter of conscience and judgment. The Gospel had been made a handle for sedition, the destruction of learning, and the rupture of friendships. It bade fair to become the occasion of a bloody revolution, and he can on no account consent to make it a pretext for the play of human passions. He had hitherto not written against him for fear of hindering its advancement, and had contented himself with repudiating the charge that he was in secret agreement with him in all his opinions. If he had consulted his private advantage, nothing would have brought him greater favour and fortune. It might even be of more advantage to the Gospel to do so in opposition to the writings of certain stupid scribblers, who champion Luther's cause and bring discredit on the Gospel. On this account alone he cannot consent to be a mere spectator of this tragedy.[74]

It did Luther no harm to be reminded that others had a right to their opinions, even if they differed from him, and that there might be more than one view of the Gospel and a different way of serving it from that of the more rabid of his professed adherents. On the other hand, by his heroism in risking all for his convictions and spurning compromise on the essential issue, Luther had certainly won the right to rebuke him for his tendency to hedge on this issue which he had himself contributed to raise, and telling him to mind his own business and keep his opinion to himself.

From the tenor of Erasmus's reply, it is evident that he had made up his mind to join in the fray on the side of Luther's opponents. The projected deliverance had, in fact, in substance, if not in form, already taken shape, though its actual composition occupied him but a few

[73] Enders, iv. 319-322, middle of April 1524.
[74] Allen, v. 451-453, 8th May 1524.

days.[75] The printing of the "De Libero Arbitrio" was completed by Froben of Basle in August 1524, and in the beginning of September Erasmus sent presentation copies to Henry VIII., Pope Clement VII., Wolsey, Duke George of Saxony, and other high patrons. "The die is cast," wrote he to Henry. "My book on Free Will has seen the light. An audacious villany, as things now stand in Germany! I expect to be stoned." [76]

### III. Erasmus against Luther

In choosing his theme Erasmus was attacking a central position of Luther's theology. Luther's personal experience of the fact of human sin and divine righteousness seemed to him to necessitate the complete impotence of the will and the worthlessness of human works for salvation, and led him to formulate the conviction as a theological axiom in the most uncompromising fashion. Both envisage the problem from the theological rather than the philosophical standpoint. It is not for either a question of the power of the will considered in itself, but of its power from the religious point of view. The specific point is whether and how far the will contributes to the attainment of eternal life ? Luther answers the question with an uncompromising negative, and the negative is for him so vital that any attempt to modify it (and this is what Erasmus attempted) seemed to endanger his whole teaching. It lay at the root both of his religious experience and his antagonism on dogmatic grounds to the teaching of the Church and the schoolmen. Erasmus alone of all his opponents, he said, had laid his finger on the cardinal point of the whole matter and had seized him by the throat.[77] Not only his reputation as a theologian,

---

[75] See von Walter, "De Libero Arbitrio," Introd. 11-12 (1910), in " Quellen schriften zur Geschichte des Protestantismus." Zickendraht shows that already in 1522 he was reflecting on the question of free will as the differentiating point between him and Luther. See "Eine Anonyme Kundgebung des Erasmus aus dem Jahre 1522," " Z.K.G.," 1908.

[76] Allen, v. 541, 6th Sept. 1524.

[77] " Werke," xviii. 786.

if not his work as a reformer, but his very salvation seemed at stake.

In the introductory part of his work [78] Erasmus claims the right to dissent from Luther, who himself exercises this right in refusing to recognise the authority of the doctors of the Church or even of Pope and cardinals. He is, therefore, unable to understand why he and his adherents should resent such a free discussion. His only object is to explore the truth and he will (and on the whole does) conduct the discussion in this spirit, though he is conscious of his unfitness for such a task. He is by nature, he says, inclined to scepticism, not to dogmatism, and whilst prepared implicitly to receive the dogmas of the Church, even when his reason revolts against them, condemns the opinionated and non-objective controversial method of his opponents He believes in a certain freedom of the will, and after reading Luther's contention to the contrary,[79] has found no reason to change his view. He recognises Luther's intellectual power, and if his adherents draw odious comparisons between Luther's gifts and his, let them remember that to their master himself the enlightenment of the Spirit of God is far more important than theological learning. He may have misunderstood Luther's teaching. But they must allow him to exercise his right to dispute with him, if only that he may thereby learn to know better. It is as a seeker of truth, not as a judge or a dogmatist, that he ventures on this debate. This is the right attitude for moderately gifted individuals like himself to adopt. There are difficult passages in Scripture which are meant to impress on us the inscrutable majesty of the divine wisdom and the limits of human knowledge of divine things. Curious speculations about these mysteries are reprehensible. The imperative thing is to strive, in dependence on God's help, to overcome sin, imputing the good to Him, the evil to ourselves, believing in the justice and goodness of God and eschewing these speculations about God's decrees and human freedom, etc.

[78] " De Libero Arbitrio Diatribe," edited by von Walter (1910), and in vol. ix. of " Erasmi Opera " (1540).

[79] In the " Assertio omnium Articulorum," which he has particularly in view throughout the discussion.

Many things have not been revealed or only partially made known by God, and some things, even if fully known, it is not expedient to proclaim to the multitude. This would apply to Luther's teaching even if it were true, since it tends to nurture moral laxity. As the Scripture is adapted to our understanding, so the preachers of the Gospel ought to refrain from presenting the extreme doctrine of the enslaved will to the people in view of its pernicious effects.

Since Luther admits no authority outside the Scriptures, Erasmus is saved the trouble of examining the opinions of the Greek and Latin Fathers on free will. He will, therefore, limit the discussion to the relative passages in the Old and New Testaments. At the same time, he reminds the reader that none of the ancients or the scholastic doctors has totally rejected the freedom of the will except Manicheus and John Wiclif. Though the vote of the majority is no guarantee of truth, due weight should surely be attached to the opinion of so many doctors, saints, martyrs, councils, popes, as against the private judgment of one or two individuals. Surely the Greek and Latin Fathers were better fitted by their linguistic knowledge and their holiness of life to interpret the Scriptures than these new evangelical preachers, who cannot be compared to them in either respect. The clarity of Scripture on this subject is disproved by the variety of opinions throughout the ages. Even in Apostolic times the gift of prophecy was necessary to interpret it. His opponents appeal to the testimony of the Spirit of God in them. But the Spirit is more likely to operate in the ordained priesthood than in these claimants to its exclusive possession, though he admits that in Scripture it is promised to the simple and foolish in the eyes of the world. In this case the injunction of Paul to try the spirits is imperative at a time when both sides claim the guidance of the Spirit. The age of miracles has ceased, and would God we had in place of miracles the pure life of the Apostles. To criticise the priesthood is no proof of the exclusive possession of the Spirit, and it is impossible to believe that it has allowed the Church to err for 1,300 years.[80]

[80] " De Lib. Arbitrio," 1-18, von Walter's edition.

He proceeds to examine, in the first place, the passages of the Old and New Testaments, which plainly establish the freedom of the will, and, in the second place, to explain those which seem to exclude it, on the principle that the Scripture, being inspired by the Spirit, cannot contradict itself.

Free will, from the theological point of view, he defines, following Lombardus, as the power by which man may apply himself to those things which lead to eternal life, or turn away from them.[81] According to Scripture, man was created free. But in consequence of the misuse of his freedom he lost it and became the slave of sin. The light of reason and the power of the will, which is derived from reason, were, however, not thereby completely extinguished, though the will was rendered inefficacious to do the good.[82] He retained a certain knowledge of God and power of virtuous living, as the life and teaching of the philosophers show, though he could not attain to eternal salvation without the grace which comes through faith. The fact of the law and man's responsibility for its transgression prove that he retained the power of choosing between good and evil. If the will was not free, sin could not be imputed to him. Sin involves free will. Though the will received a wound through the fall, and man became more prone to the evil than the good, it was not completely destroyed.[83] Opinion as to the extent of this freedom has varied, as a reference to the views of Pelagius, Augustine, and Scotus shows, and he declares the most probable view to be that which, differing from Pelagius, ascribes most to grace and almost nothing to free will in the attainment of salvation, whilst not totally denying its freedom. This he evidently regards, though not quite correctly, as the position of Augustine, and he contrasts it with the determinism of Luther who regards free will as an empty name (*inane nomen*), ascribes

---

[81] "De Lib. Arbitrio," 19; "Opera," ix. 1002. Porro liberum arbitrium hoc loco sentimus vim humanæ voluntatis qua se possit homo applicare ad ea quæ perducunt ad æternam salutem aut ab iisdem avertere.

[82] *Ibid.*, 22. Ad honesta inefficacem esse factam.

[83] *Ibid.*, 25. Quamquam enim arbitrii libertas per peccatum vulnus accepit, non tamen extincta est.

both the good and the evil in man to God, and holds that all that happens does so in virtue of necessity (*meræ necessitatis*). Against this extreme view he adduces a number of passages from the Old and New Testaments, which plainly imply the power to choose the good and the evil, and which are wholly meaningless without this implication. The frequent exhortations to do the good, the promise of reward, the threat of punishment are indubitably addressed to those who are capable of moral action, and are not merely the mechanical instruments of the divine will. Moreover, sayings of Jesus and Paul as well as of Moses and the prophets, which he quotes and examines, allow of no other conclusion, in spite of the contentions of Wiclif and Luther to the contrary.[84]

But what of the passages which seem to militate against the freedom of the will and ascribe to God's decree all the good and evil we do ? What, for instance, of the hardening of Pharaoh's heart and Paul's reasoning in the ninth chapter of Romans on this and similar passages of the Old Testament ? In such passages Paul does seem to attribute nothing to human agency and to exclude free will. It is absurd, he replies, following Origen, to make God, who is just and good, the author of human wickedness. God only makes use of Pharaoh's wickedness to attain His purpose. In virtue of this wickedness Pharaoh could only do evil, just as rain can only bring forth thorns and thistles out of bad soil and good fruit out of good. It depends on the disposition of the individual what God does with it. God only foresaw what would happen in Pharaoh's case. But he did not foreordain it. Foreseeing a thing is not the same as foreordaining it. He is not, therefore, the cause of Pharaoh's action. The ultimate causality of God in relation to human action is, indeed, a very difficult question. What God foresaw He must in some way have willed, since He did not hinder it, though it was in His power to do so. He really willed that Pharaoh should perish, and justly so by reason of his wickedness. Nevertheless, it was not because of God's will that he persisted in his wickedness and perished,

<hr>

[84] " De Lib. Arbitrio," 19-46.

but of his persistence in his evil course, due to his wicked
nature. God co-operates with human action. But the evil
in this action does not proceed from Him, but from the
human will.[85] To posit that man acts in virtue of a pure
and perpetual necessity is to take away the possibility of
merit and all distinction between good and evil. In opposition to this monstrous determinism he expounds this and
other passages in order to harmonise the fact of God's grace
and man's free will.[86] With the aid of Bishop Fisher's
" Confutatio," [87] he then reviews the passages which Luther
adduces in his " Assertio " on behalf of the dogma of the
total impotence of the will and the utter nullity of man's
works. He thinks that the overwhelming testimony of
Scripture is against this extreme dogma and, in virtue of
this test, claims to have the best of the argument.[88]

In the concluding part he seeks to uphold his own
moderate position against the extremists on both sides—
those who assume the complete freedom of the will, on the
one hand, and the total suppression of it, on the other. He
has no little sympathy with Luther's teaching, which tends
to lead man to depend wholly on God, to humble himself
before Him, to subject himself wholly to the divine will,
to magnify His immense mercy freely bestowed, to realise
his own weakness and misery, to confide entirely in God's
grace and not in his own merits, to give all the glory to His
grace and goodness, and frankly acknowledge the working
of His grace within him. All this evokes his whole-hearted
appreciation, and one feels that, but for this unfortunate
dogma, Erasmus is inclined to go with Luther rather than
his opponents, is really, as he himself confessed to Zwingli,
almost at one with his evangelical teaching, in spite of his
repeated prudent disclaimers to the contrary. But he
strongly objects to his determinism which makes man act

[85] " De Lib. Arbitrio," 53. Negari non potest quin ad omnem
actum concurrit operatio divina. . . . Ceterum actus malitia non
proficiscitur a deo, sed a nostra voluntate.

[86] Ibid., 45-61.

[87] Zickendraht has shown his indebtedness to Fisher's book against
Luther's " Assertio," " Der Streit Zwischen Erasmus und Luther "
(1909).

[88] " De Lib. Arbitrio," 61-77.

in virtue of absolute necessity, represents him as so much clay in the potter's hands, destroys the belief in his moral personality, declares all his works, even the pious ones, to be sinful, and does away with merit and reward. How can this harmonise with the language of Scripture, which speaks of God's children walking righteously before Him, which praises those who keep His commandments and punishes those who break them ? How can man be judged for what he does if he cannot do otherwise than as God has decreed ? What is the meaning of all these exhortations, threats, warnings, punishments ? What is the use of praying for anything, if He has resolved to give or not to give according only to His pleasure ? Why speak of reward if there is no such thing as merit ? How can it be just to give grace to some and eternal damnation to others, if, on the theory of the unfree will, all are incapable of doing anything good and must do what they do in virtue of God's decree ?

He sympathises, too, with the emphasis laid by Luther on faith as the source of and the important thing in the religious life. But he holds that faith springs from love, if love also springs from faith and is nurtured and maintained by faith. Nor can he accept Luther's doctrine of original sin, which exaggerates sin to such a degree that man by nature cannot but hate God and that even the works of those that are justified by faith are necessarily, in themselves, sinful. All such exaggerations are obnoxious to him, and he deprecates Luther's tendency to dogmatise so rashly on the divine decrees which are to us inscrutable and insoluble, especially as Luther and his adherents (Carlstadt) are not at one in their dogmatism. This dogmatism makes God a cruel tyrant and is fitted to produce, and does indeed produce, the worst moral effect. Luther in his just reaction from the errors, exaggerations, and evils rampant in the Church and the schools has gone to the other extreme and himself fallen into error and exaggeration. Hence this torrent of disputation and recrimination, this conflict between Achilles and Hector, which, being waged with equal fierceness, death alone can end. In the quest for truth this extreme virulence is out of place, and for himself he will follow the middle way of moderation. " Pelagius," he concludes,

" seems to attribute more than enough to free will ; Scotus rather abundantly. Luther began by only mutilating it, but, not content with this, erelong strangled it and rejected it entirely. For my part, I prefer the opinion of those who attribute something to free will, but most to grace." [89] This conclusion, he thinks, is not antagonistic to the essential part of Luther's teaching on faith and works, and whilst warning against the rash rejection of the teaching of so many doctors of the Church for the sake of so paradoxical a dogma, ends, as he had begun, in a conciliatory tone.[90]

The " De Libero Arbitrio " is in some respects a remarkable performance. Erasmus adopts a reasonable and moderate tone which lends a well-merited distinction to his work compared with the theological polemics of the day. He refrains from personal objurgation, and in this he shows both his scholarly taste and a due sense of the true method to be adopted by a searcher after truth. His rebuke of the noisy and contentious dogmatism of some of the evangelical preachers is, from this point of view, very much to the point. Granting Luther's position, though not quite assenting to it, that Scripture is the sole authority on a question of this kind, he subjects the sources to a careful and scholarly review, and strives to bring to bear on the solution of the problem the testimony of the evidence relative to it. He arrives at his conclusion as the result of this painstaking investigation, and there is no reason to doubt that he is, on this ground, a conscientious believer in the relative freedom of the will, theologically considered. There can be no doubt, for instance, that in emphasising the moral character of the divine government of the world and the indubitable evidence of the Mosaic law and the moral teaching of Scripture in support of man's moral personality, he was expressing a strongly felt conviction.[91] He strives

---

[89] " De Lib. Arbitrio," 90.  [90] *Ibid.*, 77-92.

[91] Zickendraht thinks that he was at heart a sceptic on the dogmatic aspect of free will, and only entered on this aspect of the question, in the main part of the work, in deference to the desire of his high patrons that he should do so. But while, on his own confession, inclined to scepticism, he does seem to be expressing certain definite convictions on the subject.

to be fair to Luther and, in spite of the odium of his name in orthodox and exalted circles, does not hesitate to emphasise the good side of his teaching, and even betrays the fact that he to a large extent sympathises with it and the Reformation movement.  On the other hand, it is evident that his judgment of Luther and the evangelical movement is not a purely objective one.  He is incapable of understanding or appreciating a train of thought springing from a religious experience so different from his own, or a personality which could only express itself and achieve its mission in the elemental fashion so distasteful to him.  Moreover, he is apt to view Luther in the light of the personality and conduct of some of his followers, and make him responsible for the actions or excesses of which he disapproved and which he explicitly condemned.  To judge from his representation of it the Reformation was pure and simple a destructive force, an anarchic movement subversive of order and morality.  He ignored too much the constructive side of it, the profound religious genius and high ethical ideal at the back of it, the quickening of the spiritual and moral life which it brought about in the case of the better type of its adherents.  He saw the shadow rather than the light.  He does not realise that Luther's conviction of the impotence of the will to do the good sprang from his high ideal of the divine righteousness as well as from a pessimistic and too dogmatic conception of human nature, and that it was in the attempt to realise the high standard of this righteousness in the sight of a perfectly righteous God that he felt so keenly the utter insufficiency and impotence of his efforts.  He does not realise the seriousness of the problem from this point of view, because he had not, like Luther, wrestled with it in conflict with the terrible reality that sin appeared to him, with his vivid imagination and consummate command of drastic expression.  He is not, like Luther, obsessed with the necessity of being sure of his salvation, and does not appear to understand this frame of mind.  Luther was no doubt guilty of exaggeration.  But for the deeper thing that lay behind this characteristic and rather questionable gift, Erasmus has no adequate understanding.  He fails, too, to do justice to the practical tendency of Luther's teaching.  Luther is

not out to demoralise his generation by teaching a crass
and immoral determinism.   He was not so much concerned
with the speculative aspect which, indeed, as he expounded
it, and as Erasmus himself pointed out, was fitted to lead
to very questionable results.   He is out to bring man to God
in Christ and, whilst emphasising the divine as against the
human will, lays equal stress on the imperative necessity
of self-discipline and service for others, as the result of
the regeneration wrought by faith, which, if due to grace
and not to works, is inherent in the new relation of the
soul to God.   Nor is Erasmus quite true to his principle
of keeping solely to the evidence of the sources in discussing
and judging the subject.   While formerly waging war on
the scholastic theology, he shows himself in this work a
more receptive disciple of the schoolmen as well as the
Fathers.   He works with the apparatus of the scholastic
theology as well as the original languages in interpreting
the evidence of the Scriptures.   He makes use of the conventional scholastic idea of prevenient, co-operative, effective
grace, and has, unlike Luther, made no original contribution
to the subject.   He has, in fact, assimilated a good deal
from this interminable argumentation and has thus considerably mitigated his former preference for the Gospel itself,
apart from later variations of it.   His exegesis of certain
passages is sometimes fashioned to get over a difficulty
and his profession of absolute submission to ecclesiastical
authority, even against his reason, is irreconcilable with
his professed desire to seek only the truth.   In his desperate
attempts to meet the objections or explain away the
difficulties that bristle around the problem, he is not always
consistent.   The will, for instance, is inefficacious to do
the good, and is, because of the fall, the slave of sin, yet
we are told that its power of choice is not completely
nullified.


## IV. LUTHER AGAINST ERASMUS

Luther by no means relished the " De Libero Arbitrio,"
although he did not consider it in itself a formidable per-

formance.[92] He had not read far, he tells us, before he felt inclined to pitch the volume under the table. But the reputation of Erasmus and the impression it made on both friends and foes, if not its intrinsic importance, made it necessary to reply to it.[93] Pressure of work and other cares prevented him from carrying out his purpose for nearly a year, and it was only in September 1525 that he found time to devote himself to this task.[94] He worked incessantly at it for the next two months, and in December it was issued from the press under the title of " De Servo Arbitrio." [95]

Whilst recognising his great literary and intellectual gifts, and his own inferiority to him in this respect, he tells him that his book contains nothing new [96] and is not to be compared with Melanchthon's " Loci Communes." He is sorry that he has wasted his literary talent in such a concoction which has both disgusted and angered him. His defence of free will is so worthless that he thanks him for having thereby strengthened his own belief to the contrary. He treats him as a novice in theology and vigorously rebuts his dislike of dogmatism and his tendency to scepticism. No one can be a Christian who is not certain of his beliefs and prepared whole-heartedly to confess his faith before men. " Take away this dogmatism and you deprive us of Christianity." [97] The Spirit is given in order that it may convict and convince. Luther has no patience with the tendency to see both sides of the question in an essential matter of this kind. Scepticism is here absolutely inadmissible. It is all the more reprehensible inasmuch as Erasmus is prepared to accept the decrees of the Church even if he cannot comprehend or agree with them, merely because the Church prescribes what he is to believe and for the sake of peace, or to avoid personal danger. In this respect he is no better than sceptics like Lucian or Epicurus who

[92] Enders, v. 46.
[93] *Ibid.*, v. 52.          [94] *Ibid.*, v. 245 and 247.
[95] " Werke," xviii. 600 f. It is also given in " Opera Latina," vi., ed. by Schmidt.
[96] *Ibid.*, xviii. 600-601, in tanta re nihil dicis quod non dictum sit prius.
[97] *Ibid.*, xviii. 603. Tolle assertiones et Christianismum tulisti.

scoff at truth and regard all dogma as mere human opinion. He may, if he pleases, imitate the example of those who say, " They say and therefore I say ; they deny and therefore I deny." But this way is not the Christian way. The Holy Spirit is no sceptic.[98] He holds that in all essentials of Christianity, of which this dogma is one, the testimony of Scripture is perfectly clear, though the enlightenment of the Spirit is necessary for a true spiritual understanding of it, and it contains obscure passages due to the difficulty of understanding the true meaning of the words. Its teaching is unmistakable and, in denying this, Erasmus is merely reflecting the sophistic view of the scholastic theologians who, under the inspiration of Satan, have displaced it by their pestiferous philosophy and, under this false pretext, have prevented the people from reading it. This is merely to shut one's eyes and say the sun is dark.[99] You should quarrel not with Scripture, but with these sophists.

Erasmus raises the question of authority. The doctors differ in their interpretation of Scripture. Where is the absolute test of the truth ? Authority, replies Luther, is twofold—internal and external. It lies in the first place in the judgment of the individual believer, enlightened by God's Spirit, though he refuses to recognise the claim of the Zwickau prophets to the enlightenment of the Spirit. " The spiritual man judges all things." In the second place it resides in the public ministry of the Word, by which we judge not only for ourselves, but for others, and are thus enabled to strengthen the weak and confute the opponents of the Word.[100] Nor is it of any avail for Erasmus to say that the Church cannot have erred. The Church which does not err, replies Luther, is not the historic papal Church, but the secret body of God's people—the few whom He has chosen, not the many. Moreover, the mere opinion of saints and martyrs on such a subject decides nothing. As the proverb has it, The souls of many esteemed to be saints and deemed to be in heaven are now in hell.[1] Saints like Augustine and Bernard forget and despair of themselves and

[98] " Werke," 605. Sanctus spiritus non est scepticus.
[99] *Ibid.*, xviii. 606-607.
[100] *Ibid.*, xviii. 653 f.          [1] *Ibid.*, xviii. 641.

their own will and merits when they approach God in prayer and attempt anything in His service. Their only thought is their dependence solely on God's grace.[2]

To Erasmus the dogma of the impotence of the will is merely a curious and superfluous speculation. To Luther, on the contrary, it is of the very essence of the Christian faith. " Without it neither God, nor Christ, nor the Gospel, nor faith, nor anything is left us." [3] How can it be described as a superfluous speculation to seek to know whether the will can effect anything or not in regard to those things which belong to man's eternal salvation. Erasmus himself asserts both that without grace the will is inefficacious to do so, and that, nevertheless, it can do something. At the same time, he deems it superfluous to inquire whether it can or not. What is this but weakly to evade a real and fundamental problem in deference to human prudence ? [4]

To Luther this is the vital and essential thing.[5] If we are in ignorance on this point we can know nothing of Christianity and are worse than pagans. " For if I am ignorant, what, how far, and how much I can do in relation to God, I shall remain equally ignorant and uncertain what, how far, and how much God can do and does in relation to me." We cannot worship or serve God unless we know in what relation we stand to Him and He stands to us. " Hence the necessity of being able to distinguish definitely between the power of God and our own, between His work and ours, if we wish to live piously." [6] By evading this fundamental problem Erasmus has written the most worthless book on the subject, apart from its literary elegance, he has ever come across. He is a mere rhetorician and is much inferior to the schoolmen in his superficial treatment of the subject. Luther will supply his deficiencies as a theologian and a metaphysician by teaching him what the subject really means and involves, in the hope of bringing him to repent of his foolish venture.

Against " the figment " of free will he adduces the eternal and immutable will of God, by which He foresees, determines,

---

[2] " Werke," xviii. 644.     [3] *Ibid.*, xviii. 610.     [4] *Ibid.*, xviii. 611 f.
[5] *Ibid.*, xviii. 614.   Cardo nostræ disputationis.
[6] *Ibid.*, xviii. 614.

and effects all that happens, and which excludes the assumption that He foresees anything contingently. From the immutable nature of God it follows irrefragably that what He has willed is immutable, and that all that we are, all that happens, happens in virtue of an immutable necessity, as far as God is concerned, though it may seem to us mutable and contingent.[7] In demonstration of this thesis he proceeds to refute the distinction between absolute and conditional necessity (*necessitate consequentiæ* and *necessitate consequentis*), which he pronounces to be a mere play of words. Without the belief in this absolute necessity, faith and the worship and service of God would be impossible, since we could not trust God's promises or be certain of our salvation, and the Gospel would cease to afford us any real consolation amid the trials of this life.[8]

It is from this point of view that Erasmus's teaching is so obnoxious. It cuts at the root of faith and the Gospel. It is, therefore, irreligious and even blasphemous, though he admits that this is not his intention, and agrees with him in so far as his scepticism applies to the vain and sophistic argumentation of the scholastic theologians. But it is absolutely inapplicable to the teaching of the Scriptures, which is a very different thing from the theology of the schoolmen, and he objects to being placed in the same category with those hair-splitting sophists. He rebuts his comfortable advice that the truth of Scripture should not be indiscriminately preached to the people. If it is so harmful to preach on this subject to the people, why has he written a book on it? Luther admits that some preachers indulge in noxious ranting on this and other subjects. But why should this prevent earnest and pious preachers from expounding Scripture doctrine to their hearers or inveighing against the tyranny of the ecclesiastical institutions, by which the conscience is enslaved, merely for fear of the abuse of liberty? Luther refuses to suppress his convictions

[7] "Werke," xviii. 615. Eo quo sequitur irrefragabiliter omnia quæ facimus, omnia quæ fiunt, etsi nobis videntur mutabiliter et contingenter fieri, revera tamen fiunt necessario et immutabiliter, si Dei voluntatem spectes.

[8] *Ibid.*, xviii. 618-619.

for such opportunist reasons.  He scorns the egotistic advice
to cease disturbing the world for the sake of peace on a
question which is not a mere speculation, but concerns the
salvation of the soul so vitally.  For him it is a fundamental
question of faith and conscience, which concerns the glory
of Christ and God Himself, and on this serious, imperative,
and eternal issue he is ready to defy the whole world and
face death itself.[9]  " By the grace of God I am not so
foolish or mad as to have undertaken this cause for money,
which I neither have nor wish, or for glory, which, even if
I desired, I could not obtain in a world so hostile to me,
or on account of the life of the body, of which I am not sure
one moment.  Nor is it for objects of this kind that I have
maintained it with such courage, such constancy, which
you are pleased to call perversity, through so many dangers,
hatreds, snares, in brief, against the fury of men and demons.
Think you that you alone have a breast which is troubled by
these tumults ?  We also are not made of rock or born with
skins of marble.  But since it cannot be otherwise, we,
joyful in the grace of God, prefer to cause this violent
collision on account of the Word of God, which is to be
maintained with invincible mind, to being crushed with
intolerable suffering by an eternal tumult under the wrath
of God." [10]  He will not, like Erasmus, sacrifice or destroy
the Word and the cause of Christ for the sake of peace
or the favour of Pope and princes.  Christ admonishes us
rather to despise the whole world in such a cause.  He
came not to give peace, but a sword.  The function of the
Word is to change and make a new world as often as it
comes, and unless there were strife and tumult, we should
conclude that the Word was not in the world.  It will
certainly not cease its function till the kingdom of the Pope
with all his adherents is overthrown.  This tumult is far
more tolerable than the old and evil state of things, which
Erasmus himself has often enough exposed.  How much
better to lose the world than to lose God.  This tumult
is unavoidable, inasmuch as the Pope and the priesthood
will not grant a reasonable liberty from their tyrannical

[9] " Werke," xviii. 625.        [10] Ibid., xviii. 625.

laws, but insist on taking captive and binding the conscience to their will and their human traditions. This is a conflict between God and Satan, which must be fought out to the bitter end. Has not Erasmus himself had to fight against the obscurantist enemies of sound learning ? How much more must we fight for the Gospel against its corrupters ! Not preach the whole Word of God to the people ? Did not Christ command to preach the Gospel to all the world ? And did not Paul say that the Word is not bound and that God is no respecter of persons ?

He next deals with the awkward questions arising from the dogma of the impotent will, which Erasmus had raised in the last part of his introduction, and which showed the danger of teaching such a dogma to the people. Who, asks Erasmus, will strive to amend his life, if every one can only act in virtue of necessity ? " No one," answers Luther, " for no one can. Only the elect will amend themselves by God's spirit. The others will perish unamended." Who, asks Erasmus further, will believe that God loves him, if he is condemned merely in virtue of a divine decree ? " No one," answers Luther, " will or can believe except the elect, but will perish in their raging and blaspheming against God, as you do in your book." But, urges Erasmus, does not such a doctrine open a door to impiety ? " So be it," answers Luther. " This is part of the evil that is to be borne. But at the same time there is opened for the elect a door to righteousness, an entrance into heaven, a way to God." [11] Without such teaching the people would not humble themselves before God, or despair of self and be led by fear to seek His grace and live, and recognise that salvation depends wholly on God's will, not on theirs. To all such objections his answer is, God wills it so, and it is not ours to inquire into the reason of His will, but simply to adore Him, believing that He is just and wise and does injury to none. It is a matter of faith and spiritual experience, not of understanding, and the difficulties involved serve only to stimulate faith. Formerly, as we have seen, the thought of predestination had filled him with despair. Now that he is sure of his salvation, it is an essential of faith, and the

[11] "Werke," xviii. 632.

thought that salvation depends solely on God's immutable will fills him with an unfailing confidence.

He next proceeds to criticise and controvert in detail Erasmus's conception of free will, as defined by him. Erasmus has faultily defined what for Luther does not exist. Free will, in the religious sense, man does not possess. Being absolutely dependent on God for salvation, as far as God does not operate in him, his works are necessarily evil and he can do nothing for his salvation.[12] His will is not in itself free. It is dominated either by God or Satan. It is like a beast of burden. If God is seated in the saddle, it wills and goes whither God wills. If the devil is in the saddle, it wills and goes whither the devil wills. Both are striving for the possession of it and it is powerless to choose between them.[13] Free will is the prerogative of God alone.[14] It is a misnomer when applied to man, and only tends to deceive the people, to the greatest danger of their salvation. Will power man has, and it may be permissible to speak of free will applied to ordinary things, though even in this case God is the ultimate disposer of all.[15] But in relation to God—in those things which concern his salvation—he is not free, but the slave of the will either of God or Satan. Erasmus, while assuming a certain measure of freedom in the will, says that it is inefficacious to do the good without grace, and that it even became through the fall the slave of sin. He thus, retorts Luther, gives away his whole case. For, if the will cannot do the good without grace, it is not free, but the slave of evil, and cannot turn of itself or apply itself to what pertains to salvation.[16] If Erasmus had not in their eyes the merit of writing against Luther, the scholastic theologians themselves would condemn such stuff and send him to the stake.[17] There can be no attempt to do the good where there is no power to will the good and man is the slave of sin. No middle course is here possible, as Erasmus would have us believe. If God is present in us, the devil is absent and one cannot but will the good. If God is absent, the devil

[12] " Werke," xviii. 634.

[13] Ibid., xviii. 635.

[14] Ibid., xviii. 636, 662.

[15] Ibid., xviii. 662 f.

[16] Ibid., xviii. 636, 664-665.

[17] Ibid., xviii. 665-666.

is present and one cannot but do the evil.[18]  Free will is
nothing but an empty name (*inane vocabulum*), since if the
will has lost its liberty by sin, it is a mere delusion of words
to speak of its liberty.[19]  It is beside the point to appeal
to the law as a proof of free will.  God has given the law
in order to bring home to us the moral impotence of human
nature.  Nor does it avail to adduce the testimony of reason
and carnal wisdom, which only tend to nurture human pride
and mislead and blind us to the truth of Scripture.  The
Scriptural passages by which Erasmus attempts to substantiate his case he interprets wrongly.  Rightly interpreted they prove, not what man can, but what he ought to
do.[20]  The radical weakness of his exegesis consists in the
fact that he fails to distinguish between the Law and the
Gospel.  The Law commands and exacts.  The Gospel
exacts nothing, but offers us the grace of God.[21]  In thus
wrongly interpreting the Scriptures on behalf of a certain
measure of freedom in the will, Erasmus really lands himself in the same position as Pelagius, who believed in the
full freedom of the will, and from whom he nevertheless
dissents.[22]  That the testimony of Scripture is against him
on this question he asserts in the most uncompromising
fashion.  " Not only the Law, but the whole Scripture is
opposed to free will." [23]

He maintains this contention even in the face of passages
like Ezekiel xviii. 23, " The Lord willeth not the death
of the sinner, but that he should turn and live," which
Erasmus adduces in evidence of the exercise of free will.
How can it be said that God willeth not the death of the
sinner, if it is true, as the opponents of free will insist, that
the sinner can do nothing but as God wills and works in
him, and that, therefore, the fate of those who are lost is
due to Him ?  God, indeed, returns Luther, wills all to be
saved, to experience His grace.  Scripture is replete with
this teaching, and he duly emphasises this fact, whilst

---

[18] "Werke," xviii. 669-670.       [20] *Ibid.*, xviii. 671 f.
[19] *Ibid.*, xviii. 670-671.        [21] *Ibid.*, xviii. 682.
[22] *Ibid.*, xviii. 675 ; *cf.* 683.
[23] *Ibid.*, xviii. 684.  Non solum omnia verba legis contra liberum
arbitrium, sed universam Scripturam contra illud pugnare.

sticking to his determinist doctrine that it is only as He wills and works in us that we are saved. But if God does all and man nothing, and if He wills all to experience His grace, how is it that some experience His grace and others do not ? This, replies Luther, is a mystery. The solution of this mystery He has reserved to Himself. He seems so far to agree with Erasmus that the question of free will is a baffling one, though he does not accept his conclusion that it is, therefore, superfluous for us to trouble ourselves or others with it. It is at all events not superfluous as far as it concerns us to know whether or not we can do anything to attain salvation. In spite of this ultimate impasse, he will hold to his conviction on the subject and will believe and adore where he cannot understand. He takes refuge in the distinction between the revealed and the secret will of God, between the Word of God and God Himself.[24] God in His revealed Word wills and seeks all to be saved. But He has not revealed His whole will in the Word. Behind the Word is the realm of the divine majesty and nature, the secret mind of God which is above our knowledge or comprehension, and of which it is not our business to dispute. It is enough to quote the words of Paul, " Nay but, O man, who art thou that repliest against God ? "[25] (Rom. ix. 20).

In reply to Erasmus's contention that if man acts in virtue of necessity, merit and reward are excluded, and it is therefore useless for Scripture to speak of these, Luther appeals from the Old Testament—the Law and its threats—to the New, which proclaims the grace of God for the remission of sin, freely bestowed through Christ. The Gospel excludes all thought of merit. Man merits only damnation, and only as he is justified through God's mercy is he capable of good works and actually exercises them in bearing the Cross and the tribulations of life. " This is the sum and substance of the New Testament, yea, even of the Old Testament," of which Erasmus with his moralism knows nothing. He is thus incapable of understanding the new birth, the regeneration, the renewal of corrupt human

[24] " Werke," xviii. 685. Distinctio inter Deum prædicatum et absconditum, hoc est, inter verbum Dei et Deum ipsum.
[25] *Ibid.*, xviii. 686.

nature by the Spirit and mercy of God. His assertion of merit and reward, based on free will, agrees with this Gospel as little as darkness with light. The children of God do the good gratuitously and not for reward, in obedience to the will of God and for the glory of God. They are prepared to do so even if there were no heaven and no hell.[26] Our works are not ours, but God's, from whom we receive all that we do.

He next proceeds to vindicate his teaching on the unfree will from the objections urged by Erasmus.[27] He disclaims the exegesis of certain Scripture passages which Erasmus unjustifiably attributes to him. He maintains, in reference to the hardening of Pharaoh's heart, that the words of the text are to be taken literally and not merely tropologically, as Erasmus asserts. Thus Paul interprets them in the ninth chapter of Romans, and the testimony of Origen and Jerome to the contrary proves nothing, since among all ancient ecclesiastical writers none treated the Scriptures more ineptly and absurdly than those two Fathers.[28] God did not merely furnish the opportunity for the hardening of Pharaoh's heart. He actually did so for the purpose of showing His power through human wickedness. There is no use of trying to evade this evident fact by saying that God, being not only just, but good, could not have acted thus. Nor to adduce the revulsion of reason from such an interpretation. " As applied to the works and words of God, human reason is blind, deaf, impious, and sacrilegious in presuming thus to judge in divine things." [29] From the standpoint of reason it would be necessary to reject every article of the Creed as an absurdity. These things are above reason and can only be grasped by faith, and through the enlightenment of the Spirit which enables us to believe that God is good, even if He were to destroy the whole world.[30] God, he proceeds to explain, is omnipotent will, whilst man, on the other hand, is absolutely impotent to do His will and can only, in virtue of original sin, which has corrupted his nature,

---

[26] "Werke," xviii. 696.
[27] Ibid., xviii. 699 f.
[28] Ibid., xviii. 703.
[29] Ibid., xviii. 707.
[30] Ibid., xviii. 708.

will what is opposed to God.    But he is not thereby removed from the activity of God's omnipotent will, which embraces all created things.    In virtue of this omnipotence, God acts in every creature, even in Satan and the wicked.    He does so as He finds them, though, as perfectly good, He is not, in so acting, the author of evil.[31]    The evil is in the instrument, not the user of it, and is not to be ascribed to Him, who is absolute good, but to corrupt human nature, which He uses for His glory and our salvation.

Thus God, acting on Pharaoh's evil nature, which is subject to His omnipotent will and which leads him to persist in his wickedness, is truly said to harden his heart, to really will that he shall perish.    If you ask why God did not change his heart, or why He did not intervene to prevent the fall of Adam, Luther here also replies that this is an inscrutable mystery into which we have no right to inquire, though the elect will abide in their assurance that what God wills is right.    Our complaints cannot change God's immutable purpose.    No rule or limit can be set to His immutable will.    Otherwise it would not be divine.    We cannot say of it that it ought to will so and so and, therefore, what it wills is right, but, on the contrary, because it wills, it must be right.    To distinguish between foreknowing, as the scholastic theologians and Erasmus do, and fore-ordaining, in order to get over the difficulty of ascribing to God's will what seems evil, is a mere quibble.    Divine foreknowledge involves divine fore-ordination.    Nor have we any right to complain in reference to Paul's reasoning in the ninth chapter of Romans that if God's will, in virtue of His omnipotence, is irresistible, we are punished for acting as He wills.    God has the absolute right to do whatever He wills.    He owes us nothing; has received nothing from us; has promised us nothing except as it pleases Him.[32] The reasoning of Paul puts this beyond question.

He admits that this is a hard doctrine and offensive to natural reason and common sense.    He himself, he tells us, had formerly experienced the offence of it and had been

---

[31] "Werke," xviii. 709.   Quia ipse bonus male facere non potest.
[32] *Ibid.*, xviii. 717.

driven to the deepest abyss of despair in wrestling with the specious scholastic reasonings on the subject. Yea, he had wished that he had never been born until he discovered how salutary was this desperation in leading him to trust the whole thing to God and how near it is to God's grace.[33] Natural reason itself would be compelled to come to this conclusion, even if there were no Scripture to reveal it. " For all men discover this doctrine written in their hearts and acknowledge and approve it (albeit unwillingly) when it is thus expounded to them. Firstly, that God is omnipotent not only potentially, but actually. Otherwise He would be an absurd God. Secondly, that He knows and foreknows all things, nor can He err or be deceived. These two principles being conceded by the heart and understanding of all, they are compelled to admit the inevitable conclusion that nothing happens by our will, but by necessity, and that we do nothing by right of free will, but as God foreknows and brings to pass by His infallible and immutable decree and power." [34]

After dealing at length with the Scripture passages against free will, which Erasmus had attempted to invalidate, he confronts him in the concluding portion of the work with Paul and John, and elaborates against his moralism his doctrine of justification by faith alone. Paul, he holds, is a convinced opponent of free will. For him free will and grace are absolute antitheses. All men are by nature ignorant of God, enemies of God, bent on evil and helpless to do the good. From the religious point of view reason is blind and the will impotent. Without the grace of God Satan rules in man, even in his good works. Paul's words admit of no exception or modification. They apply to the best as well as the worst of mankind. " By the works of the law shall no flesh be justified in His sight " (Rom. iii. 20). These words do not refer only to the ceremonial law, as Erasmus, following Jerome, contends. This is to misunderstand Paul and falsify the Gospel. They include the whole Law, by which comes the knowledge of sin. Here is the crushing answer to the question, What is the use of the Law with its precepts and threats, if free will is a delusion ? To give the

[33] "Werke," xviii. 719.    [34] *Ibid.*, xviii. 719.

knowledge of sin, says Paul, not to prove the possession of free will.[35] The Law makes us conscious of the disease of our nature and brings us to despair of ourselves. It does not help us or heal the disease. Here it is that the Gospel comes in, proclaiming Christ as the deliverer from this disease by making us partakers of the divine righteousness, freely bestowed through faith and justifying us without the works of the Law. For the righteousness that avails before God, Christ alone suffices. The will of man may to some extent promote the righteousness demanded by the civil or moral law. It cannot suffice for the divine righteousness.[36] To believers God gives His righteousness ; from unbelievers He withholds it. Paul and Luther, as his follower, conceive of righteousness from the divine, not from the human standpoint. This righteousness is attainable only through faith, without which no righteousness can avail in the sight of God. Any other is only sin in His sight. Paul's alternative is, "Righteousness, if faith is present ; sin, if faith is not present." "As you believe, so you have."[37] "Justified freely by His grace" excludes free will and merit and all the scholastic talk of *meritum condignum* and *meritum congruum* in order to reconcile grace and merit is a mere play of words. By ignoring the plain teaching of Paul on grace and works, the Church and its theologians have radically erred, and the testimony of the Fathers and doctors of so many centuries is utterly worthless as against the Apostle's explicit teaching.[38] The whole of Paul's reasoning is based on the conviction that outside faith in Christ there is nothing but sin and damnation, and it is confirmed by that of the fourth Gospel. And what need of Christ if our salvation is not solely due to Him and not to us ? These champions of free will have transformed Christ the Saviour into the terrible Judge who must be propitiated by the intercession of the Virgin and the saints, by a whole system of penitential works, rules, vows, etc., in order that He may bestow His grace on us, which He has already obtained for us by the shedding of His blood.[39]

[35] "Werke," xviii. 766.

[36] *Ibid.*, xviii. 767-768.   Ad justitiam Dei tamen non promovetur.

[37] *Ibid.*, xviii. 769.      [38] *Ibid.*, xviii. 771.      [39] *Ibid.*, xviii. 778.

In conclusion, he claims to have unanswerably proved his case, and ends on a note of personal reminiscence which clearly shows that this grim doctrine has its root, not so much in his logic as in his religious experience. Even if free will were possible and his salvation depended on himself, he would rather not have it so, because he could have no assurance thereby of acceptance with God. Not only would the power of the demons, the trials and dangers of this life be too much for him. Even if there were no demons, dangers, adversities to face, he would be plunged into a sea of uncertainty and vain strivings. The old question which had haunted him in the monastery at Erfurt, How can I find a gracious God? would start up and rob him of peace of conscience, and if he tried and worked to all eternity he could never be sure of the answer by his own efforts. " No matter how perfect the work, the old doubt would remain whether it was sufficient to satisfy God and whether God would not require something more, as the experience of all who strive for salvation by works proves, and as I myself learned through so many years of bitter suffering. But now that God has removed my salvation beyond the power of my will and has charged His will with it and has promised to save me not by my works and ways, but by His grace and mercy, I am serene and certain that He is faithful and will not lie, and that no demons, no adversities can prevail against His power and might and can snatch me away from Him. . . . Thus are we certain and secure that we are acceptable to God, not by the merit of our works, but by the goodness of His mercy, promised to us, and that even if we do little or evilly, He does not impute it to us, but paternally pardons and amends." [40]

In this assured mood he thanks Erasmus that he has not troubled him with such questions as the Papacy, purgatory, indulgences, and such trifles, with which his opponents have hitherto in vain pursued him ; but, alone among them all, has seen where the whole thing hinges and has seized him by the throat. If the others had done so there might now have been less sedition and division and more peace

40 "Werke," xviii. 783.

and concord.  Now that he has vindicated his cause against even an Erasmus, whose learning and genius he highly extols, he hopes that he will return to his literary studies and give up disputing on a subject for which God has not endowed him.[41]

In the " De Servo Arbitrio " Luther appears at his best as a controversialist.  It is moderate and measured in style and free from the reckless abuse of too much of his controversial writing.  He treats Erasmus courteously, though he at times asperses his lack of conviction and what he considers his misrepresentation of the Gospel. It is a sustained piece of reasoning of a high order.  In fertility of thought and dialectic power he is greatly superior to his opponent.  Erasmus is a scholar and a critic, rather than a thinker.  Luther is a thinker, rather than a scholar and a critic.  Erasmus has the inquiring, Luther the dogmatic, temperament.  To the one doubt is a condition of the truth, to the other it is anathema.  A teacher, says Luther, must assert definitely what he believes and not reason in a vacillating fashion.[42]  Either we have free will, or we have it not, is the alternative he constantly holds before his opponent.  Whilst Erasmus examines and weighs the evidence and concludes accordingly, with an eye to both sides and a distinct disinclination to commit himself too definitely one way or the other, Luther thinks the matter out with the most persistent grasp and resource, and will not cease his grasp till he has got to definite results.  He is far more in earnest as well as more penetrative in thought and logic than his opponent, and he is by far the more powerful reasoner.  With the eye of the experienced dialectician he picks out the weak points of his opponent's arguments.  He constantly, for instance, points out the contradiction between his admission of the enslavement of the will by sin, in consequence of the fall, and the assumption of its capacity to do the good.  He shows again and again that even the restricted freedom that he ascribes to it is practically equivalent to complete freedom.  What Erasmus proves from certain passages of Scripture is not a restricted but a full

freedom. His reproach of the lack of logical consistency
is certainly not undeserved at times. Equally telling the
reproach of his principle of suppressing or evading the truth
for the sake of expediency. Truth is for Luther too great
a thing for trifling or diplomacy of this kind.

Erasmus treats free will as a speculative question. For
Luther it is primarily a soteriological question—one with
which his personal salvation is vitally bound up. Its religious
aspect is ever present to his mind and he realises this aspect
far more vividly than his opponent. His exalted idea of the
divine righteousness seems to him to involve the utter
incapacity of man to attain to anything approaching it
or anything worthy of the name of righteousness ideally
considered, as embodied in God. He and Erasmus are on
a different plane in this respect, though both of them felt
a revulsion from the work-righteousness of the mediæval
Church, which tended to foster a superficial religiosity and
was based on a low religious ideal, a wrong religious principle
—so much reward for so much formal merit and a bargain-
ing with God for salvation on this principle. But Luther
took the ideal of the divine righteousness with desperate
seriousness, and was not disposed, like Erasmus, to accommodate himself to Church practice or teaching in this vital
matter. Real fellowship with a perfectly righteous God,
God alone can effect, is for Luther a fundamental axiom.
Where Erasmus is more matter of fact, more rational,
Luther is mystic, emotional. His soul is more attuned
to the ideal spiritual world which transcends sense and
reason. He has an overmastering sense of God and His
perfect righteousness, and a corresponding sense of man's
littleness, weakness, unrighteousness in relation to God.
For him the thought of God as the absolute good dominates
this relation. This thought is not a mere abstraction of
reason. It is the ever-present, haunting reality it was to
the Hebrew prophet at his best, and it conditions his attitude
on the question at issue. It is the religious, not the intellectual or moral aspect of the question that appeals to him.
The old problem, started in the Erfurt monastery, How,
on what conditions can I find a gracious God and attain
the divine life ? is the decisive thing. In view of what

God is and what man cannot be—the perfect good—the conclusion is for him inevitable. God alone can make me worthy of the divine fellowship, and only as God works in me can I be assured of this fellowship. Every human effort must necessarily fall short of the perfect good. There is none good but God. Therefore only as God works in me can I will the good in the absolute sense. The good in the relative sense, even if it were possible, which he refuses to admit, is of no avail in the realm of the highest, the absolute good. So conceived, there can be no feasible relation between him and God, except as God Himself creates it. This is the strong side of Luther's position as against Erasmus with his matter-of-fact notion of a certain efficacy in the will, especially as he combines this notion with the assumption of a total inefficacy in virtue of original sin. Logically as well as religiously Erasmus's definition and his argumentation were, from Luther's standpoint, inadequate, wrong, impossible.

On the other hand, Luther's attempt to substantiate his determinism to the extent not only of denying even a relative good to man's action, but of asserting that God, not the human will, is responsible for the evil as well as the good man does, is far from convincing. Here he seems to be arguing not from a necessary axiom, but from certain prepossessions begotten of his personal religious experience, his tendency to interpret all Scripture solely in the light of this experience, rather than of its own testimony, the mediæval belief in demoniac agency, the influence of scholastic dogma, the theological assumption of the original perfection of created man, the fall of Adam, and the effects of original sin, which has influenced theology, especially since Augustine's time. To represent man as the passive agent of the divine decree is, to say the least, rather compromising for the divine righteousness. It does not sufficiently answer objections on this score to protest that God is nevertheless not the author of the evil in human action, or to adduce the secret as distinct from the revealed will of God. The secret will of God only puts the difficulty a step further back. It does not remove it, since all the same man acts by God's foreknowledge and decree. Is it

not far more reassuring to base the conviction of acceptance
with God, salvation on the divine love rather than on the
assumption of a mysterious divine decree, on which salvation
or damnation ultimately depends ? Nor does this determinism accord with human personality. It practically reduces
man to the level of a machine in the hands of an inexorable
will outside himself. It destroys his personality in its most
essential point—the expression of responsible moral action—
even if Luther's object in thus destroying it is to recreate it
in a new relation to God. Thus to make man the object and
even the victim of a fore-ordaining omnipotent will is, in any
case, to make him a mere automaton, bereft of the power
of free self-development, neutralising his innate faculties of
reason and conscience. The possibility of the freedom of
the will, despite the handicap of heredity, is a cardinal
condition of the training of human character, of the development of man's moral and spiritual nature. It is an essential
of the divine method of achieving the moral and spiritual
progress of the individual and the race. Without it the
race would remain static. Luther has no adequate conception of this side of the question. It is vain to look in his
purely theological reasonings for a treatment of the problem
from the scientific psychological point of view, as the modern
mind envisages it. His doctrine has, moreover, a questionable pantheistic bearing in the objectionable sense of the
word. Luther rightly emphasises the immanence, the all-
working of God in the universe. But he leaves very little
room for human responsibility in transforming this immanence into the realisation of an absolute decree of the divine
omnipotence, though his object is not really to destroy
human responsibility and worth, but to bring about a fuller
realisation of the divine life in man.

In doing so he disclaims all dependence on the scholastic
theology and follows Erasmus in professing to go by the
testimony of Scripture. But equally with Erasmus he works
with ideas borrowed from this theology. His whole reasoning on the subject is vitiated by the Scotist idea of God as
absolute, unlimited will. It is, as he admits, a sort of theological replica of the Greek Fate, though, of course, it excludes
the element of chance.

Nor does it invalidate the legitimate objections of reason and conscience to denounce reason as a blind and impious rebel and discant on man's natural ignorance of God and the good.   Here again his mind still works too much under the influence of the scholastic (Occamist) antithesis between reason and faith, science and religion.   He forgets that reason, though it may be abused, and, so abused, is a terrible agent of error and evil, is nevertheless an essential equally of divinity and humanity, and that it has its inherent rights and responsibilities.   An irrational faith cannot after all be a substitute for reason, and reason in a question of this kind cannot be silenced by the obscurantist objurgation, when awkward problems are suggested for solution, to which he is far too prone.   His book is, in fact, a *tour de force* of reasoning of a very remarkable order, and he himself could find a place for reason with no little effect when defending his cause at Worms and in other utterances, though his general principle came to be that reason is the enemy of God.   " In divine things reason has no authority. In these things only divine authority is valid." [43]   Its temerity is to be repressed.[44]   By the neglect of reason he, too, could be inconsistent and contradictory.   His pessimistic conception of it and human nature in general is undoubtedly influenced by the mediæval notion of the world as the plaything of the devil, who is ever seeking to establish his rule over it in his ceaseless conflict with God.   This conflict of good and evil may be true enough, though not in his naïve acceptance of the demoniac world in which the superstitious spirit of his time saw the devil, in every conceivable shape and form, in the ordinary happenings around it.   If the power of evil is indeed a terrible reality in this misgoverned world of ours, we need not seek farther for an explanation of it than in the misuse of human reason and will, due to the ignorance, selfishness, self-will, and the influence of heredity with which not God but man persists in misgoverning himself and it.   Even Luther does not as a thinker always succeed in avoiding some of the pitfalls which beset so passionate a seeker of truth and righteousness.

[43] " Werke," xviii. 692.        [44] *Ibid.*, xviii. 695.

He does not, for instance, use it aright in identifying Erasmus's position with that of Pelagius on this question. Like Erasmus he can at times press his texts to yield his conclusions, and does not always fairly face the arguments of his opponent. Is it, for instance, a reasonable argument to contend that in the passages of Scripture which seem to teach free will God only makes use of such language in order the better to make us realise our impotence, or to spite the blindness and pride of an accursed reason ? Would it not be much more forcible, in view of the evident meaning of the text, to believe that He meant what He said, even if it makes Him appeal to the responsible human will ? Again, if the reason for rejecting the free will exegesis of a text is that to grant it would be to acknowledge that Pelagius was right, is this a sufficient proof that the anti-Pelagian one must be right ? The question for the scientific exegete is not whether Pelagius was right or wrong, but what the writer actually meant.

Nevertheless, apart from such criticisms, the " De Servo Arbitrio " is a great book—great as a piece of sustained reasoning, great as the offspring of a deeply religious spirit, optimistic, in spite of its pessimism, in emphasising the love and grace of God even in the face of this terrible, omnipotent, and inscrutable divine decree, inciting to the highest moral effort in reliance solely on God, wonderfully inspiring if also at times greatly depressing. There is something grand, heroic, in its attempt to see behind the universe the great secret, the mystery of the divine will which is gradually being unfolded in its history, though the process may appear to us in a different light from that which fell upon the eyes of Luther. Likewise of great historic, practical significance. Luther takes the problem out of the academic atmosphere of the schools. It is, as he rightly emphasises, not a merely speculative one for the doctors to exercise their ingenuity on. It lies at the root of morality and religion. Moreover, his book did an immense service to the Reformation by confirming and strengthening it in the eyes of its adherents and well-wishers. Its message, delivered in such assured tones, that salvation depends not on the claims or pretensions of Pope or Church, but on the divine decree and the operation of God's grace in the individual soul was a sledge-hammer blow to the papal and priestly form of Christianity. Hence the rather generous space we have allotted to the controversy.[45]

Erasmus felt the weight of the blow and did not relish the book or its author. It exasperated him, and in spite of Luther's comparative moderation towards him personally he saw in its sledge-hammer arguments a violent personal attack. His temper and his conservatism got the better of his judgment, and his attitude was henceforth irreconcilably hostile. God preserve me from Luther and all his works, is the tone of the letter he wrote him on the 11th April 1526,[46] as well as of the counterblast which he published under the title of " Hyperaspistes." [47] Pique, as well as incompatibility of temper and tendency, doubtless contributed to this result. Erasmus had been displaced by a bigger personality as the leader of an international move-ment  Theology had taken the place of humanism in the interest even of a large section of the cultured class, whose idol and leader he had hitherto been. It was developing a driving force which humanism lacked. The fact contributed to prejudice him against the Reformation, in which he could now only see darkness and destruction. Formerly it had appeared to him as " a tragedy " of momen-tous import. Now it was a comedy which (with a thrust at Luther's marriage) ended in a wedding !

To Luther, on the other hand, Erasmus is now " a viper,"

---

[45] The " De Arbitrio " is edited by Freitag with introduction and notes for the Weimar edition of Luther's works. Translations in German, in addition to that of Justus Jonas (1526), in Walch, xviii., by O. Scheel in Luther's " Werke," edited by Buchwald (1905), and Gogarten (1924). English translations by Cole (1823) and by Vaughan (1823). Mono-graphs by Taube, " Luther's Lehre über die Freiheit " (1901) ; Katten-busch, " Luther's Lehre vom unfreien Willen und von der Predestina-tion " (1875) ;  " Deus Absconditus bei Luther " (1920) ; Peisher, " Zum Problem von Luther's De Servo Arbitrio," " Theol. Stud. und. Krit." (1926), 212 f. ; Walter, " Das Wesen der Freiheit nach Erasmus und Luther " (1906) ; Murray, " Erasmus and Luther " (1920), gives a very summary account of the free-will controversy ; P. Smith, " Erasmus," 336 f.

[46] Enders, v. 335-336.          [47] " Opera," ix.

an open and reprobate enemy of the truth.[48] He doggedly held to his belief in the enslaved will, though, unlike Calvin, he subsequently refrained from placing predestination, at least in its more speculative form, in the forefront of his teaching on this subject.[49] Fully ten years later there were, he said, only two of his works that he would perhaps not wish to consign to the waste basket—the " De Libero Arbitrio " and his " Catechism " [50]—in reference to the proposed collected edition of his works. The breach between them was a sore trial to Melanchthon, who erelong dropped Luther's determinist doctrine and would fain have healed the breach between them in the interest of learning and the Reformation. It is, however, debatable, in view of his opportunist tendency, his ingrained fear of " tumult," whether it would have been of much practical service on critical occasions to have Erasmus as a friend rather than an enemy.

[48] Enders, v. 329. To Spalatin, 27th March 1526.
[49] See Seeberg, " Dogmengeschichte," iv. 153-155.
[50] Enders, xi. 247. Luther to Capito, 9th July 1537.

# CHAPTER VIII

## CONSOLIDATION OF THE EVANGELICAL MOVEMENT

### I. THE FIRST DIET OF SPIRES

WITH the overthrow of the peasants, in which Romanist and Lutheran princes had combined, the antagonism between the two religious parties reappeared. On the part of the Romanists, in fact, the work of repression was at the same time a crusade against Lutheranism, to which they ascribed the Rising. Luther might protest, in refutation of this assumption, that Electoral Saxony had remained almost free from the revolutionary contagion and that it was just in the ecclesiastical principalities that the people had been driven to desperation by the oppression and misrule of their ecclesiastical overlords.[1] He would have served his own cause better had he borne this fact in mind when inciting the princes indiscriminately to slaughter the insurgents. In acting on this wild manifesto in behalf of established authority, the Romanists were not slow to take advantage of the opportunity to turn their vengeance against his adherents even if they had taken no active part in the revolution. Their victims included, for instance, not a few of the evangelical preachers, and thus in inditing his summons to kill without mercy he was unwittingly giving scope to the persecution of many of his own followers. Whilst alienating the sympathy of the people by his violence, he had failed to gain the goodwill of his antagonists among the princes. The overthrow of the peasants had shattered the hope alike of a national emancipation from Rome and the establishment of a new social order which the evangelical

---

[1] " Werke," 63, 23 (Erlangen ed.); Hausrath, " Luther," ii. 92-93.

movement in its earlier stage bade fair to realise. Luther was denounced by his old antagonist Emser as alike the instigator and betrayer of the peasants,[2] and before the butchery of the insurgents was completed, the Romanist princes of the north, following the example set by those of the south at Ratisbon in the previous year (1524), were taking steps to vindicate the old faith as well as the old social order. To this end, Duke George of Saxony, the Electors of Brandenburg and Maintz, and the Dukes of Brunswick-Wolfenbüttel met at Dessau in July 1525 to concoct a league against the Lutherans. Six months later they deputed Duke Henry of Brunswick to Spain to negotiate the active assistance of the Emperor.[3]

The international situation seemed favourable to the speedy realisation of their project. Charles had not only conquered and captured his rival, Francis I., at Pavia. He had extorted from him, in the Treaty of Madrid, the recognition of his supremacy in Italy and his co-operation in the suppression of the Lutheran heresy in Germany (January 1526).[4] The time had come for putting in force the Edict of Worms, as well as convening the long-talked-of Council for the reformation of ecclesiastical abuses.

The outlook seemed gloomy enough for the cause of Luther, which had besides, by the death of the Elector Frederick in the previous May, lost its most powerful protector, who had so effectively promoted it by his skilful diplomacy and his active goodwill, and who died a professed evangelical Christian. Fortunately at this critical juncture it found in his brother and successor, the Elector John, not merely a prudent patron, but a confirmed and steadfast champion. Still more fortunately, it had gained a formidable recruit in the Landgrave Philip of Hesse, whom Melanchthon had won over in the previous year. The Landgrave was a man of forceful personality and a resourceful politician as well as an ardent convert, and though his personal morality

[2] See Hausrath, ii. 64-65.
[3] Gess, " Akten und Briefe," ii. 352-353; Ranke, " Deutsche Geschichte," ii. 160-161, 173-174, 180-181, 195-196 (1925 ed.); Hausrath, " Luther," ii. 91 ; Kolde, " Luther," ii. 221-222.
[4] Ranke, ii. 245, 272 (1925 ed.).

did not tally too well with his new faith, the Lutheran cause gained in him a gifted adherent whose political ability materially contributed to save it from being overwhelmed by the threatened reaction. Under his forceful auspices a counter-league eventually took shape as the result of a series of conferences at Torgau, Gotha, and Magdeburg, which included, besides the Elector and the Landgrave, the Dukes of Lüneburg, Grubenhagen, and Mecklenburg, the Prince of Anhalt, Count Albrecht of Mansfeld, and the city of Magdeburg (12th June 1526).[5] Luther himself was dubious about this militant policy, which was a distinct departure from his principle of the inadmissibility of rebellion against constituted authority and the use of force in the service of the Gospel.[6] He believed in the co-operation of the secular authority in furtherance of the evangelical cause, and in his " Ermahnung " had assigned to it, not to the people, the initiation of reforms. He had, in fact, at the instigation of Christian of Denmark and in the hope of securing the active co-operation of the English king, written a humble apology to Henry VIII. for the violent tone of his book against him.[7] But he was not yet prepared to sanction the right of rebellion of the princes of the empire against their overlord the Emperor even for the sake of the Gospel.

The influence of this combination made itself felt in the Diet which met a fortnight later (25th June) at Spires to consider once more the religious question. In the absence of most of the leaders of the anti-Lutheran League—Duke George, the Elector Joachim, the Dukes of Bavaria and Brunswick-Wolfenbüttel—the Lutheran princes and the moderate Catholics obtained the upper hand. They not only insisted on the effective reform of ecclesiastical abuses [8]— the gravamina which had figured so conspicuously in the deliberations of previous Diets—they proposed a religious

[5] Ranke, ii. 247-248, 274-277 (1925 ed.).

[6] See his tract, " Ob Kriegsleute auch in seligem Stande sein können," " Werke," xix. 636 f. (1526).

[7] Enders, v. 231-233, 1st Sept. 1525. See also " Werke," xxiii. 17 f., for his retort to Henry's contemptuous reply (1527).

[8] See the list in Walch, xvi. 250 f.

compromise between the two parties, which went a long way towards the Lutheran standpoint. A committee of the princes declared in favour of the marriage of the clergy, of communion in both kinds, of a reduction in the number of fast and festival days and of the mendicant Orders, of the abolition of private Masses, of the use of the German as well as the Latin language in the baptismal and communion services, and of the principle, in the matter of preaching, of the interpretation of Scripture by Scripture (*Scriptura Scripturæ interpres*). " Never before in any Diet," wrote Spalatin, " was there such free and independent and outspoken criticism of the Pope, the bishops, the clergy, as in this one." [9] On the submission of these proposals to a committee of all the Estates, however, the Emperor's commissioners, chief of whom was the Archduke Ferdinand, intervened with an instruction from the Emperor, of date 23rd March 1526, which vetoed any innovation of the traditional ecclesiastical usages, and demanded anew the execution of the Edict of Worms.[10]    In this deadlock the representatives of the cities, who emphasised the impossibility of carrying out the Edict,[11] drew attention to the fact that the international situation had undergone a complete transformation since the issue of this reactionary missive.[12]    And not without reason.    Not only had the French king broken faith with the Emperor by disowning the Treaty of Madrid; the Pope had absolved him from his treaty obligation, had transferred his alliance from the Emperor to his enemy, and had engineered a hostile league against him (the League of Cognac, May 1526), which combined himself, Francis, the Swiss, Venice, Florence, and Duke Sforza of Milan, with the goodwill of Henry VIII.    Pope and Emperor were now, therefore, enemies instead of allies, and the alteration in the international situation justified the assumption that the imperial instruction no longer represented the religious policy of the Emperor.

[9] Bezold, " Geschichte der Deutschen Reformation," 577 ; Hausrath, ii. 95.

[10] Walch, xvi. 244-247, communicated 3rd Aug.

[11] *Ibid.*, xvi. 249-250.

[12] Ranke, ii. 255, 284 (1925 ed.).

Nor was this assumption ill-founded. In this emergency Charles was already considering the religious question in the light of the altered political situation. By adopting the expedient of a General Council he could embarrass the Pope, and, by conciliating the Lutheran princes to the extent of at least modifying the Worms Edict, he could secure their co-operation in the struggle with the combination which the Pope had formed against him. On his own initiative he, therefore, dispatched a new instruction on the 27th July annulling the penal clauses of the Edict and referring the further consideration of the religious question to a General Council.

Meanwhile the Diet had reached a decision in virtue of its own authority.[13] Whilst resolving to send a deputation to Spain [14] to request the convention of a General, or at least a national, Council and the suspension meanwhile of the Edict of Worms, it simply decreed that, until the convocation of this Council, each Estate should so act in the matter of the Edict of Worms as its members should answer to God and the Emperor.[15]

This decision or Recess (*Reichstagsabschied*), as it was officially termed, was undoubtedly but a temporary arrangement. It was not, as Ranke assumed,[16] a constitutional enactment which conferred on the Lutheran princes the legal right henceforth to establish reformed territorial churches apart from any further interference on the part of Emperor or Diet. It expressly recognised, in fact, the responsibility of the various Estates to the Emperor as well as to God in this matter, and it is evident that neither Charles nor the Romanist princes would forego their right to revise this decision when the political situation should permit them to do so. At the same time, it foreshadowed the principle on which the religious problem in Germany was ultimately to

[13] Ranke assumes that the Diet had received the second imperial instruction before coming to its final decision, ii. 258, 288 (1925 ed.). This was evidently not the case, as the Diet had already separated before the arrival of the second communication to the imperial commissioners.

[14] In the Recess of the Diet the Estates mention that they have sent this deputation, Walch, xvi. 267. But it does not seem to have actually gone.

[15] Walch, xvi. 268.

[16] " Deutsche Geschichte," ii. 261, 290 (1925 ed.).

be settled—the principle of territorial sovereignty—and was in accordance with the dominant political tendency in the empire.  This tendency was, and had long been manifesting itself in the growth of particular territorial sovereignties at the expense of the general sovereignty of both the Emperor and the Diet, and in the Recess of Spires we may see the virtual, if temporary, recognition of it in the sphere of religion as well as politics.  As applied to ecclesiastical matters, it was, however, a startling departure ; for whilst, politically, the trend in the empire had been towards particularism, the mediæval conception of ecclesiastical uniformity had hitherto been supreme, though the princes had been striving to assert their power in matters ecclesiastical and the popes had been fain to reckon with the fact.  Moreover, on both political and ecclesiastical grounds, it was the interest of the Emperor to withstand the tendency towards disintegration which the Reformation was thus threatening to intensify, and it was not difficult to foresee that the alteration of the international situation in his favour would be followed by a determined attempt to reverse the Recess to the advantage both of the imperial authority and the traditional Church.

Happily for the Reformation the respite afforded by the Recess of Spires enabled the Lutheran princes to materially extend the movement and consolidate it within their territories.  It had, the year before the meeting of the Diet, received a notable recruit in Albrecht of Brandenburg, Grandmaster of the Order of Teutonic Knights, who, as we have seen, transformed East Prussia into a secular duchy, with which the King of Poland, whom he agreed to recognise as feudal superior, invested him in April 1525.  The Brandenburg or Hohenzollern family furnished other influential recruits in the Margraves Casimir and George of Ansbach-Baireuth.  Within the next four years it extended its sway over Silesia, part of Pomerania (one of whose dukes, Barnum, became a Lutheran), Schleswig, Holstein, East Friesland.  The greater part of north Germany, as well as a large number of cities in the south, was professedly Lutheran.[17]  It had penetrated to such outlying regions of

[17] For the rapid extension of Lutheranism in the north during this period, see Ranke, ii. 322 f., 354 f. (1925 ed.).

the empire as Bohemia and the Netherlands and had taken a hold in lands beyond its borders—in Denmark and Sweden, in Scotland and England, in France, and even in Spain and Italy.

Its rapid spread in the northern German principalities was due in part to the preaching of zealous Lutheran propagandists like Bugenhagen. It was due, too, to the policy of secularisation, which transferred to the territorial sovereign the ecclesiastical lands, and in too many cases helps to explain the facility with which these petty sovereigns professed submission to the Gospel. The greed of ecclesiastical property was not indeed all on the Lutheran side, and it is significant of the mercenary spirit of an age in which zeal for the old faith contrasts with zeal for the new, that such professedly staunch Romanists as the Archduke Ferdinand and the Duke of Bavaria were ready enough, on occasion, to help themselves to the lands and wealth of the old Church as the price of their devotion to the Pope and the hierarchy. Even the Emperor was advised by his aunt Margaret, the Stadholderin of the Netherlands, to propose to the Pope the extensive confiscation of Church lands in order to furnish the means for the war against the Turks,[18] and Charles's Spanish councillors are found suggesting the seizure even of the temporal possessions of the Papacy, in the imperial interest, in Italy.[19]

## II. The Organisation of the Evangelical Church

Luther's conception of the Church, of which the germ is already apparent in his early lectures on the Psalms and the Epistle to the Romans, i.e., before 1517,[20] had gradually

---

[18] Bezold, 564.

[19] Ibid., 547; Berger, " Luther," ii., Pt. II., 122-125.

[20] Holl, "Aufsätze," 288 f., and with him Kattenbusch, "Die Doppelschichtigkeit in Luther's Kirchenbegriff," " Theol. St. und Krit." (1928), 197 f., maintain that he had already thus early attained to his distinctive conception of the Church. Whilst this is so far the case, as it was an implication of his doctrine of justification by faith, this implication is not fully developed, and Luther, in writing of the Church in these early works, is not conscious of any real divergence from the current Roman Catholic one. He is not yet in conscious opposition

taken distinctive form in the conflict with his Romanist opponents. This conflict had resulted, as we have seen, in a complete revulsion from the papal-hierarchical conception and the substitution of that of the community of believers, directly subject to Christ, its head and lord. The Church, as thus ultimately conceived, is the communion of saints or believers (*Communio Sanctorum aut Fidelium*)—of those who believe in Christ through the Word of God, appropriated by faith. In formulating this conception Luther thus conjoins the two articles of the Apostles' Creed, " I believe in the Holy Catholic Church, in the Communion of Saints," and, in accordance with his doctrine of justification, the emphasis is on faith in the Word or Gospel as the source of faith. In virtue of their common faith in the Word and their mutual and active love, as the fruit of faith, believers form a spiritual community [21] or people (*Volk der gläubigen*). Otherwise expressed, they are a mystical body (*corpus mysticum*), of which Christ is the head and they are the members. The great protagonist of individual faith in the sense that the believer must for himself enter into direct personal relation to God in Christ, Luther nevertheless does not lose sight of the relation of the individual believer to other believers. Hence, alongside the emphasis on individual faith, the additional emphasis on the common faith in the Word, or Gospel, which binds all believers together in the spiritual community, the Church, or as he prefers specifically to term it, the *Christenheit*,[22] in the sense of the sum total of believers.

The Church in this spiritual sense is the necessary and indispensable corollary of the personal faith which is shared by all believers, and by which they are bound together in the one communion or community. It is the antithesis of the papal-hierarchical Church—the visible, legally constituted

---

to the traditional Church even in criticising the abuses rampant in it, and can, therefore, hardly be said to be fully conscious of the differentiating principle of the Church that was to separate him from the Roman communion.

[21] For Luther communio and congregatio are identical terms. Kattenbusch, 225.

[22] Kattenbusch, 230 f.

institution through which grace, salvation is mediated by the clerical hierarchy under its supreme head, the Pope. Being based on faith in the Word, or Gospel, which belongs to the spiritual sphere, it is essentially spiritual, invisible. To differentiate between the invisible and the visible Church is, therefore, really inaccurate, though Luther himself may do so at times in speaking of the Church and its outward form. The invisible and the visible are rather to be considered as two aspects or sides of the same thing. In so far as it exists for the preaching of the Word and the dispensation of the sacrament (the *verbum visibile*) by those entrusted with this function, it takes a visible, external, regulated, though not necessarily an identical form.[23]

Luther's conception of the Church thus differs from that of Zwingli, Calvin, and ultimately that of Melanchthon as well as from that of the Romanists. Whilst the Romanists identify the invisible with the visible Church, Zwingli, Calvin, and Melanchthon differentiate sharply between them. The former consists of the elect known only to God (*soli deo cognita*), the latter is the actual Church as existing on earth. For Luther, on the other hand, the invisible is at the same time the visible Church inasmuch as it is both the totality of believers in the Word, and therefore, faith being spiritual, an invisible reality perceptible only to believers, and the visible manifestation of this spiritual reality in the common life of believers.[24]

The practical result of this conception of the Church as a spiritual association, based on the Word and bound together by a common faith, would have been an organisation free from State control, if to a certain extent accepting, for practical reasons, the co-operation of the secular authority. Theoretically the Church, which consists of all true believers, is subject only to Christ and is ruled only by His Word, in contrast to the papal hierarchical development of it and the kingdoms of this world. It has nothing to do with either

[23] Rietschel, " Luther's Anschauung von der Unsichtbarkeit und Sichtbarkeit der Kirche," " Theol. Stud. und Krit." (1900), 404 f.; Kattenbusch, " Doppelschichtigkeit," *ibid.*, 1928, 206 f.

[24] In both cases it seems to be perceptible to, or apprehended only by faith.

canon law or secular law.  Canon law is the work of the
devil and must be destroyed root and branch, and in this
spirit he had thrown a copy of it into the flames along with
the papal Bull.  Nor has it anything to do with civil or
common law, because it is a spiritual association.  The only
rule pertaining to it is that which derives from the Word of
God, as expressed in the preaching of the Word and the
administration of the sacraments.  So conceived, the Church
has no need of anything of the nature of a man-made
constitution, involving a legal, coercive jurisdiction.  It has
all that it requires for its corporate life in the spiritual rule
of Christ and the Word and such organisation as is necessary
for the election and ordination of the pastor or bishop,
the maintenance of preaching and the administration of the
sacraments.  According to this conception each congregation
is an independent spiritual unit, living its religious life and
regulating this life under the headship of Christ and in
accordance with His Word as its all-sufficient law, if maintaining fellowship with all other communities of believers
in virtue of a common faith and love.  Anything of the
nature of ecclesiastical law (*Kirchenrecht*) with the force
of State sanction behind it is inapplicable to it.[25]  The State
has no coercive jurisdiction in relation to the Church, even
if its co-operation in furthering its interests may be
accepted.

How, then, did it come about that Luther is found, in
his early period as a Reformer, assigning to the secular
power an active part in the Reformation of the Church and
ultimately inviting the Elector to direct the organisation
of the Saxon Church ?  Sohm finds the explanation of this
difference between theory and practice in the fact that
Luther retained the mediæval conception of the Church
and the State [26] as the two sides of the one Christian common-

[25] This conception is elaborately worked out by Sohm, " Kirchenrecht," i. 460 f. (1982).

[26] " Kirchenrecht," 542 f., particularly 558 f.  See also his more
recent work, " Weltliches und Geistliches Recht " (1914).  Luther
generally uses the term Obrigkeit to denote the secular power.  It is in
this concrete fashion rather than in the modern sense of the State, which
did not exist in his day, that he differentiates between the two powers,
spiritual and temporal.

wealth or kingdom of God (the two swords or powers, the ecclesiastical and the temporal). On this conception Rieker based his thesis that at the outset (particularly in the "Address to the Nobility") he contemplated the establishment, not of a purely voluntary, autonomous Church of believers independent of the secular authority, but of a Church in close alliance with it as an integral part of the Christian body (*Corpus Christianum*),[27] or, as Luther termed it, the *Christenheit* in the mediæval sense. It was, he thinks, under the influence of this conception, that in the "Address to the Nobility" he summoned the State to undertake the Reformation of the Church. Whether Luther was so consciously influenced by the mediæval conception of the close relation of Church and State as jurists like Rieker suppose, is not explicitly apparent from the "Address" itself. The reasoning on which he based the right of the State to intervene in the affairs of the Church is theological, not juristic. The jurists are, in fact, as a rule the objects of his special aversion. This right rests mainly on his specific doctrine of the priesthood of all believers, by which the State, as an integral part of the Christian body, is entitled, nay, is under obligation to exercise its function in the Reformation of the Church, which the ecclesiastical power had hitherto failed effectively to undertake. In thus empowering the State to intervene in matters ecclesiastical, Luther, according to Rieker, laid the foundation of what ultimately became the accepted ecclesiastical polity in the Lutheran principalities (*Landesherrliche Kirchenregiment*). This thesis has given rise to an elaborate discussion on the question whether or not Luther's ideal was a Reformed Church virtually independent of the State. In this discussion both jurists and theologians have participated down to the present time without reaching

[27] " Die Rechtliche Stellung der evangelischen Kirche Deutschlands " (1893). Drews energetically, but by no means convincingly, controverts his thesis. " Entsprach das Staatskirchenthum dem Ideale Luther's ? " "Zeitschrift für Theologie und Kirche" (1908), Ergänzungsheft, 1 f. See Hermelink's criticism, " Z.K.G." (1908), 479 f. Holl rejects the phrase Corpus Christianum as not historically applicable to the mediæval conception of Church and State. This is merely a modern expression. He thinks that respublica Christiana or populus Christianus comes nearer to the mediæval idea. " Aufsätze," 341-342.

anything like an exact agreement on Luther's view of the relation of Church and State.[28] Müller, for instance, contends that in the "Address" Luther conferred on the secular power only a very limited jurisdiction in matters ecclesiastical, and carefully distinguished between the ecclesiastical and the secular sphere. Whilst the secular power should take the initiative in the reformation of practical abuses, its function does not extend to purely spiritual things, which are reserved for the reforming ecclesiastical Council to be convened by the secular authority.[29] With this contention Holl agrees.[30] Kohlmeyer, on the other hand, argues that in the "Address" Luther attributed to the State in relation to the Church a wider jurisdiction in the matter of reform than these writers are prepared to admit, and the evidence seems to me to bear out his contention.[31] If the constituted authorities of the Empire, to which the "Address" was directed, had undertaken the Reformation to which he summoned them, if they had accepted his evangelical teaching, the State would evidently, in virtue of its evangelical character, have acquired an intimate relation to the Church and played an active part in its organisation and government, though this is not definitely set forth in the "Address" itself. Luther, for instance, in speaking of the ecclesiastical reorganisation of the local community, assigns to the town authority an important position in relation to this community.

The hope of such a Reformation in virtue of the active intervention of the secular power proved, however, illusory.

[28] See the works of Foerster, Sehling, Brandenburg, Karl Müller, W. Köhler, Rade, Troeltsch, Holl, Drews, Hermelink, and others. For a careful review of the literature of the subject see Kattenbusch, "Doppelschichtigkeit," and that of W. Köhler in "Z.K.G." (1917-18), 1 f. Other recent discussions are those of Jordan, "Luther's Staatsauffassung" (1917); Meinecke, "Luther über Christliches Gemeinwesen," "Hist. Zeitschrift" (1920), 1 f. (an illuminating criticism of Holl's view); Bredt, "Neues Evangelisches Kirchenrecht für Preussen," i. (1921); H. A. Preus, "Luther's Doctrine of the Church in His Early Writings," Edin. Univ. Thesis (1928).

[29] "Kirche, Gemeinde, und Obrigkeit nach Luther," 19 f. (1910).

[30] "Luther und das Landesherrliche Kirchenregiment," 26 (1911); "Aufsätze," 326 f. (1927).

[31] "Entstehung der Schrift Luther's an den Christlichen Adel," 21 f. (1922); Mackinnon, "Luther and the Reformation," ii. 245.

Within little more than six months from its publication,
the proceedings of the Diet of Worms proved incontestably
that the demand for an evangelical Reformation at the
hands of either the State or a General Council was merely
crying for the moon, in spite of the fact that the national
sentiment was largely favourable to his cause.  No wonder
that Luther, in view of the hostile Edict of Worms and the
reactionary attitude of the Reichsregiment and the second
Diet of Nürnberg, abandoned the idea of a Reformation
carried out by the Estates of the Empire and became much
less disposed to recognise their functions in matters
ecclesiastical.  In the tract on " The Secular Power " and
other writings of the years 1521-25, he sharply
differentiated, as we have seen, between the temporal
and the spiritual spheres.  In the task of organising the
evangelical Church he now turns, not to the princes, but
to the community of believers, though he still leaves room
for the co-operation of the territorial or the local authority.
The secular power—princes, counts, local superiors, town
councils—may and, in fact, ought to co-operate to a certain
extent in this task.  But to the Christian community itself
belongs primarily the right and the duty to organise and
govern itself under the lead of its pastor or bishop, with
the goodwill and, within certain limits, the co-operation of
the secular authority.  His ideal of the Christian community
is a voluntary association of believers free from State
control, if, for practical reasons, accepting the assistance
of the secular authority in the actual work of organisation.[32]
    It was this ideal that he sought to realise in his missives
to the Church at Leisnig and to Hausmann, pastor at Zwickau,
in 1523, in which the organisation of the local community
is based on the Christian-democratic principle that its
members have the right to make the proposed changes.[33]
Similarly in the missive to the senate and people of Prague,
written in the same year, he recognises the right of the
Christian community to elect and depose its ministers and
asserts the priesthood of believers, which invests them with

    [32] See Holl, " Landesherrliche Kirchenregiment," 37 f. ; " Auf-
sätze," 354 f.
    [33] " Werke," xi. 408 f. ; xii. 11 f., 205 f.

the power to confer all ministerial functions on the person or persons who perform them in their stead.[34] He was even prepared to carry his ideal of an autonomous Church the length of establishing at Wittenberg and elsewhere a Church in the more spiritual sense within the Church in the more popular sense. The former should consist of all real Christians who are prepared to subject themselves wholly to Christ and His Word ; the latter of all professed Christians who have not attained to this advanced stage of the Christian life. The former should have their particular assemblies for worship and edification, and should submit to a strict discipline exercised by the members over one another ; for the latter the ordinary services should suffice. The former forms the *Bekenntniskirche*—composed of those confessing Christ in the fullest sense—the latter the *Volkskirche*, embracing the people in general.[35] He was, however, fain to confess that this ideal was in present circumstances impracticable, and was debarred from attempting to realise it by the lack of the means to do so and the fear of thereby fostering mere sectarianism.[36]

Such attempts to devise and bring into operation a democratic organisation of the local Christian community did not, however, prove successful. Besides, the outbreak of the Peasant War, which supervened on them, appears to have shaken his faith in a religious democracy.[37] The Rising not only intensified his mistrust of the people, but so aggravated its misery and demoralisation that any further practical attempt to organise the local community on a

---

[34] " De Instituendis Ministris Ecclesiæ," "Werke," xii. 172, 178, 190-191.

[35] See the preface to the " Deutsche Messe," " Werke," xix. 72 f. (1526) ; Sehling, " Die Evangelischen Kirchenordnungen," i. 10 f.

[36] See preface to " Deutsche Messe," 12 ; Holl, " Landesherrliche Kirchenregiment," 37 f. ; and " Aufsätze," 358 f. ; Karl Müller, 39-40 ; Hermelink, " Luther's Gedanken über Idealgemeinden," " Z.K.G." (1908), 312 f.

[37] Holl (" Landesherrliche Kirchenregiment," 41 ; " Aufsätze," 361) and Hermelink (" Z.K.G." (1908), 320) think that the experience of the Peasant Rising had no appreciable effect on Luther's undemocratic organisation of the Saxon Church. This seems to me a very doubtful contention.

democratic basis might well seem hopeless. Moreover, in the work of organisation Luther had not entirely discarded the co-operation of the secular power where this was available. Even if he had been disposed to revive the primitive Christian ideal of a self-governing community wholly independent of the State, he could not ultimately ignore the territorial prince, if only because the territorial prince had become the dominant power in the empire and without his sanction and co-operation the Reformation could hardly be consolidated. The territorial prince had, moreover, been asserting his power in matters ecclesiastical long before the Reformation, and this even with the papal sanction.[38] In view of this tendency there was, in any case, not much chance of the realisation of the theory of a purely spiritual Church independent of the State and of any human polity. An autonomous Church on the basis of the Word could hardly develop in the face of the political trend towards princely absolutism, especially as Luther, whilst emphasising the distinction between the spiritual and the temporal sphere, preached the divine right of the secular authority, the *Obrigkeit*, and in the political sphere was a staunch supporter of this absolutism.

It is, therefore, hardly surprising that he disapproved of the democratic polity which was proposed by Francis Lambert, the ex-Franciscan monk of Avignon, whom Zwingli had won for the Reformation and who became the Reformer of Hesse, at a Synod convened by the Landgrave Philip at Homberg in October 1526. According to this scheme, which is an anticipation of the Presbyterian system of polity, the Church, which is founded on the Word of God, consists of the whole body of believers.[39]    It

---

[38] Bredt, " Neues Evangelisches Kirchenrecht für Preussen," i. 163 f. (1921); Pallas, " Die Entstehung des landesherrlichen Kirchenregiments in Kursachsen vor der Reformation " (1910); Dietrich Schäfer, " Deutsche Geschichte," ii. 38 (1916); Bezold, " Geschichte der Deutschen Ref.," 565; Hashagen, " Die Vorreformatorische Bedeutung des spätmittelalterlichen landesherrlichen Kirchenregiment," " Z.K.G." (1922), 63 f.; and " Landesherrliche Ablasspolitik vor der Reformation," *ibid.* (1927), 11 f.

[39] Ecclesia autem dei congregatio fidelium, Richter, " Die Evangelischen Kirchenordnungen des 16ten Jahrhunderts," i. 61.

recognised the right of each congregation to elect its pastor, elders,[40] and deacons, and excommunicate unworthy members, and committed the general oversight and government of the whole Church to a synod or general assembly, consisting of the pastor and elected representatives of each congregation, which should meet once a year. For the supervision of the churches of the various districts, visitors or superintendents are to be appointed annually by the synod. The prince and the nobles may attend the synod and vote, and the prince fixes the place of meeting. But the Church, as a religious association founded on the Word of God, is an autonomous body. The scheme was an anticipation on paper of what ultimately became the presbyterian system of Church government. It contemplated the organisation of a practically autonomous Church in alliance with the State (the co-operation of the prince in the government of the Church, though not his supremacy over it, being recognised), and it was ultimately destined to be realised in the Reformed Churches of Switzerland, France, Holland, Scotland, America. But it did not commend itself to Luther, who objected to such an elaborate legislative scheme,[41] and owing to his opposition it was not adopted in Hesse or in the other Lutheran principalities. Ranke ascribes its rejection in these principalities to the fact that the princes took an active part in directing and controlling the establishment of the Reformation, whereas in France, Holland, and Scotland it was largely a popular movement and it perforce acquired a more democratic character.[42] He ought to have added, however, that even in Germany the constitution and organisation of the Church varied with the character of the civil government. In the Free Imperial cities, for instance, the government was based on the representative principle, to a certain extent at least, and this principle made itself felt in the government of the Church, which thus reflected the

[40] He usually refers to the ministry of a congregation as consisting of the bishop, *i.e.*, the pastor, and the deacons (episcopus et diaconi). But he refers also to elders (seniores, veteres, presbyteri), *ibid.*, 60, 63, 66.

[41] Letter to the Landgrave, 7th June 1527, " Werke," 56, 170 (Erlangen ed.) ; Enders, vi. 9.

[42] ".Deutsche Geschichte," ii. 307-308 ; ii. 340 f. (1925 ed.).

democratic spirit of Luther's teaching, in this matter, in a way that could not apply in the States under absolute princely rule.

Despite his theoretical conception of the Church and his doctrine of the priesthood of believers, Luther was thus fain to make a virtue of expediency and to seek the aid of the secular power in the organisation of the Church in Germany. His recourse to the Elector was really a step towards the subjection of the Church to the State and to a system of Protestant ecclesiastical law imposed by the State and dependent on it for its validity. The necessity of taking measures to bring order into the chaos resulting from the situation produced by the Reformation, rendered it impossible to carry out the theory of the Church as a spiritual institution on the basis of the Word alone. Moreover, Luther was disposed to be less revolutionary in practice than in theory, and was prepared, on certain conditions and on grounds of expediency, to recognise what he combated in principle. He was even prepared to tolerate the papal hierarchical jurisdiction as long as the Gospel was preached and the freedom of the individual conscience recognised. The ecclesiastical constitution, though it rested on man-made law, might be suffered to exist as part of the historic inherit-ance, if the faith and conscience of the individual Christian were left in freedom. The fact is that he had not the genius of the ecclesiastical statesman and did not lay anything like the same stress on ecclesiastical as on purely religious questions. This was his strength, but it was also his weakness. As Döllinger aptly says, " He was the founder of a religion rather than of a church." In this respect he differed from men like Calvin and Knox, who were born organisers as well as reformers, and left their impress on institutions as well as doctrines.[43] Luther, on the other hand,

[43] Hermelink ("Z.K.G." (1908), 408) thinks that Luther had far more organising talent than is usually ascribed to him. He thinks that, in practical sense, he deserves a place alongside a Bismarck and other great German *Realpolitiker*. This may be true in the sense that he was remarkably ready to adapt himself to circumstances with a sort of high-minded opportunism. But it is perfectly evident that he had not, like Calvin or Knox, the organising genius in the sense of formulating and systematically applying in practice a set of clear-cut constitutional principles.

was less inclined to legislate in such matters. In the preface to the German Mass of 1526, for instance, he still emphatically disapproves of legislating uniformity of worship in the Saxon Church. Though he would be glad to see this uniformity freely adopted, he would not dream of restricting the conscience of the individual by a general law on the subject.[44] The personality and genius of the various reformers had, in fact, not a little to do with the constitutional form which the Reformed Church assumed in the lands in which the Reformation triumphed. The existing political situation was also a moulding factor. " Our decisions," said Melanchthon, " are mere platonic laws if the Court does not give them its sanction and protection."

Luther saw in the decision of the first Diet of Spires on the religious question the recognition of the right of the evangelical princes to organise the territorial Church on reformed lines.[45] Accordingly, in November 1526 he besought the Elector John, as head of the State, to initiate measures to this end within the Saxon electorate.[46] He adduces the miserable state of religion and education in the electorate as the result of the prevailing religious anarchy and demoralisation. Now that the old system has been undermined, the people are lacking in a sense of responsibility for the maintenance of the preaching of the Word and the education of their children. Each one is disposed to live as he pleases. Hence the necessity for the prince to take upon himself the lapsed ecclesiastical function of the bishops as far as the work of organising a new order of things is concerned. He seems, indeed, to have contemplated only the temporary exercise of this function, until, that is, the work of reformation and organisation should be completed (Notepiscopat).[47] The prince, as the possessor of the supreme power in the State, is to use his authority in the interest of the Church, and is not assumed to exercise the episcopal authority in purely spiritual matters. In reality,

[44] Sehling, i. 10-11.
[45] Sohm, " Kirchenrecht," 576.
[46] " Werke," 53, 386-388 (Erlangen ed.), and the Elector's favourable reply, Enders, v. 407-408.
[47] Sohm, 585.

however, the prince takes the place of the bishop in taking the initiative in ordering the affairs of the new Church, and the first step is made in subjecting the Church to the State.[48]

In response the Elector appointed four visitors—two of his councillors, Planitz and Haubitz, and two Wittenberg professors, Melanchthon and Schurf [49]—and drew up an " Instruction and Command " for their guidance. In this document (16th June 1527) the Elector assumes the right as well as the duty to make such a visitation, which is carried out by the visitors in virtue of his ordinance. They are directed to investigate the teaching and life of the clergy and schoolmasters, to displace those who are found incapable, to punish those who preach error and all sectaries, especially those who hold erroneous views of the sacrament and thus disturb public order, with banishment in both cases. The Elector professes, indeed, not to prescribe what anyone is to believe and to disallow sects only in the interest of order.[50] But practically he leaves no alternative but to believe and act as he prescribes, or quit his territory, and makes his will the arbiter of permissible belief. This inquisition is to apply to the laity as well as the clergy. They are, further, to make an inventory of all ecclesiastical revenues and teinds, on which, apparently, the nobility and the municipal authorities are laying hands; [51] to provide for the maintenance of the clergy out of these revenues, and where these are insufficient, to arrange a yearly contribution from the parishioners; to introduce as far as possible uniformity of worship; to take measures for the proper administration of the poor funds; to appoint district

[48] Burckhardt, Kawerau, and others see in the recourse of Luther to the Elector a renunciation by him of his idea of the Church as a purely spiritual institution. Sohm, on the other hand, combats this assumption (587-588), and Müller and Holl agree with him in holding that it was merely a temporary expedient, rendered necessary by the situation.

[49] Enders, v. 407-410, 26th Nov. 1526. He requested the university to suggest two names, whilst he himself nominated the other two and commissioned them on the 4th and 13th February 1527.

[50] Sehling, i. 144.

[51] Luther in his letter to the Elector, in Nov. 1526, expressly says that this was the case, " Werke," 53, 388 (Erlangen ed.).

superintendents over the clergy; and to see that public order and morality are maintained by the local authorities.[52] In accordance with this Instruction the visitors carried out a preliminary visitation in the summer of 1527. The investigation revealed a shocking state of disorder and demoralisation and emphasised the necessity for a more thorough inquisition and a systematic organisation of the Saxon Church. To this end Melanchthon, at the Elector's request, drew up and Luther and Bugenhagen revised the "Church Ordinance," or "Kirchenordnung," for a practical and constitutional Reformation.[53] In the preface which he wrote for it, Luther adduces, in vindication of the visitation, the practice of the Apostles and the ancient Church, which the bishops have neglected with disastrous results to religion and morality. He would fain have invested the evangelical preachers with this function. But the necessary authority for making such changes being lacking, the Elector, following the example of the Emperor Constantine in dealing with the Arian heresy, must temporarily take it on himself in virtue of his divinely ordained office as head of the State. At the same time, he expressly disclaims his right "to teach and exercise spiritual rule," and bases his action on the duty of the prince "to prevent division, sects, and tumult among his subjects." [54] This limitation is not, however, in keeping with the terms of the "Instruction," in which the prince does assume the right not merely to prevent division and tumult, but to direct, sanction, and enforce the reformation of teaching and ecclesiastical institutions as well as practical abuses. Luther evidently did not approve of this far-reaching extension of the secular jurisdiction over the Church, and sought by this disclaimer to safeguard its spiritual rights. For him it is merely a temporary and exceptional measure. Practically, however, in spite of his caveat, the "Kirchenordnung" is the work of the Elector

[52] Sehling, i. 35, 142 f.

[53] "Unterricht der Visitatoren, 1528," Sehling, i. 149 f.; Richter, "Die Evangelischen Kirchenordnungen des 16ten Jahrhunderts," i. 77 f.; "Corp. Ref.," xxvi. 48 f.; Lietzmann, "Der Unterricht der Visitatoren, 1528," Kleine Texte, 87 (1912).

[54] Sehling, i. 151.

and the officials appointed by him, and marks a farther step in the direction of subordinating the Church to the State.[55]

Whilst striving to preserve the independence of the Church, as an ideal at least, Luther has become less tolerant of conscientious religious opinions that differed from his own. In 1524 he was still prepared to allow even the prophets to express their views and to leave truth to vindicate itself. In 1526 he stresses the necessity of unity of belief, and supports the Elector's policy of penalising dissent from approved doctrines and institutions. In February 1526, for instance, he tells the Elector, in reference to the recalcitrant canons of Altenburg, that it is his duty to suppress the old ceremonies. "A secular ruler may not tolerate that disunity and division should be fostered by insubordinate preachers. Revolt and sectarian dispeace would be the inevitable result. Therefore only one doctrine should be preached in every place. With this argument the Nürnbergers silenced the monks and closed the monasteries." [56]

The "Kirchenordnung" forms alike a confession of faith, a directory of public worship, and a scheme of educational reform. The doctrinal sections set forth in simple language the main points of Luther's evangelical teaching, which the pastors are to teach the people. They are to preach the whole Gospel and nothing but the Gospel of repentance, the forgiveness of sins through faith in Christ, the helplessness of the will and man's dependence on God, etc. It is, however, evident that his doctrine of faith and freedom had to be somewhat modified in accordance with the condition of the people. The visitation revealed in truth a lamentable state of demoralisation—an ignorant, starved, indifferent, immoral clergy ; a peasantry still more ignorant and largely estranged from religion. No wonder, after the bloody repression of the emancipation movement, that the

[55] K. Müller's attempt ("Kirche," etc., 72 f.) to reconcile Luther's preface with the Instruction is not very forcible, and Holl recognises (47 f. ; "Aufsätze," 373 f.) that the Instruction practically established the territorial Church under the Elector's supremacy.

[56] "Werke," 53, 386 (Erlangen ed.). On Luther's lapse from his characteristic principle of toleration from 1526 onwards, see Murray, "Erasmus and Luther," 255 f.

people in Spalatin's words, "despise us as they formerly despised the Papacy." Hence, whilst the characteristic evangelical doctrines are enunciated, the stress laid on the necessity of preaching the law as well as the Gospel, which gave offence to zealous Lutherans like Agricola, who angrily challenged Melanchthon's legalism and was with difficulty meanwhile pacified by Luther. The Ten Commandments are to be diligently taught and stress laid on works, a good Christian life, practical piety as the fruit of faith. The people is evidently in a state of rudeness and ignorance in which the gospel of freedom is apt to be mistaken for a gospel of licence. The late rising, which is pointedly referred to, explains the emphasis laid on subjection to the *Obrigkeit* and the dominant social system. Any attempt to revolt against the law of the land is to be denounced and exemplarily punished as a subversion of the divine ordinance, though the *Obrigkeit* is reminded of the duty of ruling justly, and against those who would repress the Gospel the command to obey God rather than man is emphasised. In regard to the sacraments, that of penance is retained, but whilst repentance is emphasised and confession is to be made to the pastor before communion, the doctrine of penitential satisfaction is rejected and the satisfaction made by Christ substituted. Baptism is to be performed in the fashion hitherto usual, without quarrelling about chrism, on the understanding that the true chrism is that of the Holy Spirit. The sacrament of the body and blood is explained in the sense of consubstantiation, and communion in both kinds is to be positively preached and practised, with liberty, provisionally, to weak brethren, who have conscientious objections, of communion in one kind. Those who adopt an attitude of obstinate opposition to such teaching are, however, to be debarred from communion. The Mass, on the occasion of the communion, is to be sung by preference in German on the model of the German Mass composed by Luther for this part of the service in 1526.[57] But Masses for the dead and prayers to the saints are abolished, though the saints may be honoured as examples of God's grace and for the

---

[57] Deutsche Messe und Ordnung Gottesdiensts, "Werke," xix. 44 f.

quickening of faith and good works. The chief Church festivals are to be observed as giving greater opportunity for instruction in God's Word, not as if they were in themselves a special means of grace. Prayer, the importance of which is dwelt on, does not consist in repeating so many paternosters and psalms, but in diligently seeking the fulfilment of God's promises in faith and sincerity of heart. Such ordinances are to be observed as having the sanction of the civil authority, though it is not the function of the *Obrigkeit* to ordain a new worship (which, however, it practically does), but to enforce the observance of them for the maintenance of peace and love among its subjects.

In the matter of worship, the people are to assemble every morning in the church to sing these psalms in Latin or German, to hear the Word of God read, followed by the Lord's Prayer, a German hymn, and a collect. Similarly in the evening, with the addition of the singing of the Magnificat, or the Te Deum, or the Benedictus, or Quicumque Vult. On Wednesdays and Fridays, besides Sunday, and on special festival days, sermons are to be preached in which the Gospel, the Ten Commandments, the Creed, the Lord's Prayer are to be explained. In their sermons the preachers shall refrain from vituperation against the Pope and the bishops, and only refer to such subjects in as far as this is necessary for instruction and example. Those guilty of notorious sins are not to be admitted to communion and, after several warnings, are to be excommunicated, if they do not amend their conduct. There is to be no disputing on practices indifferent in themselves. On, for instance, the practice of ringing the church bells as an invitation to prayer on the outbreak of storms, which may be continued. The pastor shall, however, instruct the people against the superstitions connected therewith—the notion, for instance, that in virtue of consecration the ringing of the bell has the effect of driving away the storm.

In order that the Word of God may be purely and faithfully preached, the sacraments rightly dispensed, and a good Christian life in subjection to the *Obrigkeit* maintained, the superintendents shall exercise a careful supervision of the clergy. They are empowered to instruct those of the clergy

who are lacking in doctrine and life and, in case of disobedience, to advise the local officials who shall bring the
matter to the notice of the Elector. In the case of the
filling of vacant churches, they are to examine those
nominated by the patron to vacant charges in order that
the people may have capable and fit preachers.

Finally, for the better education of the clergy and also
in the interest of the service of the State, the training of the
children must be improved. To this end an outline is given
of a scheme of lessons adapted to the various stages of
instruction in the schools. The course includes, for the
lower classes, besides a careful grounding in the Latin
grammar and portions of Latin authors, religious instruction
and singing. In the highest class the more apt pupils shall
receive intensive instruction in Latin, including the reading
of Ovid, Virgil, Cicero, and a training in dialectic and
rhetoric.

The visitation was not only the beginning of an urgently
needed practical reformation of the religious life. It proved
to be the first step towards the establishment of the consis-
torial constitution which invested the government of the
Church, under the supremacy of the territorial prince, in a
body of State officials or consistory, composed of theologians
and jurists. The definite introduction of this system into the
Saxon Church dates from 1538, though it was only subsequently developed. Under the Roman Catholic system
the government of the Church was in the hands of the
bishops and ecclesiastical lawyers under the supreme
authority of the Pope. Under the reformed Lutheran
organisation this system was so far retained in the régime
of a consistory of theologians and jurists under the supremacy
of the State.

## III. THE SECOND DIET OF SPIRES AND THE PROTESTATION

Whilst a beginning was thus being made with the
organisation of the evangelical churches, the Landgrave
Philip was striving to negotiate an extension of the league
in their defence against the day of reaction. To this end he

entered into communication with the south German cities, with Zwingli, with Zapolya, the rival of Ferdinand for the crown of Hungary, with Denmark and Sweden, and even with Francis I. of France. With the political activity of the Landgrave, which Zwingli actively seconded, the Reformation enters as a force into international politics from the side of the reformed party itself, and this party tends to become a political as well as a religious one, with which the European rulers are fain to reckon. It is no longer merely a case of the Reformation being a movement to be used for political purposes by a Charles V. or other potentate. It tends to become a political power which was erelong to find corporate expression in the Schmalkald League and to make its weight felt in the chanceries of Europe.

The Spires Recess, which enabled the Lutheran princes to consolidate and organise the evangelical movement, left the Romanists free to repress it within their territories, and the continuation of the persecution of the Lutherans, the beginnings of which we have already noted in Austria,[58] Bavaria, and the Netherlands, and which inspired one of the most rousing of Luther's songs,[59] seemed to emphasise the necessity of the Landgrave's precautionary diplomacy. A meeting of the leaders of the anti-Lutheran party—Duke George of Saxony, the Elector Joachim of Brandenburg, and the Archduke Ferdinand—at Breslau in May 1527, aroused the suspicion of an aggressive Romanist combination, and this suspicion, though in reality unfounded, seemed to find confirmation in the revelations of Otto von Pack, an official of Duke George's chancery. This adventurer produced a document purporting to be a copy of an agreement between the leaders of the anti-Lutheran party for a concerted attack on the Elector of Saxony and the Landgrave, and the confiscation of their territories.[60] The document was a forgery, but the impulsive Landgrave, who paid the forger 4,000 gulden, without taking the precaution to test its genuineness by making representations to the parties concerned on the subject, set about concerting a counter-

[58] See Ferdinand's mandate against the Lutherans in Walch, xvi. 433.

[59] Ein neues Lied wir heben an.

[60] See the document in Walch, xvi. 445-452.

attack with the Saxon Elector. The Elector went the length of collecting a force, but refrained from actually beginning hostilities in deference to the opposition of Luther who, as usual, deprecated the use of force and urged the desirability of at least waiting until they were attacked.[61] The Landgrave was, however, less pliable, and whilst sending the compromising document to his father-in-law, Duke George, threatened, on the strength of his intrigues with Zapolya and Francis I., to invade [62] the bishoprics of Maintz, Bamberg, and Würzburg (May 1528). He discovered too late that he had been the dupe of a crafty scoundrel, whose concoction Duke George and the other members of the would-be conspiracy indignantly rebutted,[63] and aggravated his blunder by making the bishops pay the costs of the preparation for his impulsive policy.

His rashness, which only intensified the persecution of the Lutherans in Romanist territories, was all the more impolitic in view of the international situation. Charles had once more had the best of it in the renewed war with his rival, Francis. The Pope had paid dearly for his hostility in engineering the League of Cognac in the capture and sack of Rome in May 1527, by a German-Spanish force under Bourbon, and his flight to Orvieto. Charles's brother, Ferdinand, had succeeded in getting himself elected King of both Bohemia and Hungary in 1526, and in thus founding the Austro-Hungarian state in spite of the opposition of Zapolya and the ill will of the Duke of Bavaria. In these circumstances the fugitive Pope was fain to enter into a negotiation with the Emperor, which was concluded at Barcelona in June 1529 and included the co-operation of both in a crusade against the Turks and the heretics. Francis was disposed to follow suit, and ultimately came to terms with his rival in the Treaty of Cambrai (August 1529).[64] The international situation had, therefore, once more taken an

---

[61] " Werke," 53, 447 f. and 54, 1 (Erlangen ed.) ; cf. Enders, vi. 258 f.

[62] He did not actually invade Würzburg, however, as Ranke asserts (iii. 34).

[63] See their disclaimers in Walch, xvi. 457 f.

[64] For these negotiations see Pastor, " History of the Popes," x. 32 f.

adverse turn for the evangelical party in Germany, which was both divided and discredited by the Landgrave's rash enterprise and lost the support of Duke Henry of Mecklenburg and the good will of the Elector Palatine.

Charles was thus free to attempt, without any effective opposition, to reverse the Recess of Spires at a second Diet which convened in the same city in March 1529. To this end he directed his commissioners to promise the speedy convention of a General Council, which he has reason to believe that the Pope will agree to summon, to require, in virtue of his imperial authority, the various Estates of the empire to maintain meanwhile the traditional faith and usages under pain of the imperial ban, and to declare the Recess of the former Diet null and void.[65] The autocratic tone of this communication, which was an unwarrantable infringement of the rights of the Estates, was ill-fitted to rouse the enthusiasm of the assembly. But the Romanist party was present in full force on this occasion, and in its zeal for the faith, which was intensified by recent events, was not disposed to resent this unconstitutional imperial dictation. The evangelical party, on the other hand, was weakened by the doctrinal differences which had begun to estrange the adherents of Luther from those of Zwingli, who by this time could count on a considerable following in the south German cities. Its representatives on the Grand Committee, to which the discussion of the question was, in the first instance, referred, were in a hopeless minority, and were powerless to prevent a reactionary decision which, though it did not go the length of ostracising the evangelical faith outright, allowed it to exist only on sufferance. Whilst in Roman Catholic States the Edict of Worms was to remain in force as heretofore, no further innovations were to be made on the Lutheran States, pending the meeting of the promised Council or, failing this, a German national assembly. In these States Roman Catholics were not to be prevented or forbidden to attend Mass in the traditional form, which shall not henceforth be abolished,

---

[65] Kaiserliche Proposition presented to the Diet by the Archduke Ferdinand and his fellow-commissioners, 15th March 1529, Walch, xvi. 318-322.

evidently even in cases where the local congregation might adopt the evangelical faith and desire to observe the evangelical rite. Zwinglians, who deny the real presence, and Anabaptists as fomentors of sedition, shall not be tolerated throughout the whole empire, and the Anabaptists shall be summarily punished in accordance with an imperial mandate to this effect. The decrees of the Diets of Nürnberg relative to preaching and the press shall be rigorously observed. Nor shall any Estate presume to infringe the rights of another under penalty of the imperial ban—a proviso which might enable the episcopal jurisdiction to be restored in the Lutheran principalities and cities in which it had been practically abolished.[66]

Without actually declaring the illegality of the evangelical faith, as the Emperor demanded, the decision of the Committee assured the exclusive supremacy of the old religion in the Romanist States and paved the way for a Romanist reaction within the Lutheran principalities and cities, whilst absolutely prohibiting the profession of any other form of the evangelical faith. The differentiation between Lutherans and Zwinglians was a skilful device for playing off the one against the other and thus paralysing the evangelical opposition. In his alarm for the future, the nervous Melanchthon,[67] who accompanied the Elector John, was ready to play the game of the Romanists and advised him to sacrifice the Zwinglians. This pusillanimous tactic was happily frustrated by the Landgrave Philip, who was less hampered by dogmatic bias than the theologians, and realised the importance of presenting a united front to the enemy. At his instigation the evangelical princes, at the sitting on the 12th April, united in appealing, on their own behalf and that of their subjects and all adherents of the Gospel, against the decision of the Committee, on conscientious grounds, and also on the strength of the Recess of 1526. In this Appellation, and the reasons adduced in support of it, they aver that they are actuated solely by consideration of the honour of God and His Word and the salvation of their souls and by

[66] Walch, xvi. 323-328.
[67] For his anxiety see letters in " Corp. Ref.," i. 1039 f. ; Ellinger, " Melanchthon," 238 f.

fidelity to conscience. Whilst they are ready to render due obedience to the Emperor and to further the welfare and peace of the empire, they cannot act against their conscience in a matter involving the honour of God and their salvation. Nor can they be a party to the execution of the Edict of Worms even in the territories of the Romanist princes, since such acquiescence would be equivalent to the approval of the Edict on their part and the condemnation of what they hold to be the truth. Nor, further, can they agree to the restriction of their liberty relative to the Mass, which they hold to be contrary to the plain teaching of the Word of God and which, as contrary to the institution of Christ, they cannot conscientiously suffer to exist within their territories. Such demands are unjust and are incompatible with the Recess of 1526, which they have undertaken to observe and the majority of the present Diet has no right to override, pending the meeting of a General Council, to which both parties have agreed to relegate the religious question. On these grounds they cannot accept the proposed Recess, though they are ready to come to an arrangement relative to the Anabaptists and the control of preaching and the press.[68]

These arguments failed to shake the Romanist majority of the Diet, which voted in favour of the decision of the Committee (12th April), and on the 19th the Imperial Commissioners formally accepted it in the Emperor's name and requested the opposition to acquiesce.[69] Whilst the evangelical princes retired to consider their answer, they abruptly left the sitting. Whereupon the princes handed in a Protestation, in which they declare their determination to adhere to the Recess of the former Diet ; protest against its unwarrantable supersession by the present Diet, without their consent ; deny the right of the majority to impose its decision in this matter on the minority, and refuse on conscientious and constitutional grounds to recognise its validity or regard it as binding on them. Otherwise they

[68] Walch, xvi. 364 f. ; Ney, " Die Appellation und Protestation der Evangelischen Stände auf dem Reichstag zu Speier " (1529), 27 f. ("Quellenschriften zur Geschichte des Protestantismus," 1906).

[69] Walch, xvi. 380 f. ; Ney, 46 f.

are prepared to accept the clauses of the new Recess relative
to the Anabaptists, the censorship of the press, and respect
for the rights of the various Estates. They request that the
Protestation be included in the Acts of the Diet, and declare
their intention to forward it to the Emperor and publish
it along with a detailed statement of the reasons of their
refusal to recognise the decision of the majority.[70] In
the vain hope of securing the reconsideration of this decision
they sent the Protestation on the following day to King
Ferdinand, who forthwith returned it. Equally vain the
negotiation with the representatives of the more moderate
members of the majority, the Margrave Philip of Baden
and Duke Henry of Brunswick, to bring about an accommodation, which the evangelical princes were prepared to
accept. King Ferdinand and the majority rejected the
proposed modification of the terms of the Recess, and at
the sitting of the 22nd April, from which these princes
absented themselves, it was finally signed and sealed and the
request for the inclusion of the Protestation in the acts of
the Diet refused.[71]

The Protestation bore the signatures of the Elector of
Saxony, the Margrave George of Brandenburg, the two
Dukes of Lüneburg, the Landgrave Philip, and Prince
Wolfgang of Anhalt. On the 25th of April it received the
formal adhesion of fourteen cities, including Strassburg,
Nürnberg, Ulm, and Constance, and three of them—
Strassburg, Nürnberg, and Ulm—joined the Elector and
the Landgrave in a secret pledge to support one another in
its defence. Whilst Luther approved of the Protestation
and joined with Melanchthon in adducing reasons in support
of the Elector's attitude,[72] he strongly disapproved of any
alliance in its defence. He was content to entrust the
maintenance of his cause to Providence, who would know
how to defend the right. His conscience would not permit
him to defend the Gospel by force. Nor did he believe that
the Romanists had either the force or the heart to face a
civil war. Moreover, such a league would only beget a

[70] Walch, xvi. 383 f.; Ney, 50-53.
[71] Walch, xvi. 387 f.; Ney, 53 f.
[72] Walch, xvi. 360-364.

counter-league and might easily lead to a conflict which they would otherwise rather avoid. He was, too, afraid, after the experience of the previous year, that the impulsive Landgrave would make use of such a combination for attack instead of defence. In any case, an alliance with the south German Zwinglians, who differed from him on the Sacramentarian question, and whom he intolerantly regarded as " enemies of God and His Word," was for him absolutely indefensible.[78]

From the constitutional point of view, the contention of these " Protestants," as they came to be termed, that the majority of the present Diet could not reverse the decision of the previous one, or require their adherence to a deliverance of this kind to which they had not consented, was of dubious validity.[74] The Recess of 1526 was after all but a temporary agreement, and though it was to hold till the convention of a Council, it left the Emperor, who had not consented to it, free to convene another Diet to deliberate anew on the question. It evidently did not contemplate the final disruption of the Church by the establishment of independent evangelical churches in Lutheran territories and cities. Moreover, it was within the province of a regularly constituted Diet to legislate further, or not, on the question, if the Emperor should submit proposals for its consideration, and revise or reverse the law according as the majority should decide.

The real strength of the Protestation lay, not in the right of the minority legally to defy the will of the majority, but in the appeal to the higher law of conscience, to the duty of obeying God rather than man in the matter of the soul's salvation. " We fear God's wrath more than we fear the Emperor's ban." It was in opposing this conviction to the will of the majority that the real significance and the real justification of the action of the minority lay. It was the repetition on a larger scale of the protest of Luther at Worms on behalf of the individual conscience, of which it was the fruit, and though it was still but the protest of a comparatively small minority, the principle for which this

---

[78] " Werke," 54, 72-74. Letter to the Elector John, 22nd May 1529.
[74] Ranke adopts the view of its validity, " Deutsche Geschichte," iii. 107-109. Also Hausrath, " Luther," ii. 233 f., and others.

minority stood had made a very material stride towards its ultimate vindication.

Unfortunately its champions had not advanced to a true apprehension of the principle they professed. They rightly objected, on conscientious grounds, to be deprived of the right henceforth to abolish the Mass in their territories in favour of the evangelical faith should the local congregation so desire. They forcibly pointed out the injustice and intolerance of prohibiting the evangelical faith in Romanist territories, whilst obliging them to maintain the Mass in their territories, and disallowing their right to debar anyone from participating in its celebration. Roman Catholic historians like Janssen in charging them with intolerance conveniently ignore the intolerance on the other side. But apart from this aspect of the question, their assumption of the right to override the conscience of their Romanist subjects in the matter of the Mass was entirely inconsistent with their insistence on the imperative claims of conscience in their own case. Moreover, while protesting on behalf of liberty of conscience for themselves, they declared their readiness to acquiesce in the repression of Anabaptists, though happily their names do not appear in the list of those who signed the savage mandate which consigned them to fire and sword, and which the Diet accepted,[75] and it found at least one dissident in the Landgrave Philip, who appears to have protested against it.

[75] Walch, xvi. 351 f.  On the Diet of 1529 see, besides the documents in Walch and Ney, Ranke, " Deutsche Geschichte," iii.; Janssen, " Geschichte des Deutschen Volkes," iii.; Ney, " Geschichte des Reichstags zu Speier, 1529 " (1880); Brieger, " Der Speierer Reichstag " (1909); and the older works of Müller, " Historie von der Evangelischen Ständte Protestation und Appellation "; and Jung, " Geschichte des Reichstags zu Speier."

# CHAPTER IX

# THE DISRUPTION OF THE EVANGELICAL PARTY

## I. THE SACRAMENTARIAN CONTROVERSY

THE cleavage in the evangelical party had its origin in the divergence of view on the question of the real presence in the Lord's Supper. In the "Babylonic Captivity" Luther had controverted the doctrine of transubstantiation and substituted for it that of consubstantiation, *i.e.*, the bodily presence of Christ in the bread and wine, not the miraculous transmutation of their substance into the body and blood. On his own testimony he had first been led to doubt the traditional doctrine on reading a passage in D'Ailly's commentary on the Sentences, and had finally rejected it for the more rational one of consubstantiation. More rational, that is, in so far as it enabled him to discard the artificial distinction between the substance and the accidents of the bread and wine by which the scholastic theologians had sought to render plausible the notion that while the substance of the bread and wine was miraculously changed into the body and blood of Christ, their accidents—form, colour, taste, etc.—remained intact.

But the theory of consubstantiation, if simpler and comparatively more rational, was still mysterious and irrational enough, and Luther would fain have found a still simpler explanation of the words, "This is my body" (*Hoc est corpus meum*). Only the difficulty of wholly emancipating himself from the scholastic teaching on the subject and his ingrained reverence for the letter of Scripture kept him from advancing a step farther and accepting the words of institution in a spiritual, symbolic sense. This step was taken by the Netherland jurist Hoen, or Honius, who, under the influence of Wessel Gansfort's treatise on the Eucharist, interpreted the words in this sense. In the summer of 1522 (the probable date) he argued, in a letter to Luther, in behalf of this interpretation, and along with the letter sent him the works of Wessel.[1] Christ, he explained in words that show that he had read Luther's sermon on the Sacrament (1520), had ofttimes promised His disciples the forgiveness of sins, and in the Last Supper He gave them a pledge (*pignus*) in confirmation of this promise and for the strengthening of their faith. The words, "This is my body," are, however, not to be taken literally, but figuratively. The "is" here means "signifies," "represents," as in other figurative sayings of Christ, and must be read in the light of the Eucharistic discourse in John vi. and other figurative passages. Christ is present only in a figurative sense to believers for whom He has given His body and blood, and who distinguish between the bread received into the mouth and Christ Himself, whom they have received in their hearts by faith. The passage does not, therefore, warrant the doctrine of transubstantiation, which is a figment of the scholastic theologians.[2]

Luther was by no means prepared to accept this interpretation. He had already expressed doubts about the view of the Bohemian Brethren,[3] who emphasised the spiritual rather than the bodily presence of Christ, though he was disposed to leave the question of the adoration of the host, to which they objected in particular, an open one.[4] These communications from Hoen and the Brethren

---

[1] He entrusted the letter and Wessel's works to his friends Rode and Saganus who were proceeding to Wittenberg, Enders, iii. 423. There is not sufficient ground for questioning (with Göbel, "Studien und Kritiken," 332, 1842) Hoen's authorship of the letter and regarding it as the composition of Wessel himself. See Enders, iii. 424. The probable date is, as Dieckhoff has shown, 1522 ("Die Evangelische Abendmahlslehre im Reformationszeitalter," i. 278 f.); Enders, iii. 424-425. Clemen thinks it was written in the spring of 1521, "Z.K.G.," xviii. 353 f.

[2] Enders, iii. 412-421.

[3] *Ibid.*, iii. 364.

[4] *Ibid.*, iii. 363-364, 397-399. Letters to Speratus, 16th May and 13th June 1522, on the Bohemian view, on which his correspondent had written to him, and which, as these letters inform us, was communicated

impressed him with the necessity of clearly defining what
he deemed the true doctrine.   Hence the treatise, " On the
Adoration of the Sacrament of the Sacred Body of Christ,"
which he addressed to the Brethren in the spring of 1523.[5]
In the first half of it he joins issue with Hoen in his most
dogmatic tone, though without actually naming him.[6]   The
words, " This is my body," are not to be figuratively but
literally understood.   That reason cannot comprehend how
the real body and blood can be in the bread and wine does
not invalidate the plain testimony of these words.   That we
cannot understand the fact of the real presence is no reason
why we should not believe it on the strength of this testimony.
Without an express declaration of Scripture to the contrary,
we are bound to accept the passage as it stands, and have
no alternative but to believe in the bodily presence.   To
substitute without this warrant " signifies " for " is " is to
deal arbitrarily with the text, and this principle of exegesis
would endanger the whole truth of Scripture.   He further
controverts the argument for a spiritual interpretation
based on the words of Paul in the 10th and 11th chapters of
1 Corinthians, to which Hoen appealed, and concludes a
laboured argumentation by insisting on the literal sense as
the only admissible one against both the Spiritualists and
the Romanists.

Carlstadt, on the other hand, was disposed to adopt a
more receptive attitude on this, as on other questions on
which he differed from Luther.   It is not quite clear whether
he had read Hoen's letter,[7] though this seems to me probable.
At all events, from 1523 onwards he appears as the convinced
champion of the spiritual as against the bodily presence,
and as the result of the interview with Luther at Jena,
he attacked the Lutheran position in the series of tracts which

by a deputation of the Brethren.  In these communications he assumes
that the Brethren believe in the real presence, though he is not satisfied
with their mode of expression on the subject, especially their tendency
to interpret it in the light of John vi.

[5] " Von Anbeten des Sacraments des heiligen Leichnams Christi,"
" Werke," xi. 431 f.

[6] " Werke," xi. 434 f.

[7] See Barge, " Karlstadt," ii. 150-151.

he published at Basle after his banishment from Saxony in the autumn of 1524. Christ's sacrifice, he contended, was made on the Cross on which He gave His body and blood for our redemption, not in the Supper, and the breaking of the bread, the drinking of the wine, are a symbolic and commemorative celebration of this sacrifice. In proof thereof he explained that Christ in the words, " This is my body which is given for you," did not refer to the bread, but pointed to his actual body. This exegesis is certainly a strained one in view of the preceding words, " Take, eat," etc. But while explaining the words differently from Hoen, he agrees with his contention that there can be no bodily presence of Christ in the bread and wine. Christ can only be spiritually present, since the body in which He ascended is in heaven and will not reappear on earth till He come again. Luther's doctrine of the real presence is merely the Romanist doctrine in a modified form, and is both un-scriptural and unevangelical. He draws the same conclusion from the relative passages in 1 Corinthians, John vi., etc.[8]

Carlstadt's doctrine was keenly discussed by the Strassburg theologians—Capito, Bucer, Hedio, and their colleagues—who, on the 23rd November 1524, wrote to Luther on the subject. Whilst condemning Carlstadt's personal attitude towards him, they clearly indicated that they practically shared his view of the spiritual presence, and begged him to explain his position with a view to the cessation of this distressful strife, which was causing such jubilation among the Romanists.[9] In reply he sent a letter warning them against this radical teaching.[10] At the same time, he confesses that he would fain have adopted the spiritual view and that it had cost him a hard struggle to reject it. " I confess that if Dr Carlstadt or any other could have convinced me five years ago that there is nothing in the Sacrament but bread and wine, he would have done me a great service. I have been sorely tempted on this point and have struggled hard to bring myself to look at the matter in this light, because I saw that I could thereby

[8] Barge, ii. 151 f.  [10] " Werke," xv. 391 f., 17th Dec.
[9] Enders, v. 59 f.

deal the Papacy the hardest blow.  I read the views of two
writers who treated the subject more skilfully than Carlstadt
(*i.e.*, Hoen and Francis Kolb, pastor at Wertheim), and did
not wrest the Word in accordance with their own imagination.
But I am taken captive and cannot believe otherwise.   The
text is too mighty for me and will not be wrested from its
sense in this fashion.  Yea, if to-day anyone would show
me on sufficient ground that there are only bread and wine,
it would not be necessary to attack me with so much
animus as Carlstadt has done, since I am only too disposed
to believe it as far as the old Adam is concerned.  But
Carlstadt's vapourings have only led me to hold more strongly
the opposite view." [11]

He promised to deal more exhaustively with the question
in a future work, and this promise he straightway fulfilled
in his counterblast, "Against the Heavenly Prophets,"
which is alike a vindication of his relations with Carlstadt
during the previous two years and a counter-attack on his
radical teaching.[12]  The Strassburg theologians had begged
him to eschew his opponent's acrid style and discuss the
subject without animus.  Unfortunately by this time the
very name of Carlstadt, who ascribed to him his expatriation
from Saxony and had latterly denounced him as a new
papist, a false teacher, and a follower of Antichrist, had
become as the red rag to the bull.  He belabours him with
abuse as well as argument in his most objurgatory style.
Carlstadt is the very devil who strives, through him, to
subvert the divine ordinance and the truth of Scripture.
He hotly resents and refutes the charge that, while he has
rejected the Mass as an offering, he has retained the word in
his modified liturgy and also the elevation of the host, and
has thus perpetuated the old superstition.  In striving to
maintain this contention, Carlstadt shows himself an
ignoramus in both Greek and Hebrew.  He makes sport
of his exegesis of the words, " This is my body," and insists
anew that they must be taken as they stand without evasion

[11] "Werke," xv. 394.

[12] *Ibid.*, xviii. 62 f.  It appeared in two parts, at the beginning and
end of Jan. 1525 respectively.

or exegetical sophistry of this kind. " It is a hard and clear saying which compels assent by its own plain testimony." [13] It is confirmed, not invalidated, by Paul in the 1st Epistle to the Corinthians. How, he asks, for instance, can they who eat and drink unwittingly be guilty of the body and blood of the Lord, if these are not in the bread and wine? To appeal to reason against such an interpretation is to subvert faith and fall into the sophistry of the schoolmen. In thus rationally reading the text in the light of John vi. 63 and other passages, which seem to tell against the real presence, Carlstadt has surrendered himself to the wiles of Frau Hulda, that " devil's bride," [14] as he calls Reason, who is the personification of demonic lying and error. It is this hellish seducer that suggests a variety of sceptical questions in confutation of the real presence. Carlstadt asks, for instance, how the real presence consists with Christ's saying, " The flesh profiteth nothing "? Luther replies that the saying refers not to Christ's sacramental flesh, but to the fleshly disposition of the Jews, though he had previously referred it to Christ's own body. This certainly is suggestive of a tendency to make the text suit the argument. Again, how could Christ call the bread His body, if, on Luther's own reasoning against transubstantiation, the bread nevertheless remained bread? The schoolmen had attempted to solve the puzzle by miraculously transmuting the substance of the bread into the body, leaving only the accidents, and thus practically eliminating it altogether. Luther, in discarding transubstantiation and substituting for it consubstantiation, had previously attempted to render his doctrine intelligible by the illustration of red-hot iron which constitutes both fire and iron. Since his opponent persists in rejecting this illustration, he now resorts to the figure of speech known among the grammarians as *Synecdoehe*,[15] by which, whilst speaking of the whole of an object, we really have in mind only the part. Christ in using the word " This " means that His body forms part of the object in question, and it is this part (body) that He emphasises without thereby excluding the

[13] "Werke," xviii. 148.    [14] *Ibid.*, xviii. 205.    [15] *Ibid.*, xviii. 186 f.

other (bread). He uses the term "This" inclusively, not exclusively. Both body and bread are there and make up the whole, though the emphasis at the moment is on the part rather than on the whole. This exegesis as proof of the real presence seems, however, to the dubious reader as far-fetched as that of Carlstadt in proof of the spiritual presence, though it was destined to become a distinctive feature of the Lutheran argumentation on the subject. Again, Carlstadt, under the prompting of that seductive devil's bride, asks how the real presence in the Sacrament harmonises with Christ's saying that it is needful for Him to go away and that He would only come again at the last day? Christ's glorified body, retorts Luther, is not limited to any place. It is ubiquitous, everywhere present, and His presence in the Sacrament is an indispensable source of comfort to the believer. For this reason also he controverts Carlstadt's contention that Christ obtained for us the forgiveness of sins on the Cross, not in the Sacrament. Whilst this is true, it is in the Sacrament that He communicates it to the believer, who eats His body and drinks His blood, and thus imparts to him an inestimable consolation in the face of the recurring sense of sin and condemnation. Hence the cardinal significance, the absolute necessity of the literal, as against the symbolic interpretation of the words of Christ, which Carlstadt by his imaginary spiritualism, his emphasis on the inner Word at the expense of the outward Word, would rob of its supreme validity and substitute for it his own arbitrary subjectivism.

Once more in this lengthy effusion, written with red-hot conviction, Luther gives proof of his wonderful dialectic resource. In his onslaught on the mediæval sacramental system, he had strongly opposed the notion of inherent grace in the Sacraments, and emphasised faith as the essential which renders them efficacious as means of grace. Now the accent is on the Sacrament itself as embodying grace in virtue of the real presence, though faith is indispensable to a participation in this sacramental grace. In controversy with Carlstadt he seems to have reverted to the idea of inherent sacramental grace, whilst repudiating its mere mechanical operation    To us this seems a lapse towards

mediæval materialism.  To Luther it was a vital element of
the religious life, inasmuch as it is in the Sacrament that
the Word of Christ becomes effective in saving and
sanctifying the soul.  Hence the fierceness, the implacable
intolerance with which he pursues his opponent throughout,
as if his salvation depended on the interpretation of a single
text.  As in the case of the controversy with Erasmus it is
a question of only one alternative.  As to believe, with
Erasmus, in free will, so to believe, with Carlstadt, in a
merely spiritual presence is to play the devil's game and be
damned accordingly.

As in the one case, so in the other, Luther's one-sided
vehemence tended to defeat itself.  The Strassburg theologians had asked him to give them a dispassionate discussion
of the subject.  Instead of this, he had allowed his one-sided
dogmatic predilections to betray him into a wild, if brilliant
philippic against Carlstadt, which was in some respects
unfair to his opponent as well as outrageously vituperative.
The luckless Carlstadt had, indeed, given him no little
provocation in the matter of abuse and misrepresentation.
But apart from this particular controversy, the question
at issue was exciting widespread interest and concern,
and to overwhelm Carlstadt by his brilliant dialectic and
fierce invective was by no means to say the last word on
the subject.  Carlstadt's exegesis might be absurd.  But
Luther's was not necessarily irrefragable or fitted to carry
conviction to others, who might find it difficult to share
that of either.  Moreover, Luther's contempt for reason,
in spite of his own wonderful dialectic, his way of turning on the devil's bride when confronted with awkward
questions was certainly not likely to commend itself to those
who, like Zwingli, had been trained in the school of Erasmus.

Zwingli, as well as the Strassburg theologians and
Oecolampadius of Basle, was, in fact, very unfavourably
impressed by the violent and one-sided tone of the discussion.
On the question of the spiritual versus the bodily presence
they agreed with Carlstadt, if not with his exegesis, and thus,
instead of disposing of the question, Luther had merely
widened the controversy over it.

In Zwingli it brought into the field a more formidable

opponent than Carlstadt.  His early teaching on the subject
was influenced by that of Erasmus,[16] whose disciple he was
before he became the active evangelical reformer of Zürich.
Erasmus, whilst not directly attacking the doctrine of
transubstantiation, went beyond the schoolmen to Augustine
and Paul, and in his Paraphrases on the New Testament and
the "Enchiridion" emphasised the symbolic, commemorative
aspect of the Sacrament, the mystical union and communion
of the soul therein with Christ, who, to faith, is really present
in the elements, the fellowship of believers with one another,
and the ethical significance and value of the rite.  This is
the teaching that is reflected in the writings of Zwingli up
to 1524, in addition to the open rejection of transubstantiation.  So far, he had reached the conclusion that the Lord's
Supper is a commemoration, not a repetition, of the sacrifice
which Christ offered once for all on the Cross and by which
He obtained for the believer the remission of sin.  In it
Christ is really present, and the believer in a certain sense
(not exactly defined) eats His body and drinks His blood.
" There is no dispute," he says in the Exposition of his
sixty-seven *Schlussreden*, or Articles (July 1523), " whether
the body and blood are eaten and drunk (for no Christian
doubts this), but whether it is a sacrifice, or only the commemoration of the sacrifice on the Cross."  Christ is really
present in the bread and wine to faith, which is thus the
essential thing and which brings the believer into a mystical
union and communion with Him.  The bread and wine
are, therefore, for him not yet purely symbols of Christ's
body and blood, but are evidently apprehended in the
Lutheran sense of the real presence.  He is, in fact, on his
own confession, at this period in agreement with Luther.  It
is thus hardly accurate, as far as the early period is concerned, to say, with Seeberg, that for Zwingli " the Sacrament
is merely, on the one hand, a commemoration of the redemption wrought for us by Christ, and, on the other, a confession
of adherence to Him in the face of the congregation and
thereby an obligation to live a Christian life." [17]  It evidently

[16] Staehelin, " Zwingli," ii. 220-223 (1897);  Köhler, " Zwingli
und Luther," i. 51 (1924).
[17] " Dogmengeschichte," iv. 378;  *cf.* 377 (1917).

involved a more mystical experience than these words suggest.[18]

In the supervening period of controversy with Luther and his adherents (1525-29) it is, however, the symbolic, commemorative aspect of the Sacrament that is in the foreground. In his early period Zwingli had already arrived at a spiritual interpretation of the words of institution. But he had not attained to an exegesis of the text which would establish this conviction. This exegesis he found in the letter of Hoen, which was brought to him by Rode and Saganus in the summer of 1523.[19] The letter made a profound impression on him, and, unlike Luther, he at once adopted the equation of " is " with " signifies " as the correct exegesis. He was not the man to surrender his reason, in deference to a dogmatic conviction, to what seemed to him an irrational interpretation when a more rational one was open to him. He was not disposed to divorce reason from faith in deference to Luther's disparagement of rational criticism. In this respect he remained a humanist after he became an aggressive evangelical reformer.

Apart, however, from the difference in their attitude towards reason and rational Scriptural interpretation, the difference between their respective theological standpoints could hardly fail to bring the two reformers into collision on this question. Zwingli maintained that salvation is

[18] The standard work on Zwingli's early conception of the Sacrament is that of Walter Köhler, " Zwingli und Luther," i., 1924. He shows by an elaborate investigation that in his earlier teaching Zwingli, following Erasmus, held the doctrine of the real presence, and that only after becoming acquainted with the view of Hoen did he expressly enunciate the symbolic interpretation of the words of institution. In his review of the book in the " Theolog. Blätter " (1926), Karl Bauer contended that Zwingli held from the outset the symbolic interpretation. Köhler's reply in the " Z.K.G." (1927), 397 f., seems to me to have disproved his contention. See, however, Bauer's reply, " Z.K.G." (1928), 97 f. A recent discussion in English is Barclay's Ph.D. Thesis of Edin. Univ. (1926), published under the title of " The Protestant Doctrine of The Lord's Supper " (1927).

[19] The letter could not have reached him as early as 1521, as Bauer (" Zwingli's Theologie," ii. 279) contends. See Staehelin, " Zwingli," ii. 228-229; Clemen, " Z.K.G.," xviii. 346 f. ; Barclay, 54 (51-52).

attainable by faith in the atoning death of Christ on the Cross, and is not conditioned by any belief such as that of the bodily presence in the Sacrament. Faith needs no material prop of this kind to attain the assurance of the forgiveness of sins and eternal life accruing from Christ's sacrifice. Salvation comes through faith in this sacrifice, not through the Sacrament, though in the later phase [20] of his teaching he again laid more stress on its mystical aspect. Luther, on the other hand, could not quite shake himself free from the mediæval notion of the inherent efficacy of the Sacrament, the necessary channel for the operation of God's grace in the soul, though faith is necessary to the reception of the grace which it conveys. Thus, while to Zwingli it is a commemoration, a consecration, and a communion with Christ, who is spiritually present to the believer, to Luther it is the objective embodiment of the sacrifice of Christ, who is bodily present and with whom the believer comes into actual contact—actually eats His flesh and drinks His blood and experiences the grace of forgiveness which it conveys. "The antagonism of the two views," says Staehelin, "appears in the fact that Zwingli places the meaning of the Sacrament in the historic atoning death of Christ, Luther in the communication of the bodily present Christ to the believer. According to Zwingli, Christ instituted in the Lord's Supper the memorial of His suffering and death ; according to Luther, a communion in which He continually offers Himself to man as the Word became flesh for his salvation, in order not only to strengthen his faith through this objective presentation of His redeeming work, but also in this miraculous fashion to communicate Himself to him bodily in His whole human-divine being." [21] Moreover, whilst he regarded the notion of the real presence in the bread and wine as a materialising one and derogatory to the transcendental, spiritual nature of God, to Luther it was a comforting and convincing assurance of the divine mercy and goodness towards helpless, fallen humanity. However much stress he might lay on faith as the means of

---

[20] In the "Brief Exposition of the Faith," dedicated to Francis I., 1531.
[21] "Zwingli," ii. 237.

salvation, he could not give up the notion of a substantial and sensuous experience of it, though he had cast away belief in the miracle of transubstantiation by priestly incantation.

The excitement aroused by the Carlstadt-Luther polemic impelled Zwingli to declare himself. He wrote a letter to Matthew Alber, one of Luther's adherents in the controversy with Carlstadt,[22] in which, whilst finding fault with Carlstadt's exegesis and adopting that of Hoen, he expressed his approval of his spiritual conception of the ordinance and, on the ground of the figurative meaning of the words of institution and the saying of Christ in John vi. 63, condemned the doctrine of consubstantiation. He expounded his own view more at large in a treatise on " True and False Religion " (1525). His patronage of Carlstadt as much as his attack on the real presence called Luther into the arena, who, unfortunately, had no first-hand knowledge of his writings,[23] and in his wrath identified his teaching with the extreme tendency of the prophets and declared both alike possessed of the devil. His embitterment was increased by the fact that many of the south German as well as the Swiss theologians, and of the south German cities preferred Zwingli's teaching to his and became its strenuous propagandists. The result was a fierce pamphlet warfare in which, besides the two principals, Oecolampadius [24] of Basle, and with some modification the Strassburg divines, Bucer and Capito, took an active share on the side of Zwingli ; Melanchthon, Osiander, Brenz, and Bugenhagen on that of Luther.

The two main questions on which the controversy turned were the ubiquity or omnipresence of Christ's body,[25]

[22] "Opera," iii. 569-603, Nov. 1524.

[23] On this point see Köhler, " Zum Abendmahlsstreit zwischen Luther und Zwingli," " Lutherstudien zur 400 Feier der Reformation," 115 f. (1917).

[24] On the part taken by Oecolampadius in the controversy up to the end of 1526, see " Briefe und Akten zum Leben Oecolampads," ed. by E. Staehelin, i. (1927). His chief contribution to the subject up to this time is his " De genuina verborum Domini Expositione " (1525).

[25] Luther had already touched on this question in his philippic against Carlstadt, " Werke," xviii. 206, 211.

and the relation of the two natures—the divine and human—in Him, which was involved in the former question. Zwingli, in a series of controversial tracts against Luther,[26] denied that Christ's body, which is in heaven, can also be in the bread, and maintained that what is said about His flesh and blood has reference to His divine, not to His human nature. He sought to make out his point by adducing the figure of speech known as *Alloiosis* (rhetorical exchange, *Gegenwechsel*),[27] by which in speaking of the one nature in Christ we use the terms that properly belong to the other. Luther, on the other hand, maintained the omnipresence of Christ's body and denied the contention that what is said of the flesh and blood is to be referred only to the divine nature. Whilst Zwingli emphasised the distinction of the natures, which excluded the notion of Christ's bodily ubiquity, Luther emphasised their union, which made the bodily ubiquity possible, and strove to give plausibility to his contention in terms borrowed from the scholastic theology (Occam and Biel) in which, unlike Zwingli, he was an expert. Zwingli's contention that what is said of the flesh and blood really applies to the divine nature is an unwarrantable invention suggested by that devilish enchantress Frau Hulda (godless reason).

Luther's contributions[28] to this paper warfare were marked by his characteristic vehemence as well as by his resourcefulness in argument. For him Zwingli and Oecolampadius are not only possessed by the devil. He denies them the name of Christians and regards them as no better than Münzer and worse than the papists. Although

---

[26] The series comprises " Underrichtung vom Abendmahl " (1526); " Fründlich Verglimpfung " (1527); " Dass dise Worte Christi," etc. (1527); " Ueber Luther's Buch Bekenntnis " (1527); " Opera," ii. and iii. For a detailed examination of them see Staehelin, ii. 289 f.

[27] Or Commutatio idiomatum, " Opera," iii. 525; iv. 379.

[28] The two "Vorreden zum Schwäbischen Syngramm " (1526), "Werke," xix. 447 f. The " Syngramma Suevicum " is a statement of their belief issued by Brenz and a number of Swabian preachers, of which Luther approved. " Sermon von dem Sacrament des Leibes und Blutes Christi, wider die Schwarmgeister" (1526), "Werke," xix. 474 f. (1526); "Das diese Worte Christi noch fest stehen "(1527), "Werke," xxiii. 38 f.; " Vom Abendmahl Christi Bekenntnis " (1528), " Werke," xxvi. 241 f.

he had so stoutly denied the right of the Romanists to make
of transubstantiation an article of faith, he insists on their
accepting his own view of the real presence, which was
little less irrational, as an essential of the Gospel, and would
have no fellowship with such perverters of the Gospel.  " The
fanatics throttle Christ and God the Father in His words,
and my mother Christianity and my brethren in addition.
They would furthermore have me dead, and after that they
say I shall have peace and that they will live in charity
with me." [29]  " Cursed be such charity and such unity to
the very bottom of hell, since such unity not only miserably
disrupts Christianity, but makes sport and foolishness of it
in devilish manner." [30]  In view of such outbursts the
fanaticism of which he accused his opponents might more
forcibly be retorted against himself.  So fanatical and
furious was he, that he was ready to stake the whole reform
movement on the acceptance of the notion that the communicant actually eats the body and drinks the blood of Christ
under the semblance of a morsel of bread and a sip of wine.

Zwingli, on the other hand, whilst giving vent to his
indignation under the strain of such outrageous vituperation
and stoutly vindicating his own view as the Scriptural and
truly evangelical one, was ready to tolerate difference of
opinion on the subject in deference to the obligation of
Christian charity and for the sake of unity.  If he insisted
as dogmatically as Luther on his view of the question, he
felt still more keenly the detriment and discredit which
the controversy was bringing on the evangelical cause, and
the clamant necessity of agreeing to differ and uniting in the
defence of the essentials of their common faith.  The controversy was driving the wedge of sectarian dispute into the
ranks of the evangelical party at a time when it was suffering
from the shock of the social revolution and exposed to the
menace of an aggressive Romanist reaction.  It was on this
ground that, in spite of Luther's vituperative and irreconcilable attitude, he eagerly welcomed the proposal of the
Landgrave Philip to hold a conference on the subject at
Marburg in the beginning of October 1529.

[29] " Werke," xxiii. 82.        [30] *Ibid.*, xxiii. 80.

## II. The Marburg Conference

In proposing this expedient the Landgrave was actuated by concern for the defence of the Reformation, in its bearing on the political situation, rather than by a keen interest in the theological question at issue.[31] He saw the expediency of widening the defensive union, which the hostile decision of the second Diet of Spires had forced the Protestant princes and cities to form, so as to include Zürich, Berne, and the other Swiss Protestant cities as well as those of south Germany. On the other hand, the active antagonism of the Roman Catholic cantons to the evangelical cause, backed as it was by the Hapsburg power, emphasised for Zwingli the urgent desirability of an alliance on religious as well as political grounds between the south German cities and the Protestant cantons. In his apprehension of an aggressive Romanist reaction he even contemplated the disruption of the Swiss Confederation and the political as well as the religious union of the Protestant cantons with south Germany. Hence the alacrity with which he welcomed the proposed Marburg Conference as a means not only of putting an end to the threatened schism of the evangelical party, but of cementing a great Protestant combination against the aggressive designs, both in Switzerland and in Germany, of the Emperor and the Romanists. Luther, on the other hand, could only with difficulty bring himself to confer with an antagonist who, in his eyes, was a diabolic enemy of the faith and, whilst ultimately yielding to the Landgrave's insistence, backed by the Elector John, expressed his conviction that no good would come of the meeting.[32] He had, moreover, no liking for the policy of defending the evangelical cause by force, and had not this additional motive to whet his zeal for union, which appealed so powerfully to the more robust, practical Swiss reformer.

[31] On the negotiations and the motives underlying them, which preceded the Marburg Conference, see Von Schubert, " Beiträge zur Geschichte der evangelischen Bekenntnis und Bündnisbildung " (1529-30), " Z.K.G." (1908), 323 f.

[32] Enders, vii. 121-123, 29th June 1529.

The conference, which took place in the castle at Marburg and lasted from the 1st to the 3rd October,[33] brought together all the more notable divines on either side. With Luther came Melanchthon, Justus Jonas, Cruciger, Myconius, Brenz, Osiander, Agricola ; with Zwingli, Oecolampadius, Bucer, and Hedio. The brunt of the debate was, however, borne by Luther on the one hand, and Zwingli and Oecolampadius on the other, after Melanchthon had spent the first day conferring privately with Zwingli and Luther with Oecolampadius.[34] The Wittenberg theologians were surprised to learn that their opponents were not the fanatics and heretics they had taken them for. Zwingli emphatically averred his adherence to the Nicene and Athanasian Creeds, and admitted a spiritual manducation by faith, and thus reverted to the more mystical view of his earlier teaching. His declarations on these subjects tended to produce an atmosphere more favourable to friendly discussion.[35]

In public conference on the 2nd, Luther from the outset, however, declared that he would abide by his conviction of the bodily presence and the real manducation, though, like Paul, he was ready to give a reason for his faith. On the table before him he had chalked *Hoc est corpus meum*, which he insisted on taking in the literal sense. Oecolampadius reminded him of the use of figurative language in Scripture, and quoted John vi. 63, " It is the spirit that quickeneth, the flesh profiteth nothing," in proof of his contention that Christ could only have spoken figuratively of eating His body, and that He referred to spiritual not to carnal eating. Luther denied that this interpretation applied to the words of institution, and maintained that the Christian is not to ask for explanations of Christ's assertion, but implicitly to believe it. If God

[33] Jackson wrongly says that it began on the 30th Sept., " Huldreich Zwingli," 314 (1901).

[34] Enders, vii. 169.

[35] This private discussion ranged over the main doctrines of the Christian faith, besides that of the Lord's Supper, and thus served the useful purpose of showing Luther and Melanchthon that, apart from this doctrine, the parties were in general agreement on these doctrines. Von Schubert, " Z.K.G." (1908), 377 f.

ordered him to eat dung he would do it and ask no questions.[36]

Zwingli took exception to such an unreasonable notion of what is required of faith. He maintained that Scripture must be collated with Scripture in order to arrive at the meaning of such figurative expressions. So doing, the words of institution could only be rightly understood by substituting " signifies " for " is." John vi. 63 showed conclusively that this is the only possible interpretation. Luther had demanded that they should prove their contention, and Zwingli held that this was proof positive that in the Sacrament the believer could only eat Christ's body spiritually and not actually. " The words *Hoc est corpus meum*," retorted Luther, doggedly, " are not ours, but Christ's ; *da kan der teuffel nicht für*, the devil himself cannot make it otherwise. I ask you therefore to leave off your tampering with the Word and give glory to God." " And we," retorted Zwingli, " ask you to give glory to God and leave off your quibbling." [37] At this point the discussion became so hot that the Landgrave was fain to intervene, and the sitting had to be adjourned till the afternoon.

On resuming, Luther, in reply to Zwingli's objection to the real manducation, maintained that while we actually eat the body, it is not food in the ordinary sense and is not digested like other food. Nevertheless it transmits itself to us. The discussion then turned on the question of its ubiquity. Oecolampadius quoted the passages referring to Christ's going away, and adduced the finitude and limitation of His human body. " How," he asked, " can one and the same body be in different places at the same time ? " [38] " I care not for mathematics," returned Luther. " God is able to effect that the body is in heaven and at the same time in the Sacrament. I believe that it is in both and I stick to the words, *Hoc est corpus meum*. I care not that this belief is contrary to nature. It is not against faith." [39] " It *is* against faith," replied Oecolampadius, " for Christ was made like unto us. He is one with us in our humanity,

[36] " Werke," xxx., Pt. III., 116.    [38] *Ibid*., xxx., Pt. III., 128, 130.
[37] *Ibid*., xxx., Pt. III., 122.      [39] *Ibid*., xxx., Pt. III., 130-131.

whilst consubstantial with the Father in His divinity, and only as divine can He be omnipresent." "I care not for your distinction in this matter," was the reply. "Christ is substantially in the Sacrament just as He was born of the Virgin, and He does not cease to be both in heaven and in the bread." Zwingli adduced in support of his colleague's contention additional passages of Scripture, especially Hebrews iv. 15, "He hath in all points been tempted like as we are, yet without sin." Luther again retorted that, in the face of the words chalked before him, mathematics could not apply.

On resuming on the following morning, Sunday, 3rd October, Zwingli asked for proofs of the ubiquity. "My dear sirs," replied Luther, again pointing to the text, "since the words of my Lord Jesus stand there, I really cannot go beyond them, but must confess and believe that the body of Christ is there." "Surely," interposed Zwingli, "the word 'there' is an adverb of place." "The words," retorted Luther, "are 'this,' not 'there' is my body. God can make a body to be in more places than one when He pleases." The schoolmen had argued that this was even mathematically possible, as he tried to show by examples. Zwingli then quoted Augustine and Fulgentius in support of the view that a body must be in a definite space. Luther admitted that these Fathers were against him on this point, but contended that Christ is not present in a spatial sense, and that other Fathers agreed with him. Moreover, the Fathers are only to be believed in as far as they speak in accordance with Scripture. Besides, if, on the assumption of his opponents, Christ's divinity did not suffer as well as His humanity and He could not therefore be in the Sacrament both as God and man, such a Christ would be of no use to him. "If," returned Oecolampadius, "He is not present in a spatial sense, He cannot be bodily in the Sacrament, which must, therefore, be a symbol of His body." They, too, received the Scripture as the only authority, and they had only quoted Augustine to show that they taught nothing new.

By the Sunday evening the disputants had argued themselves to a complete deadlock, and agreed that further debate was hopeless. Thereupon the Chancellor of the Landgrave appealed to both sides to think better of it and make another attempt to reach an understanding. " The only way to reach an understanding," replied Luther, " is for you to give honour to the Word of God and believe as we do." [40] " As you refuse to bend to our interpretation of the text," was the retort, " so we refuse to accept yours." " Well, then," replied Luther, " we commend you to God and His judgment." In a more softened tone he thanked them for their courtesy in conducting the discussion, and asked Zwingli's forgiveness for having indulged in some acrid expressions in the course of it, seeing he was but flesh and blood. Zwingli similarly begged his forgiveness for some harsh expressions and with tears in his eyes professed his ardent desire for friendship and fellowship. There were no men in the world whose friendship he more eagerly desired. Oecolampadius urged him for God's sake to have respect to the afflicted Church, and Bucer vindicated the orthodoxy of the Strassburg theologians which he had aspersed. Luther replied with a repelling negative. " You have a different spirit from us. There can be no community of spirit between us and you who profess to accept the Word of Christ, and nevertheless condemn, controvert, and seek to undermine it with all kinds of sacrilegious arguments." [41] " Pray God," he added in conclusion, " that you may be converted." " Pray God yourself," returned Oecolampadius, " for you stand equally in need of being converted." [42]

Despite this impasse, the Landgrave, after the formal close of the debate on the afternoon of the 3rd October, made a final effort to secure unanimity. He besought both

[40] " Werke," xxx., Pt. III., 149.

[41] Ibid., xxx., Pt. III., 150.

[42] Ibid., xxx., Pt. III., 144. For the discussion see the various reports in " Werke," xxx., Pt. III., 92 f., by Hedio, an anonymous writer, Collinus, Osiander, Brenz, and another anonymous writer. For the reports of Justus Jonas and Melanchthon, " Corp. Ref.," i. 1095 f. See also Schirrmacher, " Briefe und Akten zu der Geschichte des Religions-gespräches zu Marburg," 3-29 (1876); Von Schubert, " Bekenntnis-bildung und Religionspolitik," 1529-30 (1910); W. Köhler, " Zwingli und Luther," i. The facsimile of the Marburg Articles as deposited in the Archives at Zürich is given by Usteri in " Theolog. Studien und Kritiken " (1883), 400 f.

parties to consider in private the possibility of finding a formula which both could subscribe. Luther and his colleagues expressed their willingness to do so, and Luther drew up a formula which, while asserting that " the body of Christ is truly," *i.e.*, essentially and substantially,[43] " present in the Sacrament and not merely in the remembrance of the partaker," waives further discussion on the question as to the mode of its presence, *i.e.*, " whether bodily or spiritually, naturally or supernaturally, spatially or non-spatially." On this understanding he and his colleagues were prepared to recognise their opponents as brethren.[44] This was un-doubtedly a considerable concession on Luther's part and, at first, Bucer was disposed to accept it as a feasible solution in the private discussions on the subject which took place on the following day, the 4th October. Zwingli and Oecolampadius, on the other hand, and under their influence ultimately Bucer, could not bring themselves to admit the real presence in the Lutheran sense, and held to their view that Christ is present only in a spiritual sense (*spiritualiter*).[45] Luther's formula thus failed to reconcile the contending parties. The bodily presence, as he under-stood it, could not be harmonised with the spiritual view of the presence as Zwingli conceived it. Moreover, the Swiss theologians objected to such terms as " essentially and substantially present " as unbiblical and likely to mystify and mislead the simple believer and lead to a crass notion of the presence.[46]

In view of Luther's passionate conviction of the bodily presence and his previous argumentation, his final concession represents a real stretch of principle for the sake of union. At the same time, the bodily is distinctively emphasised as against the spiritual presence, which to Zwingli is the

[43] Essentialiter et substantive.

[44] " Werke," xxx., Pt. III., 150. Osiander's Report. See also Von Schubert, " Beiträge," " Z.K.G." (1909), 67-68.

[45] Enders, vii. 354.

[46] For the details of this private negotiation see Von Schubert, " Beiträge," " Z.K.G." (1909), 60 f. He gives from the Correspondence of the brothers Blaurer, edited by Schiess, i. (1908), the actual formula as drawn up by Luther at Marburg, which Osiander only imperfectly paraphrases.

only feasible one.  On this cardinal issue the intellectual
and religious standpoints of the two chief disputants inevitably led to a collision.  Luther's disposition to divorce
faith and reason clashed with Zwingli's tendency to harmonise
them as much as possible.  For Luther the bodily presence
is an essential of saving faith—one of the relics of mediæval
belief which he carried into the Reformation.  For Zwingli
it is both an unscriptural and irrational encumbrance of
faith, on which salvation does not depend.  Such a materialist
view is not consonant with a reasonable and experimental
piety.  " We confess," he wrote a few weeks afterwards,
in words that reflect his distinctive position, " that the
body of Christ is present in the Holy Supper, not as body
nor in the nature of body, but sacramentally to the mind
which is upright, pure, and reverent towards God." [47]

The next best thing, in the interest of the Landgrave's
policy of a Protestant League, was to emphasise the points
on which they agreed, and to this end he persuaded Luther to
draw up a series of fifteen articles,[48] embracing the main
doctrines of the reformed creed.  For this purpose he used
a previous set which had been drawn up at Schwabach
as a basis of a prospective alliance of the Lutheran princes
and cities.  In that treating of the Sacrament both sides,
whilst expressing agreement on a number of specified points,
confessed their inability to see eye to eye on the question
of the bodily presence.  At the same time, they undertook
to exercise Christian charity as far as conscience would allow,
and to pray God for further enlightenment with a view to
an ultimate understanding.  To these articles Zwingli and his
associates as well as Luther and his adherents subscribed,
although in the matter of original sin and some other points
they did not exactly express the convictions of the Swiss
theologians.  They were willing to compromise to this
extent for the sake of union, in the hope that the conference
might thus result in a defensive league against the common
enemy, and obviate the scandal and weakness of disunion
within the reformed ranks.  This spirit of compromise

[47] " Opera," viii. 549;  Jackson,  " Zwingli," 334-335.
[48] " Werke," xxx., Pt. III., 160 f.

should not be ascribed, as is sometimes done, to mere opportunism, since Zwingli held that where there was substantial agreement on the evangelical faith, it was legitimate as well as advisable, for such urgent practical reasons, to agree to differ on the issue in dispute.

Both sides also agreed to refrain from controversial writing. In spite of Luther's relentless refusal to recognise the Swiss as brothers, whilst agreeing to observe peace and charity,[49] the conference thus had not been an absolute failure. If he refused to give the hand of fellowship to Zwingli and his colleagues as brethren, he had at least discovered that they were not the heretics and extremists he had denounced in his writings against them. In view of the mischievous fireworks of the previous three years, the agreement to cease controversy was a substantial gain. It tended to make further negotiation, if not with Zwingli himself, who fell at Kappel two years later, at all events with the south German theologians, and paved the way for the Wittenberg Concord of 1536. Although Luther and his colleagues saw in Zwingli's eagerness for fellowship a proof of his superior debating power, and on this ground claimed the victory,[50] he was more impressed by some of his arguments than he cared to own, and was genuinely desirous of an agreement. Melanchthon, too, if not attracted by Zwingli, who was as convinced of the truth of his own contentions as Luther was of his, and also claimed the victory, had been favourably impressed by some of those of Oecolampadius, with whom he maintained a correspondence. He ultimately, in fact, abandoned the literal interpretation of the words of institution and the oral eating, which he already in the following year ignored in the Augsburg Confession. At the same time, the failure of Luther and Melanchthon at Marburg to give the hand of fellowship to the Swiss, in spite of a difference of opinion on a question of exegesis, which after all admitted of two possible inter-

[49] Enders, vii. 169.

[50] See, besides the reports of the Lutheran writers, his letters to Agricola, 12th Oct. (Enders, vii. 169), and to Link, 28th Oct. (*ibid.*, vii. 179; *cf.* 353-354, letter to Jacob, provost of the church at Bremen, 1st June 1530).

pretations, and which Zwingli and his colleagues rightly held should not prevent them from recognising one another as brethren, perpetuated the spirit of division between the Swiss and the Lutheran Church. It also started within the Lutheran Church the tendency to a narrow and narrowing dogmatism on this question, and helped to obscure the initial grandeur of the Lutheran Reformation as an emancipation movement. Whilst engaged in the struggle for toleration for himself and his adherents, Luther had nobly championed the principle of freedom. With the growing strength of his cause he was, unfortunately, showing a corresponding diminution in tolerance and an increasing tendency to regard his own convictions as the exclusive norm of truth— a tendency which was to be only too fiercely perpetrated by the zealots of the Lutheran party against Melanchthon as well as against the Swiss. Whilst himself protesting, in his controversy with his Roman Catholic opponents, against the error of making the dogma of transubstantiation an article of faith, he was untrue to his own contention in practically demanding acceptance of his own doctrine of consubstantiation as an essential of faith.

# INDEX

## A

"Address to the German Nobility," 20, 59, 164, 171, 177, 222, 284-285

Agricola, John, 2, 4, 106, 295, 321

— Rudolf, 223

Alber, Matthew, 317

Albrecht, Archbishop of Maintz, 2, 4, 19, 37, 47 f., 234, 275

Albrecht of Brandenburg, Grandmaster of Teutonic Knights, 147, 279

Aleander, papal Nuncio, 2-4, 10, 13, 17, 128

Alsace, 190, 192

Alstedt, 183, 186, 188

Altenburg, 104-105, 294

Ambrose, 123, 126

America, 289

Amsdorf, 2, 4, 11, 52, 67, 68, 71, 76, 78, 79, 80, 92, 109, 147

Anabaptists, 301, 305

Anhalt, Prince of, 276, 303

Ansbach, Margrave Casimir of, 207, 279

— Margrave George of, 207, 279

Antwerp, 144

Aquinas, Thomas, 126, 152, 235

Arius, 17

Articles, the Thirty, 142

— the Twelve, 190-192, 193, 195-197, 199

Augsburg, 6, 146-147

— Confession, 327

Augustine, St, 7, 44, 119, 123, 126, 220, 233, 245

Augustinian Order, Chapter of, 33-34

Aurogallus, professor at Wittenberg, 13, 71

Austria, 158, 195, 298

Avignon, 288

## B

"Babylonic Captivity, The," 17, 32, 38, 59, 124, 306

Baden, 190

— Landgrave Philip of, 207, 303

Bamberg, 153, 299

Barcelona, Treaty of, 299

Barge, 97

Basle, 89, 143, 198, 212, 236, 242, 309, 313

Bavaria, Duke William of, 148, 158, 276, 280, 299

Bavaria, 158, 195, 298

Bayle, 227

Beheim, Hector, 2

Berlepsch, Hans von, 1, 9

Berlichingen, Götz von, 197

Bernard, St, 23, 119, 220

Berne, 320

Bernhardi, Barth., 19-20

Beyer, Dr, 38, 71

Biel, scholastic theologian, 318

Black Forest, the, 188, 190

Blarer, 145, 147

Bohemia, 35, 183, 280, 299

Bohemians, 215, 307

Bora, Catherine von, 131

Borna, 104

Bourbon, 299

Brabant, 145

Brandenburg, Margrave George of, 303

Brandenburg-Ansbach, Margrave of, 148

Braunfels, Otto, 145

Brenz, 147, 317, 321

Breslau, 147, 298

Brisger, Prior, 109

Brissmann, John, 130, 145

Brück, Chancellor, 36, 38

Brunswick, 190